RIGHT ON?

POLITICAL CHANGE AND CONTINUITY IN GEORGE W. BUSH'S AMERICA

Right On?

Political Change and Continuity in George W. Bush's America

edited by

Iwan Morgan
and
Philip Davies

British Library Cataloguing-in-Publication Data
A catalogue record for this book is available
from the British Library

ISBN   1 900039 69 9   (paperback)
          1 900039 63 X   (hardback)

INSTITUTE FOR THE STUDY OF THE
A M E R I C A S
UNIVERSITY OF LONDON · SCHOOL OF ADVANCED STUDY

Institute for the Study of the Americas
Senate House
Malet Street
London WC1E 7HU

Telephone: 020 7862 8870
Fax: 020 7862 8886

Email: americas@sas.ac.uk
Web: americas.sas.ac.uk

CONTENTS

THE CONTRIBUTORS

Philip Davies is professor of American Studies at De Montfort University, Leicester, and director of the British Library's Eccles Centre for American Studies. He has also served two terms as chair of the British Association of American Studies. Among his publications are: *Elections USA*; *An American Quarter-Century*; *Representing and Imagining America*; *Political Parties and the Collapse of the Old Orders*; and (co-edited with George Edwards) *New Challenges for the American Presidency*.

John Dumbrell is professor of American politics and director of the Centre for Diplomatic and International Studies at the University of Leicester. He is a former chair of the American Politics Group of the UK Political Studies Association. Among his books are: *The Making of United States Foreign Policy*; *American Foreign Policy: Carter to Clinton*; *The Carter Presidency: A Re-Evaluation*; *A Special Relationship: Anglo-American Relations in the Cold War and After* [winner, Cambridge University Donner Book Prize]; and *President Lyndon Johnson and Soviet Communism* [winner, American Politics Group's Richard Neustadt prize].

Martin Durham is senior lecturer in Politics at the University of Wolverhampton. He has written extensively on moral conservatism in both Britain and America. Among his books are *Moral Crusades: Family and Values in the Thatcher Years*; *Women and Fascism*; and *The Christian Right, the Far Right, and the Boundaries of American Conservatism*.

Godfrey Hodgson is an eminent journalist, who has written for many newspapers on both sides of the Atlantic, was formerly a member of the *Sunday Times* Insight team and has co-written and presented a number of television documentaries. He recently retired as director of the Reuters Foundation for journalists at Oxford University. He is presently an associate of the Rothermere American Institute at Oxford University. Among his books are: *An American Melodrama: The Presidential Campaign of 1968*; *In Our Time: America from World War II to Nixon*; *The World Turned Right Side Up: A*

History of the Conservative Ascendancy in America; The Gentleman from New York: A Biography of Daniel Patrick Moynihan; and *More Equal than Others: America from Nixon to the New Century.*

Steven Hurst is Senior Lecturer in Politics at Manchester Metropolitan University. He has written extensively on US foreign policy since 1945. In addition to numerous journal articles, his books include: *The Carter Administration and Vietnam; The Foreign Policy of the Bush Administration: In Search of a New World Order;* and *US Cold War Foreign Policy: Key Perspectives.*

Klaus Larres is Professor of International Relations and History at the University of Ulster. In 2000–01, he held the Henry A. Kissinger Fellowship in International Relations in the Library of Congress. An expert on the US and Europe since 1945, his books include: *Churchill's Cold War; Uneasy Allies: Britain, Germany and European Integration;* and *The Cold War: Essential Readings.*

Robert McKeever is head of the School of Politics and International Relations at the University of Reading. He is the author of *Raw Judicial Power: The Supreme Court and American Society* and *Politics USA.* His articles on the Supreme Court have appeared in numerous scholarly journals and he is currently working on civil liberties in the United States after 9/11.

Iwan Morgan is professor of United States Studies and deputy director of the Institute for the Study of the Americas in the University of London's School of Advanced Study. Among his publications are: *Eisenhower versus 'the Spenders': The Eisenhower Administration, the Democrats, and the Budget, 1953–60; Beyond the Liberal Consensus; Deficit Government: Taxing and Spending in Modern America;* and *Nixon.*

John Owens is professor of American Politics at the University of Westminster. He is on the editorial boards of *Presidential Studies Quarterly* and *Legislative Studies Quarterly.* He is a former chair of the American Politics Group of the UK Political Studies Association and has been a guest scholar at the Brookings Institution. Among his publications are [co-authored with Michael Foley] *Congress and the Presidency: Institutional Politics in a Separated System; The Republican Takeover of Congress* (special issue of *Politics and Policy,* co-edited with Erwin Hargrove); and his numerous articles on Congress have appeared in *British Journal of Political Science, Legislative Studies Quarterly, Political Studies* and *Politics and Policy.*

Robert Singh is Professor of Politics at Birkbeck College, University of London. Among his publications are: *Governing America: The Politics of a Divided Democracy*; *The Farrakhan Phenomenon*; and *The Congressional Black Caucus*. His most recent publication [co-edited with Mary Buckley] is *The Bush Doctrine and the War on Terror*. His current project is a study of Anti-Americanism since 9/11.

Alex Waddan is lecturer in Politics at the University of Leicester. He has written extensively on US politics and public policy. In addition to numerous journal articles, his books include *The Politics of Social Welfare: The Collapse of the Centre and the Rise of the Right*; and *Clinton's Legacy: A New Democrat in Governance*.

Introduction

Right On?

Political Change and Continuity in George Bush's America

Iwan Morgan

In view of the controversial circumstances of George W. Bush's election in 2000, many analysts forecast that his presidency would be constrained by problems of legitimacy and compelled to pursue a modest agenda in the interests of rebuilding national consensus. From the moment he took office, however, Bush confounded such expectations through his manifest determination to plot a bold course in both foreign and domestic policy. The transformative significance of his leadership was already taking shape before the 9/11 attacks changed the strategic context of American politics and gave him the opportunity to forge a singular presidency in the midst of national crisis. In 2000 Bush was being compared to the obscure and undistinguished Rutherford B. Hayes, the victor in the disputed presidential election of 1876. With his re-election in 2004, the comparisons now being made of him were with Franklin D. Roosevelt and Ronald Reagan, arguably the two presidents who had done most to shape the course of modern American politics. Whereas FDR had laid the basis for the 50-year ascendancy of liberalism, Bush was evidently engaged in a project to consolidate a new conservative ascendancy that had blossomed but never fully flowered under Reagan.

The genesis of this book was a symposium, 'The George W. Bush Administration's Second-Term Agenda', held on 8 March 2005 and organized jointly by the University of London's Institute for the Study of the Americas and the British Library's Eccles Centre for American Studies. The essays in this volume build on the original symposium to consider the Bush administration in terms of its historical context, first-term record and second-term prospects. In addition to the wide-ranging overview of the issues and likely problems of Bush's second-term by Godfrey Hodgson, four of the essays focus on Bush's foreign policy, three examine aspects of

Bush's domestic policy and leadership and three explore the changes in the
partisan and electoral landscape of American politics during the Bush era.
The contributors consider the Bush administration from the perspective of
its engagement in an ideologically driven project to consolidate conservative ascendancy over US politics and public policy and to promote
America's interests and values in the unipolar world of the early twenty-
first century. Within this context they consider the elements of political
change and continuity in George Bush's America. To this end some essays
focus on the extent to which the Bush agenda is new or whether it is better seen as a continuation of trends that predated Bush's presidency. In
addition, most contributors examine how far Bush has succeeded at time
of writing (mid-2005) in overcoming political, institutional and international resistance to his conservative agenda and assess his prospects for further
success during his remaining years in office.

Bush as Reagan's Ideological Legatee

Bush is the only president of modern times (and only the second in US history) whose father also held the office. Nevertheless, he is widely perceived
as the political son of Ronald Reagan, the conservative ideologue who challenged the established order, rather than of George Bush Sr., the moderate
conservative who built a political career as an establishment insider
(Friedman, 2001; Keller, 2003). Reagan was the representative of the new
Sunbelt conservatism that emerged in southern California and the Southwest
in the post-war era. Bush, who has been described as the first southern conservative to be elected president since James Polk in 1844, represented the
late twentieth-century transformation of his region into a bastion of
Republicanism and a hive of new business entrepreneurialism (Lind, 2003).
Both presidents had a visceral dislike of the cultural changes of the 1960s,
which Reagan had encountered as California governor and Bush as a student
at Yale — where he also acquired an aversion to elitist liberalism (Muntaglio,
1999). Like Reagan, Bush eschewed the pluralist Neustadian model of the
presidency, which holds that the way to get things done in Washington is
through bargaining and persuasion. Reagan held fast to a few core beliefs in
challenging the prevailing liberal orthodoxy — taxes were too high, government was too big and communism was an evil that had to be resisted through
massive defence expansion (Heclo, 2003). Bush acted, in Joel Aberbach's
words, as 'an election and legacy maximizer', who prioritized command and
sought to dominate the political system in order to fulfil his own ambitions
and meet the public's need for strong leadership (2004, p. 47).

Like Reagan, Bush adopted a populist conservative style, applied an ideological litmus test in making Cabinet and sub-Cabinet appointments,
adopted a similar approach to judicial nominations and sought to capture
the domestic bureaucracy through appointment of officials unsympathetic
to their agency's regulatory mission (Aberbach, 2004; Arnold, 2004).
Moreover, both aspired to restore the powers and prerogatives of the presidency, which they deemed to have been weakened under their Democratic
predecessors. According to Shirley Anne Warshaw, 'More so than any
modern president ... Bush has successfully governed without Congress'
(2004, p. 101). Most notably, he paid little heed to the legislature in conducting the 'war on terrorism' and whenever possible invoked executive
privilege to limit its oversight of administration operations. In addition, he
employed a host of administrative techniques such as executive orders,
proclamations, bureaucratic management, signing statements, sanctions
and treaty abrogation to accomplish his conservative agenda. As one commentator noted, 'Bush has flexed all the muscles the Constitution gave him
and, some say, a few it didn't' (Simendinger, 2002). In this regard, former
Clinton aide Sidney Blumenthal more critically described the Bush strategy
not as an extension of Reaganism but as 'the highest stage of Nixonism'
in its determination to concentrate governmental power in an imperial
presidency, politicize the bureaucracy and invoke national security to wage
partisan warfare (2005).

Nevertheless Bush had to overcome a weakness that never troubled
Reagan. The president's claim to hold a unique mandate as the only nationally elected official has been an essential element of modern presidential
power (Tulis, 2003). Bush's failure to win a popular-vote majority and the
disputed nature of his electoral-college majority in 2000 appeared to deny
him this instrument of leadership. However he refused to concede the
legitimacy issue and operated from his first day in office as if he were the
possessor of a mandate to advance his conservative agenda (Frum, 2003).
As Office of Management and Budget director Mitchell Daniels commented in the early days of the administration, 'It's not going to be a presidency of miniature gestures' (Balz, 2001). The events of 9/11 tilted the balance decisively in favour of Bush's strong leadership and erased remaining
doubts about his legitimacy. Yet he had already demonstrated his mandate-
claiming resolve prior to this crisis, not least in fulfilling his election pledge
to enact a huge tax cut. In this sense, Bush's experience appeared to prove
that a president's capacity for bold and effective leadership was not diminished by the circumstances of his election (Rae, 2004).

Bush as an 'Orthodox Innovator'

Stephen Skowronek's historically-based model of presidential leadership argues that, in spite of the constitutional prescription for three co-equal branches of government, the presidency has been the 'chief point of reference for evaluating the polity as it moves through time and space'. Endowed with unity, dynamism and popular support, this inherently disruptive institution was the 'battering ram' of political change. Skowronek classified presidents according to whether they were opposed or affiliated to the ascendant political regime, broadly defined as the prevailing orthodoxy in terms of ideology, polcy and resources (1997, p. 30). In his typology, Ronald Reagan figured as a president opposed to a vulnerable regime, who took office with the goal of repudiating the failing order and reconstructing a new one. Using Skowronek's model, George W. Bush can best be identified as an 'orthodox innovator', a president intent on continuing and fulfilling the policy agenda of the successful regime with which he is affiliated. However, Bush's task differed from that of other orthodox innovators — notably James Polk, William McKinley, Theodore Roosevelt, Harry Truman and Lyndon Johnson — because it entailed completing the construction of the successful regime rather than just maintaining its dominance. As Stephen Schier has observed, 'The primary project of the Bush presidency is to complete the political reconstruction of national politics, government and policy begun by Ronald Reagan in 1981' (2004, p. 4).

The incomplete nature of the Reagan reconstruction posed particular challenges for an orthodox innovator affiliated to the conservative regime that emerged in the 1980s. The Reagan presidency was significant in changing the terms of political debate but had only moderate success in fulfilling its conservative agenda (Hill et al., 1990; Hodgson, 1995; Sloan, 1999). Reagan legitimized conservative solutions to the nation's problems as alternatives to the liberal ideas dominant since the 1930s. Also, his conservative vision of low taxes, small government, military strength and traditional values was appealing to voters. In policy terms, however, Reagan's greatest accomplishments were in the international arena, notably his contribution to the collapse of the Soviet Empire. In the domestic arena, he only managed to slow the growth of government rather than roll it back. His proudest achievement was to cut personal income taxes, but he raised business taxes in order to control the budget deficit. The Reagan reconstruction was constrained domestically by what Skowronek dubbed 'institutional thickening', namely the Washington power relationships that developed outside presidential control as the twentieth century progressed (1997, p. 413). Its transformative agenda encountered the powerful opposition of an iron triangle of groups — the Democrat-controlled House of Representatives (and the Democratic majority in the Senate in 1987–88), liberal interest groups and federal bureaucrats — that identified with the New Deal regime.

In Skowronek's model, orthodox innovators promise 'to continue the good work of the past and demonstrate the vitality of the established regime to changing times' (1997, p. 41). In its purview, they have often done so 'most effectively when asserting American power in international affairs' (1997, p. 245). In this regard, George W. Bush followed in the footsteps of Polk, McKinley, Teddy Roosevelt, and — most notably — Harry Truman. In common with Truman, he seized the opportunity presented by crisis to define new threats to national security and offer a strategy to combat them. Bush's new sense of national purpose brought to an end the period of drift, uncertainty of threat perception and lack of coherence in post-Cold War US foreign policy (McCormick, 2000). His warnings about the gravity of the threat facing America, the need for enhanced homeland security, and the necessity to assert US primacy through massive defence expansion formed the basis of a new foreign policy consensus. Bush's insistence in linking terrorist groups with rogue states under the threat concept of weapons of mass destruction transfer also won broad support from Americans, even if his pre-emptive use of military force to neutralize this danger in the particular case of Iraq did not. Moreover, his vigorous prosecution of the war on terror enhanced conservative regime legitimacy at home. To this end it reinforced the American public's belief that Republicans were more reliable stewards of national security, which Reagan's 'peace through strength' approach had firmly established in the wake of Jimmy Carter's foreign policy failures.

There were also clear continuities between the domestic agendas of Reagan and Bush. Indeed the latter showed greater devotion to some of the conservative regime's commitments, notably by cutting business taxes in the face of a growing deficit rather than raising them like his predecessor. Bush also looked to make the conservative regime relevant to the present by supporting unsuccessful Reagan initiatives that were deemed to be ahead of their time. Among these were social security reform, restriction of abortion rights, reduction of environmental regulation and educational vouchers. Bush also demonstrated greater commitment than did Reagan to building a new Republican majority that would perpetuate the conservative regime and safeguard his own legacy.

Guided by chief campaign strategist Karl Rove, Bush made the mid-term elections of 2002 a referendum on his handling of homeland security and campaigned on behalf of key Republican Senate candidates. This was a risky strategy because every first-term president had seen his party lose ground in mid-term contests since 1934. In this instance Bush's boldness was duly rewarded when the GOP regained control of the Senate and increased its majority in the House of Representatives. The president was also assiduous in wooing the Republican base and sought to energize those elements of it, notably evangelicals, whose turnout rate in the 2000 election was relatively low. Christian Right groups and other organizations with a socio-moral agenda, which Reagan had largely taken for granted, found the Bush White House ready to consult and support them. As veteran conservative activist Paul Weyrich observed, 'I've been through five Republican administrations, and the effort to communicate with conservatives and to understand our concerns and address our concerns and involve us in the process is the best of any Republican administration, including Ronald Reagan. In fact, far superior to Ronald Reagan' (Toner, 2001).

In addition, Bush co-opted some Democratic issues into his Republican agenda in an effort to appeal to voter groups contested by both parties (Beachler, 2004; Price and Coleman, 2004). His administration promoted accountability reforms in education to draw votes from suburban families, farm price supports to attract rural voters and steel tariffs to protect blue-collar jobs in battleground states like Pennsylvania and Ohio. Bush's strategists also recognized the key significance of senior citizens. Having lost some ground with them in the 1990s, Democrats made a concerted effort to regain it in the 2002 elections by portraying the GOP as the enemy of social security. To counter this, in a videotape distributed for use by Republican candidates, the president promised social security recipients, 'No changes, no reductions, no way' (Toner, 2002). He also supported prescription drug benefits for Medicare recipients, a measure enacted with bipartisan support in 2003.

Though Bush characterized such initiatives as 'compassionate conservatism', they were regarded as transgressions from the true faith by many on the right. The conservative *National Review* voiced its concern in an editorial entitled 'Left Turn: Is the GOP Conservative?' Though allowing Bush a passing grade on national security, tax reduction and judicial appointments, it expressed doubt that he would deliver the rest of the conservative agenda to reduce government (2003, p. 7). Former congressman Newt Gingrich, still an important voice of Republican conservatism, remarked that those who sought to transform Washington in the early twenty-first century should look for guidance to the Contract with

America, the radical manifesto on which the GOP had won control of the House of Representatives in the 1994 mid-term elections (2005, p. 4).

Regardless of such concerns, Bush's agenda was fundamentally conservative, but differed markedly from the Contract with America in some instances. Fiscal discipline was at the heart of the latter's drive to reduce government. In contrast, Bush emulated Reagan in tolerating a rising deficit as a trade-off for attainment of his core goals of tax reduction and increased defence spending. A fundamental aim of the Contract with America was to make government more accountable through enactment of timetables for the achievement of key objectives, rules to make Congress less elitist and more transparent, and constitutional amendments to require balanced budgets and congressional term limits. Bush showed little interest in pursuing this aspect of the Contract with America agenda because his aim to restore presidential dominance of government entailed reducing executive accountability and transparency. Finally, the stunning Republican victories in the 1994 mid-term elections convinced proponents of the Contract with America that the conservative revolutionary moment was at hand, but this proved something of a false dawn. Still faced with the task of completing the construction of a new Republican majority, Bush sometimes put pragmatism ahead of ideological purity.

The Tight Electoral Environment of Bush's America

Bush's failure to win a popular-vote majority in 2000 only confirmed the fragility of the Republican coalition. This was also the third consecutive presidential election in which the Republican candidate had failed to win 50 per cent of the votes cast. The glory days of the 1980s, when the Republicans won sweeping popular-vote victories in three presidential elections and aggregated more electoral-college votes than any party had ever won over a single decade, showed no signs of returning. The GOP's position in Congress, where it effectively enjoyed majority status for the first time since the 1920s, was stronger but hardly secure (Davies, 2003). Its majorities in both houses continued to be relatively small after 1994. Indeed the Republicans briefly lost control of the Senate in mid-2001 when the defection of James Jeffords of Vermont gave the Democrats a single-vote majority for the remainder of the 107th Congress.

In these circumstances, Bush's ambition of regime consolidation required him to engage in a permanent campaign for public support. It also put a premium on maintaining party unity in support of his programme. To this end, the White House focused on promoting enactment of a small

number of core goals, such as tax reduction, educational reform, and prescription drug benefits, and eschewed taking positions on less important
legislative matters facing Congress. Even on its core goals, the administration was willing to compromise, such as accepting removal of the school
vouchers proposal from the 2002 education bill and taking a smaller tax cut
than sought in 2003, in order to achieve its broad objectives. Moreover, as
indicated above, the White House engaged in its own version of Bill
Clinton's triangulation strategy in appropriating some Democratic issues as
its own. Bush made tactical feints to the middle to peel off voters from key
Democratic constituencies in pursuit of his strategic goal of creating a stable Republican majority that would ensure the durability of the conservative regime (Brownstein, 2002).

The Republican clean sweep in the 2004 national elections meant that
George Bush became the first GOP president since Calvin Coolidge to begin
his second term with his party also in control of both houses of Congress.
Whether this added up to the consolidation of the conservative regime was
another matter. Bush won 50.7 per cent of votes cast in the presidential election, but his popular-vote margin of victory was only 2.4 per cent, the smallest by which any US president has won re-election (the previous low was
Woodrow Wilson's 3.2 per cent in 1916). Nevertheless, Bush swept aside all
doubt about the meaning of the election, just as he had done in 2000, in
promising a bold second-term agenda. 'I've earned capital in this election',
he avowed, 'and I'm going to spend it for what I told the people I'd spend
it on ... social security and tax reform, moving this economy forward, education, fighting and winning the war on terror'(Harding, 2005).

If Bush succeeds in achieving his second-term goals and the presidency passes on to a like-minded Republican in 2008, he will have done much
to achieve his aim of conservative regime consolidation. He will also have
demonstrated that the presidency still has the capacity to develop an ideological agenda through partisan means. Although Bill Clinton employed
similar tactics in the shape of the permanent campaign, issue triangulation
and emphasis on key issues beneficial to his prospects, he did so only to
shore up his personal position rather than for broader political purpose and
party benefit. Nevertheless, the obstacles facing Bush in his second term
were still significant.

In Skowronek's analysis, the political time in which the presidency has
an opportunity to effect political change has waned because of changes in
the broader political environment, notably the decline of party loyalties,
issue fragmentation within the electorate and the rise of the mass media as
political intermediaries. As a result, latter-day political regimes were likely

to be more fluid, of shorter duration than the 30 years or more enjoyed by earlier ones and more vulnerable to institutional resistance. If this assessment is right, the kind of pre-emptive and personal politics practised by Clinton has more chance of success than Bush's ideological leadership (Skowronek, 1997, pp. 49–58). Moreover, Bush's prospects of regime consolidation, regardless of other factors, depend on the continuing relevance of his administration's core commitments in foreign and economic policy. Failure on one of these fronts, as exemplified by Jimmy Carter, could undermine the viability of the conservative regime.

Overview of Chapters

A substantial amount of the analysis in the subsequent chapters of this book agrees that Bush is engaged in a project of conservative regime consolidation. With regard to this venture, some contributors place more emphasis on the elements of conservative change that build upon the Reagan reconstruction (and in one case the ideas of the old Republican right). Others put greater stress on its transformational aspects that move beyond the Reagan legacy, particularly in the foreign policy field. All the contributors regard Bush's re-election in 2004 as a significant staging post in his project, but none see it as a guarantee of the final achievement of his ambitions. All are agreed that powerful forces of continuity and resistance to change still have to be overcome at home and abroad. There is some disagreement among them as to the extent of Bush's first-term success but they are unanimous that the problems to be faced in the second term could well inhibit his hopes of bequeathing a viable conservative regime as his political legacy. In addition, the contributors of the foreign policy chapters are broadly in agreement about the likelihood of international difficulties restraining Bush in his second term from pursuing the kind of ambitious initiatives to which the world became accustomed in his first term.

In his chapter on 'President Bush's Second Term Agenda', Godfrey Hodgson adjudges the risk of failure to be high in a number of policy areas, including the pacification of Iraq, management of the budget deficit, promotion of social security reform and appointment of conservative judges. He also draws attention to the constraints of lame-duck status as Bush's time in office draws to a close. While Hodgson accepts that the centre of gravity of American politics has been moving rightward since the 1970s, he argues that the polarization of the public is clear evidence that the triumph of conservative Republicanism is far from assured. In addition, he expresses concern that the Bush administration will remain unpopular abroad for as long as it clings to the view that America has a unique duty 'to redeem the world in accordance with its own political religion'. As such, his analysis is highly sceptical that Bush's conservative legacy will be as significant as many of the president's supporters on the right believe.

Steven Hurst's chapter on 'Conservatism Resurgent: The Foreign Policy of the Bush Administration' takes issue with the conventional view that Bush embarked on a neo-conservative crusade for democratic globalism after 9/11. While acknowledging the sincerity of the Bush administration's commitment to reconstruct Iraq as a democracy, he emphasizes that its principal motivation for intervention in the first place was concern about Saddam Hussein's possession of weapons of mass destruction. As such, Hurst believes that Bush foreign policy — both pre- and post-9/11 — traces its ideological roots to the early Cold War beliefs of the old Republican right, whose conservative nationalist world-view emphasized hegemony, military power, unilateralism and security against attack — if necessary through pre-emptive action. The moderate majority of the GOP rejected such ideas as unrealistic in the bipolar world of the mid-twentieth century and opted instead for multilateral containment of communism. According to Hurst, the old right's ideas have flowered anew in the post-Cold War era to gain the support of the now conservative mainstream of Republicanism, but he anticipates that the realities of a complex world and the limitations of US power will ultimately restrain Bush's capacity to pursue them.

John Dumbrell offers a different perspective to Hurst in his chapter, 'President Kerry's Foreign Policy: Continuity and Discontinuity in Contemporary US Foreign Policy'. He accepts that the first Bush administration was influenced by neoconservative ideas, but also emphasizes its inheritance from the second Clinton administration of a foreign policy already moving in a unilateralist direction. Moreover, his analysis of John Kerry's 2004 campaign statements suggests that the election of a new Democratic administration would not have produced significant changes in US foreign policy in terms of rapid withdrawal from Iraq, forging new multilateral agreements and modifying America's pro-Israeli position. Dumbrell accepts that there are important differences of tone and — in some cases — substance between the parties and that experience and personality are instrumental in shaping presidential response to unexpected international developments. However, he perceives an underlying bipartisan foreign policy consensus based on acceptance that American primacy in the world is the key to securing US interests. On the other hand, he recognizes that this is not a blank cheque for new interventions in the Middle East or elsewhere. In his estimate, the difficulties encountered in Iraq and the domestic demands of regime consolidation will result in a somewhat more pragmatic and less risky second-term foreign policy.

In his chapter on 'The Bush Administration and Europe', Klaus Larres analyzes the deterioration of US relations with continental Europe's two most influential nations, France and Germany, in Bush's first term and assesses the prospects for second-term rapprochement. The fissures that Bush's unilateralism generated within the transatlantic alliance rank among the most significant consequences of his foreign policy. Despite the promising signs of thaw that culminated in the newly re-elected Bush's visit to various European capitals in early 2005, Larres anticipates the likelihood of continuing disagreements over the Middle East, China and North Korea. In his assessment, US relations with Germany remain especially problematic because of the deep gap in the foreign policy values of the two nations. Whether justified or not, American policymakers for their part evinced some concern that Germany aspired to make the European Union the champion of liberal internationalism as a rival to American primacy.

Robert Singh's chapter, 'The Bush Administration and the Middle East', offers at least partial confirmation for the view that the Bush Doctrine has revolutionized US foreign policy. Until the 9/11 attacks moved it to centre-stage, US attention to the region was spasmodic, limited in scope and reactive. According to Singh, Bush's new Middle Eastern policy mixed Wilsonian ideals with realist means to focus on regime change, pre-emption as well as deterrence of assaults against the US and preserving American primacy. Overall, however, he argues that the invasion of Iraq, in spite of its overthrow of Saddam, failed to assuage regional anti-Americanism by a demonstration effect of democratization and generated a deep schism in American opinion, as revealed by voting patterns in the 2004 presidential election. On the other hand he acknowledges that the Bush administration has made more progress in advancing the cause of democracy in the Middle East than any of its predecessors. In Singh's view, further significant success in the second term appears unlikely, but Bush (and most probably his successors) will continue to address the region's problems in pursuit of American security because crisis management and purchasing stability at the price of justice are no longer viable options.

Iwan Morgan's chapter, 'The Bush Administration and the Budget Deficit', discusses the new manifestation of an issue that previously haunted the Reagan presidency. He attributes the return of large deficits mainly to Bush's first-term prioritization of higher spending and huge tax reduction over balanced budgets. Bush held his conservative nerve steadier than had Ronald Reagan to reduce business taxes in the face of a rising deficit in pursuit of a supply-side

strategy of economic growth. In terms of spending, he promoted the greatest military expansion since the 1980s defence build-up, but unlike Reagan he
also increased domestic outlays to enhance his appeal to groups beyond the
Republican base. In a key change from the first term, debt-funding concerns
and the need to preserve his core conservative goals of strong defence and
low taxes from budget-balancing pressures impelled Bush to announce that
he would cut the deficit in half during his second term. His strategy of achieving deficit reduction wholly through non-defence retrenchment indicated a
more conservative direction in fiscal policy. In Morgan's estimation, however,
it was unlikely to succeed because proposed extensions of temporary first-
term tax cuts would cause further haemorrhaging of revenues and domestic
retrenchment of the scale envisaged would be politically difficult to enact.

In his chapter, 'American-Style Party Government: Delivering Bush's
Agenda, Delivering the Congress's Agenda', John Owens analyses one of
the most significant political changes in the Bush era. Following a prolonged period of institutional competition, the early twenty-first century
has seen the re-emergence of traditional American-style party government
in presidential-congressional relations to its strongest level in over a hundred years. Owens presents this as the product of increased party competition, ideological homogenization of the two main parties and the willingness of Republican congressional leaders to co-ordinate their actions with
the president to enact their common party agenda. GOP loss of control of
the Senate in mid-2001 delayed full implementation of the governing party
strategy until the 108th Congress. Though Republicans showed greater
unity in support of the president in the more hierarchical House of
Representatives than in the more decentralized Senate, the congressional
party was remarkably successful in enacting Bush's core goals in 2003–04.
In Owens's estimation, however, controversial elements of Bush's second-
term agenda, notably social security reform, further tax cuts and domestic
retrenchment, were certain to test Republican unity to its limits

Robert McKeever's chapter on 'Constitutional Issues, Rights, Supreme
Court Appointments', analyses a core element of Bush's conservative
agenda. Reviewing the first-term record, he shows that the combination of
personal conviction and political need to broaden his appeal to evangelicals drove Bush's combative strategy of nominating controversial federal
judicial nominees, which provoked filibusters by Senate Democrats to
block their appointment. The president's determination to press his case
in the second term generated further confrontation, which was resolved
— at least temporarily — through a compromise negotiated between
Senate moderates of both parties. McKeever also evinces scepticism that

the president would fully achieve his goal of creating a conservative majority on the Supreme Court when vacancies arose on this body. Similarly, his assessment of judicial changes regarding issues like abortion rights, homosexual equality and the rights of 'unlawful' combatants suggests that Bush has had only partial success in achieving conservative goals in these substantive policy areas. In his estimation, the institutional factors that constrained Bush's first-term progress, such as Senate opposition to his conservative judicial nominees, the problems of enacting constitutional amendments and the Supreme Court's current moderation, were likely to continue to do so in the second term.

Philip Davies suggests in his chapter, 'A New Republican Majority?' that the Bush White House has made progress in its electoral project to consolidate the conservative regime, but questions whether it has effected full-scale realignment. As he shows, America remains polarized, with Bush carrying only 50.7 per cent of the popular vote and the Republicans aggregating only 50.1 per cent of the House vote in 2004. Nevertheless Davies also points to certain advantages that benefit Republican prospects of eventually achieving a stable majority. These include better campaign funding, incumbency advantage in the House, stronger support in small states that exert disproportionate influence within the Senate, signs of growing appeal to groups outside the party's base, and greater ability to mobilize core voters. Nevertheless, the Democrats, who remain strong in the populous states, may benefit if Bush fails to satisfy the second-term demands of Christian Right groups, particularly if they can develop a more popular stance on the values issues that lost them votes in 2004. For Davies, a key indicator of whether the Republican majority is at hand will be the GOP's performance in the 2008 elections when its ticket will not be headed by an incumbent president and it holds two-thirds of the Senate seats being contested.

Martin Durham's essay, 'Evangelicals and the Politics of Red America', assesses the opportunities and problems arising from the close links that the White House fostered with this faith-based constituency to assist the president's re-election. He shows that three forms of mobilization took place to boost evangelical support for Republicans in 2004. The White House made a concerted effort to court this group; evangelical organizations were themselves active in urging followers to turn out in support of Bush in greater numbers than in 2000; and the holding of simultaneous referenda on gay marriage in eleven states also enhanced evangelicals' electoral participation in those states. Believing they had been crucial to his re-election, Bush's Christian Right allies were determined to collect their due rewards in his second term. However, the president was reluctant to invest political capital in a doomed effort to enact a Federal Marriage Amendment, a key evangelical concern. In Durham's estimation, failure to appoint conservative judges and Supreme Court justices was certain to cause further rifts. As he notes, Bush's hope of solidifying strong evangelical support for his party in the long term depends on his capacity to achieve substantive changes that have so far proved elusive.

Finally, Alex Waddan's essay on 'Whither Blue America?' considers the condition and prospects of the Democratic Party in Bush's America. He evinces scepticism of the view advanced by some analysts that the insecurities of a post-industrial economy would have transformed US politics to the Democrats' advantage had not 9/11 refocused attention on security issues to Republican benefit. Instead, he finds the so-called 'two majorities' thesis more convincing in its portrayal of an American public that had a majority preference for Democratic liberal policy options on socio-economic issues and for Republican conservative prescriptions on security and cultural issues. With security issues likely to feature prominently for the foreseeable future, Waddan argues that the best Democratic hope to regain lost ground lies in crafting a compromise position on cultural issues that defuses their exploitation by Republicans but without alienating the party's own base. Nevertheless his review of four core Democratic groups — women, African Americans, Latinos and the white working class — indicates that the party is losing ground with all except blacks. Of the others, the Latinos represent the most significant test case for the Democrats' ability to win votes on economic issues while not losing them on cultural concerns.

Evaluating Bush's Achievement

As the preceding chapter review indicates, it is reasonable to claim that George W. Bush has generated political and policy change on a greater scale than most analysts anticipated at the time of his inauguration. It is equally the case that Bush must be credited for rising above the unpromising circumstances of his 2000 election to establish himself as a political leader of historical significance. But in contrast to a reconstructionist president like Reagan, whose success could be evaluated in terms of having started the process of political transformation, Bush must be judged on whether he has extended and consolidated the regime launched by his conservative predecessor.

Like Reagan, Bush has enjoyed most success in asserting America's primacy in the international arena, but he has no prospect of emulating Reagan's Cold War victory on his watch. The war on terror that he initiated may well take decades before anything truly resembling victory can be declared. Bush's own hubris in declaring the Iraq war won in May 2003 soon acquired a hollow ring as American casualties mounted during the post-war occupation to establish a stable Iraqi democracy. Even with the successful holding of elections for a new government in early 2005, Iraq remained a boil that American power had still not lanced.

Bush's ability to consolidate the conservative regime requires him to achieve a second-term withdrawal from Iraq on terms that justify America's vast military effort and the not inconsiderable loss of American soldiers' lives. Moreover, Bush's claim that his foreign policy activism has made America safer will lose legitimacy if it were to fall victim to another terrorist attack on his watch. In this context, it should be noted that only William McKinley among other 'orthodox innovators' strengthened his political regime as a result of involvement in foreign war. The modern Democratic Party paid a heavy price for the unpopularity of military ventures initiated by Democratic presidents. Public disillusion with Harry Truman on account of the Korean War stalemate helped to elect Dwight Eisenhower as the first Republican president since Herbert Hoover. Lyndon Johnson's Vietnam War created the bitterest divisions in his party over foreign policy since James Polk's acquisition of western territories as a result of war with Mexico split the mid-nineteenth century Democrats over the issue of slavery expansion. The political fallout from their foreign wars fatally undermined the successful regimes with which Polk and LBJ were affiliated.

As the experience of George Bush Sr. demonstrated, even leadership in a successful and broadly popular foreign war is no guarantee of political success if a president is deemed too involved in foreign policy at the expense of domestic matters. The requirements of regime consolidation make it likely that George W. Bush will prioritize completion of his domestic agenda ahead of bold new ventures abroad in his second term, a reversal of the normal trend that presidents become more internationally engaged the longer they are in office. Yet, as the chapters in this book on domestic policy and politics have demonstrated, success on the home front looked uncertain as the second term progressed. Bush claimed to have political capital to invest in pursuit of his domestic goals, but polls showed that his approval ratings remained at historic lows for a president at the start of his second term. Moreover, the administration's inept response to Hurricane Katrina's battering of the Gulf Coast and the consequent flooding of New Orleans dented the president's post 9/11 image of confidence and competence.

Whatever one's view of Bush, few can doubt that his presidency is a high-stakes enterprise that has pursued large but risky ambitions. In June

1826, as the United States prepared to celebrate its fiftieth year of independence, the aged Thomas Jefferson declared in the last letter he ever
wrote that the American form of republican self-government would eventually become every nation's birthright. As Michael Ignatieff has suggested, Bush is the first American president to have risked his presidency and
his own place in history on the premise that Jefferson might have been
right. If democracy plants itself in Iraq and spreads through the Middle
East, he will be remembered as a visionary. If the Iraq project ends in failure, however, 'it will be his Vietnam and nothing else about his time in
office will matter very much' (Ignatieff, 2005, p. 25).

Without decrying the significance of Iraq, one could argue to the contrary that there is more at stake in the Bush presidency than success or failure in this venture. Bush also has the chance to mould the nation's highest
court in his conservative image and shape its outlook for a generation. The
decision of Sandra Day O'Connor's, a moderate conservative, to return to
private life laid bare the political fault-lines over how the nation's
Constitution should be interpreted. According to Jay Sekulow, counsel of
the conservative American Centre for Law and Justice, 'This is probably
the most significant Supreme Court resignation and nomination we'll see
in our lifetimes'. Nan Aron of the liberal Alliance for Justice likewise commented, 'The stakes are now enormous' (Fineman and Rosenberg, 2005,
p. 29). Others worry more about the long-term implications of Bush's
budget deficits and the corollary growth of the current account deficit for
the nation's economic wellbeing. According to former Clinton Treasury
Secretary Robert Rubin, redress of the nation's fiscal imbalances is 'an
immediate and critical imperative' and failure to do so would place America
in 'great peril' (2005). Somewhat more pithily but in like vein, former
Nixon Commerce Secretary Peter Peterson warned, 'As a nation, we are
running on empty' (2004, p. xiii). Nor should any assessment of Bush's
importance lose sight of his project to establish what America has lacked
since the 1920s, namely a conservative Republican majority as the dominant force in national politics.

George W. Bush has challenged the orthodoxy that bargaining, compromise and consensus-building is the way to get things done in American politics and has tested the limits of American primacy in world politics. It remains
to be seen whether his assertive and ideological style of leadership creates a
final legacy that future historians may dub the Bush Revolution or whether he
will be remembered mainly for polarizing America and the world in vain pursuit of his ambitious agenda. Whatever the outcome, the significance of his
presidency is certain to be debated for years to come.

1

President Bush's Second Term Agenda

Godfrey Hodgson

I

The conventional wisdom has been that American presidents have very little time to make an impact, and that second terms, if a president is lucky enough to earn one, are all too likely to be times of frustration, disappointment and even disaster. 'You've got to give it all you can that first year', Lyndon Johnson told Harry McPherson. 'Doesn't matter what kind of majority you come in with. You've just got one year when they treat you right' — he was thinking about the Congress, of course, as ever — 'and before they start worrying about themselves... So you've got one year' (McPherson, 1972, p. 268)

Johnson's unpopularity within his own party over the Vietnam War persuaded him not to seek renomination in 1968 for another term as president. Richard Nixon's second term was spoiled and in the end curtailed by his involvement in covering up the foolish actions he had encouraged his people to take in order to win it. Ronald Reagan offered a handful of large ideas, and in his first term he made some progress in moving the centre of gravity of American politics in his direction. But in his second term, he too was all but crippled politically by the antics of his staff. Had it not been for the national desire to avoid the trauma of another Watergate, Iran-Contra could well have destroyed Reagan's presidency in the same manner that the earlier scandal had destroyed Nixon's. As for Bill Clinton, personal indiscretions exposed him to impeachment proceedings that blighted his second term. Even Franklin D. Roosevelt, arguably the greatest president of the twentieth century, had more than half a century earlier experienced a disappointing second term after the defeat of his plan to reform the Supreme Court left him politically weakened.

My purpose here, however, is not to trace the frustrating second-term history of the modern presidency, but to emphasize George W. Bush's determination to break this syndrome. Bush did not approach his second term with the lame-duck mindset of his fellow Texan, Lyndon Johnson, that he had only a year to achieve his goals before his political capital ran out. Nor did he regard the presidency as a weakened institution. More concerned with reputation than survival, he intended to pursue an ambitious second-term agenda that reflected his deeply held personal beliefs. Even when political caution might have suggested restraint, he chose to interpret his relatively narrow re-election victory as a mandate for strong, unapologetic action.

From the outset of his presidency Bush intended to be at least as conservative, and at least as revolutionary, as his personal role model, Ronald Reagan. To many, in the 'blue' states and even more in Europe, the younger Bush appeared gauche, naïve, somehow not quite qualified to be president. That was not how his followers saw him. And that was not how he saw himself. He meant to be a great president, great in his willingness to follow the dictates of his ideological and religious beliefs, and to dare greatly. Deaf to his critics, Bush's supporters came to see him as a man of destiny, worthy of having his image carved on Mount Rushmore as one of the greatest American presidents.[1]

In some respects Bush appeared to be even stronger at the start of his second term than at the beginning of his first, when he faced doubts about his legitimacy because of the disputed nature of his election. He had no need to feel constrained by Congress. Although his fellow-Republicans still did not have a large enough majority in the Senate to enable them to do whatever they wanted, their numbers had grown over the course of Bush's presidency. Meanwhile, House Republicans held a comfortable majority, and their leaders were, if anything, more conservative than the president. Although Bush came quite close to losing the 2004 election in the electoral college, and his majority in the popular vote was not overwhelming, he claimed a popular mandate for strong, controversial policies. He and his supporters felt sure that, as Bush's campaign strategist Karl Rove put it after the 2002 mid-term elections, 'something is moving out there'. Bush believed himself the leader and the beneficiary of a tidal movement in American public opinion and, even more, in American political emotion. Accordingly, rather than being moderate, or centrist, or even cautious, he fully intended to be confident, assertive, in some respects radical in his second term.

There is, of course, room for legitimate discussion whether any such tidal movement in American values was taking place. Some interpreted President Bush's re-election in 2004 as evidence of some such profound shift in American values. Others dismissed it as merely the result of some ruthlessly efficient electoral management by Rove and others, of hesitant

and at times downright inept campaigning by the Democrats and of a successful Republican campaign in the crucial state of Ohio.

The truth, it seems to me, is somewhere in between. No one can easily
deny that the centre of gravity of American politics has indeed been shifting rightward at least since the late 1970s. More than a generation ago the
'liberal consensus' was shattered, and the Roosevelt coalition disintegrated.
Yet the nation has not undergone a mass conversion to Republican conservative values. Rather it is both deeply divided, and indeed in some ways
polarized. Poll data repeatedly showed, for example, that harshly nationalistic foreign policy did not represent a majority view.[2] In domestic affairs,
too, while support for interventionist government policies to try to solve
social problems has indeed declined rather dramatically, on most issues that
arouse strong public feeling — abortion, healthcare, marriage and divorce,
education, retirement pensions, tax policy, affirmative action, the death
penalty, to take only the most obvious examples — public opinion was
divided and indeed confused.

In his 2000 campaign, George W. Bush successfully contrived to give
many voters the misleading impression that he was a moderate or at least a
'compassionate' conservative. In fact, from the moment of his arrival in
the White House, Bush consistently promoted a strongly ideological conservative agenda. He pressed ahead with tax cuts that went disproportionately to the well off and did not conceal that he had a pro-business agenda. The night after the mid-term elections of 2002 one of its more influential supporters, Grover Norquist, predicted, accurately, that the Bush
administration's policy would favour 'the investor class'.[3]

Bush mainly sought advice from conservative ideologues, rather than
professional Republican politicians. The most influential members of his
administration have been from the Right: Vice President Richard Cheney,
Defence Secretary Donald Rumsfeld, and in the first term Attorney General
John Ashcroft. This strong right wing flavour has been particularly clear in
foreign policy. Even before 9/11, President Bush promoted people who
accepted the agenda of the Project for a New American Century. Since 9/11
the 'war on terror' and the war in Iraq, inspired as it was in large part by a
'neo-Wilsonian' ambition to bring democracy to the Middle East by
American intervention, armed if necessary, have reinforced that preference.

It has often been remarked that Bush is much more the political heir of
Ronald Reagan than of his own father, George H. W. Bush. Indeed, one
way of looking at his presidency is to see him as a restoration president
intent on rebuilding and extending the legacy of his conservative predecessor, for whom he has frequently expressed his admiration.[4] The Reagan

Revolution, in its supporters' eyes, was interrupted by the first Bush presidency. George Bush Sr. was more of a traditional Republican than an ideological conservative. In the event his time in the White House was largely occupied with foreign policy issues, first, with the impact of the fall of communism and the reunification of Germany, and, second, with the Gulf war. There followed the even greater interruption of the Clinton presidency. It became the target of ferocious conservative attacks, exemplified by wild insinuations on the editorial page of the *Wall Street Journal* after the suicide of Vincent Foster and the frenzied attempts to find Bill and Hillary Clinton guilty of something, of *anything* in the Whitewater affair. Such extreme partisanship reflected a feeling among conservatives that the Clinton administration was a deeply illegitimate reversal of the Reagan Revolution's salvation of America from the sins and aberrations of liberalism.

The conservative mindset regarding the legitimacy (and to some on the right, divinely ordained nature) of the Reagan Revolution provides an essential context for understanding George W. Bush's presidential perspective. With his own legitimacy confirmed by his re-election, it was hardly surprising that Bush in his second term, even more than in his first, regarded his presidency as giving expression to a deep movement of public opinion and national values in its mission to fulfil the Reagan revolution. This chapter seeks to answer two questions that are important for the world as a whole: Is Bush right in this? And what are his prospects of succeeding in this conservative crusade? To address these issues, we should look first at the details of his policies under three headings: domestic, fiscal and economic policy; foreign policy; and constitutional and judicial policy. Finally, and more generally, we must try to understand the ideological thrust of how this president sees the world, and what he wants to achieve. Only then can we assess his chances of achieving what is beyond doubt an exceedingly ambitious agenda.

II

The president's domestic strategy and his budget plans are undeniably bold, some — even among Republicans in Congress — would say to the point of rashness. Bush's first-term fiscal policy, particular the large tax cuts of 2001 and 2003 that mainly benefited the better-off, did much to transform the budget surplus inherited from Clinton into a large deficit. There was a historical irony in this. Traditionally Republicans have favoured economic caution and fiscal prudence. A substantial strand in the party's thinking has long argued for balanced budgets, even for a constitutional amendment mandating them. However, Bush followed a different course originally plotted by

Ronald Reagan, who came into office as a champion of balanced budgets but went on to run record deficits.

The reason for Reagan's fiscal about-face was simple. He cut taxes, as he had promised to do. But he also increased defence spending. And he failed to cut domestic spending, mainly because entitlement expenditure was sacrosanct and the Democrat-controlled House of Representatives resisted retrenchment of discretionary programmes (Anderson, 1988; Niskanen, 1988). As a result the federal deficit reached record dimensions. Reagan's own budget director, David Stockman later acknowledged that before its first year in office had ended the new administration was headed not for its 'rosy scenario' and the brave new conservative world of the Reagan Revolution but for a fiscal catastrophe (1986). Instead of stamping down on liberal profligacy, the Reagan administration created a structural deficit that exceeded four per cent of GDP for most of its time in office and added US$1.3 trillion (nearly a 200 per cent increase) to the publicly-held national debt.

Moreover, and this is less well remembered, like George W. Bush, President Reagan also tried to reform social security, and ended up failing miserably. Early in his administration, he approvingly showed aides an article in the conservative journal *Human Events* that portrayed social security as a failure. Reagan favoured a plan for replacing compulsory social security pensions with incentives to workers to make their own investments (Cannon, 2000, pp. 205–7). He was only rescued from the damaging political consequences of carrying out these ideas, which had been popular among conservative theorists since the 1960s, by the caution of his advisers, notably James A. Baker and Richard Darman, and Republican Senate leader Howard Baker. Social security reform was safely handed to a bipartisan commission, which recommended modest amendments that met broad acceptance but denied Reagan substantial budget savings.

Bush has followed in Reagan's footsteps by incurring large deficits through tax reductions, increased defence and homeland security spending and — in his case — bigger domestic outlays. In the 2004 election campaign, he promised to begin putting fiscal matters right by cutting the deficit in half by the time he left office. This pledge has been subject to two criticisms not only from Democrats but also from some congressional Republicans, the Congressional Budget Office, academic economists and not a few Wall Street analysts. One charge holds that the deficit can only be cut in half with smoke and mirrors. The other is that the shortcomings of Bush's fiscal strategy will fall heavily on his successor — so heavily that some presidential aspirants may have second thoughts about running for office in 2008 to avoid the responsibility of sorting out the budgetary mess inherited from the outgoing administration.

The President's Office of Management and Budget insisted that the plan to cut the deficit in half in his second term was realistic. For a start, the administration meant to measure its success against the FY 2004 deficit of US$521 billion it predicted in February 2004, not against the actual shortfall of US$413 billion (Andrews, 2005). It also estimated a record increase in tax revenues in FY2005 based on questionable forecasts of the scale of economic growth. Moreover, the White House's fiscal planning did not allow for the costs of its proposed extensions of first term temporary tax cuts nor for future outlays on the wars in Afghanistan and Iraq. Unsurprisingly, therefore, many competent analysts voiced scepticism about Bush's deficit-reduction prospects.

Even if Bush were to achieve his personal goal of cutting the deficit in half over the course of his second term, it looked probable that the fiscal situation would get significantly worse after he left office. The full impact of three major costs — tax cut extensions, social security reform and the addition of prescription drug benefits to Medicare — will only kick in fully after 2008 (Weisman and Baker, 2005). The tax cuts approved in 2001 and 2003 (set to expire respectively at the end of 2010 and 2008) were to cost no more than $1.7 trillion in aggregate, but if made permanent would cost a further $2 trillion through FY 2015. Provision of free prescription drugs for the elderly, which was supposed to cost US$400 billion over ten years when enacted in 2003, carried a price tag of nearly double that once the programme came fully into effect in 2006. Finally, Bush's social security plan, if enacted, would cost a total of $79.5 billion in his last two years in office, but US$675 billion in the following five years. If the tax cuts were made permanent and Bush's social security reform went through, the Congressional Budget Office estimated that the deficit would bottom out at US$250 billion in FY 2008 but then climb to US$335 billion by FY 2015. Even more pessimistically, analysts at Goldman Sachs forecast that the yearly deficit would average US$500 billion from FY 2006 through FY 2015.

Reform of social security is Bush's boldest second-term domestic initiative, on which he has staked his biggest pot of political chips. The pension programme has a place in American political hearts analogous to that reserved in Britain for the National Health Service. To tamper with social security, the 'third rail' of American politics, it has been widely held, was to court political electrocution. That, after all, was why President Reagan's advisers shied away from the reforms Reagan himself wanted. At the same time, there has been widespread concern that social security will incur annual deficits so large that the system will eventually have to be reformed through means of benefit reductions or higher payroll taxes. In popular discussion, attention has focused on the idea that the case for reform is based on the passing of the post-World War II 'baby boom'. But in his 2004 economic report, President Bush's advisers point out that, even when the last surviving baby boomer has died, social security will still be in danger of imbalance and ultimate collapse. In America, as in Europe, people are having fewer children and living longer. More retired people will have to be supported by fewer of their economically active children (*Economic Report of the President*, 2004, pp. 129–47).

Bush's plan for social security sought to avoid bequeathing an ever-growing tax burden to future generations to pay for retirement benefits. It intended the creation of 'personal retirement accounts', into which a portion of retirement savings of Americans under the age of 55 would be placed for investment in the stock market. Current social security recipients and Americans approaching retirement age were to be exempt from this change. Bush and his advisers believed that the profits from the privately managed equity investment plans would safeguard future retirement incomes without need for payroll tax increases. Their agenda also had an ideological dimension: to privatize the single most important, and most popular, of the remaining New Deal programmes, and in so doing to liberate Americans from one of the last chains of their dependence on Big Government.

The plan, of course, was enticing for the financial services sector, which gave it a ringing endorsement. Administration spokesmen also claimed prestigious Democratic endorsement, particularly in the case of President Clinton's acknowledgement that social security needed to be reformed. The truth appears to be that at times President Clinton said he thought it did, while at other times he was not so sure. Attempts to recruit Daniel Patrick Moynihan, who died in 2003, to the cause were even more problematic. The former New York senator, a member of the 1983 Bipartisan Commission on Social Security Reform, thought future programme beneficiaries should be allowed to invest an additional sum in equities on grounds that the working people should have the same chance as the rich to own equity portfolios. But, as his widow and daughter pointed out with some indignation, there was all the difference in the world between allowing people to invest in equities over and above an inviolate government pension and taking a substantial part of the existing state obligation and privatizing it (Stevenson, 2005).

As with the tax cuts and prescription drug benefits, the full cost of Bush's social security plan would not be felt until 2011, after he himself had

left office. It would cost US$1.4 trillion for the first ten years, rising to
US$3.5 trillion in the second decade. As one wag quipped, the president
appeared to believe that if you took care of the billions, the trillions would
take care of themselves. Undeterred by warnings of the excessive cost,
Bush went on the road to campaign for his plan at the start of his second
term. He delivered a forthright message that unless the system was fundamentally reformed, future generations of Americans could not count on a
pension remotely comparable with the present comfortable arrangements.

By no means everyone agreed with the president. According to Princeton
economist and *New York Times* columnist, Paul Krugman, those who argued
for privatization were caught in a 'Catch-22' (Krugman, 2005). Actuaries predicted that economic growth, which averaged 3.4 per cent per annum over
the last 75 years of the twentieth century, would slow to below two per cent
over the first three-quarters of the present century. Accordingly, the Bush
plan's assumption that investing in stocks would yield a return of 6.5 per
cent, or even higher after inflation, looked fanciful at best. By 2050, in
Krugman's estimate, it would require a price earnings ratio of 70 times earnings, five times the historical ratio of 14 times earnings, to achieve this. From
this it follows that privatizing social security could only work if the economy
were to grow fast enough to deliver such huge returns, but if it did do so,
there would be no urgent need to reform the system.[5]

Many politicians, Republicans as well as Democrats, who may not
accept the Cartesian logic of Krugman's calculations, still seem to feel
instinctively that the president, in proposing to replace the existing social
security pension with private savings, was heading into fiscally and politically dangerous waters. In March 2005 the *Washington Post* reported that the
president's campaign had succeeded in convincing two-thirds of those
polled that social security was headed for a crisis, but had failed to persuade
them that his approach for dealing with it was the right one (Weisman,
2005).[6] It was no surprise that Congresswoman Nancy Pelosi (California),
the Democratic minority leader in the House of Representatives, accused
the president of forcing senior citizens to live at a 1940s standard of living
(Birnbaum, 2005). It was more notable that Pelosi's opponent, Republican
majority whip Roy Blunt (Missouri), confided to the *Washington Post* that
'almost everything has to go right to get anything this hard done' (Balz,
2005). Even Senate majority leader Bill Frist (Tennessee) initially seemed in
two minds about whether to back the president's plan (*Fox News*, 2005).
Washington has learned to have a healthy respect for the effectiveness of
the combination of President Bush's fervour and the loyalty of his congressional legions. But many within the Beltway feel that in seeking to pri-

vatize social security, he may have bitten off more than even he can chew.

Other issues of macro-economic policy added to the president's difficulties. The first Bush administration was apparently untroubled by the weakness of the dollar. This was predominantly seen as a bonus for US exporters. It has also, of course, added to the bill for America's growing imports, though not as much as might have been imagined. As a number of commentators sympathetic to the administration have pointed out, several factors made the trade deficit and the pressure on the dollar less serious than they would be for other countries. For one thing, both massive US oil imports from the Middle East and imports of manufactured goods from China were in effect denominated in dollars. (The *renminbi*, or yuan, China's currency, is pegged to the dollar.) Moreover the USA is not dependent only on exports from US ports: most major US manufacturers, such as General Motors, Ford, IBM and their peers produce more for foreign markets from factories abroad than from US plants. There is some reason to believe that foreign exporters to the United States are willing to absorb lower profit margins in order to hang on to a share of the world's largest, and on the whole most promising, market. Moreover, so long as US Treasury bills and bonds are seen as safe and the profitability of US equities is buoyed by confidence in the growth of US productivity, foreign investors — both public and private — are likely to continue investing in America (Coy, 2005).

However, the growing trade deficit continued to put the dollar under pressure. By the spring of 2005 it was running at more than US$60 billion a month. Major US manufacturers, notably of automobiles, were running big losses. Their poor sales were presumably due to poor design and quality as well as to their competitors' cheaper costs. In spite of this, Treasury Secretary John Snow argued that the trade deficit was proof of the success of America's economy because it reflected the ability of US consumers to buy more imports (Becker, 2005). In contrast, Paul Volcker, the highly respected former chairman of the Federal Reserve, warned that the present 'seemingly comfortable pattern can't go on indefinitely. I don't know of any country that has managed to consume and invest six per cent more than it produces for long … I think we are skating on increasingly thin ice' (2005). His successor at the Fed, Alan Greenspan, was more optimistic in declaring, 'I have argued elsewhere that the US current account deficit cannot widen forever, but that, fortunately, the increased flexibility of the American economy will likely facilitate any adjustment without significant consequences to aggregate economic activity.' Yet even he warned of the dangers of excessive complacency in the face of America's trade, current account and fiscal deficits.[6]

In effect America benefited from the willingness of foreign governments, especially Japanese and Chinese public bodies, and private investors
in Taiwan, Hong Kong, the Middle East and Western Europe to keep their
funds in dollars. The availability of the Euro, in particular, as an alternative
reserve currency and the failure of the Bush administration to confront its
international monetary difficulties together raised the question as to how
much longer international investors would continue to support the dollar.
These are technical questions, of course, that will be decided by markets,
not by economists, however eminent.

Two conclusions can be tentatively stated. It is plain that the Bush
administration, as it entered its second term, motivated perhaps more by
the same nationalistic confidence that guided its foreign policy than by hard
analysis, was less concerned by the twin budget and trade deficits than most
other observers. This apparent insouciance, as the second term went on,
was likely to incur domestic political penalties as American workers continued to lose their jobs to foreign competition either because of loss of markets or because of the outsourcing that corporate management adopted as
its own response to the competitive problem. The loss of a comparatively
small number of jobs in automobile plants in Ohio, for example, could
affect Republican prospects in the state that was decisive in Bush's 2004
presidential victory.

III

There are, as I have said, those who attribute Bush's re-election to a deep
subterranean movement to the Right in American public opinion, to a shift
in values at least as profound as that accompanying the New Deal, though
in the opposite direction. Others on the contrary maintain that the outcome of the 2004 presidential election was essentially a reaction to the
9/11 atrocities: to a congruence, that is, between a deep sense of national
outrage and Bush's instinctive response that this was a time that called for
national solidarity and for war.

My own instinct is that there is some merit in both schools of thought.
It seems to me undeniable that the decision to strike at Afghanistan as at
the lair of a dangerous wild beast was in harmony with instincts that were
very widely shared indeed, and was realistically inevitable. It is this, I suspect, that has muted criticism of such departures from the traditional
American respect for the rule of law as the incarceration of 'enemy combatants' without trial at Guantanamo, and the rather un-American climate
of angry ruthlessness that led senior officials, including legal officials, to

condone methods tantamount to torture. It is remarkable, and I would say a break with the best of American tradition, that Presidential Counsellor Alberto Gonzalez was not punished by his boss for describing the Geneva conventions against the torture of prisoners as 'quaint', but was instead promoted to Attorney General at the start of the second term.

The same instinct, I believe, muted domestic criticism of the Bush administration's decision to invade Iraq and of how that decision has worked out. The suspicion that Saddam Hussein possessed and might use nuclear, biological and chemical weapons was the initial justification for war. This gave way to the accusation that the Iraqi dictator was helping Al Qaeda. Finally, when it became clear that there was no truth in either of those charges, the Bush administration fell back on the claim that removal of a brutal regime made the war worthwhile. The habitual and healthy scepticism of the American media was muted by fear of falling out of step with the national mood after 9/11.

The purposes, and the tone, of the Bush administration's attitude to the rest of the world cannot, however, be wholly explained by the terrorist atrocities in Washington and New York. For one thing, as long ago as June 1997, long before they came to power, many of the key members of the Bush circle were planning a 'project for a new American century' that envisaged a massive build-up of military power and the aggressive pursuit of universal American hegemony.[7] It is clear, too, that this project was not imposed, as some on both sides of the Atlantic have assumed, by a half-secret cabal of 'neo-conservatives', obsessed by their desire to help Israel. After 9/11, a new, harder foreign policy, impatient of foreign doubts, became popular in many quarters in Washington and was shared by many of the elements of the coalition that returned Bush to power in 2004.

The roots of this development go back a long way. They can be traced, certainly, at least as far back as 11/9, that is, to 9 November 1989, the day when the Berlin Wall fell. From that moment, Americans felt that they had won the final of the world power championships. Many were of the view, too, that they no longer needed to take much notice of the feelings of captious and unreliable allies. Few noticed that those allies, as a result of precisely the same great change in the world, no longer felt the need to avoid upsetting the Americans for fear they would not defend them against a Soviet Union that soon ceased to exist. Conversely, few in Europe understood how contemptuous many Americans were of their failure to deal effectively with genocidal brutality in the former Yugoslavia. It became fashionable in circles close to the Bush administration to stress the decline of Europe with something like *Schadenfreude*. Conservative commentators liked to point out that native populations in Europe exhibited low birth rates, so that much of the continent's demographic expansion came from immigrants, many of them Muslims. They failed to appreciate that much the same was true in the United States, where immigrants from Mexico and Central America acted the same role as newcomers from Turkey, the Maghreb and the former Soviet empire in Western Europe.[8]

Perhaps the roots of a new, impatient American attitude to the rest of the world go back even further still to the disappointments of the 1970s. There was the shock of losing a war in Vietnam. There was the shock of learning that the United States, once abundantly self-sufficient, needed to import energy, and might therefore be vulnerable to the power of foreigners, including the Muslim Arabs of the Middle East. It was shocking, too, to watch the United Nations, created as forum for bringing American ideals to the world, turned into an arena for bullying America's ally, Israel.

To be sure, in the 1980s, Ronald Reagan did much to heal the fears of the 1970s. He not only made it morning again in America but also laid the foundations of final victory over Soviet communism abroad. National success in the Reagan era generated a new confidence that the US could once again bring to the world the benefits of the American way — and not now just the benefits of democracy, but of an American version of capitalism as well. Though from the opposite end of the ideological divide from Reagan, Clinton and his aides spoke repeatedly of their 'neo-Wilsonian' belief that it was America's duty and destiny to share its political beliefs with the world. Possibly the fact that they did so in a less abrasive tone than officials of the succeeding administration caused the international community to look back on the 1990s as a rosy era of multilateral co-operation.

The Bush people who came to office in 2001 displayed open contempt for foreign governments, and especially for those of Western Europe. It would no doubt have been impossible for any American administration to get support for the Kyoto Treaty through the United States Senate. But where previous administrations might have sought compromise, Bush showed no sign of understanding that many people, in many parts of the world, saw the United States, not as the beacon of enlightenment, but as a society that brooked no restraint on its standard of living. The chasm between American attitudes and those of most other countries on Kyoto, on the proposal for an International Criminal Court and on trade policy, had already transformed attitudes to the United States in many countries, before ever a plane flew into the World Trade Centre.

The newly re-elected President and new Secretary of State Condoleezza Rice made plain their desire to improve relations with fractious European governments. During Bush's visit to Europe in January 2005, briefings and press reports focused on the prospects of improving relations in respect of a number of specific causes of friction. Iraq was one, Iran and its apparent nuclear ambitions another. Europe's desire to end the embargo on arms sales to China was a third. Most European statesmen themselves wanted to improve relations with Washington. However, the gap between the two sides was not one that could be easily bridged.

Despite being the 'lone superpower', the US cannot altogether do without allies and cannot afford to ignore the interests and sensitivities of the rest of the world. It is dependent on foreigners for imports of energy, of raw materials and of cheap manufactured goods, for markets and for investment. It needs foreigners, especially the Chinese and the Japanese, to buy American bonds and so to fund America's trade and budget deficits and prop up the exchange rate of the dollar. It needs immigrants, for old stock Americans, like Western Europeans, are not reproducing themselves in sufficient numbers. Americans, like the rest of us, live in an interdependent world.

The question is, however, whether the president, his administration, and its supporters fully understand this. For one thing, Bush made a number of second-term appointments that appeared less than tactful. Among these were the nominations of Paul Wolfowitz, one of the architects of war in Iraq, to be head of the World Bank, and the abrasive John Bolton, who had gloried in his contempt for international institutions, as his ambassador to the United Nations. These selections suggested, at the very least, that the president was more concerned to please conservative opinion at home than to reassure opinion abroad.

Moreover, the successful holding of elections in Iraq in January 2005 seemed to convince Washington that American-style democracy would soon sweep the Middle East and so justify its military invasion of a sovereign country. The formation of a provisional Iraqi government, the popular demonstrations that brought Syrian military occupation of Lebanon to an end and exceedingly modest steps taken towards reform in Saudi Arabia and Egypt were postulated as further harbingers of regional change. It still seems more likely, however, that the invasion of Iraq will have on balance a negative effect on American influence not only in the Middle East but also the whole Muslim world from Algeria to Indonesia. The US occupation, at time of writing, had not won hearts and minds in Iraq, except perhaps in Kurdistan. The record in terms of practical efficiency was not brilliant. Military tactics had been inept and the political side of the occupation had not been well handled. The restoration of utilities and the repair of the oil industry have been disappointingly slow.

There is at least a danger that the invasion's principal political consequence will not have been to bring Wilsonian progressivism to Iraq, but to install in power there a Shia majority with deep resentments of the United States and strong ties to Iran. If that is the case, Bush's war will turn out to have been, as a French wit said of Napoleon's murder of the Duc d'Enghien, 'worse than a crime: it was a mistake'.[9]

Whatever happens in Iraq, in Egypt and Saudi Arabia, Algeria and Pakistan, not to mention Uzbekistan, democracy looks as far away as ever in these countries. The spread of democracy may well turn out to be compatible with deep suspicion and resentment of the United States. From this perspective, the Bush administration could well be accused of deceiving itself about the benefits of its invasion of Iraq. Its outlook echoes illusions cherished by the Reagan administration and its conservative admirers about American paternity of the democratic revolution in Eastern Europe, a change that that was essentially internally generated.[10]

The heart of the American problem in the Middle East is the widespread resentment of US policy towards the conflict between Israel and the Palestinians. The dilemma is a genuine one. It is perfectly true that Israel remains, compared to its Arab neighbours, a relatively democratic country. It is equally the case that the United States could not honourably withdraw support for Israel, because that might really lead to its destruction. Nor has Washington always backed its ally uncritically over the decades. Having said all that, the United States is almost universally seen in the Middle East as the chief ally both of Israel and of reactionary regimes in Egypt and Saudi Arabia, and as indifferent to the injustices done to the Palestinians.

It is at least arguable that the administration's emphasis on the Middle East distracted policy-makers from a number of equally important and potentially dangerous issues elsewhere. There is, on the one hand, the complex of policy choices posed by the new economic advance and political assertiveness of China in East Asia. These include the possibility of Sino-American co-operation to contain North Korea, clearly much closer to being a nuclear power than Saddam Hussein's Iraq was, at least since the imposition of UN sanctions. The US also has to deal with Chinese sabre-rattling towards Taiwan and bad relations between China and Japan, quite possibly exacerbated by the Chinese government in order to divert attention from growing social unrest at home. Finally, the Bush administration, like its recent predecessors, seems systematically to exaggerate the power and the friendliness of China in comparison with the potential in both respects of India, an established English-speaking democracy. The Communist dictatorship in China attracts American conservatives because of its expansive capitalist aspect, but China remains in many respects, like India, an underdeveloped country with widespread poverty, gross inequalities and serious political unrest.

On the other hand, perhaps in deference to the attitudes of its own supporters, the Bush administration seemed unlikely to grasp successfully the great transnational issues that increasingly preoccupied both the developing continents and, to a lesser extent, European governments. It appeared torn between an instinct that hunger, poverty, global warming and environmental problems are of concern only to more or less socialist sentimentalists and a conviction that the United States had a mission to bring enlightenment and freedom to the developing world, but only in its own, entrepreneurial way. Once again, it is important to be reminded that, in this as in other respects, the administration's attitudes and those of its more strident political partisans appear to be far from representative of American opinion as a whole.

Beyond the specifics of policy in particular regions or on specific topics, in fact, there was a larger question about the Bush administration's capacity to understand, and therefore to manage successfully, America's relations with the rest of the world. This arose out of its ideology, which was both strongly held and genuinely seen as a guide to action. The Bush foreign policy, like the 'Project for a New American Century', was fundamentally rooted in the set of beliefs often referred to as 'American exceptionalism'. This does not just mean that the United States is an exceptionally rich and powerful country, one that now spends more on the military than all the rest of the world put together. More significantly, this concept embodies a belief that the United States is morally different, that is, morally superior, to the rest of the world.

It used to be said that everyone had two countries, his or her own and France. The same, for many of us, can now be said of the United States. My deepest fear, however, is that it will not be easy to maintain good relations between on the one hand American conservatives who seriously think they are morally superior and 'lesser breeds' on the other. The allusion to Rudyard Kipling[11] reminds us that many peoples in the past have believed themselves to possess the mandate of heaven. The British, the French, the Germans, the Russians, the Spanish, the Chinese, the Japanese and many others have fallen into this delusion. It has always proved more or less disastrous, both for them and for those on whom they sought to impose their will.

The Bush administration and its supporters certainly hold the exceptionalist view very deeply. Even Condoleezza Rice, for all her charm, has spoken of pursuing 'optimal goals even if they seem at the time politically infeasible', a formulation of conviction politics Margaret Thatcher could endorse (Sestanovich, 2005). 'If people want to say we're an imperial power,' the influential conservative pundit, William Kristol, airily remarked, 'fine.'[12] President Bush, in his first reaction to 9/11, avowed, 'You're either with us or against us'. That, of course, was in the context of the shock of the terror- ist attacks on New York and Washington, but it does reflect a belief in the moral right of America's supranational authority.

Global American power is undeniable. But the Bush administration, I think, has gone further than merely asserting US power. It assumes that others have a duty to acknowledge American hegemony. The Bush admin- istration may become less truculent than in its first term, but its fundamen- tal mindset showed little evidence of change in the early months of the sec- ond term. In adhering to the 'exceptionalist' view of America's unique duty to redeem the world in accordance with its own political religion, the pres- ident will find popularity with some at home, but will be less effective — except in strictly military terms — abroad.

IV

Early in George W. Bush's second term a number of events seemed to presage difficulties unanticipated by his ecstatic supporters at the time of his re-election. The Bush airliner passed through turbulence on Capitol Hill severe enough to hint that he might not be able to count on automatic sup- port from his increased majorities. The difficulties House Majority Leader Tom DeLay of Houston encountered with the Ethics Committee were uncomfortably reminiscent of the troubles of that earlier Republican *wun- derkind*, Speaker Newt Gingrich. The acrimonious Senate confirmation hearings over the provocative nomination of John Bolton, an outspoken critic of the United Nations, to be US ambassador to that body showed that the upper house would not rubber-stamp presidential choice. The case of Terri Schiavo, tragic and passionately divisive, reopened deep fissures within the conservative movement itself. Bush's most ominous problem, however, was the coming battle with the Democrats over judicial nomina- tions, against the background of increasingly shrill denunciations of 'liber- al judges' from those on the right. That conflict threatened his domestic agenda, at a time when economic difficulties might well require congres- sional support for unpopular action. It was foreseeable by the spring of 2005 that Bush's second term would likely prove a bumpy ride.

Unlike his father, or Ronald Reagan, or Richard Nixon, or indeed, unlike his own position until 2002, Bush began his second term with his own party in control of both branches of Congress. The GOP had effective working control of the House of Representatives. It could count on a clear majority in the Senate, though not on the 60 votes required to defeat a filibuster. As far as Congress is concerned, the president ought to be able to carry out most of his sweeping programme if he has truly restored American-style party government to the extent that some analysts believe. But under the Constitution, there is another separated power, that of the judiciary, which may be harder to control. Indeed, as of the spring of 2005 it looked as if the process of seeking to establish conservative ascendancy over the federal bench might create tensions that would make it hard for the president to achieve his other goals.

One of any president's most important powers is his constitutional right to nominate federal judges, subject to the advice and consent of the Senate. Because of their power of judicial review, judges, and especially the justices of the Supreme Court and the judges in the Court of Appeal, who are the court of last appeal in more than 99 per cent of the cases they hear, have great power over public policy (Rowland and Carp, 1996; O'Brien, 1988). From its outset, Bush's second term promised controversy over judicial appointments because of the acute political and emotional sensitivity of moral issues like abortion and gay rights that were likely to come before the courts

In the past, confirmation of judicial nominations by the Senate, while not automatic, was generally dignified and non-partisan. That began to change with the bitter resistance of southern senators to President Lyndon Johnson's nomination to the Supreme Court in 1967 of Thurgood Marshall, the African-American advocate who had won the great civil rights victory in *Brown v. Board of Education, Topeka*. In the later twentieth century, judicial confirmation became embroiled in the ideological conflict between a Republican Party that was increasingly conservative and Democrats who were more or less identified as liberal.

President Nixon was advised by his staff[13] to remember that 'the decision as to who will make the decisions affects what decisions will be made' (Maltese, 2004, p. 2). With this in mind, he deliberately nominated two very conservative southern candidates to the Supreme Court,[14] so conservative, indeed, that both of them were rejected by the Senate. Ironically, he succeeded in appointing Harry Blackmun, a Minnesota judge of conservative reputation who shocked Republicans by writing the majority opinion in the *Roe v. Wade* judgement that legalized abortion. It was not, however, until 1987, when President Reagan nominated Nixon's former solicitor-general, Robert Bork, a suspected opponent of *Brown* and a declared foe of *Roe*, that ideological lines were drawn as never before. Bork was offensive to liberals and to Democrats for several reasons, but he was a distinguished lawyer and legal scholar and there was no serious question that he was qualified. So when Democrats launched a ferocious attack on him and succeeded in blocking his appointment, Republicans and conservatives deeply resented what they saw as a perversion of the confirmation process. They determined to retaliate in kind for the liberal offence of so-called 'Borking'.

The Reagan administration introduced the ideological screening of judicial candidates by establishing the President's Commission on Federal Judicial Selection, which Attorney-General Edwin Meese said was intended to 'institutionalize the Reagan revolution' (O'Brien, 1988, pp. 21–4). Reagan made a number of what were seen at the time as conservative nominations to the Supreme Court, including those of William Rehnquist as Chief Justice and Sandra Day O'Connor, Antonin Scalia and Anthony Kennedy as Associate Justices.

President Clinton seemed less interested in the ideology of judicial candidates than in their gender or minority status. Even so, Republicans, including Robert Bork, charged that Clinton's appointments to the federal bench came almost exclusively from 'the ranks of the liberal elite' (Weinstein, 1997; Maltese, 2004). In retaliation, Senate Republicans deliberately slowed down confirmation of Clinton's nominees, with the result that 42 of them had not been confirmed when he left office and 38 never received a hearing. The political temperature was further heated up by the Supreme Court's decision, by five to four, in *Bush v. Gore*, which — by ending recounts in Florida — handed the presidency to George W. Bush, even though Al Gore carried the popular vote by more than half a million votes.

In his second term, Bush faced the requirement of appointing a successor to octogenarian Chief Justice Rehnquist, who died from cancer in September 2005. The resignation of Sandra Day O'Connor in June also presented him with the opportunity to tilt the balance of power on the Court towards the right. The Rehnquist Court had a nominal five to four majority in favour of its 'conservative' members over its 'liberal' ones. However two justices supposedly affiliated with the 'conservative' bloc — Anthony Kennedy and O'Connor — were better characterized as 'swing voters'. Therefore, the replacement of the latter with a reliable conservative would have significant effect on the balance of the Court, but the successful nomination of such a true believer could not be taken for granted. Although Bush made clear his intention to seize every opportunity to build a genuine conservative majority on the Supreme Court, the Democrats made equally plain their determination to use every weapon at their disposal to thwart the confirmation of nominees they deemed ideologically objectionable.

Pro-choice partisans assumed that the whole issue of the legality of abortion in the United States would be at stake in any Supreme Court confirmation hearing. 'They have been dancing around on the basic issue,' declared Senator Barbara Boxer (California), 'which is they want *Roe v. Wade* repealed and to take away a woman's right to choose' (Toner, 2004). The Democrats consequently threatened to use their filibuster powers as widely as possible to block action on Republican bills in the Senate. 'I will, for want of a better word,' promised Senate minority leader Harry Reid (Nevada), 'screw things up' (Dewar and Allen, 2004). In turn the Republicans threatened what is called the 'nuclear option', though they understandably prefer the phrase, the 'constitutional option'. That means that they would secure an opinion from Vice-President Cheney, as the presiding officer of the Senate, that it would take only a simple majority of 51, rather than 60 votes, to confirm a judicial nominee.

To be sure, the likely deadlock in Congress must be kept in perspective. The politicization of judicial confirmation is a cause, but also a consequence, of political polarization. But the onset of trench warfare in the Senate would make it more difficult for Bush to enact his tax programme and probably rule out any chance of social security reform in which he had invested so much of his political capital.

The extraordinary case of Terri Schiavo only added to the combustibility of the political environment (Goodnough and Yardley, 2005; Milbank, 2005; Richey, 2005). In February 1990 Terri, the young wife of Michael Schiavo, collapsed with a heart attack. She was partially resuscitated, but her cerebral cortex, the part of her brain that controls conscious thought, was largely destroyed and replaced by spinal fluid. She entered a permanent vegetative state, kept alive by a feeding tube. Both doctors employed by her husband and independent doctors concluded that there was no hope of recovery. While acknowledging the severity of Terri's condition, her parents claimed to detect signs that she recognized them, which inspired their hope that if she could be kept alive, medical science might come up with a cure.

In 1998 Michael Schiavo filed a petition in a Florida court to remove the feeding tube and end Terri's life. The case generated enormous and highly politicized interest. In October 2003 the lower house of the Florida state legislature passed what was known as 'Terri's law', which authorized the state governor to order that doctors continue to feed Terri. In September 2004 the Florida Supreme Court struck down the law, and in March 2005 a Florida court allowed removal of the tube. Four days later a federal judge rejected an appeal by Terri's parents, and the next day a federal appeals court confirmed the district court's decision. In the meantime, in an atmosphere of intense national media excitement and ideologically charged emotion on Capitol Hill, Congress rushed through a statute ordering the doctors to keep Terri alive. President Bush hastened back to Washington from Texas and, in his pyjamas, signed the bill into law before dawn.

Armed with this Federal statute, Terri's parents filed an emergency appeal to the Supreme Court, asking it to order the feeding tube reinserted. The Court, for the sixth time, refused to intervene. The appeals court judgment, rejecting the Schindlers' appeal, was only one sentence long. In a concurring opinion, a federal judge, Stanley Birch, who had been appointed by the first President Bush in 1990, ruled that federal courts had no jurisdiction in the matter and deemed the law allowing the Schindlers to seek review in federal court unconstitutional. He also rebuked the president and the Republican majority in Congress in unusually severe terms for acting 'in a manner demonstrably at odds with our founding fathers' blueprint for the governance of a free people'.

At the height of the excitement, House Majority Leader Tom DeLay (Texas), one of the most powerful voices in Congress, appeared to threaten judges handing down decisions that he did not approve. 'The time will come,' he warned, 'for the men responsible for this to answer for their behaviour.' DeLay subsequently apologized for his remarks, but on this occasion at least the decision of the courts could not reasonably be blamed on the subversive tendencies of 'liberal judges'. Republican presidents had appointed seven of the twelve members of the supposedly errant appeals court. Nor could the Democrats be subject to righteous condemnation. Aware of the inflammable quality of the issue, they went out of their way to keep quiet as the legislation was rushed through Congress. Moreover the public was overwhelmingly critical of the emotional reaction by the president, his brother Jeb (the Governor of Florida) and the Republican majority in Congress. A poll commissioned by CBS News found that 82 per cent of the American public opposed the president and the Congress getting involved, and 75 per cent thought Congress acted as it did because of 'politics' rather than principle.

The Schiavo case reinforced the conviction of many on the right that federal judges have been attempting for years to impose liberal values through judicial decisions. Conservative politicians and their media allies had long fanned the flames of popular resentment against court judgements on race, abortion, gay rights and patriotism (saluting the flag and the like). Senator John Comyn (Texas), a right-wing Republican, for example, suggested that a number of recent attacks on judges by deranged persons could be blamed on, if not justified by, the liberal opinions of the judiciary. Justice Anthony Kennedy also came under attack from those who found foreign influence in his opinion banning the execution of minors in the *Roper v. Simmons (2005)* judgement.

The most significant effects of the Schiavo affair, however, may well be on the conservative coalition itself. The conservative ascendancy drew on different elements with different priorities — libertarian conservatives, authoritarian conservatives, religious, patriotic and pro-business conservatives, for example — making common cause and working together. The new religious Right (including, it would seem, at least on this matter, the president and his brother) embraced the cause of keeping Terri Schiavo alive not out of 'politics', but because they identified the termination of Terri Schiavo's life with the termination of pregnancy in abortion. In the process, they utterly ignored other principles traditionally sacred to American conservatives and to Republicans. One, as Judge Birch pointed out, was the separation of powers. Even more at odds with traditional conservative beliefs, especially in the South, was the way that the majority in Congress and the president trampled on states' rights by enacting a federal statute to nullify a state court's decision. Issues as emotionally agonizing as the Schiavo case are fortunately not frequent. Yet it was a dramatic illustration of how far — to quote former Republican senator and Episcopal clergyman John Danforth — 'Republicans have transformed our party into the political arm of conservative Christians' (2005).

President George Bush entered upon his second term as if his re-election has given him a renewed mandate for bold, ideologically robust action both at home and abroad. At first, he may, thanks to Al Qaeda, have had such a mandate in America for his foreign policy, however unpopular it made him abroad. Certainly he was helped by the unwillingness of the Democrats to challenge him robustly either on the Iraq war or on the generally 'unilateral' (read 'bullying') style of his foreign policy.

Crucial to the ultimate success or otherwise of the Bush presidency will be the unfolding of events in Iraq. At the time of writing, its efforts to claim success there are unconvincing. This is not because the terrorist opposition to the coalition appeared likely to succeed. It was more the case that the political solution Washington tried to impose on a country it seemed not to understand very well was not likely to work out as hoped. Then, too, America's attention span in foreign policy is notoriously short. There is the danger, from the administration's point of view, that public opinion at home will weary of keeping 150,000 troops in Iraq. There is the probability that, so long as the Republican project is for a new American century in which the United States attempts to exports its ideals or impose its preferences almost everywhere, other priorities will jostle Iraq down the agenda. It is not hard to imagine what they might be: political upheaval in Egypt, Saudi Arabia or Pakistan or a crisis over North Korea or Taiwan are among the more obvious candidates.

The domestic prognosis depends on whether George W. Bush's vision of his role as the fulfiller of a Reagan revolution is shared by the majority of a deeply divided American public opinion. It is a bold and idealistic vision. It depends for success not only on converting opponents but also on keeping together the coalition that won the president re-election.

As Bush began his second term, the first priority for his domestic agenda, 'reform' of social security, seemed not to have fired the popular imagination. His management of the economy, with the budget, trade and foreign exchange deficits all apparently out of control, was not impressive. Congress and the Republican Party were restive, and the conservative movement was to some extent divided. The president's second-term changes in his team were in the direction of rewarding loyalty and excluding challenging differences of opinion. His standing in the polls offered little reassurance that he commanded widespread popular support. Bush's supporters may dream that he will be commemorated as a great president by having his image carved in South Dakota rock on Mount Rushmore along with Washington and Jefferson, Lincoln and Theodore Roosevelt, but second-term portends suggested that he was headed, not North by North-West, but South.

Notes

1   The first to promote this prominently was Thomas Sowell in the *Wall Street Journal*, 7 January 2005. 'Now that President Bush has twice gotten himself to the White House', he declared, 'the question is whether he wants to try for Mount Rushmore.' This was also suggested previously by the political consultant, Dick Morris, on 17 May 2002.

2   The Program on International Policy Attitudes at the University of Maryland found in 2003 that only 12 per cent of Americans wanted to see the US as 'the pre-eminent world leader' and 76 per cent wanted the US to 'share in efforts to solve international problems with other countries'. Other surveys by the Chicago World Affairs Council reported similar findings.

3   In an interview with Gwen Ifill on 4 November 2002 Norquist said, 'Watch for lots of legislation to address the investor class.' To be sure, Norquist repeated the Republican assertion that this class is a large and growing one. The fact is that fewer than half of Americans have an

interest, direct or indirect, in the stock market, and a substantial proportion of those that do have an interest worth less than US$5,000. The great majority of significant stock market investments are owned by a small group of the relatively wealthy.

4   See, for example, Bush's eulogy for Reagan at the National Cathedral in Washington after Reagan's death in June 2004.

5   Krugman expanded his analysis of the Bush administration's policy for social security reform in his article, 'America's Senior Moment,' *New York Review of Books*, LII, 10 March 2005. This was a review of Laurence J. Kotlikoff and Scott Burns (2005) *The Coming Generational Storm: What You Need to Know about America's Economic Future* (Cambridge, MA: MIT Press).

6   See Greenspan's speech to the Advancing Enterprise conference, London, 4 February 2005, and referring to his own speech at the European Banking Congress, in Frankfurt, 19 November 2004.

7   The project was signed by many future members of the Bush administration, including Governor Jeb Bush, Deputy Secretary of Defence Paul Wolfowitz and Assistant Secretary of Defence Douglas Feith, as well as by influential neo-conservative intellectuals such as William Kristol. It declared, 'American foreign and defence policy is adrift. Conservatives have not confidently advanced a strategic vision of America's role in the world'. To remedy this, the New American Century called for increased military expenditure to ensure that the United States remained the dominant power in the world.

8   See, for example, a column by George F. Will (2005), 'Suicide by Secularism?' *Washington Post* (4 April). This cited the views of George Weigel, a Roman Catholic commentator on ethics close to Eliot Abrams, a prominent member of Bush's national security staff for the Middle East. It quoted Weigel's opinion that Europe's 'demographic suicide' would cause its 'welfare states to buckle' and was creating a 'vacuum into which Islamic immigrants are flowing'.

9   Often attributed to Talleyrand, this mot was in fact coined by Boulay de la Meurthe (1761–1840).

10   See, among many perceptive criticisms, an article by Jackson Diehl in the *Washington Post*, 19 April 2005. According to him, 'The politics of this Arab Spring are not that simple, either [in Lebanon] or in the other countries where change is stirring. The old autocracies ... are manoeuvring to postpone or rig the democratic elections that are scheduled in the next six months. Powerful Islamic movements — Lebanon's Hezbollah, Egypt's Muslim Brotherhood and the

Palestinian Hamas — waver over an embrace of democratic politics while trying to preserve their violent options. Outside actors, including the United States, grope for the best means to apply their leverage.' See also Jonathan Steele, 'The US is failing — and hatred of the occupation greater than ever,' *The Guardian*, 19 April 2005.

11   Rudyard Kipling, *Recessional*: 'If, drunk with sight of power, we loose, Wild tongues that have not Thee in awe, Such boastings as the Gentiles use, Or lesser breeds without the law'.

12   Kristol said this on Fox Television in November 2003. See Gary Dorrien (2004) 'Benevolent Global Hegemony,' *Logos*, no. 3 (Spring).

13   The aide in question was none other than Tom Charles Huston, responsible for domestic intelligence and security in the Nixon White House, whose recommendations played an important part in setting off the sequence of events that led to 'Watergate'.

14   Clement Haynsworth in 1969 and G. Harrold Carswell in 1970.

2

Conservatism Resurgent?
The Foreign Policy of the Bush Administration

Steven Hurst

Finding critics of George W. Bush's foreign policy is not the world's most demanding research project. Attacks on Bush's 'imperialism' from the left were, and are, predictable. Nor would one expect mainstream liberals to be enthusiasts, though it is more surprising to find them voicing criticisms almost as damning as those of the left: John Ikenberry, for example, has condemned Bush for abandoning a half-century old strategy blending liberalism and realism, in favour of a 'neo-imperialist vision in which the United States arrogates to itself the global role of setting standards, determining threats, using force and meting out justice' (Ikenberry, 2002, p. 44). Most surprising, however, is the extent of criticism by self-defined conservatives, a tendency most prominently represented by Stefan Halper and Jonathan Clarke's *America Alone*. In their view, Bush has deserted the pragmatic conservatism of his Cold War Republican predecessors, with its emphasis on the balance of power, alliances and deterrence, in favour of a radical, utopian programme to remake the world peddled by 'neo-conservative' parvenus (Halper and Clarke, 2004).

What links the criticisms, and what explains the unusual degree of liberal antipathy and the unexpected sight of conservatives attacking a conservative president, is the perception that Bush has abandoned tried and tested practices and principles in favour of a dangerous foreign policy radicalism. This is not a radicalism of ends — the fundamental purpose of US foreign policy, to create a democratic capitalist world order with the US as the leading global power, remains unaltered — but of means. The 'Bush revolution' in foreign policy is 'not a revolution in America's goals abroad, but rather in how to achieve them' (Daalder and Lindsay, 2003, p. 2). The administration has embraced unilateralism whilst demonstrating a barely concealed contempt for international law and institutions. It has elevated a strategy of preemptive war to doctrinal status while dismissing traditional strategies of deterrence and containment as outdated (*National Security Strategy of the United States*, 2002). Established allies and alliances have been treated in a contemptuous fashion with little or no attempt made to acknowledge their interests or concerns. And leadership through co-operation and negotiation has been replaced by the open pursuit of global hegemony and the injunction that 'you're either with us or you're against us'. Whilst all of the above developments represent inclinations which are not wholly new to US foreign policy, nevertheless, under this administration, they have been taken to a 'different, almost philosophical plane' (Cox, 2002, p. 276).

The explanation for this transformation in US foreign policy was typically located in the combination of the events of 11 September 2001 and the influence of 'neo-conservatives' within the Bush administration. Critics asserted with dismay that Bush had become 'the callow instrument of neo-conservative ideologues' or that there had been a 'neo-conservative coup' within the administration (Epstein, 2003; Lind, 2003). Meanwhile, self-proclaimed neo-conservatives proudly trumpeted the alleged triumph of their ideas (Kaplan and Kristol, 2003, pp. 72–5). However, whilst the Bush foreign policy does indeed mark a break with those of preceding administrations, the claim that this is a result of the president's embrace of neo-conservative ideas after 11 September 2001 is largely misconceived. As the first part of this chapter will seek to demonstrate, neo-conservatism has thus far been a rather marginal influence on a foreign policy characterised primarily by continuity rather than change following 9/11. Moreover, whilst unilateralism, pre-emption and hegemonism may be novel in practice, they are far from new to the worldview of American conservatives, the protests of Stefan Halper and Jonathan Clarke notwithstanding. On the contrary, and as the second part of the chapter discusses, these principles represent deep-rooted ideological commitments on the part of the Republican Right.

Neo-Conservatism and Conservative Nationalism

In order to assess the extent of neo-conservative influence on the Bush foreign policy, it is necessary to establish just what neo-conservative ideas are and what distinguishes them from other strands of conservative thought. Most analyses of conservative thinking on foreign policy in the 1990s utilised a threefold categorization:

1   **Isolationists/abstainers/minimalists** — a mixed bunch of libertarians and paleo-conservatives, divided on matters economic but united in rejection of US global leadership and support for a unilateralist focus on self-defence.

2   **Realists/shapers** — concerned primarily with the maintenance of international order and stability, they seek to achieve this through a traditional balance of power maintained by the use of alliances and international organizations.

3   **Controllers/maximalists/internationalists** — optimistic about US power and wisdom, they advocate a benevolent US hegemony, whereby America uses its overwhelming power — unilaterally if necessary — to create a world order conducive to its interests and its values (Garfinkle, 2001; Maynes, 2001; Muravchik, 1996, pp. 9–18).

In these terms, the complaint of Halper and Clarke and like-minded conservatives is that sensible 'group two' thinking has been superseded by crazy 'group three' thinking. The problem with this argument, and the above categorization, is its treatment of the third group as a unitary phenomenon and the identification of it with neo-conservatism (e.g., Podhoretz, 1999). In fact, group three is a conflation of two distinct sets of beliefs, one neo-conservative and the other termed here, and elsewhere, 'conservative nationalist' (Daalder and Lindsay, 2003; Halper and Clarke, 2004; Hoffman, 2003). Whilst the conflation of these factions is not altogether surprising given the extensive degree of consensus between them, it serves, nevertheless, to conceal disagreements which are of considerable significance to any effort to interpret the Bush foreign policy. The following discussion will explain the distinctions between the two groups.

Neo-Conservatism and Conservative Nationalism: Consensus

The broad area of consensus binding neo-conservatives and conservative nationalists comprises the following key beliefs:

1   **Realism:** The realist theory of international relations and its claim that world politics is characterized by a lawless struggle of power-maximizing states is a basic tenet of the worldviews of both factions. The world is assumed to be a dangerous place in which there will always be new threats to American security. Realism further asserts that in this dangerous world the state remains the primary actor and military strength the fundamental source of power. Throughout the 1990s, conservatives repeatedly attacked the idea that economic globalization was ushering in a world in which state power was being steadily eroded and where armed force was increasingly irrelevant (Rice, 2000, p. 50). The urgent need to increase the defence budget in order to sustain a US military capable of enforc-

ing international order was a staple of conservative nationalist and
neo-conservative thinking (PNAC, 2000).

2   **Global predominance:** Neo-conservatives and conservative nationalists alike argue for a 'foreign policy premised on American hegemony'
(Kagan and Kristol, 2000, p. 13). The traditional multi-polar balance of
power is, they aver, inherently unstable, and 'only a hegemonic power
is able to guarantee peace, stability and freedom of commerce among
major powers' (*National Review*, 1995). The demise of the Soviet Union
had left the US as the lone superpower and 'America's grand strategy
should aim to preserve and extend this advantageous position as far
into the future as possible' (PNAC, 2000). As a 'peaceful and non-
aggrandizing' hegemon that seeks to promote an international order as
beneficial to others as it is to itself, US hegemony will be welcomed by
other states (Muravchik, 1996, pp. 30–1).

3   **Unilateralism:** A predilection for unilateralism is a logical corollary
of the first two sets of beliefs. If the world is an anarchic, lawless
place of self-aggrandizing states in which force remains the basic
currency, the mere creation of multilateral rules and norms is point-
less. Those who wish to challenge the international order will simply
ignore the rules. 'No international agreement can possibly be relied
on, by itself' to enforce norms of behaviour (Kristol and Kagan,
1999). Rules only work if they are backed by a credible threat of
force. Whilst many would argue that such threats should only be
made under the auspices of the United Nations (UN), these conservatives note that this subjects US policy to the whims of tyrants and
international renegades. Efforts to enforce the rules of the international order can be hampered by those who are violating them.
Given this assumption, and the fact of America's benign nature,
neo-conservatives and conservative nationalists contend that the
best solution is simply for the US to enforce the peace unilaterally.

4   **Rogue States and WMD:** Finally, neo-conservatives and conservative nationalists agree that 'the proliferation of weapons of mass
destruction and their means of delivery will constitute the greatest
single threat to world security for the rest of our lives'
(Krauthammer, 1991, pp. 31–2). In particular, it is the possibility of
these technologies getting into the hands of so-called 'rogue states',
that is most alarming, and it was generally agreed in the 1990s that
'Iraq ... is the prototype of this new strategic threat' (Krauthammer,
1991, p. 31–2; see also Perle, 2000).'

The primary concern was not that rogue states would launch an unprovoked attack on the American homeland, but rather that they were 'rushing to develop ballistic missiles and nuclear weapons as a deterrent to American intervention in regions they seek to dominate (PNAC, 2000)'. If Saddam Hussein acquired WMD 'the safety of American troops in the region, of our friends and allies like Israel and the moderate Arab states, and a significant portion of the world's supply of oil will all be put at hazard' (PNAC, 1998) because the US would be deterred from responding to Iraqi aggression. Rogue states with WMD represented a fundamental threat to America's hegemonic role.

The threat thus posed was deemed to require a twofold response. Firstly, the US had to develop a National Missile Defence (NMD) system sufficiently effective to deal with the kind of small scale missile attack a rogue state might be able to launch. Such a system would be 'the vital shield that would free the United States to play its leading role undeterred by the threat of nuclear annihilation or of attack by rogue states' (Kagan and Schmitt, 1998, p. 25). NMD, in short was the 'sine qua non' of the whole hegemonic strategy (Kagan and Kristol, 2000, pp. 16–17). Even better, however, and a far more certain method of eliminating the danger of rogue states, was 'regime change'. NMD ought to be sufficient to deter rogue states from aggression, but it offered no guarantee. Moreover, once they had WMD, the elimination of such regimes would become too dangerous to contemplate. All things considered, therefore, 'the most effective form of non-proliferation' was 'an effort to bring about the demise of these regimes themselves' (Kagan and Kristol, 2000, p. 19).

Neo-conservatives and conservative nationalists are thus agreed on the essentially conflictual nature of international relations and the centrality of military power to those relations. They believe that the US can best maintain its own security, and international order, by unilaterally securing its position as global hegemon rather than by seeking to create a balance of power or a multilateral, rule-based system. They believe rogue states armed with WMD represent a grave threat to that project and one that must be eliminated. It is not surprising, therefore, to find them working side by side in interest groups like the Project for a New American Century (PNAC) and within the Bush administration itself.

Neo-Conservatism and Conservative Nationalism: Dissensus

Nevertheless, neo-conservatives and conservative nationalists have a marriage of convenience rather than a true union of shared beliefs.

1   **Ideas, Values and Democracy:** The key division between the two
      factions centres on the importance of ideas and values in US foreign
      policy. In simple terms, neo-conservatives insist that the promotion
      of 'American values' must be central to that policy, while conserva-
      tive nationalists disagree. The neo-conservative position is that it is
      both morally right and in American interests to do this because 'in
      foreign policy, principle *is* realism' (Bauer, 1997, p. 14). This is so,
      they suggest, for a number of reasons, but above all because of the
      validity of the 'democratic peace' theory, which argues that democ-
      racies tend not to initiate war and, in particular, do not go to war
      with each other (Doyle, 1986; Russett, 1993). The primary objective
      of US foreign policy should thus be 'worldwide democracy, for only
      its endless expansion could truly guarantee peace and American
      security' (Abrams, 1995, p. 9).

      Conservative nationalists are not indifferent to democracy, nor do
      they doubt the superiority of US values. They are sceptical, never-
      theless, about whether democracy promotion is a solution to inter-
      national conflict and whether the US is able to achieve it. William F.
      Buckley argues that 'the business of government is to concern itself
      with vital threats to its own interest and to reject the Wilsonian alter-
      native as quite simply beyond our powers' (Buckley, 1997, p. 62).
      One survey indicated that just under half of self-identified neo-con-
      servatives thought US efforts at democracy promotion have been a
      success, whilst only 30 per cent of conservatives agreed (Noonan,
      1999, p. 626).

2   **Humanitarian Intervention, Peace-Keeping and Nation-
      Building:** The distinction between these two perspectives can be
      clarified by examining neo-conservative/conservative nationalist
      divergences in a range of overlapping policy areas, the first of which
      is humanitarian intervention. Michael Noonan's survey showed 59
      per cent of neo-conservatives favoured promoting human rights
      abroad compared to just 38 per cent of conservatives. In the case of
      peace-keeping, 79 per cent of conservatives in Noonan's survey said
      it should not be a key mission for the US, whereas only 44 per cent
      of neo-conservatives agreed. Similarly, 75 per cent of conservatives
      said US forces should not stay in Bosnia for as long as it was neces-
      sary to keep the peace in that country whilst only 47 per cent of neo-
      conservatives concurred (Noonan, 1999, pp. 626, 628, 630). These
      statistics reflect disagreement over both the importance and the fea-

sibility of shaping the internal development of states. According to the conservative nationalist *National Review*, America's first purpose must be 'to advance America's interests abroad; the US military is not a corps of armed social workers' (1995, p. 12). Neo-conservatives, in contrast, not only see peace-keeping as a valid use of US forces but believe nation-building should be as well. Their confidence in the universality of American values leads them to assume that, given the chance, others will embrace them, with the post-war reconstruction of Germany and Japan seen as the paradigmatic example. Moreover, given their faith in the validity of the democratic peace theory, neo-conservatives necessarily regard (democratic) nation-building as vital to US national security.

The Bush Administration Pre-9/11

Having identified the key areas of agreement and disagreement between neo-conservatives and conservative nationalists, we can now examine the policies of the Bush administration in their light.

If anything, Bush's foreign policy statements during the 2000 election campaign indicated a more cautious and traditionally realist foreign policy position than either faction advocated (Dunn, 2003, pp. 282–3). Nevertheless, the core conservative/neo-conservative consensus was broadly articulated. Candidate Bush's commitment to American predominance was made clear in his repeated insistence on the need for big increases in defence spending and especially by his stress on the 'revolution in the technology of war'. By harnessing America's technological superiority, he argued, the US could make itself so powerful that it would be able to 'extend the current peace into the far realm of the future' (Bush, 1999). A predilection for unilateralism was also evident. Bush expressed support for the US Senate's rejection of the Comprehensive Test Ban Treaty (CTBT), and indicated a willingness to abrogate the 1972 Anti-Ballistic Missile (ABM) Treaty without Russian agreement (Balz, 1999). In an article in *Foreign Affairs*, Bush's top foreign policy adviser, Condoleezza Rice, dismissed the 'symbolic agreements' and 'illusory norms' pursued by the Clinton administration and denied that the imprimatur of the UN was required to legitimate the exercise of US power. The US had a 'special role in the world,' she argued, and it should feel free to act unilaterally whenever necessary (Rice, 2000, pp. 47–9).

Finally, the danger of rogue states with WMD was a central theme of the campaign. Rice identified the three states that would later come to constitute Bush's 'Axis of Evil' (Iran, Iraq and North Korea) as the principal danger to the US (Rice, 2000, pp. 60–2). The necessity of developing NMD to counter the threat they posed was the most insistent theme of Bush's national security platform. Moreover, in the specific case of Iraq, Bush and his team were clear that 'nothing will change until Saddam is gone, so the United States must mobilize whatever resources it can ... to remove him' (Rice, 2000, p. 60). Asked what he would do if Saddam Hussein was found to be developing WMD, Bush replied that he would 'take him out' (Buni, 1999, A12).

In the areas where conservative nationalists and neo-conservatives diverged, Bush came down firmly on the side of the former. Democracy promotion was non-existent as a campaign theme. Bush was equally unequivocal when it came to humanitarian intervention and nation-building. He declared that the US 'should not send our troops to stop ethnic cleansing and genocide in nations outside our strategic interest' and that 'I don't think our troops ought to be used for what's called nation-building, I think our troops ought to be used to fight and win war' (Mufson, 2000, A1; Presidential Debate, 2000).

The first eight months of 2001 saw no significant ideological shifts. None of the national security principals appointed by Bush (Vice-President Dick Cheney; Secretary of Defense Donald H. Rumsfeld; National Security Adviser Condoleezza Rice; Secretary of State Colin Powell) were identified with neo-conservatism, and the administration's initial actions conformed to established themes. Unilateralism was a marked characteristic of its early initiatives; it rejected the Kyoto Protocol on global warming, repeated the threat to unilaterally revoke the ABM Treaty and opposed the setting up of an International Criminal Court (ICC), an international small arms pact and enforcement of the 1972 Biological Weapons Treaty.

Outlining the administration's national security strategy to Congress, Rumsfeld revealed its hegemonist worldview. He declared that 'the security and stability that the US armed forces provide is the critical underpinning of [the] peace and prosperity' that the world currently benefits from. If rogue states developed WMD it would give them 'the power to hold our people hostage to nuclear blackmail — in effect to stop us from projecting force to stop aggression'. Such states, he went on, were not constrained by diplomacy or international agreements, nor could the US rely on traditional deterrence. Only NMD would ensure their inability to strike the US and thus free America to maintain international order (Rumsfeld, 2001a).

The second aspect of the strategy for dealing with rogue states was also clearly under consideration. Paul Wolfowitz spoke for a majority of senior administration officials when he insisted of Saddam Hussein that 'there will be no peace in the region and no safety for our friends there ... as long as he remains in power' (Wolfowitz, 2001). After consulting his advisers at his first National Security Council (NSC) meeting on 30 January 2001, Bush decided to release US funding for the Iraqi opposition (cut off by Clinton in 1996) and encouraged them to resume their activities (APS Diplomat Recorder, 2001). Significantly, however, not a single statement about the importance of promoting democracy was made by any senior administration official.

The Bush Administration post-9/11

For many observers, 11 September 2001 marked a decisive turning point in the Bush foreign policy. According to this line of argument, the events of that day allowed neo-conservatives within the administration to persuade the president of the necessity of bringing democracy to the Middle-East in order to eliminate the causes of 'Islamic' terrorism.

The basis for this claim lies primarily in a change in George W. Bush's rhetoric. Having said nothing about democracy promotion before 9/11, the president subsequently raised the concept regularly in key speeches. In his 2002 State of the Union address he declared that 'we have a great opportunity during this time of war to lead the world towards the values that bring lasting peace' (Bush, 2002a). Then, in his West Point address in June the same year, he stated that 'we will extend the peace by encouraging free and open societies on every continent' (Bush, 2002b). The official version of the new 'Bush doctrine', the *National Security Strategy of the United States*, published in September 2002, included as one of its three basic objectives the intention to 'extend the peace' by working 'to bring the hope of democracy, development, free markets and free trade to every corner of the world' (*National Security Strategy*, 2002). And as the administration moved towards war with Iraq in late 2002, Bush told the UN General Assembly that 'liberty for the Iraqi people is a great moral cause and a great strategic goal ... Free societies do not intimidate through cruelty and conquest, and open societies do not threaten the world with mass murder' (Bush, 2002c).

Despite this change in rhetoric, however, the fact remains that US foreign policy since 9/11 is more readily explicable as a logical evolution of pre-existing views than as the result of a sudden conversion to neo-conservative notions of democracy promotion. The *National Security Strategy of the United States* may have had a section on democracy promotion, but the basic thrust of the document was wholly consistent with pre-9/11 thinking. Its first line is a bold hegemonist declaration that 'the United States possesses unprecedented — and unequalled — strength and influence in the world' and that that power 'must be used to promote a balance of power that favours freedom'. Nor had the events of 9/11 changed the focus of the administration with regard to the primary threat to that balance of power. Despite the complete absence of any connection between the events of that day and the danger of rogue states with WMD, it was the latter which remained the central concern. The document reiterated the administration's unilateralism in its insistence that 'we will not hesitate to act alone, if necessary' to deal with that threat.

One element that did appear novel, and which garnered much attention, was the doctrine of pre-emption. The administration now asserted that defending US national security meant 'identifying and destroying the threat before it reaches our borders' (*National Security Strategy*, 2002). Yet, while not stated in such bold terms, this position had always been implicit in its worldview. In testimony to Congress in June 2001, Rumsfeld had said that without effective missile defences the US might 'be forced to take pre-emptive action' to eliminate the threat posed by a rogue state developing WMD (Rumsfeld, 2001a). 9/11 seemingly demonstrated that NMD could not deter or eliminate the threat. In the case of Iraq, of course, few in the Bush administration had made any secret of their belief that only 'regime change' would be sufficient to eliminate the danger.

The administration's immediate response to 9/11 — the invasion of Afghanistan — was principally an act of retaliation rather than the first step in some grand design to remake the world. Nevertheless, the Bush administration's actions were consistent with its pre-9/11 worldview. When, several weeks into the planning of the military campaign, Bush asked his advisers, 'who will run the country?' after the war, it turned out that no one had given the question much thought (Woodward, 2003, p. 195). Rumsfeld, for his part, was clear that 'I don't think [the US attack] leaves us with any responsibility to try to figure out what kind of government that country ought to have' (Rumsfeld, 2001b). Bush apparently agreed, telling his advisers that 'once the job is done …we ought to put in place a UN protection force and leave' because 'we don't do police work' (Woodward, 2003, pp. 237, 310).

The administration's actions largely accorded with its words. The task of nation-building was swiftly handed over to the UN and an International Security Assistance Force (ISAF) composed of non-US forces. In fact, not only did the Bush administration pass the buck on nation-building and democracy promotion, but it actually hindered the process. US troops remained in Afghanistan after the war for the purpose of hunting down the remnants of Al-Qaeda and the Taliban. In order to make that task easier, they tolerated the continued dominance of co-operative warlords in the areas of the country beyond Kabul. The US also resisted the expansion of the remit of ISAF beyond Kabul until September 2003 because of fears that it would disrupt US military operations (Gannon, 2004; Naeck, 2004). That successful presidential elections were held in October 2004, in short, was in spite, rather than because of, US efforts, and the warlords remain powerful whilst President Karzai's authority barely exists beyond the suburbs of Kabul.

It is the war against Iraq, nevertheless, which is seen by most as *the* defining evidence of the influence of neo-conservative ideas. According to this argument, neo-conservatives saw 9/11 as an opportunity to persuade Bush to implement their grand design for democratizing the Middle East. Iraq's function in this project was to serve as an example. By removing Saddam Hussein, and replacing him with a democratic regime, the administration would send a warning to the rest of the tyrants in the region, provide a demonstration of successful Arab democracy and encourage Arabs across the region to demand the same for themselves (Dunn, 2003, p. 291; Kaplan and Kristol, 2003, pp. 95–111).

The two main problems with this argument are the paucity of evidence to support it and the extensive evidence that the Bush administration's decision to remove Saddam Hussein from power was entirely consistent with previously offered rationales. The Bush administration did seize on 9/11 as an opportunity to justify the elimination of Saddam Hussein and his regime, but — for reasons already given — this course of action did not constitute some post-9/11 epiphany.

The first weakness in the 'neo-conservative coup' argument lies in the reasons offered by the administration for the war against Iraq. Bush's UN speech apart, the democratic peace theory was notable chiefly by its absence. In contrast, the three most detailed articulations of the case for war, made by Vice-President Cheney and Secretary Rumsfeld in the autumn of 2002 and by President Bush in his 2003 State of the Union address, contained the same arguments that had underpinned their desire to eliminate Saddam Hussein before 9/11. Containment and deterrence of Saddam Hussein would no longer work. Saddam was a 'brutal dictator, with a history of reckless aggression, with ties to terrorism' (Bush, 2003) who had broken every agreement he ever signed. Nothing that had been done in the last decade had dealt effectively with the danger he posed. If allowed to develop nuclear weapons he 'could then be expected to seek domination of the entire Middle-East, take control of a great portion of the world's energy supplies, directly threaten America's friends throughout the world and subject the United States or any other nation to nuclear blackmail' (Cheney, 2002). The only option, therefore, was to eliminate him before he had the chance to develop WMD (Rumsfeld, 2002). Apart from the tacit admission that NMD was not the panacea they had claimed, every part of this argument had been extensively articulated by the administration principals not only before 11 September 2001 but before they had even taken office.

Undaunted, believers in neo-conservative influence can nevertheless argue that spreading democracy was the real reason for going to war and WMD merely a convenient rationale for selling that war to the US public. Paul Wolfowitz's comment that WMD were emphasized 'for reasons that have a lot to do with the bureaucracy' has been seized on in this context (Wolfowitz, 2003). But this argument requires us to believe that a rationale for action that had been developed and articulated for several years was simply superseded by an entirely new logic overnight. More importantly, it requires us to ignore the fact that, later in his interview, Wolfowitz stated that freeing the Iraqi people from Saddam's tyranny and creating a democracy in Iraq was 'not a reason to put Americans at risk', and that WMD were the number one reason for going to war (Wolfowitz, 2003).

It is certainly the case, nevertheless, that the Bush administration's commitment to post-war Iraq has been much greater than that in Afghanistan, and that it has seen the country through to elections at some considerable cost to itself. Nor is there any reason to doubt that the administration is sincere in its efforts to foster democratic government in Iraq. Yet neither fact need alter our assessment of the basic motivations for the war. Quite obviously, if Saddam Hussein's regime was to be eliminated then it would have to be replaced, and simply installing another dictator was hardly a serious option. It would have been virtually impossible to find a likely candidate untainted by association with the previous regime. It would have risked a repeat of the circumstances that had led to war in the first place, and it would have been a public relations disaster on a global scale. In addition, it should be noted that the complete and total failure to find WMD has left the administration with regime change as the only shred of justification for its actions. For all these reasons, the Bush administration's commitment to creating a viable democracy in Iraq is quite understandable. None of them, however, support the claim that the creation of a democracy was the reason for going to war in the first place.

Conservatism Resurgent?

George W. Bush is not, therefore, pursuing a neo-conservative foreign policy. Nevertheless, that fact does not detract from the radicalism of his foreign policy, whose key characteristics — unilateralism, contempt for international institutions and law, an open embrace of hegemonic ambitions and a readiness to ignore traditional allies and to use force in a pre-emptive fashion — mark a departure from post-1945 practice. It does not follow, however, that this worldview is novel *per se*, or that it is somehow alien to the traditions of the Republican Party or the conservative movement in the United States. Indeed, a brief overview of the past century or so indicates that the policies of the Bush administration represent the resurgence of tendencies deeply-rooted in both.

In the traditional mythology of US foreign policy, the 'Old Right' of the pre-World War Two Republican Party was described as 'isolationist'. Yet the Republican Party dominated US politics between 1865 and 1932, and in that time presided over expansion into Latin America and the Pacific, the 1898 war with Spain and the occupation of Cuba and the Philippines. Under the Roosevelt corollary to the Monroe Doctrine, the US made repeated military interventions in Latin America. The Old Right was not, in short, anti-interventionist as such. Rather, it opposed overseas entanglements in the form of alliances and multilateral and collective security arrangements. The most famous, or infamous, demonstration of this was the Senate's rejection of US membership of the League of Nations. Whilst some of those who opposed membership of the League were isolationists, the majority were not. Their objection to the League was that it was a wrong-headed and ineffective vehicle for the pursuit of US national interests that threatened to tie American hands and subject US foreign policy to the whims of foreigners. Senator Henry Cabot Lodge summed up this position when he asked his colleagues, rhetorically, 'are you prepared to put your soldiers and your sailors at the disposition of other nations' (Paterson et al, 1995, p. 112)? The Old Right was not isolationist; it was unilateralist.

The emergence of the Cold War created a dilemma for the Old Right, as it found itself torn between a profound anti-communism and a fear of entangling alliances, high defence spending and big government. Anti-communism (and political pragmatism) won the day and the Old Right adopted an aggressive, interventionist 'new nationalism' committed to the total defeat of communism (Nash, 1996, pp. 74–5). That transformation, however, in no way implied a total break with past principles. The new nationalism was driven by a hatred of communism, not by an enthusiasm for the liberal internationalist vision of world order underpinning the Democrats' policy of containment. The Republican right retained its old predilection for unilateralism, its hostility towards collective security organizations and its suspicion of alliances. It also developed contempt for the policy of containment, which it regarded as an insufficiently aggressive and decisive response to the communist threat.

These tendencies were clearly evident in the Republican right's response to the Korean War, a catalytic event in its transformation. Within months of the North Korean invasion, the right was attacking the Truman administration's policy of limited war as half-hearted appeasement. It called for the reunification of Korea rather than the mere restoration of the *status quo*, on the grounds that, in the words of Senator William Knowland (California), to do otherwise would leave the US 'living under the gun' and facing an ever present North Korean threat. Korea also saw the Republican right abandon its fear of big government, attacking the Truman administration's US$42 billion defence budget as inadequate to the task at hand. A willingness to take pre-emptive action was manifest in support for General Douglas MacArthur's desire to extend the war to mainland China. Meanwhile continued disdain for collective security organizations was clear in repeated verbal assaults on the UN. According to Senator Robert Taft (Ohio), this body 'has proved that it is not only an utterly ineffective weapon to check military aggression, but that it is actually a trap for those nations that rely on it to secure action against aggressors' (Caridi, 1968, pp. 72–4, 112–16).

Probably the most important intellectual representative of the new nationalism was James Burnham. In a series of books and articles, he outlined a strategy for the defeat of communism which clearly prefigures the worldview of the Bush administration. In his view the policy of containment instigated by the Truman administration was simply inadequate to the task at hand. It did not eliminate the threat or go to its source. It was purely defensive and posed no real threat to the enemy. It allowed the USSR to enlarge its war machine, develop atomic weapons and become stronger and more dangerous. 'To try and contain [the USSR] is as futile as to try and stop a lawn getting wet by mopping up each drop from a rotating sprinkler … To stop the flow we must get at the source.' What was required, therefore, was not containment, but 'a policy of liberation' (Burnham, 1953, pp. 36–7, 69–70, 138).

Burnham was also an unabashed champion of US global predominance. Technological change had shrunk the world, and atomic weapons, in particular, had rendered global dominance by a single power a real possibility. Since the US and USSR constituted the only realistic candidates for that role, it was imperative that the US act decisively:

> The United States has power, greater relative power in the world today than has ever been possessed by any single nation … A positive and adequate policy for the United States would presuppose first of all that the United States should face the fact and the responsibility of power. That done, there would follow at once the realization that the United States must itself, openly and boldly, bid for political leadership of the world (Burnham, 1947, pp. 140–1).

Some people argued, Burnham noted, that if there was to be a world government then it should be organized under the auspices of the UN. He vehemently disagreed, having once described the UN building as that 'East River Madhouse … where the patients wear fancy dress and think they're Napoleons'. In his opinion the UN was an institution which allowed third class nations who had no business involving themselves in major issues of world affairs to obstruct US foreign policy. 'The obvious solution', he avowed, 'would be to give up the UN as a bad job and forget about it.' If that was not possible, then the US should certainly make sure that it got what it wanted from the UN because 'without us … there would be no one to pay the bills and the UN wouldn't matter a damn' (Burnham, 1965, pp. 219, 153, 170).

Burnham was no more enamoured of international law, arms control treaties or any of the other paraphernalia of liberal internationalism than he was of the UN. 'Treaties have never lasted' because there was no world state to effectively enforce them and the communists just cheated anyway. Arms control was nonsense because it was the threat of war that produced arms, not *vice versa*. And the US should certainly not sign up to a Test Ban Treaty because it would be wholly ineffective in halting nuclear proliferation whilst simultaneously undermining the ability of the US to develop better nuclear weapons and Anti-Ballistic Missile (ABM) systems (Burnham, 1947, p. 155; Burnham, 1965, pp. 85–8).

All of these views, of course, are to be found in the worldview of the Bush administration. And that worldview can therefore be seen not to be 'neo-conservative' so much as a contemporary manifestation of the 'new nationalism' that emerged out of the Old Right of the Republican Party in the early Cold War. The reason for the apparent novelty of the Bush worldview is simply that, for as long as the Cold War lasted, the views of Burnham and the Republican Right were destined to remain marginal factors in US foreign policy, for two basic reasons. In the first place, they remained a minority within their own party and so were unable to dominate its policy positions. More fundamentally, and not unrelatedly, the reality of Soviet power, and the ever-present danger of nuclear war, made the policies of global hegemony, aggressive military action and liberation a fantasy. This was nowhere more readily demonstrated than during the Hungarian revolution of 1956, when Burnham and others who had called for military action to liberate Eastern Europe were to be found rapidly and embarrassingly rowing back from that position into advocacy of vague peaceful alternatives.

In the early twenty-first century, however, neither of these conditions pertains. In the first place, the Republican Party has been transformed. The liberal and internationalist wing of the party, which formed a centrist alliance with internationalist Democrats that dominated Cold War foreign policy, has become a steadily diminishing minority. What was the right of the party has now become its centre, and the ideological descendants of those whose views were marginal in the 1950s and 1960s dominate policy-making. Whilst the ideology of the Republican Right may not have been preserved in aspic (economic protectionism is less *de rigueur* these days and evangelical Christianity rather more so), many of its traditional inclinations have clearly survived to reappear in the foreign policy of the Bush administration. Moreover, the principal obstacle to the untrammelled exercise of US power, in the shape of the USSR, is no more. Under conditions of effective 'unipolarity', ideas that during the Cold War looked lunatic or suicidal now appear to many to have entered the realm of the distinctly possible and eminently desirable.

Conclusions

The radical nature of the Bush foreign policy, and its divergence from post-1945 patterns, was not the result of an internal coup by ex-liberals with wild utopian ideas about converting the world to democracy. Rather, it is the logical product of the rightwards evolution of the Republican Party over the past half century, combined with a permissive international (and, after 9/11, domestic) environment. Far from the administration's philosophy being alien to Republican thinking, it is bred deep in the bone of the right of the party.

There may even be a case for arguing that, rather than the Bush foreign policy being the aberration, it was the Republican internationalism of the Cold War which was the oddity. Facing the inescapable fact of Soviet military power abroad and a dominant New Deal consensus at home, conservative Republicans were marginalized and forced to compromise their principles and trim their ambitions. With the collapse of domestic liberalism and Soviet communism, they have been able to recapture both their party and political power and been freed to pursue their ambitions in their preferred fashion both at home and abroad.

None of which is to say that the Bush second term will therefore conform to the patterns of the first. In the first place, it is almost certain that the wars against Afghanistan and Iraq will prove to be the exception rather than the rule. The former was a unique response to the specific events of 9/11, while the latter, although much longer in gestation, was also exceptional. Despite being lumped together with North Korea and Iran in the so-called 'Axis of Evil', Iraq was clearly different to the other two. Above all, it was 'doable', in contrast to North Korea, because of its possession of nuclear weapons, and Iran, given the long term commitment of US forces to Iraq. Barring another 9/11 or similar, the second Bush administration appeared unlikely to engage in further wars.

Secondly, and ironically, in view of the conventional explanation of the war against Iraq, neo-conservative ideas about democracy promotion may be *more* prominent in the second term than in the first. With the Iraqi 'threat' dealt with, US foreign policy needs a coherent public rationale. Certainly, President Bush has been pushing the argument that democracy is the answer to the twin threat of rogue states and terrorism ever more strongly since his re-election (Bush, 2005a; 2005b). To a considerable extent, this is simple opportunism. The regime of Saddam Hussein was eliminated for strategic reasons, but its overthrow presented an opportunity to push for the spread of democracy in the Middle East. The elections in Palestine and events in Lebanon created a further momentum which the administration has sought to exploit. Whether anything significant will result from this, however, is doubtful. The Israeli-Palestinian conflict is not going to suddenly resolve itself because of the election of Abu Mazen, and other hints of change in the region remain vestigial at best. Moreover, an appropriate scepticism must be maintained with regard to the sincerity of the administration's commitment to spreading democracy. Given the record so far, there seems little reason to doubt that when democracy is seen as incompatible with US strategic and economic interests it will come a poor second to both. US support for authoritarian regimes in Pakistan and Uzbekistan, its encouragement of the attempted coup against the democratically elected Hugo Chávez in Venezuela, and its unwillingness to deal with elected Palestinian leaders who do not conform to its preferences, all suggested that this will remain the case.

There are also reasons to believe that a certain degree of pragmatism may come to temper the tendencies demonstrated by the administration in its first term. Even in the absence of the USSR, the world is not as malleable as US conservatives, with their instinctive preference for the swift and absolute solution of any problem, would like. The ongoing conflict in Iraq is likely to tie down US troops and demand considerable expenditure for some time to come. The budget deficits run up in the first term will have an impact (both political and economic) at some point. As 9/11 grows more distant, so Congress is likely to become less supine, and the American public's instinctive lack of enthusiasm for unilateralism and grand hegemonic ambitions is likely to reassert itself. In the face of these considerations the utility of co-operative allies, at least, may become more apparent to the administration, as indicated by the tone of President Bush's trip to Europe early in 2005.

Any such shifts in policy, however, will probably be limited and purely utilitarian. The administration's realism, unilateralism, hegemonism, contempt for the UN and disdain for allies who dare to question its judgement will remain essentially undimmed. Nor should we expect things to be otherwise, for these tendencies do not reflect a temporary coup by a bunch of wild-eyed ex-Democrats whose crazy ideas will soon be marginalized once the Republican Party regains its senses. On the contrary, they reflect the rightward evolution of the Republican Party in the past half century and the consequent resurgence of a deep-rooted and decades-old conservative worldview that is, and is likely to remain for the foreseeable future, the dominant tendency in the Republican Party.

3

President Kerry's Foreign Policy: Continuity and Discontinuity in Contemporary US Foreign Policy

John Dumbrell

Introduction: Clinton, Gore and George W. Bush

Shortly before the 2000 presidential election, Jacob Heilbrunn published an article entitled 'President Gore's Foreign Policy' (2000). At one level, the following discussion is offered as response to that excellent, if prophetically inaccurate, piece. More generally, this chapter engages with this book's themes of change and continuity. Would a Kerry Presidency have greatly changed the style and shape of post-9/11 US foreign policy? Is there now a governing, bipartisan consensus which any president in the foreseeable future will be unable or unwilling to challenge? Were there substantial shifts, not only in tone but in content, between the first and second George W. Bush administrations?

The Heilbrunn article postulated a major, though largely unreported, foreign policy debate between 2000 presidential candidates Al Gore and George W. Bush. It described the latter as a likely international disengager, unilateralist and even neo-isolationist. Heilbrunn particularly noted Bush's disinclination openly to condemn the conservative nationalist views of the victor in the 1996 Republican presidential primary in New Hampshire, Pat Buchanan. In contrast, he presented Gore as the internationalist candidate: a liberal hawk who might be expected to intervene internationally for humanitarian purposes. Though the public proved fairly indifferent to the foreign policy aspects of the election campaign, Heilbrunn depicted the Gore-Bush battle as a pivotal moment in the development of post-Cold War American foreign policy. He also considered a major influence on both candidates to be their respective fathers: the anti-Vietnam War Senator Albert Gore and President George H. W. Bush. (As is the way in these matters, fatherly influence may be discerned sometimes as much in reactive as in duplicative terms.) Heilbrunn saw public and congressional neo-isolationist sentiment as President Gore's major problem, and identified

Colombia as the likely site of his most challenging foreign policy crisis. Vietnam memories would also continue to play a major role.

Before moving to the 2004 presidential election, we may pause briefly to consider the issue of Clinton-Gore-Bush continuity. Heilbrunn, along with most commentators, anticipated that a President Gore was likely to act generally in the spirit of a Clinton third term. There would have been different emphases, possibly reflecting Gore's personal interests and priorities — as with matters relating to the environment. The general expectation was, however, that Gore would have worked with veterans of the Clinton foreign policy and retained its second term focus and priorities. What is perhaps less often observed is that this focus and these priorities had already shifted from those of the Clinton first term.

Faced with a Republican-controlled Congress from 1995 onward, the Clinton administration had moved towards unilateralist positions on some issues. This was notably the case regarding its opposition to US participation in the International Criminal Court, a stand that the president only reversed for symbolic reasons in his very final days in office. The second Clinton term also reflected the confidence engendered by undisputed American international primacy. As such it showed itself willing — as in the 1999 bombing of Kosovo — to act militarily without United Nations Security Council sanction. The second Clinton administration also increased the defence budget and, under Republican pressure, revived the National Missile Defence programme.

The tone of the new Bush administration — unilateralist, 'Americanist', nationalist — was very different from that of Clinton's second administration. In many areas, for example the virtual disengagement from the Israeli-Palestinian peace process, it departed from the likely Clinton-Gore track. In a sense, the post-9/11 Bush foreign policy, with its ditching of any pre-9/11 neo-isolationist inclinations, almost represented a return to the unapologetic internationalism of the second Clinton administration. However, we should be cautious about ascribing too much discontinuity between Clinton-Gore and George W. Bush. This should be borne in mind when considering the putative Bush-Kerry transition, and, of course, the actual transition between first and second George W. Bush administrations (Dumbrell, 2002).

Moving on four years from the Bush-Gore contest, we can see that all has changed, and all has not changed. The 2004 election, for example, saw another 'battle of the fathers'. Candidate Kerry invoked those passages in President Bush Sr.'s book warning of the perils of a sustained invasion of Iraq in 1991. Commentators examined former US diplomat Richard

Kerry's book advocating a cautious, post-Vietnam multilateralism for clues as to his son's likely foreign policy. (Bush and Scowcroft, 1998; Kerry, 1990.) Vietnam memories also dogged the Bush-Kerry contest. In contrast to 2000, however, 2004 was in many ways an election more like 1968: one with foreign and national security policy at its centre. Although exit polls and journalistic comment tended to add weight to the importance of moral/conscience issues in securing Bush's 2004 victory, both pre- and post-election surveys pointed up the centrality of (widely defined) War on Terror concerns. A Pew Research Center survey, released in August 2004, for example, found 41 per cent of Americans citing international and security concerns as the most important problems facing the US (Small, 2004; Pew Research Center, 2004; Chicago Council on Foreign Relations, 2004).

Without straying too far into the murky swampland of counter-factual history, this chapter seeks briefly to review the 2004 foreign policy debate, focussing particularly on the promises and likely trajectory of a Kerry success. It then addresses the related issue of the continuity between the foreign policy of the first and second George W. Bush administrations.

Kerry's Background and Record

At times, the 2004 campaign seemed to be more preoccupied with Vietnam than with Iraq. Despite major differences between the two conflicts, debates about one war shaded into concerns about the other. Kerry's history of war heroics *and* anti-war leadership gave his campaign an extraordinary degree of resonative weight and complexity. It clearly also pushed the candidate into the position, especially at and following the Democratic Convention, of prioritizing foreign and security over economic issues. This decision, though responsible and worthy in itself, left the candidate open not only to attacks from Swift Boat Veterans, but also to perils of fighting the election on grounds — national security and War on Terror — which would ultimately favour the president.

Since we cannot peer into his soul, we cannot foresee how Vietnam memories would have affected the foreign policy outlook of a President Kerry. After all, even now, it is far from clear exactly what the 'lessons of Vietnam' are. Should a president avoid limited war altogether? Should he always take the war to the enemy? Should America always fight for something tangible — like oil — or is simple 'freedom' enough? Some insight into the lessons John Kerry drew from the Vietnam War may be gleaned from an interview that he gave to *The New Yorker* in May 2004. Vietnam, he declared, 'taught me about the promises you make to Americans; about telling the truth about what you're into and not lying — about obligations

to those who serve.' The interview offered some backing for the view that
Kerry's lessons of Vietnam included an extreme caution about messianism
in foreign policy, along with an awareness of the dangers of veering irre-
sponsibly between the extremes of assertive power-projection and intro-
spective, guilt-ridden caution. Kerry took issue with Madeleine Albright's
remark about America being 'the indispensable nation', commenting: 'It
has fallen to us to be that country. It's not romantic, it's not arrogant, it's
just a reality, that we've been needed to deal in so many situations to make
something happen.' (Gourevitch, 2004, pp. 57–8). The outlook of Kerry,
and of figures associated with his campaign, such as Senator Joe Biden
(Delaware), has been well described as embodying the determination not to
allow foreign policy failure to derail responsible internationalism (Starobin,
2004; see also Kranish, Mooney and Easton, 2004; Brinkley, 2004).

Kerry's Senate voting record, of course, became prime hunting ground
for Republicans attempting to consign him to the 'far left bank' of American
politics (Martinez, 2004). As a senator representing Massachusetts for nearly
20 years, Kerry had by 2004 cast around 6,000 votes — many on procedural issues, and of a complexity that defies simple generalization (Clinton,
Jackman and Rivers, 2004). Most famously, of course, Kerry voted against
authorizing the 1991 Gulf War — he invoked Vietnam memories at the time
and quoted from the antiwar novel, *Johnny Got His Gun* — but *for* authorizing
war in 2002. Initially cautious about attacking the president's war, Kerry was
branded 'Bush lite' in the Democratic nomination campaign. A change of
tone was evident by December 2003, when he condemned Bush foreign
policy as 'the most arrogant, inept, reckless and ideological' in recent memory. 'How is it possible', he asked, 'to do what the Bush administration has
done in Iraq: win a great military victory yet make America weaker?'
(Gourevitch, 2004, pp. 50–1).

Kerry's shift against the war reflected both the deterioration of the situation in Iraq and the opening of electoral opportunities. Howard Dean's primary campaign showed the possible benefits of moving beyond 'Bush lite'
to the assumption of a more robust anti-war position. In a campaign with so
many Vietnam War echoes, Dean thus played the role of Eugene McCarthy
to Kerry's Bobby Kennedy. Kerry's vote against the $87 billion appropriation
for the military in Iraq and Afghanistan caused problems on the campaign
trail. It was, at one level at least, the product of procedural complexity — an
amendment offered by Senator Joe Biden. At another level, the vote was a
response to Dean's anti-war challenge, and became a hostage to the fortune
of candidates playing to core party support in the primary campaign and
then facing a more centrist electorate after nomination. In yet another

Vietnam War echo, Kerry's final description of the Iraqi invasion as a 'colossal error' recalled all the 1960s/1970s debates over whether the earlier war was a mistake, the product of deliberate deception, or just the inevitable expression of American imperialism.

On the basis of his Senate record, Kerry may reasonably be described as a 'learning peacenik'. His opposition to high defence appropriations continued into the 1990s. In 1994, for example, he voted to divert B-2 bomber funds to domestic spending. In 2000 he voted to delay National Missile Defence deployment. Yet, like Biden and several of his 2004 campaign associates, he was a strong supporter of Clinton's 'liberal hawk' interventions in Haiti, in respect of the broadening of mission aims in Somalia, and in the former Yugoslavia. Kerry's record was complex. In September 2004, journalist Paul Starobin described the post-1989 'learning peacenik' view, as follows:

> The worldview of the Kerry folks [the candidate and his advisory team] can best be understood as the perspective of an East Coast, Liberal Establishment crew that overcame its own Vietnam-grounded hesitations about the political use of military power during the Balkans crises of the 1990s and now worries that liberal populists, pointing to the morass in Iraq, will force a retreat away from necessary interventions in the future (2004, p. 1281).

Kerry actually opposed the lifting of the arms embargo on the Bosnian Muslims in 1995. Less of an instinctive 'liberal hawk' than Biden, Kerry's road to support for the Kosovo bombing was difficult and beset by doubts. He certainly did not argue for anything approaching concerted intervention regarding the Rwandan genocide of 1994. By March 1999, however, he was supporting a multilateral, NATO action in Kosovo. In May, he backed the sending in of US forces: 'now that we have decided to intervene, let us at least have the courage to persevere'. Only 'our own lack of resolve' could turn Kosovo into a new Vietnam (Starobin, 2004, p. 1282).

One consistent theme in Kerry's Senate record was support for free trade. In relation to China policy, for example, Kerry was an advocate of integration rather than of strategic containment. He strongly backed Chinese entry into the World Trade Organization. On Cuba, Kerry voted consistently to keep open the possibility of normalization, attributing the retention of the embargo to the exigencies of Floridian politics.

Kerry's Campaign

Kerry's criticism of Bush on the campaign trail centred on his opponent's unilateralism and alienation of allies, especially those in Europe. He positioned himself as an opponent of administration arrogance and neo-imperialism. This stand implicitly identified him with those interpretations of the Bush foreign policy which stress its revolutionary and neo-conservative nature (Daalder and Lindsay, 2003). According to the Kerry campaign, President Abraham Lincoln's vision of America as 'the last best hope of earth' did 'not encompass and reach for global empire'. 'Instead of demeaning diplomacy', President John Kerry would 'restore diplomacy as a tool of the strong' (Council on Foreign Relations, 2003; Kerry campaign website).

Kerry's foreign policy position coalesced around four 'imperatives': military modernization, 'a new era of alliances', 'deploying all that is in America's arsenal' against terrorism, and 'freeing' the US from Middle Eastern oil dependency. He broadly aligned himself with the 'revolution in military affairs', though his criticism of the lack of planning for Iraq clearly distanced him from the Bush-Rumsfeld Pentagon. Kerry promises for his presidential watch included the following commitments. National Guardsmen would be used only for homeland duties. Military special forces would be doubled in size, with at least 40,000 more active duty forces for the army. Defence Secretary Donald Rumsfeld's technological transformation of the military would be speeded up and concluded. Accordingly, most commentators concluded that Kerry budget requests for defence spending would have been roughly similar to those issued by a second term Bush White House. Kerry repeatedly emphasized the value of multilateralism and the support of Western European allies on grounds that hostility to the US acting alone and pre-emptively had damaged global American influence. He also portrayed Iraq as a diversion from, rather than an aspect of, the War on Terror. Finally, candidate Kerry proposed to eliminate US reliance on Middle Eastern oil, by a mixture of new technologies ('hybrid' technology) and geographical shifts in supply. However unconvincing his remedy on this score, it certainly contributed to his willingness to make criticism of the ruling regime in Saudi Arabia a part of his campaign. In clear contrast to Bush, Kerry was prepared to draw attention to Saudi human rights abuses and ambivalence towards Sunni terrorism.

Though accused by Republican spokesmen of wishing to quit Iraq prematurely, Kerry in fact — in a rather unfortunate echo of Richard Nixon and Vietnam — spoke of exiting in four years time. Opponents predictably seized on his criticism of administration policy in Iraq as aiding terrorists. In reality Kerry's position on the war was inevitably cautious and exploratory: telling points about Iraq had to be made in such a way as to minimise the credibility of the inevitable charges of lacking patriotism. Kerry experimented with various rhetorical strategies: by turns, accusing the Bush team of inflexibility, ideological rigidity, while also (especially in Afghanistan) of lacking real perseverance and commitment. A promising part of Kerry's repertoire was his assertion that, in this election, the Democrat was the conservative, the believer in traditional alliance patterns, standing opposed to the 'revolutionary' Bushite unilateralists. Yet, despite scoring some good hits, Kerry failed to develop a consistent critical line that shielded him from charges of lacking patriotism in a time of war.

Inevitably, the politics of war dominated the campaign in a way, at least with the benefit of hindsight, that was always likely to favour the incumbent. Kerry presented himself as a multilateralist and supporter of diplomacy, while always emphasizing his willingness to use unilateral force when required for the national security. Regarding Cuba, he sought to exploit the unpopularity among many exiles in Florida of restrictions on travel and the sending of cash remittances to the island. However his Senate support for moves towards normalization of US relations with Cuba proved problematic for his campaign in this crucial battleground state. As a consequence he was pushed into endorsing the embargo. Nevertheless, many commentators anticipated that a Kerry presidency would see efforts to break the Cuban deadlock. Kerry also offered to re-prioritize the denuclearization of the former Soviet Union. A largely unspecified new negotiating position would be developed for North Korea. The Kyoto Protocol on global warming would be renegotiated to make Senate ratification possible. On the other hand Kerry did not challenge the Bush stance on China that combined selling arms to Taiwan while putting pressure on Taipei not to declare independence, encouraging some degree of Sino–US convergence on the War on Terror, and showing awareness of emerging Sino–US rivalries. Kerry urged greater respect for South American democracy. In the Middle East, moderate Muslim opinion would be strengthened by a newly positive attitude to the Israeli-Palestinian 'road map'. Investment — presumably a revival of Bush's Greater Middle East initiative — and public diplomacy would also be prioritized in the region. Despite Sandy Berger's comments in a much quoted *Foreign Affairs* article on a Democratic foreign policy (2004), Kerry maintained a deafening silence on Guantanamo and the International Criminal Court. Much clearer was his attitude to free trade. He attacked 'outsourcing' and promised to abolish tax breaks that encouraged companies to shift production abroad. Unlike Clinton's campaign in 1992, however, Kerry's 2004 speeches to labour audiences contained no hints of protectionism. Addresses in the industrial belt, including the swing state of Ohio, offered little beyond sympathy and the commitment on 'outsourcing' tax breaks: 'I won't come here and tell you that all the rivers of steel will flow again' (*International Herald Tribune*, 17 May 2004).

Predictions

What difference would a Kerry presidency have made? The question raises massive problems of structure and agency, and of 'levels of analysis' in international relations. Much depends on the perspective of the enquirer. No American president is going to disband the army, institute revolutionary socialism, or invade China (or, even, in contemporary conditions at least, North Korea). If one takes the view that US foreign policy is made on Wall Street, or is entirely deducible from the polar structure of the international system, a change of president is unlikely to effect big changes. At one level, current US foreign policy clearly *is* the product of military unipolarity, asymmetric threat and shifting global American economic interests.

The study of presidents — their backgrounds, likely reactions, personalities, beliefs — is just one level of analysis, yet it is an exceedingly important one. One would have to be a very arch-determinist indeed to fail to allow for personal outlooks, misjudgements and belief structures. As Kenneth Waltz, often regarded as a ultra-determinist, acknowledged: 'One cannot assume that the leaders of a nation superior in power will always define politics with wisdom, devise tactics with fine calculation, and apply force with forbearance. The possession of threat power has often tempted nations to the unnecessary and foolish employment of force...' (1979, p. 201).

Presidents do matter, and they matter especially in foreign policy. In his extraordinary study of presidential structure and agency, Stephen Skowronek portrayed the US presidency as a 'blunt disruptive force,' overturning and disturbing established structures (1997, p. 4). In foreign policy in particular, presidents — especially under conditions of declared international crisis — are able to cut through bureaucratic politics. They are able to replace the old senior foreign policy team with a new guard, to exploit (especially in the first term) the 'honeymoon' period, and also to effect change by declaration as much as by legislation. If presidents matter anywhere, they matter in foreign policy.

We need also, as ever, to look to history. There have been ten presidential transitions since 1945, eight of them in the wake of a presidential election. In examining the seven that involved (as would a Kerry takeover from George W. Bush) a change of party, one is admittedly struck as much by continuity as by abrupt change in foreign policy. The 1952 Republican platform, for example, attacked the 'futile and immoral' policy of containment. Under President Eisenhower, however, containment was not abandoned in favour of 'rollback'. Manifestly, the defining events of recent history — the onset of Cold War, the defeat in Vietnam, the end of the Cold War, 9/11 and the onset of the War on Terror — loom much larger than mere presidential transitions. There certainly were important continuities during the presidential/party transitions: between, for example, Carter's later, containment-oriented, foreign policy and the early Reagan policies; between LBJ's rather desperate search for arms control and Nixon's pursuit of détente. As already indicated, it may also be asserted that there was a degree of continuity between President Clinton's confident, increasingly unilateralist post-1996 policy and the 'Americanist' outlook of George W. Bush and his team. When incoming presidents seek to define themselves against predecessors, they often caricature or distort that predecessor's actual record. For example, President Reagan defined his policy against Carter's early 'global community' phase, George W. Bush against Clinton's 'assertive multilateralism': both ignored the extent to which policy had actually shifted in their predecessors' later years.

Clearly, arguing from history is problematic. Cases can always be made for both continuity and discontinuity. Campaign stances, especially on foreign policy, are often vague — they certainly were in Kerry's case — and provide only a modestly helpful guide. Much of foreign policy consists of responding to the unexpected and of adapting to complexity. Yet new administrations, especially if they involve a change of party control at the White House, do bring in a (usually over-confident) shift in world outlook. JFK and his 'action intellectuals', Carter and the commitments to human rights, George W. Bush and his mixture of neo-conservatives and offensive realists constituted significant, if far from absolute, breaks from the immediate past. Zbigniew Brzezinski described the early mood of any presidency as one of 'ecstatic emancipation from the past', rapidly followed by 'a discovery of continuity, and finally a growing preoccupation with Presidential re-election' (1983, p. 544). New presidents, especially in their first two years, do tend to make a difference. The precise difference, of course, is very unpredictable. Some new presidents, for example, fall victim to what may be called the 'law of over-compensation'. Leaders widely seen as leaning towards conciliation may seek to prove their mettle by following lines of aggression; their putatively pugnacious counterparts turn into conciliators.

Between Kerry's emergence as leader in the primary campaign and the November 2004 elections, predictions for a Kerry presidency were very varied and unexpected. Some commentators on the far left, for example, urged a vote for Bush on the grounds that (in the words of Gabriel Kolko) the incumbent president was 'much more likely to continue the destruction of the alliance system that is so crucial to American power' (Pilger, 2004, p. 15). In this view, Bush alone would destroy the American empire through his over-reaching hubris. More mainstream comment tended to divide into those who saw little difference between the candidates and those who, like G. John Ikenberry (and, in turn, like Heilbrunn in 2000) saw 2004 as a pivotal foreign policy election (Ikenberry, 2004; Ikenberry and Kupchen, 2004).

In some senses, the varied predictions appeared to reflect differences between America and Western Europe. Several prominent European commentators took the line that Kerry did not offer distinctive policies, and that international circumstances — and especially the involvement in Iraq — would box in the new president. In their line of thought, Kerry, unlike his two Democratic predecessors, was a Washington 'insider'. He would also have been denied the degree of policy freedom accorded to Carter by the defeat in Vietnam, and to Clinton by the end of the Cold War. Kerry was the prisoner of 9/11, the War on Terror, the 'unipolar moment', and, however unwillingly, of the war in Iraq. American hegemony was not in question. Michael Cox wrote that the Democrat was 'four square behind Israel. He had not criticized the Bush military budget. And in spite of his various attacks on the president's unilateralism, he made it clear that he would be multilateral where possible, but go it alone where necessary' (Cox, 2004, p. 15). A few days after the election, British Prime Minister Tony Blair (for a host of reasons, not all connected to the cause of objective academic analysis) played down the degree of difference a Kerry victory would have made. 'We would still have been sitting here working through Iraq, the Middle East peace process', he observed, 'all these issues would have remained' (*The Times*, 5 November 2004).

Some leading American commentators took a very different tack. For Ikenberry, the 2004 foreign policy choice was of a gigantic significance: between liberal, co-operativist, and unilateral, neo-imperialist, versions of American hegemonism (2004). For Michael Barone, 'a President Kerry would pursue a foreign policy that looked a lot more like the one that the United States had before 9/11 — and America would leave a smaller, lighter footprint in the world'. A re-elected Bush, on the other hand, 'would regard the return to office as a vindication of the approach we have seen so far' (2004, p. 27).

This apparent Western European-American dichotomy, in fact, does not survive much inspection. Jonathan Rauch, writing originally in the *National Journal*, commented trenchantly on the closeness of the candidates' foreign policy positions in the first presidential election debate:

> George W. Bush and John Kerry agreed that the leading
> problems are the Iraq engagement, North Korean mis-
> siles, Iranian nukes and loose nukes. Their main policy
> disagreement was on whether to add a bilateral compo-
> nent to current six party talks on North Korea — a tacti-
> cal nicety (Rauch, 2004, p. 13).

The idea that Europeans tended to expect little change from a Kerry victory also has to face the fact that European populations so overwhelmingly supported the Democrat. Interest in the election was very high in
Western Europe, with overwhelming popular support for Kerry. In Eastern
Europe, of course, the picture was somewhat different. Poland, for example, was widely reported as one of the very few countries whose population generally welcomed the Bush victory.

Attentive and mass publics in Western Europe looked to a Kerry presidency as a harbinger of a less abrasive US foreign policy posture. It was
argued that Western Europe was anti-Bush, not anti-American: a Kerry victory would ease transatlantic tempers and tensions. Against this vision of
Euro-American harmony under a Kerry presidency, however, it is important to appreciate that underlying problems would have remained.
Regarding Iraq, for example, Western European governments would have
been put on the spot and no longer able to hide behind the personal
unpopularity of the president as a way of ducking international responsibilities. While European Union enlargement has arguably increased EU-US
convergence of interest in the affairs of Europe's new Eastern neighbours,
tensions would have remained on a range of issues, from defence spending to Europe's UN Security Council representation. On Iran, Kerry
offered little more than a vague undertaking to try to work with the
Europeans in whatever direction US national interests dictated.

The Bush Second Term

As argued above, within the structure/agency limits imposed by the nature
of international American power, presidents do make a difference. The difference between a President Kerry and a second term George W. Bush,
however, did not look to be especially marked, at least in terms of specific
campaign undertakings. Despite Kerry's attacks on Bush's putatively neo-
imperialist and unilateralist foreign policy, we are struck more by the consensus between them, at least applying to War on Terror issues, than by the
differences. Where real divergence would have occurred was more likely to
be in the choice by Kerry of a foreign policy team — no unabashed neo-

conservatives — and in the likely reactions of either man to new challenges. How Kerry would have responded to these new challenges can only
be guessed at in the light of his own background and political record.

We turn directly now to the issue of first and second term Bush presidency continuity. Discussion here touches not only on the major themes of
this book: the broader questions of consensus, 'right on' continuity and
possible policy disjunctions between the earlier and later stages of Bush's
presidency. It also has important implications for our mini-debate about
whether Kerry's election would have made any difference. After all, to the
extent that Bush in the second term was likely to move in a more pragmatic, accommodationist, multilateral, 'Kerry' direction, the impact and significance of a new face in the White House clearly recedes. 'Pragmatism' in
this connection may be simply defined in terms of: no more invasions, a
falling away in the influence of high-profile neo-conservatives, real efforts
to restore relations with Western European allies, and generally a more cautious, *ad hoc* stance towards the politics of the Middle East. On the other
hand, a restored, newly confident second Bush administration, replete with
neo-conservative zealotry in high places, would, of course, point in the
opposite direction. With these wider contexts in mind, and with due caution about giving too many hostages to fortune, we will now attempt to
take the foreign policy temperature of the George W. Bush presidency as
it entered its second term

Personnel changes in late 2004 — Colin Powell's replacement by
Condoleezza Rice at the State Department, the circumstances of Powell's
leave taking, the retention of Rumsfeld — seemed to point to a renewed
commitment to the first term agenda and approach. The re-elected Bush
made some rhetorical gestures towards restoring international (primarily
Western European) support for his foreign policy. His tone (for example,
during his Canadian trip, where he conspicuously called for changes in
Palestinian, but not Israeli, behaviour) was, however, more frequently
unapologetic. Apparent democratic openings in early 2005 in the former
Soviet Union, Egypt, Lebanon and even Saudi Arabia — together, of
course, with the Iraqi elections – also gave encouragement to the neo-conservative cause.

It is nonetheless a contention of this chapter that the burden of evidence
for the early phase of the second term suggested a move in a more pragmatic direction, at least if 'pragmatism' is defined in the rather modest way suggested above. The appointment of Condoleezza Rice as Secretary of State
was widely interpreted as shifting the administration rightwards. Yet Powell's
first term impact on actual policy, especially Middle Eastern policy, had not

been great. His resignation for a combination of health, personal and political reasons had long been trailed in the press. Someone universally acknowledged to enjoy the complete confidence of the president replaced him at Foggy Bottom. Far from symbolizing the rejection of diplomatic options, the Rice appointment was a signal that the State Department would be a force in the new administration. Other State appointments — that of Robert Zoellick was especially welcomed in Europe — seemed clearly to point in a 'pragmatic' direction (Klein, 2005). Other appointments, notably Paul Wolfowitz to the World Bank and John Bolton as US Ambassador to the United Nations, were, of course, extremely controversial. In both cases, however, prominent right-wingers were actually removed from central War on Terror policy-making positions (Duffy and Shannon, 2005). The departure of Douglas Feith from his important position at the Pentagon also was a clear setback for neo-conservative influence in the new administration. The appointment of close Bush public relations adviser Karen Hughes to the post of Undersecretary for Public Diplomacy at the State Department was widely interpreted as embodying a change of tack. Against this general drift, a very widely read piece by Seymour Hersh argued that an invasion of Iran was being prepared and that a new concentration of power was taking place in Donald Rumsfeld's hands at the Defence Department (2005).

Numerous administration representatives in the early part of 2005 were manifestly keen to use conciliatory language, particularly towards European allies. Rice's 'charm offensive' European tour, following on from conciliatory remarks made during her confirmation hearings pointed in the same direction. According to the new Secretary of State, the US was now looking for a 'conversation not a monologue'. In April 2005, Nicholas Burns, the newly appointed Undersecretary for Political Affairs, spoke at Chatham House in London of a 'renewed spirit of purpose, compromise and unity in Trans-Atlantic relations' (2005). President Bush's own inaugural address was generally seen in Europe as signalling an aggressive push for 'freedom' and 'liberty', the frequently repeated slogans of the speech. It was less widely noticed that Bush also made an approving reference to the Koran and asserted that freedom-promotion was not primarily the task of arms.

In the early part of 2005, as the Hersh article indicated, it was possible to read the second term runes in contrasting ways. There unquestionably was now a greater commitment to public diplomacy, but was this merely the camouflage for more invasions, more unilateralism? However one interprets the appointments and the signs of conciliatory language, what cannot be denied is that, as it entered the second term, the administration did face a series of constraints, most of which pointed to the kind of 'pragmatic' policy sketched above. Leading members of the administration undoubtedly would argue that these constraints are matters to be 'managed', rather than factors which should be allowed to shape and distort the second term policy choices. That these constraints exist, however, cannot be in question.

The first constraint relates simply to the dynamics of second presidential terms. William Quandt has argued that second term presidents have only around one and a half years before mid-term election and 'lame duck' status begin to restrict their freedom of action (1986). Second terms are frequently times of frustration, scandal and the running down of political time. They also see a shift in priorities from re-election to historical legacy. George W. Bush may, of course, be less vulnerable to second-term sclerosis because of the support he commands in Congress. He may also engage in further activism in the Middle East if he wants to be remembered as the leader who took the historic opportunity provided by 9/11 to transform the region. Yet it is at least worth recalling that the first and second terms of Ronald Reagan, the only other Republican to gain re-election in the last quarter century, had vastly different characters. Bush may also be concerned at the prospect of being recalled as the US president who presided over a huge rise in global anti-Americanism.

Other constraints include the budget deficit ($412 billion in Fiscal Year 2004) which Bush targeted for substantial reduction in his second term. One very interesting feature of the late 2004 policy debate was the re-emergence of 'declinist' literature (Segal, 2004). The idea that the conflict in Iraq will be funded at any time in the near future from oil revenues appeared by early 2005 as just a Pentagon dream. A third constraint is the related problem of military overstretch. With 150,000 US forces tied up in Iraq in early 2005 and the Pentagon reportedly budgeting for at least 120,000 through 2006, it is difficult to imagine anyone outside the most ideological neocon members of the administration being enthusiastic about invading Iran. Although bombing suspected nuclear facilities or a proxy Israeli raid might come under consideration, either option would involve the raising of the stakes for possible ground action.

Our fourth constraint appears in the form of public opinion. Given that Bush was a wartime presidential incumbent seeking re-election in a non-recessionary economic environment, John Kerry actually performed very well in 2004. Bush led his opponent by only 2.4 per cent in the popular vote, the smallest re-election margin in American history. Presidential approval ratings in January 2005 hovered only just above 50 per cent. Approval of Iraq policy fell even below 40 per cent and returned to this level in May after a short-lived lift that was generated by the holding of elections in Iraq. Public opinion, at least as revealed in the Pew Research Center and Chicago Council on Foreign Relations [CCFR] surveys, points clearly to multilateralism and pragmatism as widely held preferences. To quote the CCFR executive summary: 'Majorities of the public do not support states taking unilateral action to prevent other states from acquiring weapons of mass destruction, but do support this action if it has UN Security Council approval'. CCFR surveys also record that the public generally holds a 'positive feeling towards the UN'. They also show widespread popular concern about America's international moral, high and economic standing (Pew Research Center, 2004; Chicago Council on Foreign Relations: Executive Summary, 2004, p. 1).

A further possible basis for a more pragmatic second term might be termed the 'argument from rationality', a view advanced in some form at least by analysts as varied as Robert Tucker and David Hendrickson (2004), Charles Grant (2004) and even Francis Fukuyama (2004). This argument holds that the Bush first term approach dangerously exposed and weakened the US, especially in terms of international 'soft power'. Rationality indicates a shift in the second term and the pragmatic transcendence of the 'neo-conservative moment'. Linked to this is the argument that a second Bush administration will have learned lessons in pragmatism from the failures and overreach of the first term. Typifying this view, Joe Klein commented that both Vice President Cheney and Secretary Rumsfeld were 'complicit in rose-petal scenarios in the first term. It stands to reason that each may be less susceptible to bellicose fantasies floated by Utopian underlings now' (2005, p. 25).

A final consideration is that the first Bush administration was not *entirely* inflexible and ideological. There is at least *some* pragmatic tradition — exemplified by the April 2001 handling of the dispute over China's downing of a US spy plane or the six party approach to North Korea — upon which to build. The neo-conservative project was concerned with China, but was always primarily geared in practical terms towards the Middle East, so the emergence of a pragmatic second term policy towards the Far East would not be a huge surprise.

Conclusion

To conclude by stating the heart-stoppingly obvious: we shall no more know what a President Kerry foreign policy would have been like than we can imagine what would have been President Gore's long-term reaction to 9/11. In 2004, Kerry and George W. Bush differed in several substantive areas — over Cuba, over the role for public diplomacy, over the importance of alliances — but coincided in many more. The major differences were over interpretations of past deeds, notably the invasion of Iraq, and in general approach and tone. In the reactive, unpredictable context of foreign policy, however, such differences do matter.

It was argued above that the George W. Bush foreign policy probably would, like that of the last two eight-year presidencies, those of Reagan and Clinton, have distinct first- and second-term features. Our list of Bush second-term constraints probably also contains one important omission, which it is appropriate to take up in this concluding section. This missing constraint relates to the second-term domestic agenda, and also leads directly to the chief prediction made in this chapter that post-2004 foreign policy was likely to be 'pragmatic', at least in the modest sense of the word indicated above. It was in domestic policy, where most of the constraints identified above did not apply, that the Bush administration was more likely to manifest ideology and rigidity. As other contributors to this book emphasize, the second-term domestic agenda, announced in early 2005, was highly ambitious, wide-ranging and controversial. Major battles loomed in particular over social security reform and in respect of Supreme Court and lower judicial appointments. Pursuit of this agenda will consume much of the president's time and attention. Accordingly, in the absence of another crisis on the scale of 9/11, it is very dubious that the Bush administration could muster the political energy to mount a second-term foreign policy anywhere near as controversial and activist as that pursued between late 2001 and 2004.

4

The Bush Administration and Europe

Klaus W. Larres

A t the outset of his second term as president, George Bush signalled his desire to heal the rifts that had developed between America and some of its most important transatlantic allies in his first term. Perhaps inevitably Washington's relations with the governments of France and Germany had become less close since the end of the Cold War, but the European alliance still remained the cornerstone of American foreign policy in the 1990s. However, Bush's unilateral decision to invade Iraq in March 2003 without United Nations authorization and in the face of overwhelming opposition from global public opinion provoked the most serious crisis in Western European-American relations since 1945.

The US decision to invade Iraq had essentially been taken shortly after the 9/11 attacks on New York and Washington (Woodward, 2004; Suskind, 2004; Clarke, 2004). America's allies were unaware that it did not matter to the Bush administration whether or not evidence of Iraq's production or possession of weapons of mass destruction could be found. Another nine months elapsed before it dawned on the most senior foreign policy and security experts in Britain, Washington's closest ally, that the issue at hand was not whether or not Bush would invade Iraq but how the invasion could be justified. On 23 July 2002 MI6 chief Sir Richard Dearlove informed a meeting of top security officials convened by Prime Minister Tony Blair that war was 'inevitable'. In Washington, he reported, 'the intelligence and facts were being fixed around the policy' of removing Saddam Hussein 'through military action' (Danner, 2005, pp. 70–1). The British government ultimately agreed to support the war on condition that Bush at least attempted to obtain UN authorization for the invasion of Iraq. With the predictable failure of a rather half-hearted effort to gain the endorsement of the international community, the Americans and their British allies went ahead with military action (Keegan, 2004).

Other members of the Atlantic alliance, far from lending the Americans their support, took the lead in opposing them. German Chancellor Gerhard

Schröder and French President Jacques Chirac did their best to marshal opposition against war within the UN Security Council. France possessed veto power as a permanent member of this body and Germany currently held a rotating seat as one of the non-permanent members. Though they were instrumental in denying UN authorization for the invasion, this did not deter the Bush administration from pressing ahead with it.

A detailed analysis of the development of transatlantic antagonism in the summer and winter of 2002–03 is beyond the scope of this chapter. A number of stimulating studies already offer first interpretations from both a pro- and anti-Bush perspective (Shawcross, 2003; Gordon and Shapiro, 2004). This chapter focuses instead on the deep gaps in the shared transatlantic value system that were exposed in the course of the Iraq crisis and their significance for Franco-American and German-American relations in particular. Contrary to conventional assumptions, it argues that Franco-American relations will prove much easier to reconcile in the long run than German-American relations. Paris and Washington's falling out was essentially attributable to the hard-nosed power politics practised by both Chirac and Bush and to France's geopolitical envy of the US. In contrast, Germany's quarrel with the US was rooted in a much more fundamental difference of views and values regarding the basic principles which rule — or, in the German belief, ought to rule — the international conduct of nations, including that of the world's only superpower. German-American differences were much deeper, more complex and fundamental and thus much more difficult to reconcile. Their troubled relationship is the main focus of this chapter's analysis.

Given their shared realism and political pragmatism, there was no fundamental obstacle preventing Bush and Chirac from eventually engaging in compromise and co-operation — in spite of their policy spats and personality clashes. The much more principled, if not ideological, German belief in the existence of an overarching moral code for international relations stood in the way of pragmatic rapprochement with the US. This certainly remained the case so long as Gerhard Schröder's shaky red-green coalition government remained in power. The general election of September 2005 failed to produce a clear victory for either Schröder's Social Democrats or Angela Merkel's Christian Democrats. The new 'grand coalition' that took office under Merkel's leadership after weeks of negotiations among the party leaders was undoubtedly keener on pursuing a more pro-American policy. In the last resort, however, it too had to take account of the German public's widespread support for a foreign policy based on multilateral norms and strict moral principles. Belief in such values has been deeply ingrained into the national psyche as a result of the lessons learned from Germany's Nazi past and its difficult but eventually successful re-integration into the community of nations by means of the European integration project.

Harmony and Conflict

From the vantage of hindsight transatlantic relations during the Cold War appear to have been relatively uncomplicated. Admittedly, Franco-American relations often proved tetchy, not least in the 1960s when Charles de Gaulle was French president (Wahl and Paxton, 1994). Notwithstanding some minor squabbles, however, West German-American relations were extremely close. Being located on the front line of the Cold War and entirely dependent on the nuclear and conventional security umbrella provided by the United States, the West Germans simply had no choice but to be supportive of major American policy initiatives. West Germany was in fact only a semi-sovereign country, as was indicated by its passivity during the Vietnam War. Its government provided indirect humanitarian and some financial aid to the anticommunist cause without voicing any hint of official criticism in public. Behind closed doors, in contrast, West German politicians viewed America's Vietnam policy as highly unwise and a distraction from the main task of containing communism in Europe.

Deep gratitude for Marshall Plan aid, food deliveries during the Berlin air lift of 1948–49, and gestures of support — such as President John F. Kennedy's famous 'Ich bin ein Berliner' speech shortly after construction of the Berlin Wall in August 1961 — served to ingrain a very pro-American attitude in West German popular opinion. Only in the late 1960s, under the impact of Vietnam, did a younger generation begin to view the US more critically (Larres and Oppelland, 1997; Junker, 2004). Towards the end of the Cold War, George H.W. Bush's support for German unification against initially strong opposition from Russia, Britain, France and a number of smaller countries reinforced the 'special relationship' between the two countries. In 1990 Bush Sr. even spoke of a 'partnership in leadership' linking Germany and America, but this proved the final apex of their Cold War relationship (Hurst, 1999). In the post-Cold War world relations grew more distant because the two countries simply did not need each other as much as during the Cold War.

Helmut Kohl, the long-serving Federal Chancellor whose period in power from 1982 to 1998 spanned the end of the Cold War and the early stages of German unification, was especially pro-American. He was a trained historian who recognized Germany's opportunity to make amends for its past and a member of a generation that felt deep emotional gratitude for America's protective Cold War role. He was also keenly appreciative of George Bush Sr.'s unflagging support for his country's reunification (Kohl, 2004). Gerhard Schröder and his Foreign Minister Joschka Fischer, who came to power in 1998, had an entirely different outlook. They were more sceptical of the basic benevolence of American foreign policy, which Kohl had never doubted. Indeed Fischer had played a prominent role in the anti-American youth rebellion of the 1960s. Moreover, it was their conviction that as a fully sovereign united nation, the new Germany should manifest greater independence in foreign policy. This made Schröder and Fischer ready to accept greater international responsibilities for Germany, including sending German troops abroad on peace-keeping missions. In return they expected Germany to be treated with the respect befitting an important regional European power, notably in terms of being consulted and given information on international issues by its main allies (Harnisch and Maull, 2001; Maull, Harnisch and Grund, 2003). In line with this, they claimed in 2004 that Germany and a number of other rising states ought to be given a permanent seat on the UN Security Council (Van Oudenaren, 2005).

In general Schröder got on well with Bush Sr.'s charismatic successor but he viewed Bill Clinton's tendency to embark on unilateral policies without consulting European allies with suspicion. Nor was he willing to follow America's lead in all cases. A number of serious German-American differences of opinion arose over the Kosovo war and the enlargement of NATO (Asmus, 2002). Clinton's neglect, if not disdain, for the United Nations was also much criticized in Berlin. German opinion fitted in with the feeling prevalent in much of Western Europe, with the exception of Britain, that the only remaining superpower lacked respect for its European allies, did not take their international role seriously and only deigned to consult them when it suited the United States to do so. This was hardly a novel complaint but insensitivity to European concerns appeared to have become an ingrained American habit by the late 1990s. A growingly visible European animosity — some even termed it envy — of America's unipolar power also helped push the transatlantic allies further apart. As Martin Walker observed, 'The essence of European attitudes toward America ... is a broad resentment that almost no field of human activity is left that is not dominated by the military, economic, cultural, technological and political hyperpower' (Walker, 2000).

In other words, suspicion and resentment of America's overwhelming power had begun to burden transatlantic relations long before George W. Bush came to power, but his accession to the presidency made matters worse. The Bush administration quickly embarked on an even more unilateral course in foreign policy than that of its predecessor (Larres, 2004a, pp. 196–202). It did not even pay lip service to the need to consult European allies. In her famous *Foreign Affairs* article setting out the foreign policy goals of a Republican administration, Condoleezza Rice emphasized the importance of working together with allies who shared America's 'core values'. Yet, she also avowed that the US 'will proceed from the firm ground of the national interest, not from the interests of an illusionary international community' (Rice, 2000, p. 46). It soon became evident that the latter sentiment was uppermost in the outlook of the new Bush administration.

Although the events of 11 September 2001 brought the transatlantic allies closer to each other again, this proved to be merely a temporary improvement in the steady worsening of their relationship since Bush had become president. The two sides co-operated in dislodging the Afghan Taliban regime for its refusal to extradite Osama bin Laden, the Al-Qaeda leader deemed responsible for planning and funding the 9/11 attacks. By the spring of 2002, however, divergent views about how best to pursue the 'war on terror' and, above all, whether to deal with Iraqi dictator Saddam Hussein by military pressure or the continuation of economic sanctions had given rise to renewed bickering. The invasion of Iraq in the spring of 2003 and the chaos and violence of the post-war reconstruction brought the transatlantic alliance and particularly the German-American partnership close to breaking-point (Larres, 2003, pp. 23–42).

Disharmony and Gradual Rapprochement

Public opinion in virtually every European Union member-state was either opposed to or strongly sceptical about going to war against Iraq on a flimsy pretext and without UN authorization, but the governments of these countries were hardly of one mind in this regard. In essence there were deep rifts between European leaders themselves. Some, such as Britain's Tony Blair and Spain's José María Aznar, displayed loyalty to the transatlantic alliance by proclaiming their adherence to an all-embracing 'war against terror', including the invasion of Iraq. Many others followed the Schröder-Chirac line because their personal convictions and domestic circumstances deterred them from supporting Washington's intent to topple Saddam Hussein by military force (Gordon and Shapiro, 2004; Shawcross, 2003).

Even Schröder and Chirac, Bush's most vociferous critics, exhibited some differences in their attitude towards US unilateralism in Iraq. A combination of principle and pragmatism drove the German Chancellor. His strong personal convictions induced him to regard the Iraq invasion as morally dubious. Yet he also faced a tough fight for re-election — and jumping on the bandwagon of popular hostility to Bush's military action represented his best (and perhaps only) chance of winning another term in office. Chirac's sense of realpolitik and his own predilection to make use of military force on occasion, for example when attempting to resolve difficult situations in France's former colonies, did not lend itself to moral condemnation of the Iraq invasion in the manner of his German counterpart. Instead the French president condemned Bush's abandonment of multilateralism and his refusal to make an invasion of Iraq dependent on obtaining a second UN resolution. France's long-standing resentment of US hegemony and its desire to bring about a world of multiple power centres also played a large role in Chirac's antagonism to Bush's Iraq policy. He was desperately fearful of being forever faced with a unipolar world dominated by the United States and regarded the build-up of Europe, under Franco-German leadership, as a counterweight to American power. In the last resort Chirac, like Schröder, also viewed Bush's actions in invading a country that did not pose an imminent threat and in the face of overwhelmingly hostile world opinion as setting a very dangerous precedent for pre-emptive war (Styan, 2004).

The dire state of the transatlantic alliance led US Defense Secretary Donald Rumsfeld to portray Europe as divided between 'old' and 'new'. In his construct, 'new' Europe consisted of those nations who supported the United States and included not just new EU members, such as Poland and the Czech Republic, but also long-standing EU countries, such as Britain, Italy and Spain. From this it followed that 'old' Europe corresponded not with length of EU membership but opposition to America's invasion of Iraq (*Deutsche Welle*, 2003). While Rumsfeld's ideas were much quoted in the media, their usefulness as a tool of analysis was limited. 'New' Europe did not side as one with the United States. Of the nation-states that formed this supposed bloc, Britain was by far the most loyal supporter of Bush's foreign policy and was the only European country which sent any substantial numbers of troops to Iraq. Moreover, public opinion in 'new' as much as 'old' Europe — including British public opinion — was united in its anti-war stance. Rumsfeld's concept sounded even less convincing after the Madrid bomb attacks precipitated the election of a strongly anti-war government in Spain and the ongoing unpopularity of the war helped to weaken the political position of the Silvio Berlusconi's government in Italy. In the British general election of May 2005 Tony Blair was returned to power for a third term but with his parliamentary majority substantially reduced from 161 to 67 seats. Once his party's chief electoral asset, the Prime Minister's support for the controversial war in Iraq had transformed him into its greatest liability (AlJazeera.com, 2005).

At the height of the crisis in the transatlantic alliance National Security Adviser Condoleezza Rice and Donald Rumsfeld charged that German-American relations and the Franco-American relationship had been 'poisoned' (Sullivan, 2002). Rice refused to see Foreign Minister Fischer when he visited Washington in early 2003 and Rumsfeld refused for some time to speak with his German counterpart. President Bush himself did not remain aloof from the dispute. He took the 'ice age' that had descended on German-American and Franco-American relations as a personal insult. Convinced that he had been betrayed by Chirac and blatantly deceived by Schröder in the United Nations forum, Bush did not exchange friendly words with either of them for over a year. The White House even refused to accept calls from the Chancellor's office in Berlin during this period (Szabo, 2004). It should be said, however, that the behaviour of Schröder and his party added grist to the mill of American animosity by making ill-considered remarks about a new 'German way' in foreign policy. With reference to Bush's invasion plans Schröder declared bluntly and unambiguously that his government would not participate in any foreign policy adventures (Hooper, 2002). While all this was going on, close contact between the US and its allies was being maintained at advisory and ambassadorial levels and within the intelligence community. However the depth and longevity of the conflict and what can only be termed the immature behaviour at the executive level on both sides of the Atlantic had no precedent.

The German-American crisis over the war in Iraq finally eased when Schröder paid a long overdue visit to the White House in February 2004. To make up for the severe tension and long delayed political and personal reconciliation, the two leaders did not limit themselves to expressions of mutual friendship and admiration and declarations of intent to co-operate constructively from now on. They also announced an all-encompassing 'common agenda of action' and grandly reaffirmed a 'German-American alliance for the 21st century' (Bush and Schröder, 2004). This was clearly intended to hark back to the two men's joint statement of March 2001, which posited the long-standing German-American partnership as a 'pillar of transatlantic relations' (Bush and Schröder, 2001). Yet even this earlier expression of amity could not wholly mask the frostiness that would soon become more open. Schröder's had deliberately delayed his visit to see the new president, which provided the occasion for the joint statement, as a demonstration of the independence of united Germany's post-Cold War foreign policy.

Only a blind optimist could have believed the joint statement of 2004 constituted a full and frank rapprochement. In it Bush and Schröder avowed their wish to 'open a new chapter' in their two countries' 'close relationship' and reiterated their common belief in 'freedom, democracy and human rights' (Bush and Schröder, 2004). On the other hand, little attempt was made to paper over the substantive differences that still existed between them. Admitting that they differed over the Kyoto Protocol on global warming and the International Criminal Court, which Bush refused to recognize, the president and Schröder somewhat disingenuously proclaimed that 'as good friends, we can disagree and still be good friends'(Bush and Schröder, 2004). Their recent quarrels over Iraq gave these fine words a somewhat hollow ring and the thaw in relations over this most contentious of issues was symbolic rather than substantive. Bush graciously accepted Schröder's offer for Germany to train Iraqi soldiers, albeit outside Iraq in the United Arab Emirates. Despite its incipient rapprochement with the US, the German government could not be moved to send any German military instructors to Iraq as this might easily be interpreted as expressing its belated support for the American-led invasion (*Deutsche Welle*, 2004).

The seeds of a Franco-American rapprochement were eventually sown when Bush visited France for the sixtieth anniversary of the D-Day Normandy landings. The 'worst moment between the two men' had occurred during their personal meeting at the United Nations in New York in September 2003. It took another nine months before they were ready to dine together at the Elysee Palace on 5 June 2004. At that gathering, a French journalist reported, the 'atmosphere was all for understanding and, for once, each of the two used some tact' (Jauvert, 2005, p. 2). But one convivial dinner was not enough to bury the hatchet. Franco-American relations took another turn for the worse at the G-8 meeting in Evian a few days later and at the subsequent NATO meeting in Istanbul. The death of Palestinian President Yasser Arafat in November 2004 and the reinvigoration of the Middle East Peace Process under his successor, Mahmoud Abbas, muted French criticism of America's policy towards the Palestinians. The successful holding of elections in Iraq in January 2005 also enabled the French government to focus on that country's future rather than dwell on its dispute with Washington over the war. The subsequent crisis over the assassination of former Lebanese Prime Minister Rafik al-Hariri in February furnished proof that France and the United States had mutual interests in the Middle East. The two governments cooperated to put pressure on Syria to terminate its occupation of Lebanon (Swink, 2005). This resulted in a more general reconciliation between the Chirac and Bush administrations.

The first half of 2005 saw general improvement in both Franco-American and German-American relations. European chancelleries had to face up to the reality of having to deal with Bush for another four years now that his re-election victory had put paid to any hopes of having a less unilateralist Democrat in the White House. As well as having to make do, they were encouraged by apparently substantive signs of American progress in the democratization of post-war Iraq. The holding of what the White House heralded as the first ever 'free and democratic elections' in Iraq in January 2005 eventually resulted in the formation of a sovereign Iraqi government, a long-standing French demand, and the departure of Paul Bremer, America's unpopular and controversial pro-consul in Baghdad.

Bush himself signalled his strong desire for reconciliation in announcing immediately after his re-election his intention to visit Europe early in his second term 'to deepen transatlantic co-operation' (White House, 2004). In the course of her successful preparatory trip to Europe in February 2005, new Secretary of State Condoleezza Rice told the global media that there was 'almost no dwelling on the past' in her conversations with European leaders. '[E]verybody was in a very constructive mood', she declared, 'and very much ready to move on' in order to start a 'new chapter' (Rice, 2005). On his own visit, which included stopovers at Brussels, Berlin and Paris, Bush openly called for 'a new era of transatlantic unity' (Bush, 2005).

Continuing Underlying Difficulties

Yet, German-American and Franco-American relations, and indeed transatlantic relations in general, were by no means back to normal. In particular Germany's leaders, no less than a majority of its people, remained dubious of America's ability to stabilize and reconstruct Iraq in the face of escalating terrorist attacks. In their eyes Washington's oft-stated claim that the Iraqi elections had turned the tide in favour of democracy was a denial of reality. German scepticism was legitimized by growing criticism of Bush within the United States itself, especially by respected members of the foreign policy establishment. Jimmy Carter's former National Security Adviser, Zbigniew Brezinski, for example, accused Bush of having conducted the Iraq war with 'tactical and strategic incompetence' and of pursuing a foreign policy that had left the United States 'more isolated than ever before' and 'the object of unprecedented international mistrust' (Riechmann, 2005). Behind closed doors, meanwhile, European leaders' low opinion of Bush's world vision had not abated. They remained critical of what they deemed to be his overly 'missionary' and highly unrealistic drive of bringing democracy and freedom to the Middle East. In contrast to the crisis of 2002–03, however, such scepticism was rarely voiced in public. Most

European leaders — as well as much of the European press corps accredit-
ed in Washington — now realized that Bush tended to take criticism person-
ally and could be unforgiving towards those who voiced it. (Madsen, 2005)

Bush's undiminished optimism about America's ability to turn
Afghanistan, Iraq and, essentially, the entire Middle East into a haven of freedom and democracy was not the only running sore that threatened to blight
the new transatlantic rapprochement. His haphazard way of dealing with the
Israel-Palestine crisis disappointed European leaders, who wanted him to put
more than token pressure on Israeli Prime Minister Ariel Sharon to withdraw
from Palestinian territory. This was a core requirement laid down in the 'road
map' that had been drawn up in April 2003 by the US, Russia, the EU and
the UN (the Quartet). This plan was meant to bring about a comprehensive
and peaceful resolution of the Israeli-Palestinian conflict based on a two-
state solution. However the Bush administration's initial enthusiasm for the
project soon cooled. It became apparent that Sharon would encounter great
difficulty in obtaining the support of the Israeli Parliament for the plan and
might well fall from power in the process of attempting to implement even
parts of it, such as withdrawal from the Gaza strip and abandoning some
Israeli settlements on the West Bank. Unwilling to countenance the loss of
its staunchest ally in the Middle East, Washington lost much of its interest in
the 'road map' plan that threatened his political survival.

A number of other issues also cast their shadow over the hoped for rapprochement in transatlantic relations. The Bush administration's reluctance
to openly support the E-3 (France, Germany, and the UK) in their attempts
to convince Iran to abandon its nuclear ambitions and its inflexible
approach to resolving the nuclear crisis with North Korea caused deep
concern in Europe, particularly in Germany. America's allies also resented
its willingness to let the dollar slide as a way of closing its trade gap, even
though the main burden of adjustment fell on Eurozone countries rather
than on China, which continued to run a big trade surplus with the US
because it pegged its currency to the dollar. Nor did they appreciate the
Bush administration's persistent refusal to abandon the strict arms embargo imposed on China after the Tiananmen Square massacre of 1989. A
number of economic disputes also clouded US-European relations, not
least the lingering Airbus-Boeing rivalry.

Nor was doubt about the reality of rapprochement confined to Europe.
The Bush administration remained suspicious about Germany's moral concerns regarding the 'war on terror'. It neither understood nor appreciated
the strong pacifistic streak in German society that was reflected in the
Schröder government's reluctance to sanction the use of military force

other than as a very last resort. Berlin's continued insistence on multilateral solutions for all international problems also caused irritation in Washington. Underlying these concerns, however, was a deeper American suspicion that the transatlantic crisis had finally brought into the open Europe's ambition to rival the United States as a global power. Though US leaders were sceptical that their hegemony could be challenged, they were irritated by the outpouring of books that predicted this was imminent and angered by the evident enthusiasm of some European leaders to bring about this change (Kupchan, 2003; Reid, 2004).

Moreover, the intra-German discourse during which Schröder's opposition to American foreign policy over Iraq was frequently identified as a new 'German way' in international affairs continued to cause concern in Washington. Claims that Germany was a 'great power' and had finally recognized that its foreign policy had to be made in Berlin rather than in Washington also caused unease (Schöllgen, 2003, pp. 156, 159, 161). It was impossible for Bush administration policy-makers to overlook the underlying striving of united Germany for independence from the US. They also perceived an element of anti-American populism in the independence professions of German politicians.

Assertions of Germany's new confidence may not have aroused American concern that the strident German nationalism of the past was about to flower anew, but they were still viewed with suspicion as an expression of the perceived ambition of the European Union's most important member-states to build it into a global rival. Britain's occasional temptation to join France and Germany in a European 'Big Three' directorate to guide the enlarged 25 member European Union and London's endorsement of an independent European rapid reaction force did little to reassure the Bush administration that it would be would be possible to return quickly to the *status quo ante* in transatlantic relations (Larres, 2004b, pp. 7–9).

Whether exaggerated or not, American suspicions of European aspirations subsided in the wake of the apparent collapse of the European constitution project in May 2005 and the subsequent acrimonious break-up of the meeting of European leaders to decide the EU budget. Europe had certainly become more than a geographic expression in the past 50 years, but these events showed that it was still far from becoming a unified political entity. The rejection of the proposed European Constitution by France and the Netherlands made it likely that the EU would be far more preoccupied with rebuilding its internal coherence than recalibrating the transatlantic alliance over the next few years. Moreover, Britain's apparent isolation in the European budget imbroglio offered Washington hope that it would continue to gravitate towards the US rather than seek closer relations with France and Germany. Prime Minister Blair's insistence on defending the British rebate and open demands for the abolition of the Common Agricultural Policy resulted in him replacing Bush as Chirac's favourite pariah. The fall-out from the budget dispute and Britain's determination that the EU should abandon statism in favour of flexibility in socio-economic policy may well inhibit its desire and ability to co-operate in the kind of joint foreign policy ventures that it pursued with Germany and France towards Iran (Larres, 2004b).

The fact that the European crisis salved American concerns was significant testimony that full trust in the transatlantic alliance had not been restored. Regardless of the improvements that have taken place since the nadir of 2002–03, serious differences still remained. The heart of the problem was the fundamental difference of outlook and world vision between the United States and Germany. In essence this was a conflict over 'soft' power rather than 'hard' power. America may regard itself as a benign hegemon, the first great power in global history to deploy its resources for the common good, but there was a fundamental clash between its foreign policy values and those of the new Germany.

The Aftermath of the Iraq War and the Value Problem in German-American Relations

Despite the hand-over of sovereignty to an Iraqi government in early 2005, the Schröder government remained very critical of the Bush administration's vision for the Middle East. From Berlin's perspective, the US continued to rely too much on hard military force and too little on negotiations, diplomacy and engagement with the Iraqi population. Many Germans were also dismayed by the Bush administration's rather half-hearted efforts to investigate the developments which led to the use of torture to prise information out of the detainees at Abu Ghraib in Iraq and also at various prisons in Afghanistan. This fed into broader fears that the US was actively contributing to a 'clash of civilizations' through its role in the Middle East. Compounding this unease, many Germans were suspicious that Bush was exploiting the war on terror to keep Americans in an artificial state of fear and maintain their support for his high-risk foreign policy (Heins, 2002, pp. 128–45).

On the other hand, the feeling was prevalent in Washington that Germany offered little support for the reconstruction and stabilization of Iraq. It showed no willingness for NATO to assume any role in the pacification process and, along with France and some other European countries, refused to forgive Iraq all its pre-war debts. In private, Bush administration officials expressed the conviction that Germany (as well as France) viewed America's difficulties in Iraq with a good deal of *Schadenfreude* and would love to throw the words 'I told you so' at the administration if this were not politically inopportune.

At first sight the political differences between Germany and the USA largely concerned the tactics to be employed in Iraq to stabilize the country and to win over the hearts and minds of the Iraqi people, but the tensions went much deeper. The fundamental gap in values that had initially provoked the rift in German-American relations had only been thinly plastered over. In a press conference with European media representatives shortly before his trip to Europe in late February 2005, Bush emphasized that the transatlantic allies shared 'a belief in human rights and human dignity and rule of law and transparency of government and democracy and freedom' (Bush, 2005). Nevertheless the existence of a coherent transatlantic value system was open to doubt. Bush was of course correct that some essential values were shared by all allies, but some equally fundamental values were not, particularly within the framework of the German-American partnership. Analysis of these value differences reveals the significant differences in the foreign policy outlook of the two countries.

Different Assessment of Political Leadership:

President Bush was able to build his case that Saddam Hussein had to be deposed on account of his alleged possession of weapons of mass destruction (WMD) to a large extent on the words 'trust me'. Until former weapons inspector David Kay's statements before Congress in early 2004 and subsequent revelations, the majority of Americans believed that Iraq had WMD. Despite the flimsy nature of the evidence, they were willing to trust and believe Bush's assurances on this score (Woodward, 2004; Suskind, 2004; Clarke, 2004). In Europe, by contrast, less trust was invested in leaders. Even in Britain Blair's credibility about the threat posed by Saddam proved short-lived. In Germany people were sceptical of the case from the start. Based on their collective memory of the Hitler regime's deceptions and crimes, ordinary Germans were much less willing than their American — and even British — counterparts to take any government's word on trust. In the absence of clear evidence of the existence of Iraqi WMD, they remained dubious about the claims put forward by Bush and Blair and supported Schröder's adamant refusal to be drawn into an optional and superfluous war. The Chancellor's stand was decisive in the narrow re-election of his Red-Green coalition government in September 2002. In all likelihood, the more pro-American (though also anti-Iraq war) platform adopted by the conservative Christian Democrats was the main cause of their defeat.

In contrast, Americans looked to Bush to provide firm leadership in the war on terror. To this end they supported the enhancement of his powers as a wartime president through such instruments as the Patriot Act of October 2002. Bush also used the presidential bully-pulpit to warn his fellow citizens of the dangers facing their country. As journalist Mary McGrory put it, most Americans took a 'don't mess with the Commander-in-Chief' viewpoint. They didn't 'mind his U.N.-baiting or his inconsistent approaches to Iraq and North Korea. They [were] constantly reminded of multiplying and unseen threats' (McGrory, 2002, A25). Approval of Bush's handling of the war on terror was arguably the single most significant factor that secured his re-election.

From a European perspective the level of respect accorded the US president as wartime commander-in-chief appears unhealthy for any democratic state. After all, democracy is by definition based on equality and the power of the common man rather than on the influence and the privileged position of leaders. Undue awe and admiration for a president whom the Constitution requires to share power with other branches of government appears to be a contradiction in terms. Europeans tend to be much more critical and sceptical and much less deferential to their political leaders. At least with respect to the Iraq crisis one can only conclude that a greater degree of scepticism and less trust and faith in the leaders were warranted in the US and those European countries that backed its war.

So long as different attitudes to leadership prevail in America and Europe, the transatlantic reconciliation is likely to prove shallow. On this score, the ongoing violence finally showed signs in mid-2005 of eroding support for Bush's policy in Iraq. In June a CNN/Gallup survey found that 53 per cent of respondents believed it had been a mistake for the United States to go to war in Iraq. In response, President Bush attempted to rally support by giving a nationally televised address from Fort Bragg. While he persisted in linking Saddam Hussein's regime with 9/11, his rhetoric was far more multilateral in tone than his previous statements on the war. The president even quoted with approval Chancellor Schröder on the shared interest of the international community in a stable Iraq and averred that 'Iraqi army and police are being trained by personnel from Italy, Germany, Ukraine, Turkey, Poland, Romania, Australia and the United Kingdom' (Garton Ash, 2005)

Use of Military Force and Civil Engagement

After World War II Germany increasingly became a pacifist nation and tended to view international affairs in highly moral terms. Responsibility for Hitler's rise to power, for the subsequent war, and particularly for the over six-million deaths of the Holocaust shaped its world view. No event in recent US history, not even the significant impact of the Vietnam War on the American psyche, was comparably profound. In American political life, it is conventional to use the term *war* to refer to political strategies — for example, the war on drugs, the war against crime, or the war against poverty — but this terminology is unacceptable in German politics because of its aggressive and offensive connotations.

To a considerable extent the military remained discredited in German society throughout the Cold War years, something which has changed but little in the post-Cold War era. The participation of German soldiers in the wars in Kosovo and Afghanistan generated controversy and was only approved by very slim parliamentary majorities. In the case of Kosovo, Foreign Minister Fischer had to make an impassioned appeal to his parliamentary colleagues that the use of German troops to prevent genocide would show that Germany had learned the lessons of Auschwitz and was now on the right side of history (Fischer, 1999). Nevertheless the German people continued to regard military force as a very last resort that was to be used only after all other alternatives were exhausted and if everyone involved agreed. In contrast, in US and British governmental circles, as well as in wide sections of their respective populations, the deployment of military forces at an early stage in a crisis was entirely acceptable under certain circumstances. Many Americans and Britons would be utterly surprised if they were aware of the moral hand-wringing which occurred in Germany over these and similar issues over many years.

Multilateralism and Belief in the UN System

Germany's leadership role within both NATO and the EU enabled it to become a respected member of the international community and an influential actor in the Cold War. In view of its own identification with these bodies, Berlin was angered by the Bush administration's cavalier attitude towards international organizations. The two governments were far apart on such issues as the Kyoto Protocol, the International Criminal Court and indeed the sidelining of the UN during the Iraq crisis. Washington's belated appeal for Security Council authorization to use force against Saddam Hussein on grounds of his alleged possession of WMD was viewed as a sop to internationalism not a damascene conversion in Europe. It soon became evident that Bush intended to attack with or without UN support and despite the flimsy nature of its case against the Iraqi leader (Woodward, 2004; Suskind, 2004; Clarke, 2004; Danner, 2005). This cavalier attitude bred long-lasting resentments that are not easily cast aside in the face of Washington's apparent desire for re-engagement with the international community over Iraq. It may very well be the case, as one analyst has suggested, that 'American policy has got better — more sober, more realistic — at least partly because things in Iraq have gone so badly' (Garton Ash, 2005) From the German perspective, however, Bush's new appreciation for multilateralism represents a change of tactics rather than a change of heart.

Exploitation of Nationalist Forces

The USA and Germany also hold vastly differing views of nationalism, flag-waving patriotism and how to deal with domestic and international terrorism. Owing to the disastrous consequences of the exaggerated nationalism of the Nazi years, post-1945 Germany was characterized by strong anti-nationalist and anti-patriotic sentiments. Both Willy Brandt's *Ostpolitik* of the 1970s and the frequently voiced scepticism about reunification in 1989–90 reflected the belief that it was best not to pursue a nationalist policy and not to be too proud of one's nation. Many West Germans also believed that Germany should remain divided because a large and powerful united Germany would only give rise to political temptations that were best restrained. There was a sense that Germany had to atone for World War II and the Holocaust by playing a restrained rather than assertive role in world politics.

In contrast, the United States had strong confidence in its exceptionalism and had long manifested a sense of mission to export its values abroad. It was infused with a sense of its own moral superiority. As such, America had a tendency to see its enemies as evil — whether the 'evil empire' in the case of the Soviets or the 'axis of evil' in the case of the war on terror. Nor did it have experience of terrorist attacks that Europeans had learned to live with in the final decades of the twentieth century. Interpreting the 9/11 attacks as a threat not only to America but the liberties it claimed to stand for, Bush could tell other countries that they had a duty to support the US in its war on terror. Most Europeans, however, were convinced that the western world was confronted with a severe and deep crisis but not necessarily with a real global war. While Americans are keen on addressing the symptoms of the crisis — international terrorism — Europeans, including the majority of politically aware Germans, believed that more attention should be given to the roots of the problem such as deprivation, poverty and injustice.

Conclusion

The deep value gaps that have opened rifts in German-American relations and impacted on the broader transatlantic alliance during the Bush presidency defied easy healing. The two governments can make some progress in overcoming their differences by means of co-operation in areas of common interest. The Bush administration could do much to reassure the German government that its new declarations of multilateral intent were sincere if it gave greater responsibility to the UN in Iraq and made greater efforts to arrive at a solution for the Israel-Palestinian conflict. Conversely, the German government could gain credit in Washington if it were prepared to become more directly involved in resolving the enormous difficulties in Iraq and took on a constructive stabilization role in the newly sovereign country. If both sides continue to value the transatlantic alliance, they need to make a serious effort to bridge the value gaps outlined in this essay. It will not happen by default.

5

The Bush Administration and the Middle East

Robert Singh

If social security represents the 'third rail' of domestic American politics for American presidents, then the Middle East constitutes an even more formidable third rail in international politics. The terrorist attacks of 11 September 2001, followed by the US military campaigns in Afghanistan and Iraq, made Middle East policy the defining and most controversial feature of the polarizing first term of the George W. Bush presidency. Not only did the Middle East move to centre stage in US foreign policy for the first time in America's history of fraught relations with the region but the president's public commitment to a 'forward strategy' of preventive war, regime change and democratization dramatically reversed the stability-oriented principles and relative caution of Bush's predecessors in the White House. In firmly grasping this rail, however, the president has taken a courageous, calculated and substantial gamble on his place in history, the fate of millions within and outside the Middle East and the future of international security for a generation to come.

Several regional developments at the beginning of Bush's second term offered partial vindication of the president's approach and, in particular, the central tenets of the 'Bush Doctrine' (Buckley and Singh, 2005). Libya's abandonment of its weapons of mass destruction programmes, the holding of successful elections in Afghanistan on 9 October 2004 and Iraq on 31 January 2005, followed in rapid succession by President Mubarak's declaration that he would allow multi-party candidates in Egypt's 2005 presidential election, mass Lebanese protests against Syrian occupation following the assassination of former Prime Minister Rafik Hariri, joint US-French sponsorship of UN Resolution 1559 that helped secure Syria's withdrawal of troops from Lebanon in May 2005, and local elections in Saudi Arabia together offered promising signs of significant political change in precisely the directions called for by President Bush. In an address that could have been crafted by Karl Rove, the Lebanese Druze Opposition leader, Walid Jumblatt — who had 16 months previously described Paul Wolfowitz as a 'filthy son of a harlot of Zion' and hoped for the early death of 'people like him in Washington who are spreading disorder in Arab lands, Iraq and Palestine' — told the *Washington Post* in February 2005 that an 'Arab Berlin Wall' was now falling: 'This process of change has started because of the American invasion of Iraq. I was cynical about Iraq. But when I saw the Iraqi people voting three weeks ago, eight million of them, it was the start of a new Arab world' (Ignatius, 2005). Just as Ronald Reagan's clarity had previously encouraged reformers in Eastern Europe and the Soviet Union, so Bush's bold embrace of a values-laden grand strategy emboldened Arab reformers and dissidents to demand a say in their own self-government and their nations' future.

To the chagrin of his many critics who dismissed notions of an 'Arab Spring' as preposterous propaganda, Bush — far from recalibrating the more controversial aspects of his first term — reaffirmed his radicalism by pledging in his second inaugural address and State of the Union speech of 2005 ultimately to 'end tyranny' by promoting freedom and democracy in the Middle East. Such a commitment reinforced sharply contrasting scholarly interpretations of Bush's foreign policy: between a Bush 'revolution' and substantial continuity with prior administrations; and between Bush as an ideologically driven, visionary leader and a more pragmatic — even opportunistic — president. Bush's second-term legacy may plausibly repeat the pattern wherein no post-1976 president has left the White House unscathed by the effects — intended and unintended — of US interventions in the Middle East. A combination of continuity in some of the traditional lodestars of US policy and the profound changes induced by the events of 2001–05 means that Middle East policy seemed set to dominate the second term of the Bush administration as much as it did the first. The prospects for success rely greatly on the extent to which the president's heavy investment of political capital — and the resilience or frailty of autocratic regimes in the region — together trump the broader forces typically limiting transformational presidential ambitions in foreign policy.

This chapter proceeds firstly by tracing the radicalization of Bush's foreign policy over 2001–05. It then assesses the key agenda challenges and constraints on an equally radical second term before concluding that the prospects for the success of Bush's Middle Eastern policy are not without foundation.

The First Term: A Grand Strategy for a New Era

In reviewing the legacy of one much misunderstood and 'misunderestimat-ed' Republican president's policies for the Middle East, John Lewis Gaddis remarked:

> Unilateral security guarantees could be taken as excuses for American intervention, as the hostile Arab reaction to the 1957 Eisenhower Doctrine showed: that single proclamation, pledging the United States to defend 'the Middle East' against 'overt armed aggression from any nation controlled by International Communism', dissipated overnight the goodwill Washington had won in the Arab world by opposing the British-French-Israeli invasion of Egypt the year before. And, of course, none of this ensured that nations being protected by the United States shared the administration's perception of interests and threats, or that they would turn their nationalism against communism in the way Washington wanted them to (Gaddis, 1982, p. 180).

Echoes of this sceptical analysis can be readily identified in contemporary criticisms of the Bush approach to the Middle East. The Iraq invasion of 2003 — the sole application thus far of the Bush Doctrine's embrace of preventive war — squandered what limited sympathy had existed in the 'Arab street' for the US after the 9/11 attacks. For critics who deny that a 'war on terrorism' can ever be won, or who see victory as hinging on winning over rather than alienating 'moderate' Muslim opinion, or who view secular liber-alism as ultimately incompatible with Islam, Bush's foreign and security poli-cies have retarded rather than advanced the defeat of radical transnational Islamic terrorists and the pacification of the Middle East. As numerous opin-ion surveys have demonstrated, anti-Americanism among Arabs and Muslims — including putative US allies such as Egypt, Saudi Arabia and Jordan — is at an all-time high. The depth and breadth of American unpop-ularity means, as Jonathan Stevenson argues, that:

> Negative Muslim perceptions of the United States make con-troversial but largely non-optional US policies in the Middle East, the Gulf and the wider Muslim world all the more dif-ficult to execute. Immediately after 11 September, the Qatar-based satellite television station al-Jazeera resolutely portrayed Muslims as victims of a 'crusade' in Afghanistan — a term initially and unfortunately used by the Bush administration

itself in characterizing the intervention — rather than culprits in the attacks that necessitated a self-defensive US-led intervention against the Taliban and al-Qaeda. The network also manifested a kind of cognitive dissonance, championing bin Laden as a righteous defender of Islam …while denying his involvement in the attacks that bestowed that status (2004, pp. 82–3).

It might therefore appear redundant to argue the existence of markedly competing interpretations of the coherence and effectiveness of Bush's approach. Academic analysis of Bush's Middle East policies, however, is in many ways a representative microcosm of that of the Bush foreign policy more broadly. Disagreement is strong and broad and exists as much within particular ideological or doctrinal tendencies ('conservatives', 'neo-conservatives', 'liberals') as much as between particular schools. For some analysts, for instance, Bush represents a clear departure from prior American presidents and precedents. Most notably, Ivo Daalder and James Lindsay (2003) cast the Bush foreign policy after 9/11 as a 'revolution' that de-emphasized multilateralism in favour of unilateral approaches, championed American primacy, engaged in unapologetic assertions of American military might, embraced illegal doctrines of preventive war, and rejected realist approaches to international relations in favour of a neo-Wilsonian conviction in the transformational power of democratization. Although some analysts, following this view, regard Bush politically as more Reagan's son than George H.W. Bush's progeny, traditionalist conservatives such as Stefan Halpern and Jonathan Clarke strongly dispute this assertion. They depict Reagan as a far more pragmatic, non-doctrinal and deft diplomat than the supposedly blinkered and blunt Bush (2004). Others — for better and worse — discern substantial continuity in Bush's grand strategy (Leffler, 2004). For still others, however, Bush has shrewdly married Wilsonian ideals to realist means in a timely, effective and long-overdue 'distinctly American internationalism' (Kaplan and Kristol, 2003).

Most scholars echo Gaddis in regarding the Bush Doctrine as 'the most sweeping redesign of US grand strategy since the presidency of Franklin D. Roosevelt' (Gaddis, 2005, p. 2; also 2004 and 2002). As outlined in a series of speeches from 2001 to 2003, but most succinctly crystallized in the National Security Strategy document of September 2002, the Doctrine adopted four key principles. These were: to maintain American primacy; to prosecute the war on terrorism through multiple means; to supplement traditional deterrence with preventive war if necessary; and to promote democratization. The extent to which these guiding principles — individually or collectively — represented a rupture with the past is a matter of dispute. Inderjeet Parmar, for example, has argued that the 'new more aggressive foreign policy' was 'merely made more acceptable by 9/11, not made by 9/11 itself' (2005, p. 1). Others — such as Godfrey Hodgson in this volume — identify its roots in fractious post-Vietnam and post-Cold War debates over America's role and the aspirations of the Project for a New American Century. Nevertheless the application of the Doctrine to the Middle East theatre offers at least partial confirmation of the transformational thesis.

The most obvious contrast with prior administrations can be gleaned by considering the four lodestars of US policy towards the region from 1945 to 2001. First, America's main priority during the Cold War was to prosecute a vigorous containment of communist expansion in the region — one that accepted the role of authoritarian opponents of Soviet power and that assisted Islamist resistance in Afghanistan to the Soviet occupation. Second, a commitment to support the state of Israel became steadily more central and, for US relations, made vastly more complex its dealings with the region from 1967 onwards. Third, access to energy supplies was a necessary condition of American — and global — economic growth, necessitating cordial relations with key oil-producing states in the Gulf region in particular. Fourth, support for 'friendly' authoritarian regimes, such as the Shah's Iran, Saudi Arabia and latterly Egypt was viewed in Washington as the optimal means to contain regional threats and guarantee energy access while providing a sufficient modicum of stability to an infamously volatile region plagued by conflicts of religion, tribe, clan, ideology and nationalism. Despite the impressive continuity in successive Democratic and Republican administrations' policies, however, as a priority for Washington the Middle East was invariably secondary to Europe and Asia throughout the Cold War and pre-9/11 eras. With few, though significant, exceptions, US attentions to the region were spasmodic, limited in scope and reactive rather pro-active in advancing change.

Initially, Bush's apparent commitment to a realist foreign policy, which rejected Clintonian humanitarian interventions, nation building, and 'foreign policy as social work' suggested business as usual with regard to the Middle East. Bush entered office in January 2001 with minimal interest in the region's politics and problems, being preoccupied instead with relations with Russia and China. The two partial exceptions here were Israel and Iraq. In the former, Bush's visit to Israel before becoming president compounded the pro-Israeli political dynamics of the GOP's electoral coalition to foster a clear and unequivocally pro-Israeli stance. Clinton's failure to secure a peace deal in the most propitious circumstance in 2000, the worsening nature of the subsequent second *intifada* and Israeli repression, and the personal politics favoured by Bush in his dealings with other international leaders — which cast Yasir Arafat as an unreliable and mendacious supporter of terror — together augured against a direct and consistent involvement on the Israeli-Palestinian issue. Iraq was, according to some accounts, the one example of very early presidential curiosity as to what options should be pursued, including military action (Woodward, 2004; Suskind, 2004, pp. 70–5). A number of factors combined to make Iraq a likely target for US action. These included Saddam's continued flouting of UN resolutions, the commitment to regime change favoured by the Project for a New American Century since 1997 and its status as official US policy since the Iraqi Liberation Act of 1998, and the planned assassination of Bush's father by Iraqi agents in 1993. Prospects for a direct invasion, however, appeared slim in 2001.

The transformation occasioned by the 9/11 attacks was therefore one comprising not only the region's elevated priority in US foreign and security policy but also a substantive shift in policy preferences. 9/11 highlighted three critical features of the region that could not entirely or reliably be de-linked. First, the supply of 'superterrorists' — while not exclusively or even centrally located in the Middle East — drew most directly, and to most destructive force, from the region's conflicts. Second, the nexus of terrorism and weapons of mass destruction (WMD), and the possible or potential nexus between tyrants, terror and WMD that threatened an even more costly 9/11, was most forceful and elaborate here. Third, to the extent that the domestic structures of undemocratic regimes could be linked to their bellicose and destabilizing foreign policies, the issue of democratization — and the most effective instruments to achieve this — became an urgent matter for US decision-makers. Bush's response to these challenges was to reject both the 'narrow realism' of his father's administration and the 'wishful liberalism' of Bill Clinton in favour of a 'distinctly American internationalism' (Kaplan and Kristol, 2003). This approach pared Wilsonian ideals to realist means, focusing on regime change, prevention as well as deterrence and preserving American primacy.

9/11 therefore not only caused the region to move to centre stage in US foreign policy but also rapidly to alter the direction, priorities and instruments of Bush's international agenda. Although the Bush Doctrine was global in focus, the Middle East immediately became the central arena for its practical application. The linking of 'rogue states' to terrorists and WMD proliferation precipitated the military interventions to topple the

Taliban in 2001 and to secure 'regime change' in Iraq in 2003. Both also facilitated the emphasis accorded democracy promotion as the path to long-standing regional peace. Rejection of nation-building was replaced by its (partial) embrace in both nations, even though international donors proved far more recalcitrant to foot the bills than they had been after the first Gulf War. As the NSS made clear, however (and as caricatures of Bush the Cowboy so frequently neglected), Bush's approach was neither exclusively militarist nor unilateralist. Intensive international co-operation on intelligence sharing, combating money laundering, and public diplomacy were supplemented by aggregate increases in the US foreign assistance budget of 50 per cent from Fiscal Years (FY) 2002 through 2004. The administration also committed to a Middle East Partnership Initiative that was to increase from US$29m in FY 2004 to over US$290m for FY 2005 (Stevenson, 2004, p. 88). Quiet but insistent diplomatic pressure was also exerted on a range of regional actors from Tripoli, Riyadh and Damascus to Cairo and Islamabad to co-operate in the war on terror or face the adverse consequences. This threat was made all the more credible by the deployment of the US military in Iraq and the extension of US military bases and operations to Central Asia.

If much of the counter-terrorism activity necessarily occurred in secret, the public position of the Bush administration was dramatically to repudiate the acceptability of good relations with the types of repressive regimes that had, ultimately, spawned the terrorists who committed the 9/11 attacks. In November 2003 during his visit to the United Kingdom, Bush expressly stated that, 'We must shake off decades of failed policy in the Middle East. Your nation and mine, in the past, have been willing to make a bargain, to tolerate oppression for the sake of stability. Long-standing ties often led us to overlook the faults of local elites.' As one set of critical observers commented, however:

> With the air already poisoned by Iraq and continued violence in Israel and Palestine, this *mea culpa* generated very little (if any) goodwill. Simply put, US action abroad sets the context for dialogue, and even significant shifts in rhetoric vis-à-vis the Middle East will remain a distant second to recorded votes (in the UN), the distribution of aid and observable intentions. This is particularly true when those interventions are as momentous as regime change in Iraq and tend to reinforce the prevailing views of what really drives American foreign policy (Clarke et al., 2004, p. 100).

The Iraq invasion, the first test of the Bush Doctrine's embrace of preventive war, underlined the limited prospects of assuaging regional anti-Americanism by a demonstration effect of democratization. For Arabs and Muslims within and without the region, the symbol of US-led 'emancipation' was less the fall of Saddam's statue than the torture at Abu Ghraib prison and the failure of the US-led coalition to quell the insurgency and restore order to Iraq.

Bush's narrow but clear victory in the 2004 presidential election — the first in which national security had figured prominently since 1988 — repudiated the notion that the war on terror had been 'hijacked' by a neo-conservative cabal. 80 per cent of those listing the war as the key issue voted for Bush and there is reason to attribute the president's re-election largely to the effects of the 9/11 attacks. But almost 80 per cent of voters who specified Iraq as the key issue cast their ballots for Kerry. The American electorate manifested deep schisms over both the justifications for and outcome of war in Iraq. The clear preference of most non-Americans for a Kerry victory was also evident. This combination of factors induced many observers to hope and expect that a Bush second term would necessitate a rejection of the 'neo-conservative' influences of the first, and a return to the more tempered, diplomatic and consensual approaches of prior administrations. As Gaddis notes, second terms:

> ...open the way for second thoughts. They provide the least awkward moment at which to replace or reshuffle key advisers. They lessen, although nothing can remove, the influence of domestic political considerations since re-elected presidents have no next election to worry about. They enhance authority, as allies and adversaries learn — whether with hope or despair — with whom they will have to deal for the next four years (Gaddis, 2005, p. 2).

As Hodgson notes in this volume, however, President Bush is not a leader to cut his cloth according to temporary or divided public opinion over his own convictions. In regard to the Middle East especially, declarations of the Bush Doctrine's demise appear decidedly premature.

The Second-Term Agenda: Fall of the Dictators?

The overall relationship between the US (and its Western allies) and the Middle East during and beyond Bush's second term will be shaped by the Israeli-Palestinian conflict, post-war developments in Iraq, the standoff over

Iran's nuclear ambitions, the extent of America's continued dependence on Saudi oil, and how far key regional governments — in particular Iraq, Egypt, Saudi Arabia, Syria and Pakistan — can openly assist the US while resisting popular support for bin Laden's perverted version of Islam. Crucial, too, will be two distinct but related questions. The first concerns the extent to which the US genuinely moves to promote governments across the region that are representative and inclusive of their peoples rather than mere clients of Washington. The second centres on the ability of the administration to continue to prevent a second 9/11 from occurring on the American homeland.

Faced by such complex, seemingly intractable and mutually overlapping problems, three factors condition the likely success of Middle East policies. These are, according to David Ross: 'first, every vacuum in that region is filled by violence; second, every diplomatic opening tends to close quickly; and third, the war on terrorism is actually a war against radical Islam' (2005, p. 72). More accurately, the war is against not all terrorists but against *jihadist* terrorists seeking to hijack Islam to establish non-democratic theocracies.[1] Only a carefully calibrated set of US policies that recognizes this, addresses the four concentric circles of *jihadism* — al-Qaeda, related *jihadist* groups, *jihadist* sympathizers and the broader Islamic world — and crafts country-by-country policies that accept trade-offs and collateral effects will likely yield success in the medium to long term (Clarke et al., 2004). It was in regard to this that the mix of policies, from prevention to public diplomacy, required a more deft touch by the Bush administration than was shown in its first term.

As such, and despite recent propitious developments in Afghanistan, Palestine and Iraq, Bush's second-term policy in effect marries highly ambitious goals to what may plausibly prove — in the limited frame of four years — to be more modest and uneven achievements across its three key priorities.

First, stabilizing Iraq and achieving a deliberate but phased withdrawal of US forces by the 2006 mid-terms is a prerequisite of an effective US policy. Iraq was a military triumph but an occupational disaster. By May 2005, over 1,700 American personnel had been killed, far more in the occupation than the invasion. The steady death toll exacted increasing disillusion at home over Bush's Iraq policy, while the central contradiction — how to justify the presence of 140,000 US troops in an apparently sovereign nation — remained unresolved. The bitterly polarized post-war conflict over the extent to which the original rationales for the war had been distorted both reflected and reinforced the growing distrust of government and politicians that originated in the Watergate scandal. If the erosion of trust was less for Bush than for British Prime Minister Tony Blair (the latter had focused on WMD alone, downplaying alleged Iraqi terrorist ties, repression and democratization), it nonetheless made the prospect of further preventive military invasions minimal. A US presence in Iraq throughout 2006 that is of comparable dimensions to that in mid-2005 would not only retard Iraqis' faith in their own sovereignty but also erode further the American public's support for a forward policy of freedom in the region.

It is ironic, however, that critics of Bush at once contested the applicability of 'western-style' democracy to Iraq while simultaneously dismissing the type of democracy signified by the momentous elections of 2005 as not equating to a genuine democracy synonymous with those of the West. The achievement of a fledgling and fragile democratic structure does not offset the damage done to the nation and wider region by the failure to find WMD, the botched occupation, and torture revelations. But, as Bernard Lewis notes, the two dominant fears about Iraq are — in the West — that a democratic Iraq will not work and — in the ruling regimes of the Middle East — that it will:

> Arab democracy has won a battle, not a war, and still faces many dangers, both from ruthless and resolute enemies and from hesitant and unreliable friends. But it was a major battle, and the Iraqi election may prove a turning point in Middle Eastern history no less important than the arrival of General Bonaparte and the French Revolution in Egypt more than two centuries ago (Lewis, 2005, p. 51).

Moreover, it is vital that Iraq does not become the lens through which the US views the region and the world. What occurs in Israel and Palestine, Iran, Egypt, Pakistan, Saudi Arabia and elsewhere will be at least as significant for the region. In terms of the international system, what occurs in China, Russia, India, Europe and Africa may well be at least as important as the Middle East.

If the first priority of Bush's Middle Eastern policy was to achieve withdrawal from a stabilized and democratized Iraq, the second remained the 'war on terror', broadly conceived. The key issues on this front continued to be how Iran's nuclear ambitions could be countered, how Iran and Syria could be cajoled to cease support for terrorism, how Pakistan could both counter al-Qaeda and not become a failed state and how the loose network of *jihadist* terror groups could be marginalized. The Iraq war did have one countervailing if mixed beneficial effect, in concentrating trans-national terrorism in the regional theatre and thereby bringing home the seriousness of the *jihadist* terror threat both literally and figuratively to Arab and Muslim regimes and peoples in the region. The administration's own National Intelligence Estimate of January 2005, however, effectively endorsed those Democratic Party critics who argued that Iraq was a strategic blunder of the first order that had produced more, not fewer, terrorists. The accuracy of such is difficult to gauge, given the contentions that surround the discussion and the absence of a consensus about either what constitute the 'roots of terrorism' or how best to weed these roots out. Nonetheless, the existence of the threat remains potent. Moreover, the possibility that WMD could be obtained and delivered at the US or Europe has hardly been negated by revelations of the illicit network of A.Q. Khan in Pakistan.

The third priority for the Bush administration remains the resolution — more plausibly, the downscaling — of the Israel-Palestine conflict by the establishment of a democratic Palestinian state by 2009. As with other aspects of his foreign policy, the significance of Bush's ambition has been rather neglected here by his critics. In his first term Bush became the first American president publicly to commit the US to endorsing a two-state solution to the conflict. He also emphasized the importance of a Palestinian state being not only independent but also contiguous. A number of developments combined to provide greater momentum to the peace process — albeit without activating the 'road map' — than had been witnessed since 2000. These were Arafat's death in November 2004 and the subsequent election of Mahmoud Abbas as Palestinian Authority (PA) president, the reformation of Ariel Sharon's coalition government, and the likely Israeli withdrawal from Gaza in 2005. Similarly, while the potential destabilizing roles of Hamas in the PA and Hezbollah in Lebanon augur caution, regional developments offered some grounds for cautious optimism that a second-term Bush push could indeed yield meaningful progress towards a peaceful settlement.

What is clear is that in political, economic and especially military terms, the US is now more firmly entrenched in the Middle East than it was prior to 9/11. What is more opaque is the degree to which Bush's second term will see a re-evaluation of US goals and methods in the region. While the blunt charge of 'neo-conservatism' is likely to continue regularly to be levelled at the administration, its accuracy may be tempered in substance by the reshaping of key foreign policy personnel and by five practical political realities. Together these suggest that the autumn — or fall — of all the despots of the region, however desirable, remains more distant than close at hand but that some will no longer be in power by 2009.

In personnel terms, the partial reconfiguration of the foreign policy team in 2005 offered competing signals for policy directions. The extension of White

House control, especially through Condoleezza Rice's appointment as Secretary of State, suggested more about the presidential imprint on policy than its specific contents. Not since James Baker has a Secretary of State been able to articulate foreign policy with the clear authority of the president behind her. A greater degree of pragmatism and a more sustained effort at diplomacy — a dialogue rather than a monologue, as Rice put it at her Senate confirmation hearing in January 2005 — appeared to be the likely results. Rice and Bush's trips to Europe in the first half of 2005 and their emphasis on the value placed on transatlantic ties were certainly greeted warmly. Dick Cheney and Donald Rumsfeld remain in place, however, as vice-president and secretary of defence, with the formidable political command and bureaucratic skill that they together wield. Colin Powell's departure therefore weakens the more pacific and instinctively multilateral voices in the higher echelons of decision-making. At the same time, the appointment of Paul Wolfowitz as World Bank president confirmed that the president's commitment to economic, as well as political, transformation of the Middle East was genuine. But John Bolton's controversial nomination as Ambassador to the UN suggested a continuation of the 'put up or shut up' approach of the first term towards that unloved institution. The relative balance in the second Bush administration between 'American nationalists' and 'democratic imperialists' and the ambitious rhetoric of its leading foreign policy players looked more or less similar to that of the first term. However, the practical experiences of these actors over 2001–05 recommended a more circumscribed application of their more controversial beliefs in practice.

Meanwhile a combination of geopolitics and domestic political considerations suggests a more tempered second term as far as the application of the more muscular aspects of the Bush Doctrine is concerned. According to Gaddis, the American commitment to democracy promotion as the number one priority of national security and foreign policy was 'neither rhetorical nor a cloak for hidden motives' (2005, p. 2).[2] Nevertheless it looked destined — for reasons of geopolitics — to continue bearing the taint of a selective policy aggravating Arab and Muslim grievances against American 'double standards'. The democratization strategy has won neither universal nor consistent approval even within the ranks of the administration, much less outside. Traditionalists regard the transformationalists' conviction in democratization as at best naïve and at worst foolhardy. As George Will argued, 'the premise — that terrorism thrives where democracy does not — may seem to generate a duty to universalize democracy. But it is axiomatic that one cannot have a duty to do something that cannot be done' (2004, A7). On this view, the inherent incompatibility with

separating the religious and secular spheres in Islam precludes a nation —
much less an entire region — which can be legitimately democratic and
authentically Muslim at the same time. Islamic nations have rarely known
democratic traditions in a western conception and those few entities that
have experienced forms of pluralism — Turkey, Indonesia, Lebanon —
have done so with fragility, hesitance and subject to highly contingent factors (such as the role of the army in Turkey's case). The central tenets of
constitutional liberalism — from protection of human rights, guarantees
of freedom of the press and religion, to women's equality and minority
rights — have not yet encountered fertile ground in the Middle East.
Moreover, as Europeans typically point out, however much democracy is a
necessary condition of defeating terrorism, it is clearly insufficient.

Second, co-operation in the 'war on terror' and continued access to
energy supplies will plausibly remain necessary and at times sufficient conditions of good relations with Washington for key regional actors. The
access of Europe, America and China to oil and natural gas supplies
remains central to the health of their economies and the global economy.
John Kerry's attempts to exploit reliance on the Saudi royal family in the
2004 campaign highlighted the limited extent to which Bush's policies had
altered the status quo in this regard. As such, brute realities of geopolitics
and energy needs further compromise the substantive commitment to a
strategy based on democratization, wherein certain states receive vocal
pressure to democratize — such as Iran — while others (Egypt, Saudi
Arabia, Pakistan) avoid such a fate.

Third, Bush's involvement in the peace process will hinge heavily on his
assessment of the extent to which expending political capital represents a
sensible investment. As Stanley Renshon notes, Bush invests enormous
capital in his personal relationships and his assessments of other leaders,
both positive and negative (2004). Such personal diplomacy may occlude
rather than assist clear assessments of America's vital strategic interests and
feasible options. Nevertheless its continuation meant that relations with
regimes such as Saudi Arabia and Pakistan would rely centrally on Bush's
ties to their leaders and the latter's willingness to brave domestic political
opposition — including assassination — to assist the US.

Fourth, the prospects for another preventive war appear minimal, given
the continued military commitment to Iraq and the further erosion of
America's international standing that any such action would cause. Although
the Iraq war confirmed the awesome power and skill of American armed
forces, the occupation demonstrated the profound limits to its militarism.
The prospects of the US being able to wage two wars simultaneously — a

fulcrum of defence doctrine in the 1990s — appeared decidedly less robust by 2005. A crisis on the Korean peninsula or Taiwan would pose major difficulties for a decisive US military response. Equally, while speculation surrounded US intentions towards Iran and Syria, a full-scale invasion of either was implausible. Selective strikes by either Israel or the US on Iran's nuclear production facilities were the most commonly cited strategy but such action would exacerbate the already faltering battle for 'moderate' Muslim opinion within the region. For some critics, one of the main costs of the Iraq invasion was that — in limiting the military's flexibility and alienating traditional allies — Iran and Syria were emboldened, not tempered, by the exercise of American power. The co-operation of the E3 (the UK, France and Germany) in pressurizing Tehran over 2005, while an indication of some significant movement back toward transatlantic co-operation, did not promise a certain or a non-military outcome to the confrontation.

Fifth, America's standing in the region remains subject to powerful attacks. The sources of, and domestic political usages of, anti-Americanism are varied and multiple (O'Connor and Griffiths, 2005; Rubin and Rubin, 2004). Resolution of the Arab-Israeli conflict will not eliminate anti-Americanism, however much it may partially ameliorate it. The *jihadist* vision rejects both what America does and what it is but, more importantly, regards America as a barrier to the creation of theocratic nation-states or caliphates. An existential threat is therefore one that policy and rhetorical changes cannot of themselves remove since it is partly premised on an occidentalist view of the US as a soulless nation of depraved morals, degraded women, corruption in every form, with a people dominated by the pursuit of money, technology and violence over virtue. Public diplomacy can, allied to private western efforts, perhaps partially ameliorate such antipathy but, as Barry Rubin notes, it is:

> …perceived softness of the US in recent years, rather than its bullying, that has encouraged anti-Americans to act on their beliefs. After the US failed to respond aggressively to many terrorist attacks against US citizens, stood by while Americans were seized as hostages in Iran and Lebanon, let Saddam Hussein remain in power while letting the Shah fall, and allowed its prized Arab-Israeli peace process to be destroyed, why should anyone respect its interests or fear its wrath? Further concessions will only encourage even more contempt for the US and make the anti-American campaign more attractive … If Arab anti-Americanism turns out to be

> grounded in domestic politics rather than American mis-
> deeds, neither launching a public relations campaign nor
> changing Washington's policies will affect it. Only when the
> systems that manufacture and encourage anti-Americanism
> fail will popular opinion also change (Rubin, 2002, p. xx).

Although America has demonstrated renewed will to use its military power, respect for its culture, institutions and leadership has declined in the Arab world, a trend unlikely to be reversed in Bush's second term.

Finally, domestic, as well as international, politics seems likely to pose major limitations to Bush's transformational project. The contentious domestic agenda of the second term analyzed elsewhere in this volume sharply limits the political capital available to the president for more controversial foreign interventions, especially where the justification for these hinge on intelligence claims not shared fully with Congress or the American people. It would be ironic if the principal constraints on a combative second term foreign policy derived from the consequences of the domestic choices of Bush at home.

The strategic calculations of incumbents on the Hill regarding the 2006 mid-terms and the 2008 presidential race add powerful drags on Bush's support. Bush's continued unpopularity and low job approval ratings, the constraints of the budget deficit, and the 'drip-drip' of deaths from Iraq will likely ramp up the risk averse approach of most Democrats and a sizeable proportion of House and Senate Republicans. Among the latter, especially, the appetite for further military adventures and alliance ruptures is likely to be limited. Figures such as Senators Richard Lugar, John McCain, Chuck Hagel and Bill Frist — the latter three with presidential ambitions for 2008 — are instinctively internationalist. Leading Democrats, too, are unlikely to provide the type of political cover — often from a fear of looking 'soft' on terror — that Bush received in the run-up to the Iraq war authorization of October 2002. While the imperative to demonstrate strong national security credentials remains powerful, the continuation of pronounced conflict over the appropriate mix of priorities, instruments and means by which to prosecute the war on terrorism seems likely to remain a constant.

Beyond this, the possibility of scandal engulfing a second term administration, the structural factors invariably shaping 'lame duck' presidencies, and the possibility of a second major attack on the continental US together pose fundamental problems for an audaciously ambitious White House approach. While bipartisan support for the war on terrorism remains strong, the deep and bitter fissures caused by Iraq both between and within the two main parties presaged difficult relations with Capitol Hill. Foreign policy issues rarely decide American elections, so one could logically argue that the autonomy of decision-makers is greater there. Nevertheless, the combined salience of the continued terror threat, the US presence in Iraq and the dissensus and distrust of the administration on the Hill and among the public together provide formidable constraints on the White House's room for manoeuvre.

There is good reason, therefore, to view the prospects for success of Bush's radicalism to be more bleak than bright. Optimism towards the Middle East should always be cautious and expectations of rapid progress should likewise be modest. But against this scepticism, three factors provide some reason to challenge those dismissive of Bush's policies as wholly counterproductive, lacking in intellectual sophistication and as ultimately doomed by the familiar exigencies of America's fragmented, fissiparous and hyper-pluralist politics.

First, the extent to which Bush's policies represent a 'revolution' in US foreign policy needs to be heavily qualified. The caricature of an exclusively militarist and belligerent Washington browbeating Arab regimes, lending unqualified support to its regional deputy, Israel, while stoking anti-Americanism to unprecedented levels is misleading and unhelpful. Indeed, while analysts and journalists alike regularly discuss Middle East 'policy', the stark reality is that Washington typically and necessarily tailors its policies towards the particular circumstances of each state and their inter-relations. The Iranian case, whereby an anti-American regime confronts a predominantly pro-American populace, is thus wholly dissimilar to the Saudi case, where a heavily divided regime faces a population even more hostile to the US. The political uses of anti-Americanism, similarly, differ in important respects between the nation-states of the region (Clarke et al., 2004).

Second, the threats that exist in the region to the security of America, Europe and elsewhere are serious and urgent. Political, economic and structural changes partially explain bin Laden's 'catch-all' appeal to sections of Middle Eastern opinion. Recent decades have seen the end of the Arab radicalism/nationalism that began in 1954 with Nasser's coming to power in republican Egypt and the gradual erosion of the various appeals that Arab despots such as Saddam, Gaddaffi, Arafat and Assad enlisted over time in their aid (anti-monarchism, anti-colonialism, anti-Zionism, socialisms, secularism, pan-Arabism). Conservative, rather than radical, command economies have produced disastrous consequences. The 2002 Arab Human Development Report (UN) noted that the entire Arab world had the same GDP as Spain and lower per capita economic growth than any other region except sub-Saharan Africa. Authoritarianism and nepotism ensured that changes of government are rare while repression is wide-spread. The growth of militant or 'political Islam' as the only viable expression for new radicals (though past its peak) remained a key feature of the region's supply of eager and willing terrorists. Finally, economic and political stagnation, technological backwardness (total Arab Internet usage is two per cent), the region's growing demographic crisis (the 22 Arab states plus Iran are estimated to grow from 304 to 400 million people between 2001 and 2015) together pose profound dangers. The United Nations report (2003), written by Arabs, was scathing in its denunciation of the sources of the region's failings:

> AHDR 2002 challenged the Arab world to overcome three cardinal obstacles to human development posed by widening gaps in freedom, women's empowerment and knowledge across the region. AHDR 2003 makes it clear that, in the Arab civilization, the pursuit of knowledge is prompted by religion, culture, history and the human will to achieve success. Obstructions to this quest are the defective structures created by human beings — social, economic and above all political. Arabs must remove or reform these structures in order to take the place they deserve in the world of knowledge at the beginning of the knowledge millennium.

If socio-economic and political stagnation therefore offers plentiful supplies of disaffected young men to whom militarist or terrorist appeals are seductive, the potential consequences are disturbing. A nuclear Iran, for example, would probably precipitate a chain reaction in the region that would cause hopes of non-proliferation to evaporate. The prospects for peace would not only recede rapidly but also decisively, while the potential costs of regional war would be ratcheted up. The effect of conflict on the price and supply of energy needs not only to America but to Europe, China and India would have a devastating effect on the global economy, a downturn in which would wreak graphic havoc on Asian, African and Latin American fortunes. The likelihood of trans-national terrorists gaining at least some usable forms of WMD would also be immeasurably greater with a proliferation of such weapons across the region. The stakes, therefore, could not be higher.

As such, few critics of the Bush administration — including John Kerry in 2004 — have offered coherent, convincing and substantially different alternatives that promise a more comprehensive or rapid solution. Indeed, the virile opposition to Bush witnessed the emergence of an odd — though not unprecedented — *de facto* alliance, one in which those castigating Bush for excessive idealism on both the Left and the Right now appear to have together embraced the amoral realism of Nixon and Kissinger. Yet, as Natan Sharansky argued:

> …it is hard to imagine many who would contend that if the region's tyrannies were transformed into *genuinely* free societies, the world would not be more secure. Surely, few would argue that the successful transformation of the non-democratic regimes of the Middle East into governments that respect the rule of law, protect individual rights, cherish human life and dedicate themselves to improving the wellbeing of their citizens would not be better for everyone (Sharansky, 2004, p. 23).

Moreover, the combination of approaches employed by the administration in its dealings with the region's despots had reaped significant gains by the early stages of its second term. Progress may have been less that than the Bush administration had wished for but was arguably greater than achieved by any previous US administration in the Middle East. While the balance between domestic and international influences on encouraging the growth of self-governing trends typically favours the former, the encouragement given to democratic forces by Washington's lead is invaluable. The established Arab autocracies have outwitted and outlived predictions of their demise previously, but something different has now been injected into the region's struggles. As Fouad Ajami observed, 'The United States — a great foreign power that once upheld the Arab autocrats, fearing what mass politics would bring — now braves the storm' (2005, p. 35). The environment that precipitated the collapse of tyrannical regimes in Eastern Europe depended on both dissidents who demanded their governments free their own peoples and boldness on the part of western leaders who conditioned superpower relations partly on internal liberalization, reform and progress. To castigate an American administration for not exhibiting complete coherence and constancy betrays an unsophistication about the realities of foreign policy-making far more naïve, cynical and dangerous than the Bush commitment to ending tyranny. Bush extends the tradition of historic figures such as Senator Henry Jackson in demanding that moral clarity intrude upon American foreign policy. The possibility that, to paraphrase Reagan, the West will not simply contain terror and tyrants but transcend them, relegating both to a tragic but transient chapter in human history, is one that Bush has seized upon. The will to effect such change represents a necessary, but not always sufficient, part of the capacity to do so.

Conclusion

Few analysts can venture predictions about the Middle East with confidence. Although US-China relations may well assume a more central priority by 2008, Bush's second term cannot but address the region's dangers in pursuit of America's security. Crisis management, rather than conflict resolution, no longer appears a viable US strategy. Purchasing stability at the price of justice looks a similarly barren course of action. In this respect, the profound strategic shift that has seen a conservative Republican president embrace the liberal Democratic ideal of making the world safe for democracy as a national security imperative is shrewd and timely. It is of course the case that — for historical, geopolitical, and religious reasons — comparisons with peaceful democratic revolutions in Eastern Europe have limited purchase in the Middle East. Nonetheless, Bush's bold embrace of democratization represents an important and consequential about-face in US policy. That America's prior record offers limited cause for confidence in its current approach should not obscure the significance of the shift. Bush's historical legacy stands or falls in large part on his success or failure in addressing some of the most vexing, complex and multi-faceted problems hewn over centuries of conflict. His stature — as a presidential success or failure of the first rank — rests heavily not only on the adoption of 'ideals without illusions' but also the commitment and skill to find the appropriate mix of means to advance, if not fully to realize, them by the time he leaves office.

Notes

1   While the meaning of 'jihad' in Islam is broader than fighting war and typically concerns a personal and inward struggle, radicals such as al-Qaeda proclaim themselves to be 'jihadists'.
2   In November 2004 at a reception to honour its author, Bush described Natan Sharansky's *The Case for Democracy: The Power of Freedom to Overcome Tyranny and Terror* (New York: Public Affairs, 2004), as being 'hardwired' into his 'presidential DNA'.

6

The Bush Administration and the Budget Deficit

Iwan Morgan

The huge budget deficits that were a characteristic of the 1980s again became a primary fact of government in George W. Bush's America. Republican presidents from Warren Harding to Dwight Eisenhower had made the balanced budget the symbol of their party's dedication to fiscal soundness and constrained government. Even Richard Nixon and Gerald Ford, who presided over a growing deficit in circumstances of recession in the 1970s, looked to return to what Herbert Stein dubbed the 'old-time religion' of balanced budgets once the economy showed signs of recovery (Stein, 1994, p. 189). Like Ronald Reagan, however, George Bush deviated from this gospel to place tax reduction and defence expansion at the core of his agenda — even at the cost of a rising deficit. Indeed the Bush White House initially drew on the precedent of the 1980s to fortify its case for tax reduction against the doomsayers of fiscal debacle. In response to Treasury Secretary Paul O'Neill's warning in late 2002 that the federal government was moving towards a budgetary crisis, Vice President Dick Cheney reportedly remarked, 'Reagan proved deficits don't matter' (Suskind, 2004, p. 291).

This was a dubious reading of history since the experience of the 1980s arguably proved the very opposite. The burgeoning fiscal deficit weakened America's international economic position in this earlier period, was a contributory factor to the Wall Street Crash of 1987 and eventually came to be seen as a threat to America's wellbeing (Friedman, 1988; Calleo, 1992). Moreover, the need to restore fiscal responsibility dominated the politics of the 1990s and was used by the Clinton administration to justify its 1993 tax increases, which partially reversed the Reagan cuts in personal taxation (Woodward, 1994).

Fiscal realities eventually compelled the Bush presidency at its midway point to regard the deficit as one red state that it did not want in its political column. This constituted one of the most significant political changes between Bush's first and second terms. However, the president's determination, stated in his budget message of February 5 2005, to cut the deficit in half during his final four years in office also embodied political continuity in his intent to do so without compromising the tax and defence programmes launched in his first term. In contrast to his initial expansion of domestic programmes, Bush's second term promised to feature a more orthodox Republican retrenchment of non-defence spending in pursuit of deficit control.

This chapter seeks to: explain the re-emergence of the deficit problem; assess why Bush prioritized deficit reduction in his second term; analyze his Fiscal Year (FY) 2006 budget plan's strategy to halve the deficit within four years; and evaluate his prospects of success in this goal.

The Return of the Deficit Problem

In FY 1998 the federal government balanced its budget for the first time since FY 1969 and for only the second time since FY 1960. Three further balanced budgets followed in FY 1999, 2000 and 2001, the longest consecutive sequence since the 11 balanced budgets of FY 1920–FY 1930. Having been committed from its outset to reducing the huge deficits inherited from the Reagan and Bush Sr. administrations, the Clinton administration claimed the credit for this fiscal accomplishment. In reality, it was the harvest of revenues generated by the remarkable spurt of economic growth from 1996 through 2000 that was mainly responsible for the balanced-budget sequence. Also important was the Cold War peace dividend that facilitated military retrenchment for most of the Clinton years. Having grown in every budget (measured in FY 2000 dollars) from US$250.6 billion in FY 1977 to US$398.9 billion in FY 1989, defence expenditure declined yearly from US$354.3 billion in FY 1992 to US$282.6 billion in FY 1998. Despite rising again in the final Clinton budgets, it was still lower at US$297.2 billion in FY 2001 than at the start of the Reagan defence build-up in FY 1982 (OMB, 2005a, pp. 114–16).

The Clinton administration's major contribution to the fiscal turnaround was to ensure, through its deficit reduction plan of 1993 and the balanced-budget plan of 1997, that the budget would be balanced at a high level of revenue, which permitted a correspondingly high level of expenditure. In contrast, the congressional Republicans, who controlled both houses of the legislature from 1995 onward, had vainly sought large cuts in domestic spending in order to fund tax reduction within a balanced-budget framework (Ippolito, 2003). Accordingly, in FY 2000, budget receipts amounted to 20.9

per cent of GDP, the highest level since the World War II budget of FY 1944, and expenditures totalled 18.4 per cent of GDP, the lowest share since FY 1966 but the highest ever sum measured in constant dollar terms.

At the outset of the Bush presidency, the Congressional Budget Office (CBO) estimated that the federal government would run continuous surpluses aggregating $5.6 trillion in FY 2001–FY 2011. By early 2003, however, its ten-year forecast had transmuted into a prediction of cumulative deficits of $1.3 trillion, which was revised upward to $3 trillion in the following year. As indicated in Table 6.1, the Bush first-term fiscal record constituted the polar opposite of Clinton's second-term success. For the first time since World War II federal finances underwent four consecutive years of fiscal deterioration measured as a percentage of GDP. Moreover, the fiscal deterioration of 6 per cent GDP represented by the shift from the FY 2000 surplus of 2.4 per cent GDP to the FY 2004 deficit of 3.6 per cent GDP was almost comparable to the 6.7 per cent GDP decline experienced during the early stages of the Great Depression from FY 1930 to FY 1934 (Kogan and Greenstein, 2004).

Table 6.1: Receipts, Outlays and Surplus/Deficit as Percentage of GDP, FY 2000–FY2004

Fiscal Year	Receipts	Outlays	Surplus/Deficit
2000	20.9	18.4	2.4
2001	19.8	18.5	1.3
2002	17.8	19.4	-1.5
2003	16.4	19.9	-3.5
2004	16.3	19.8	-3.6
2005 (estimate)	16.8	20.3	-3.5

Source: OMB, *Budget of the United States Government: Fiscal Year 2005: Historical Tables.*

The causes of this fiscal downturn were a matter of dispute. According to the Office of Management and Budget (OMB), 53 per cent of the FY 2002-

FY2008 deficit could be attributed to the weak economy that resulted from the stock market decline of 2001, 24 per cent to increased domestic security and war expenditure, and 23 per cent to the three tax cuts enacted in Bush's first term (Rosenbaum, 2003). The congressional Joint Economic Committee (JEC) calculated that 37 per cent of the change in the CBO's ten-year budget surplus projection resulted from the weak economy, 39 per cent came from increased federal spending, and 24 per cent derived from tax reduction (Joint Economic Committee, 2004). Nevertheless, the three-year increase in the deficit since the official end of the recession in late 2001 marked the first occasion in America's post-1929 fiscal history that this had happened so far into the recovery cycle. Other analysts therefore placed greater emphasis on structural budgetary changes, namely the effects of new taxation and expenditure measures, to explain the fiscal deterioration (Gale and Orszag, 2004b).

George Bush took office with a firm commitment to cut taxes. One of the clearest policy differences between the two main candidates in the 2000 presidential election centred on how to allocate the projected budget surplus (Wattenberg, 2004). Al Gore promised a modest tax cut targeted at middle-income Americans but proposed to set aside the bulk of the surplus in a 'lockbox' that guaranteed future social security and Medicare funding. In contrast, Bush wanted to give some of the surplus back to taxpayers in the form of a massive US$1.3 trillion in federal taxes over ten years. As he put it in the third presidential debate, 'See, I don't think the surplus is the government's money. I think it's the people's money' (Mucciaroni and Quirk, 2004, p. 164).

The Bush tax programme was enacted as the Economic Growth and Tax Relief Reconciliation Act of 2001. This measure's ten-year cost of US$1.35 trillion, equivalent to some nine per cent of federal revenue, made it the largest tax cut since 1981. Its provisions included across-the-board reduction in personal tax rates, the doubling of the child tax credit, tax breaks for education and the phasing out of the estate tax. Bush made skilful use of the presidential bully pulpit to promote enactment of his main domestic priority. He crafted a message that variously justified the tax cut as a return of the people's money, relief for middle-class families hard pressed by high energy prices and credit-card debt, and a stimulus for the faltering economy. Whether it met any of these aims was open to question. The richest one per cent of taxpayers received 45 per cent of the benefits, while the poorest 60 per cent received less than 13 per cent (Rosenbaum, 2001). The back-loading of the bulk of the tax cut towards the end of the ten-year cycle also limited the measure's expansionary effects. Its complex phase-in and phase-out rule reflected the modern congressional practice of beginning tax bill considerations with an overall dollar value in order to fit as many cuts as possible under that ceiling (Edwards, 2005). Moreover, there was little debate about the affordability of the programme, which placed absolute faith in the longevity of the surplus. To facilitate speedy enactment, the Republican congressional leadership arranged for consideration of the tax bill outside the normal budget process, thereby eschewing discussion of multi-year revenue projections (Mucciaroni and Quirk, 2004).

The disappointing growth in jobs as the economy recovered from the brief recession of 2001 prompted two further tax cuts. The US$29 billion Job Creation and Work Assistance Act of 2002 sought to encourage business investment in capital equipment. The Jobs and Growth Tax Relief Reconciliation Act of 2003, which cut taxes to the tune of US$350 billion over ten years, mandated immediate implementation of the phased-in tax cuts of 2001 and reduced the maximum tax rates on capital gains and dividends until 2008. Conservatives applauded the latter as a correction of the excessive taxing of dividends dating from the New Deal (Edwards, 2005a). Critics dubbed it a bill for the rich because 46 per cent of the dividend and capital gains cuts would flow to the 0.2 per cent of households with annual incomes over US$1 million and nearly three-quarters would go to the 3.1 per cent of households making more than US$200,000 a year (Friedman, 2005).

Nevertheless congressional concern about the deficit diminished the scale of the 2003 tax cut. The House approved a bill with a revenue cost of US$726 billion, in line with what the president requested. In contrast, the Senate — mindful of Iraq war costs — only approved a US$350 billion bill, which Bush initially derided as 'little bitty' but eventually accepted for fear of losing the measure. The tax cut also provoked a war of words between conservative and liberal economists. 110 of the former, including three Nobel laureates, signed a letter in January 2003 supporting it as necessary to stimulate the economy. Over 400 liberal economists, including ten Nobel prize winners, signed a counter-statement that it was inequitable, would not spur job creation and would enlarge the deficit (Tatalovich and Frendreis, 2004, pp. 238–9; Gale and Orszag, 2004a; Gravelle, 2005).

The Bush tax cuts continued a Republican agenda that stretched back through the 1994 Contract with America to the Reagan Revolution, but the ideological root of his spending programme was less clearcut. Its conformity to Republican tradition was most evident in the growth of military and homeland security spending to prosecute the war on terror and implement the Bush Doctrine in the wake of the attacks of 9/11. However, most other periods of defence expansion — notably World War II, the early

1950s and the 1980s — were characterized by domestic spending retrenchment or slowdown. In contrast, as Table 6.2 indicates, mandatory and discretionary domestic programme expenditure experienced substantial growth in
Bush's first term. Under Clinton, discretionary domestic spending had
declined from 3.4 per cent of GDP to 3.1 per cent and social entitlement
expenditures had fallen from 10.2 per cent of GDP to 9.8 per cent between
FY 1993 and FY 2000. However, Bush ranked with Democrats Lyndon
Johnson and Jimmy Carter as one of only three presidents since 1950 to pre-
side over the expansion of both the defence and domestic budgets.

**Table 6.2: Defence and Domestic Spending as Percentage of GDP,
FY 2001–FY 2005**

FY	Defence	Discretionary Domestic	Social Entitlements
2001	3.0	3.1	10.1
2002	3.4	3.5	10.7
2003	3.7	3.6	10.9
2004	3.9	3.5	10.7
2005 estimate	3.8*	3.8	10.8

*excludes supplemental appropriation for operations in Iraq and Afghanistan

Source: CBO, *The Budget and Economic Outlook: Fiscal Years 2006 to 2015: Tables 3-1,
3-7, F-8 and F-10*

Bush is conventionally characterized as a conservative Republican in the
Reagan mould, but there were substantial contrasts between the fiscal
approaches of these two presidents. Reagan achieved his greatest success
in budgetary policy during his first year in office, when he promoted the
largest tax cut in American history (which reduced both personal income
and business taxes), the greatest expansion of defence spending since the
early 1950s and the largest ever single-year retrenchment of discretionary
domestic spending. However the congressional Democrats regrouped to
resist further domestic cutbacks from 1982 onward. Meanwhile the revenue loss from the tax cuts and the growth in military outlays combined to

send the deficit skyrocketing from 2.6 per cent of GDP in FY 1981 to an annual average of nearly five per cent of GDP in FY 1982–FY 1985. For the remainder of his presidency Reagan encountered continuous pressure from congressional leaders, both Republican and Democratic, to scale back his defence and tax programmes in the cause of deficit reduction. To safeguard his core concerns of military strength and low personal taxes, he engaged in trade-offs that sacrificed other elements of his programme. Accordingly, Reagan approved business tax increases in 1982, 1984, 1986 and 1987, mainly in the form of loophole closures, and increases in social security taxes in 1983 to keep the pension programme solvent (White and Wildavsky, 1989; Brownlee and Steurle, 2003).

Bush reduced taxes in 2001 to dispose of an anticipated surplus, but he made no effort to change course in the face of emergent budget problems. Instead of copying Reagan's example of twice raising corporate taxes in his first term to try to limit the deficit, he promoted two further pro-business tax cuts in a bid to stimulate investment. The White House clung staunchly to the conviction that these measures would eventually offset deficits by spurring economic growth. Its stand drew support from many in the corporate community that had been uniformly hawkish on the deficit in the 1990s. While some eminent businessmen, notably Warren Buffett, continued to advocate balanced budgets, organizations such as the Business Roundtable, the US Chamber of Commerce and the National Association of Manufacturers were prepared to tolerate the deficit as a trade-off for lower personal, corporate and investment taxes. Treasury Secretary John W. Snow typified this transformation. As chair of CSX, the giant railroad corporation, he had joined other business leaders in 1995 to sign a public letter to the *New York Times* urging the federal government to balance its books within seven years. A decade later he no longer advocated a deadline for erasing an imbalance he now termed 'entirely manageable' (Ota, 2004, p. 162).

The early advocates of supply-side tax reduction despaired of Reagan's u-turn on business taxes as an abandonment of their cause (Roberts, 1984). Twenty years on, devotees of this doctrine regarded Bush as having done substantially more to advance their agenda. The flattening effect of his tax programme on the progressive structure of the tax system, which they deemed a deterrent to economic growth, investment and saving, particularly heartened them (Altman, 2004; Edwards, 2005). Like their 1980s forbears, Bush-era supply-siders regarded the deficit not as an economic problem in its own right but as a residual of the economy's performance that would be eliminated through investment-generated economic growth. In reaction against the experience not only of the 1990s but also the 1950s, a balanced budget held little appeal to them if it was achieved through high taxes. According to Stephen Moore, president of the Club for Growth — a Washington-based group that lobbies for lower taxes, Bush completed the transformation of the Republicans into a supply-side party. 'It has evolved over the past forty years,' he avowed, 'from being a party of Eisenhower balanced-budget Republicans into a party of Reaganite pro-growth advocates' (Cassidy, 2004).

On the spending side of the budget, the Bush defence build-up was in one regard more modest than Reagan's because annual military spending only averaged 3.7 per cent of GDP in FY 2002–FY 2004 compared with 6.0 per cent of GDP in FY 1982–FY 1988. In constant (FY 2000) dollar terms, however, the Bush expansion climbed steeply from US$297.2 billion in FY 2001 to $404.7 billion in FY 2004, an increase of 36 per cent. This compared with the more gradual Reagan first-term growth from US$282.2 billion in FY 1981 to US$334 billion in FY 1984, an increase of 18.3 per cent, and a total Reagan expansion from FY 1981 through FY 1988 of 41.3 per cent (Office of Management and Budget, 2005a, pp. 116–7).

However the starkest difference between the Bush and Reagan budgets was over spending on the discretionary domestic programmes that are subject to annual appropriation legislation. Discretionary domestic expenditure accounted for only 3.1 of GDP in 1989 compared with 4.5 per cent in 1981, thereby reversing two decades of almost continuous expansion in the 1960s and 1970s. In contrast it rose from 3.2 per cent to 3.5 per cent of GDP from FY 2001 through FY 2004. Real discretionary spending (in FY 2000 dollars) declined by 1.4 per cent during Reagan's presidency, and rose by 3.8 per cent under George Bush Sr. and by 2.1 per cent under Clinton. However, it grew by 4.8 per cent from FY 2001 through FY 2005, a rate outstripped in the previous 40 years only by the five per cent expansion under Nixon (Slivinski, 2005, p. 5). In the 1980s and 1990s the biggest growth in domestic spending was on mandatory entitlements like social security and Medicare. However, discretionary domestic spending grew in real terms in Bush's first two budgets (FY 2002 and 2003) by more than it did during Clinton's entire presidency.

The expansion of domestic spending indicated that Bush's conservatism differed from the anti-government conservatism of Ronald Reagan and the Contract with America. Newt Gingrich was intent on completing the Reagan Revolution through the instrument of the federal budget. In his first address as Speaker, he declared: '[T]he budget is the transformational document for this system. When you've changed the budget, you've really changed government, and until you change the budget, you've just talked about changing government' (Strahan and Palazollo, 2004, p. 103). The GOP-controlled House went on to approve a budget for FY 1996 that required elimination of more than two hundred government programmes, including three entire Cabinet agencies — Commerce, Education and Energy, but Bill Clinton's obduracy frustrated its enactment.

In contrast, Bush was willing in his first term to spend on programmes that could enhance his re-election prospects by appealing to constituencies that did not habitually identify with the Republicans — provided these measures comported with conservative ideals of enhancing individual opportunity, empowerment and responsibility. In the words of John Bridgeland, former director of Bush's Domestic Policy Council, 'We have moved from devolution, which was just pushing back as much power as possible to the states, back to where government is limited but active.' More orthodox conservatives, such as Chris Edwards of the libertarian Cato Institute, complained that this was just a case of 'big government conservatism' that 'keeps expanding the federal involvement into state and local affairs' (VandeHei, 2005). In their eyes, Bush's most dismaying first-term measure was the No Child Left Behind law of 2002 (Garrett, 2004, p. 238). Enacted with Democratic support over the opposition of 33 House Republicans, this measure enhanced federal powers to police elementary school standards and accountability. In line with this new activism, the budget of the Department of Education, once a Republican target for abolition, rose from US$36 billion in FY 2001 to US$63 billion in FY 2004. However, this expansion paled into insignificance compared to the costs of the 2003 prescription drug benefit programme to protect senior citizens from escalating healthcare charges. Its US$720 billion price tag from FY 2006 through FY 2115 will grow even bigger in subsequent years, making it the most significant expansion of social welfare since the introduction of Medicare in 1965 (Nather, 2005; Hook, 2005; Slivinski, 2005).

In general, the congressional GOP was a partner in, rather than an obstacle to, Bush's first-term spending expansion. Some analysts, such as William Niskanen, saw this as proof that fiscal restraint was more likely in periods of divided party control of government when Republicans and Democrats could check each other, as happened during the Eisenhower and Clinton presidencies (Niskanen, 2003). However divided government was associated with substantial domestic expenditure expansion during the first Nixon administration and the Ford presidency. It also contributed to the growth of the deficit in the 1980s because the Democrat-controlled House was able to limit the scale of Reagan's domestic cutbacks. Nor did the Bush-era experience of divided government encourage belief that it promotes fiscal restraint. The 107th Congress (2001–03), for all but four months of which the Democrats controlled the Senate, increased Bush's non-defence spending requests by US$29 billion aggregate in FY 2002 and FY 2003. This only looked restrained in comparison with the US$62 billion that the entirely Republican-controlled 108th Congress (2003–05) added to the president's FY 2004 and FY 2005 non-defence budget proposals (Slivinski, 2005, pp. 13–14).

Arguably a more convincing explanation than single party control of government for the growth of the deficit under Bush was the congressional GOP's loss of revolutionary fervour since the heady days of the mid-1990s. The 104th Congress (1995–97) cut non-defence discretionary spending by 3.1 per cent in real terms, but the next two Congresses raised it by 3.6 per cent and 8.7 per cent respectively (Moore, 2005, p. 64). By the 106th Congress (1999–2001), spending control had gone out of fashion with the Republicans. Almost certainly a sense that the deficit problem had been resolved in the late 1990s contributed to this development. The belief that the party had lost popular support by pursuing retrenchment to the point of government shutdown in its confrontation with Clinton over the FY 1996 budget also inclined many Republicans to favour loosening the public purse-strings. According to the National Taxpayers Union, every Republican member of the 104th Congress had cast votes for net reduction in spending, but in the last Congress of the twentieth century only two (Representatives James Sensenbrenner of Wisconsin and Ron Paul of Texas) compiled overall voting records that supported a net cut in spending (Dircksen, 2004).

Republicans' support for increased domestic expenditure in the first two Congresses of the Bush era provoked the charge that they had become 'the Grand Old Spending Party' (Moore, 2005, p. 65). Pork barrel politics to channel federal funds towards home districts and states, deemed wasteful by the Republicans when they were the minority, found new favour. The 2004 omnibus spending bill contained 7,931 pork projects, approximately twice the number typically included by the Democrats when they held power (Taxpayers for Common Sense, 2004). Perhaps no measure better exemplified the Republican embrace of domestic spending than the 2002 agricultural programme legislation, which eviscerated the Freedom to Farm Act of 1996, one of the top spending-control accomplishments of the 104th Congress. Whereas the earlier measure sought to bring farming closer to the market through phasing out subsidies, the new bill resurrected the subsidy programme and provided it with a ten-year funding increase of US$87 billion (Moore, 2005, pp. 65–7).

The Shift to Deficit Control in Bush's Second Term

The mere fact of the deficit's enlargement did not guarantee its elevation in Bush's second-term agenda. Even the FY 2004 deficit, the biggest of the first term, was significantly smaller at 3.6 per cent of GDP than every Reagan-era deficit from FY 1982 through FY 1986. Nor did Bush face popular alarm about the deficit. According to the Pew Research Center Survey, respondents who identified the deficit as 'a top priority' had risen from 35 per cent in 2002 to 56 per cent in January 2005, but this did not match its salience in 1994 when 65 per cent held this view. The Contract with America's promise of a balanced-budget amendment was in tune with the popular mood a decade earlier. However, the deficit was a non-issue in the 2004 presidential election and no figure emerged from outside the party mainstream to arouse a sense of national emergency over the condition of government finances, as Ross Perot had done in 1992. As poll analyst Nancy Belden commented, the deficit was not 'a high hot-button issue' for the public at the outset of Bush's second term (Harris, 2005).

In making deficit reduction a core issue of his second term, Bush was engaged in a strategic reassessment of his priorities in light of a combination of international, financial and political considerations. His first administration was able to operate guns-and-butter deficits without need for high interest rates to help fund its increased borrowing. In this regard it was the beneficiary of the East Asian central banks' strategy to maintain their countries' export competitiveness in the giant American market through massive purchase of US Treasury securities, which helped boost the value of the dollar against their own currencies. The down side of this was the worrying enlargement of America's current account deficit, which basically comprises the trade deficit and interest paid to foreigners holding US assets. The current account deficit grew to an estimated 5.7 per cent of GDP (US$665 billion or the equivalent of nearly US$2 billion a day) in 2004, far above the pre-Bush peak of 3.5 per cent of GDP in 1987.

Unless corrected, the US current account deficit was on course at the start of Bush's second term to expand to seven per cent of GDP in 2006 and in excess of eight per cent in 2008, by when the net investment debt could well equate to about 50 per cent of GDP and almost 500 per cent of export revenues (Roubini and Setser, 2004, pp. 4–5). There is no absolute threshold at which a country's current account deficit becomes unsustainable. Past trends suggest that these imbalances typically decline, whether due to lower currency exchange rates or economic slowdown, once they reach 4.2 per cent. The US may be able to operate higher current account deficits because of its strong economy and the dollar's role as international reserve currency, but its capacity to sustain them along the growth track projected was doubtful. Many analysts also questioned whether Asian countries would expand their reserve purchases to sustain the projected growth in the US net external debt. China and Japan, the two main buyers, would need to increase their combined holdings from US$1.4 trillion at the end of 2004 to nearly US$3 trillion by the end of 2008, an annual growth of more than US$350 billion. (Weller, 2004; Roubini and Setser, 2004)

In these circumstances the Bush administration adopted a two-track strategy to reduce the current account deficit. It initially tackled the trade deficit through a dollar-devaluation strategy that allowed money markets to determine the dollar exchange value, but this yielded limited results because East Asian countries effectively pegged their currencies to America's to maintain their export competitiveness. Yet even if the devaluation strategy had proved more effective, it carried the risk that the declining value of their dollar holdings would persuade Asian central banks to sell them off rather than accumulate more (*The Economist*, 2004; Roubini and Sester, 2004). The US could also lessen its dependence on foreign capital through enhancement of national saving — the income it has available to invest in its future. The personal savings rate collapsed as Americans went on a binge of consumption during the last boom of the twentieth century. However the net national savings rate rose from three per cent to 6.5 per cent of GDP over the course of the 1990s thanks to government finances moving from large deficits to large surpluses. The fiscal developments in Bush's first term reversed this expansion. Cutting the deficit in half in his second term would go some way to putting matters right if it laid the foundations for the achievement of a balanced budget (Rubin et al., 2004; Gale and Orszag, 2004b).

Deficit reduction also served Bush's fundamental political project, defined by political scientist Stephen Schier as 'conservative regime restoration through electoral domination and a strong policy legacy' (2004, p. 10). The public may have shown little concern for the deficit in the 2004 election, but this would almost certainly change if high interest rates became necessary to sustain government borrowing in the event of Asian reluctance to go on buying Treasury securities. More expensive credit would probably produce economic slowdown that would be harmful to Republican electoral prospects. Bush could also safeguard his policy legacy of big defence spending and big tax reduction by taking the lead on deficit reduction and targeting economies on programmes outside his core concerns. Reagan's failure to tackle the deficit offered a salutary lesson in this regard because his tax cuts and defence expansion had fallen prey to bal-anced-budget concerns after he left office.

The FY 2006 Budget Plan

Bush's FY 2006 budget plan launched the new agenda of fiscal restraint. 'It's a budget that sets priorities', he told reporters, 'Our priorities are win-ning the war on terror, protecting our homeland, growing our economy' (Baker, 2005). Projected spending was set at 19.9 per cent of GDP, down from 20.3 per cent (estimated) in FY 2005 but still the second-highest level of the Bush era. It also constituted the biggest Bush budget to date (in FY 2000 dollars) at US$2.24 trillion (US$2.56 trillion in current dollars), an increase of 23 per cent over FY 2001 (OMB, 2005a, pp. 116–17).

The president proposed a five per cent real increase in defence spend-ing and a seven per cent real increase in homeland security expenditure over FY 2005 levels. He also called for the 2003 tax cuts to be made per-manent, implementation of two high-income tax breaks enacted in 2001 but then put on hold and the introduction of new tax incentives to allow high earners to shift cash into tax shelters. The focus of the new economy drive was exclusively on domestic programmes. Nine of the 15 Cabinet departments faced cuts in funding as part of the administration's plan to cut discretionary domestic spending by US$17.2 billion (3.7 per cent) from its FY 2005 level. Savings were to be achieved through the elimination of 99 programmes (US$8.8 billion), reducing the budget of 55 others (US$6.5 billion) and spending reforms to enhance efficiency (US$1.9 billion). One third of the programmes targeted for retrenchment were in the field of education, where savings of US$4.3 billion were projected (OMB, 2005b). Vice President Cheney declared, 'This is the tightest budget that has been submitted since we got here' (Allen and Baker, 2005).

Rural America greeted with open dismay a budget that cut back rural healthcare, education, community development and transportation pro-grammes. Most significantly, the administration appeared willing to take on the farm lobby by depriving it of many of the subsidy increases awarded in 2002. Overall, the Department of Agriculture faced a budget reduction of 9.6 per cent in FY 2006, with its subsidy programme, which cost US$17.8 billion in FY 2005, earmarked for cuts totalling US$5.7 billion over ten years (Morgan, 2005). Representative John E. Peterson (Pennsylvania), the Republican co-chair of the Congressional Rural Caucus, complained, '[T]hose who are currently advocating these dracon-ian cuts would not be in office today if it weren't for rural America. These cuts disproportionately target essential programmes in rural communities while turning a blind eye to the wasteful spending that is rampant in many big cities across the country' (Milbank, 2005a, A15). But urban America felt equally hard done by in the face of projected cuts in social welfare, community and transportation programmes. Baltimore's Democratic mayor, Martin O'Malley, complained that Bush's budget constituted an attack on America's cities (Dao, 2005).

The administration's Democratic critics charged that the president had abandoned his first-term flirtation with compassionate conservatism to launch a full-blooded assault on the welfare state reminiscent of the Reagan budget of FY 1982. According to the Center on Budget and Policy Priorities [CBPP], a liberal organization, programmes that provide services or benefits to low-income families and individuals in both rural and urban areas make up some 20 per cent of all government expenditures and the increase in spending on them only accounted for six per cent of the cost in FY 2005 of legislation enacted since the budget moved into deficit in FY 2002. However, they made up 49 per cent of the budget available for deficit reduction once untouchable items like defence, social security, interest repayment and tax cuts were taken out (Shapiro and Greenstein, 2005). The CBPP also warned that the planned reduction in discretionary domestic spending from US$412 billion in FY 2005 to US$363 billion in FY 2010 would amount in real terms to cumulative cuts of US$214 billion in appropriations and US$143 billion in outlays. In a departure from normal practice, the president's budget proposal did not provide details of how the retrenchment was to be achieved in FY 2007– FY 2010. Using data that the OMB had provided to congressional budget committees, CBPP analysts estimated that if the Bush plan was implemented, FY 2010 funding would be lower in real terms than the FY 2005 level by 14 per cent in education programmes, 23 per cent in environmental protection and one third in community development. They also calculated that the reduction in federal grants to states and localities over five years would amount to US$71 billion and speculated that the latter would have to raise taxes to cover the extra costs or reduce the services affected (Parrott et al., 2005).

Prospects for Deficit Reduction

Of course, Bush's FY 2006 proposal only set the context for the fiscal deliberations of Congress, which would have the responsibility of turning the plan into the bricks-and-mortar of revenue and spending legislation that make up the real budget. Contemporary budget politics have rarely been characterized by consensus on fiscal goals between president and Congress. Every Reagan budget plan from FY 1983 onward was declared 'dead on arrival' in Congress because of antipathy, and not only from the Democrat-controlled House, to his insistence on putting the burden of deficit reduction on domestic programmes. The FY 1996 deliberations produced open warfare between the Clinton White House and the congressional Republicans that eventually resulted in two partial shutdowns of government because of failure to agree a budget. Twice in Bush's first term — in 2002 and 2004 — Congress failed to agree a budget resolution (that sets the bottom-line limits for total spending on programmes subject to annual appropriations bills, for entitlement programmes and for tax cuts, which the various congressional committees then use to craft spending and tax legislation).

Since Bush was the first Republican president since Calvin Coolidge to be re-elected with his party in control of both chambers of Congress, his ability to get the legislature to support him on the priorities of his FY 2006 budget plan was an important test of his second-term leadership. As was inevitable, elements of his plan provoked opposition from Republican congressmen whose constituency interests came under threat. In particular, the proposed cutbacks in agricultural subsidies incurred public criticism from a number of powerful senators, including Appropriations Committee chair Thad Cochran (Mississippi) and Agriculture Committee chair Saxby Chambliss (Georgia), who complained that southern rice and cotton growers had been treated unfairly. As a result, the Senate Budget Committee initially set a figure of only US$2.8 billion for farm subsidy cutbacks, just under half of what Bush wanted (Morgan, 2005; Slevin, 2005). A group of six moderate Republican senators, led by Gordon H. Smith (Oregon), initially succeeded in stripping out proposed reductions in Medicaid, the federal health insurance plan for the poor, and substituting a proposal to create a commission to study the programme's future (Stolberg, 2005a).

The House provided far readier support for fiscal restraint and approved a tight US$2.6 trillion budget that, among other things, gutted US$69 billion over five years from entitlements — including US$20 million from Medicaid. Twelve Republicans voted against the budget, which carried by a close vote of 218 to 214, but some did so because they wanted even deeper cuts. The Senate, in contrast, approved amendments to the House resolution that among other things restored US$14 billion to Medicaid, US$5.4 billion for education and US$2 billion for community development over five years. It also increased the size of the proposed tax reduction from US$70 billion to US$134 billion over the same period (Weisman, 2005a; Broder, 2005).

A lengthy impasse was finally broken on April 28 when both chambers agreed a compromise resolution that set spending at US$2.56 trillion and a deficit of US$383 billion falling to US$211 billion over five years. This represented a significant political victory for the president. Members of the administration, notably Budget Director Joshua Bolten and Health and Human Services Secretary Mike Leavitt, had lobbied furiously for a deal that secured the president's priorities but allowed some cuts to be scaled back, notably in Medicaid, agricultural subsidies and student loans. The agreement also assumed US$106 billion in tax cuts over five years, US$70 billion of which would require legislation, mainly to extend the 2003 capital gains and dividend tax cuts. In addition, it directed Congress to produce US$2.4 billion in energy revenues, a device that could be used to legislate opening the Arctic National Wildlife Refuge to oil drilling. On the spending side, the five-year provision for US$35 billion of cuts in entitlement programmes like farm subsidies, Medicaid and the federal pensions guarantee, was US$16 billion less than the president sought, but was the first time since 1997 that Congress had curbed entitlements. House Majority Leader Tom DeLay (Texas) called the FY 2006 resolution 'the best [budget plan] since the historic Balanced Budget Act of 1997'. At a press conference, Bush cited it as proof of his ability to get things done on Capitol Hill (Stolberg, 2005b; Weisman, 2005b).

While the 2006 budget resolution constituted a political coup for Bush, it also offered a broad target for Democratic charges of unfairness. House Minority Leader Nancy Pelosi (California) called it 'an assault on our values' because it cut discretionary programmes that helped low-income Americans and gave tax benefits to the rich. With revenues at a lower level of GDP than at any time from the 1960s through the 1990s, the prospective tax cuts were also inconsistent with Bush's goal of deficit reduction and contributed to the growing national debt. Indeed the congressional budget resolution sanctioned the raising of the federal statutory debt limit by US$781 billion to US$8.96 trillion, which represented a growth of US$3 trillion in the borrowing limit since Bush took office. 'If you like debt', commented Democratic Senator Kent Conrad (North Dakota), 'you've got to love this budget because it builds a wall of debt' (Weisman, 2005b).

Within the broader context of the president's intent to reduce the deficit by half, however, the strategy of economizing solely through domestic cutbacks was fraught with problems. Incremental growth has been the dominant trend in discretionary domestic programmes since 1945. The scale of five-year retrenchment planned by Bush has never hitherto been achieved. Domestic spending has previously been cut but the retrenchment was never sustained for long. The last occasion that discretionary domestic outlays were scaled back in two consecutive budgets was in the Eisenhower era. Significantly, of the 101 biggest spending domestic programmes that the Republicans slated for abolition in 1995, only 19 were eliminated. The others survived and grew — total spending on these 82 programmes was 27 per cent higher in FY 2005 than on all 101 programmes a decade earlier. 'It seems', commented one conservative analyst, 'that being targeted for elimination by the Republicans turns out to be a pretty good guarantee of eternal life' (Slivinski, 2005, p. 9).

Aside from conventional pressures for higher spending, the administration also had to deal with the fiscal fall-out from Hurricane Katrina. Congress quickly passed a US$10.5 billion package of aid to storm and flood victims in the devastated areas of Louisiana, Mississippi, Alabama and Florida. Some legislators estimated the total cost of relief and recovery could be as high as US$200 billion. The president stubbornly insisted that the federal government could foot the bill without resorting to a tax increase, but many analysts doubted that this would be possible without hugely inflating the budget deficit (Fletcher and Weisman, 2005; Concord Coalition, 2005c).

In addition, Bush's second-term drive to reform social security had significant budgetary implications. The president's plan for partial privatization of the programme through introduction of personal retirement accounts that will tie benefits to stock market performance was predicated on the belief that social security faced a solvency crisis in 2042 because beneficiaries would outnumber contributors from 2018 onward. Opponents of his proposal claimed that reform was unnecessary because programme solvency could be guaranteed through payroll tax increases to cover a shortfall that would be less than a third of the fiscal shortfall resulting from the 2001–2003 personal and business tax cuts if made permanent. They also pointed out that the Bush plan had immense transitional costs and would require a larger programme bureaucracy, all of which could add US$79.5 billion to his last two budgets (FY 2009–10) and US$675 billion in the following five years. The end result would be to enlarge rather than reduce the federal deficit (VandeHei and Weisman, 2005; Kogan and Greenstein, 2005; Concord Coalition, 2005a).

The Bush administration's practice of funding its operations in the war on terrorism through supplemental appropriations also cast doubt on the accuracy of its five-year defence estimates. Some 20 per cent of the FY 2004 defence budget was appropriated in this manner. True to form, in February 2005 the administration made an additional request for some US$75 billion additional to the agreed FY 2005 budget, of which US$72.5

billion covered costs relating to military operations and reconstruction in Afghanistan and Iraq. Its approval on 10 May pushed up expenditure on the war on terror since 9/11 to US$275 billion, including US$192 billion for the Iraq conflict, by the end of FY 2005. The Department of Defence, at time of writing, has not provided an estimate of the total likely cost of the wars and subsequent reconstruction in Afghanistan and Iraq, but the CBO calculated that outlays on operations in both these countries could amount to US$458 billion from FY 2005 through FY 2014 (Belasco, 2005). To some analysts, the administration's use of supplemental requests to fund these conflicts constituted an attempt to hide their true costs in case of domestic reaction against their prolongation. Loren Thompson of the Lexington Institute commented, 'It looks as though they want a bigger defence budget without admitting it' (Weisman, 2005c). Meanwhile other defence costs looked set to escalate after FY 2010 when new weapons programmes reached full production, existing weaponry and bases required expensive maintenance and upgrades, and improved pay and benefits needed to recruit and retain military personnel hit their peak. In the words of Robert Bixby, executive director of the Concord Coalition, a bipartisan group that advocates balanced budgets, 'Defense is going to be a deficit driver for the foreseeable future' (Kady, 2004, p. 154).

Finally there appeared to be gaping black holes in the revenue estimates on which the administration's deficit calculations were based. The total costs through FY 2015 of making permanent the tax cuts of 2001 and 2003 (due to expire in 2010 and 2008 respectively) would run (including the consequential cost of increased interest on the public debt) to US$2.1 trillion (Friedman, 2005). In addition, the revenue calculations in Bush's FY 2006 budget plan made no allowance for the costs of providing the majority of taxpayers' relief from the Alternative Minimum Tax (AMT), which is conventionally aimed at the minority of taxpayers who aggressively shelter their incomes. There was universal expectation that the customary relief would be granted, but the resultant cost of US$275 billion from FY 2006 through FY 2009 would add to the difficulty of deficit reduction.

Conclusion

Having presided over the re-emergence of unbalanced budgets in his first term, George Bush made the halving of the deficit a key test of his leadership in his second term. His strategy for achieving this goal entailed considerable political risk and questionable fiscal calculation. In its 2005 mid-session review, released on 13 July, the OMB virtually declared game won in estimating that the FY 2005 deficit would only amount to US$333 billion, US$94 billion less than projected when it released the FY 2006 budget plan in February. It further calculated that revenues would aggregate US$409 billion more than initially projected for the FY 2006–2010 period on the basis that they were US$87 billion higher than originally forecast in FY 2005. This good news was attributed to the expansionary effects of the 2001 and 2003 tax cuts and was also cited as proof that the deficit can be brought under control if Bush's second-term tax proposals were adopted. Such optimism brought forth a chorus of scepticism from the Congressional Budget Office, the Center on Budget and Policy Priorities, the Concord Coalition and financial analysts such as Goldman Sachs. They all insisted that the new five-year projections still vastly underestimated Iraq and Afghanistan reconstruction costs, the effects of providing relief from the Alternative Minimum Tax and the fiscal consequences if social security were reformed. Furthermore, these bodies all attributed the FY 2005 revenue surge to temporary factors such as a booming stock market, expiration of the depreciation bonus and a one-time incentive to repatriate offshore earnings rather than to a sustainable expansion of economic growth (Horney and Kogan, 2005). The Concord Coalition's Robert Bixby warned, 'If lawmakers get the idea that our fiscal challenges are behind us and view these numbers as a green light for new tax cuts or spending initiatives, they will make a bad situation worse' (Concord Coalition, 2005b).

The uncertainties of the FY 2006 budget plan's five-year estimates were not the only source of controversy relating to Bush's second-term fiscal programme. The president's insistence on achieving economies wholly through domestic spending retrenchment also pitched the budget back into the centre of political dispute. In the eyes of critics, his fiscal strategy was both inequitable in placing the burden of retrenchment on programmes that benefit those in the lower half of the income distribution and unworkable because of its intention to cut rather than raise taxes. The resultant polarization of opinions in the budgetary debate increased the difficulty of forging agreement on how to solve a problem that poses a significant threat to the wellbeing of twenty-first century America.

Even if the deficit were cut in half by the time Bush left office, all the signs point to its substantial enlargement rather than continued reduction in the second decade of the twenty-first century. The costs of the extended tax cuts (if enacted) and the higher payouts for healthcare and pensions necessitated by the retirement of the post-World War II baby-boom generation do not encourage optimism about America's progress to the promised land of balanced budgets.

Treated purely as a fiscal issue, the budget could actually be balanced *either* by raising taxes to generate 22 per cent more revenue by FY 2010 than projected in the Bush FY 2006 budget plan *or* by eliminating 72 per cent of all discretionary spending other than for defence and homeland security. The politics of the budget rule out either of these extremes but a compromise needs to be found. The ringing of the alarm bells of future fiscal decline is usually drowned out by the regular cacophony over more immediate issues that carry a high degree of symbolic resonance, such as Supreme Court nominations, abortion, gay rights and the like. But America's budget problems could well undermine its economic strength if they are not soon addressed in serious and substantive fashion. At an obscure but still noteworthy symposium in Washington DC in May 2005, analysts of differing political viewpoints — Stuart Butler of the Heritage Foundation, Isabel Sawhill of the Brookings Institution and Comptroller General David Walker — voiced a common concern that the ongoing deficit was a ticking time-bomb. Unless the problem was resolved, they forecast that America's power and wellbeing would rapidly unravel under the impact of massive debt and draconian interest rates from 2040 onward (Milbank, 2005b, A4). All agreed that the ideological sacred cows of conservatism and liberalism would have to be sacrificed for the common good because deficit control could only be achieved through a combination of tax increases, reduction of entitlement benefits, and discretionary programme cutbacks. This was a nettle that George Bush has been unwilling to grasp, but his successors may have less choice in the matter.

7

American-Style Party Government: Delivering Bush's Agenda, Delivering the Congress's Agenda

John E. Owens*

Scholarly analysis of congressional-presidential relations in the recent past has almost exclusively emphasized *institutional* competition between the executive and the legislature. This approach needs some considerable adjustment in the contemporary era of American politics. Greater account must be taken of the increased homogenization and polarization of the two main political parties that has resulted in the emergence of American-style party government in the twenty-first century.

In exploring congressional-presidential relations in a given historical period, political scientists have focused quite rightly on the strategic contexts that presidents encounter as they enter or re-enter the White House and on the political skills that they bring to the task of leadership. As Charles O. Jones commented, '[P]residents are not created equally, politically or otherwise' (1994, p. 27). Given America's separated system, it is logical that congresses, too, are not created equally, politically or otherwise. As a number of scholars have observed, the variations in strategic context and skills that shape presidential-congressional relations produce a regular see-sawing in the preponderance and power of the two elected branches of national government (Chamberlain, 1946; Moe and Teel, 1970; Polsby, 1983; Peterson, 1990; Jones, 1994). This is clearly evident in the post-1992 pattern of American politics. In the first two years of the Clinton presidency, there was a balance of power between president and Congress. The Republican victory in the 1994 mid-term elections ushered in a brief period of congressional preponderance, but in late 1995 this gave way to a restored balance that lasted until the terrorist attacks of 9/11 (Jones, 1999a, 1999b, 2003; Nelson, 2004; Sinclair, 2000a; Cooper, 2005). What is missing — or underplayed — in this interpretation of recent patterns of congressional-presidential relations is party.

American Style Party Government

Political parties organize to win elections in order to control government agendas, exert influence over public policy and distribute benefits to favoured constituencies (Aldrich, 1995). Logically, in a competitive system the most important factor affecting the achievement of a party's goals is the behaviour of other major parties, which in the American system is one other party. Inter-party competition stimulates party discipline and cohesion, helps resolve individual legislators' collective action problems and prompts party legislators to empower their leaders to construct effective co-ordination strategies designed to win elections and gain legislative and other benefits. *Ergo*, the closer to parity are the parties in a two-party system, the stronger the pressures to stick together (discipline and cohesion) and empower leaders to construct effective co-ordination strategies (Binder, 1997; Dion, 1997). A majority legislative party with a small plurality in a polarized system cannot afford to lose votes on legislation that is important to its brand identity. Such losses can adversely affect the electorate's perception of the party (Cox and McCubbins, 1993; Sinclair, 1983), undermine the willingness of officeholders to commit to collective action (Aldrich and Rohde, 2001), and in extreme circumstances lead to party defections that threaten chamber control.

As Table 7.1 indicates, congressional-presidential relations since 1996 have been characterized by tight margins between the parties, whether measured by party majorities in the House and Senate, or by the percentages of the popular vote achieved by each major party in House or presidential elections. Increased party competition — resulting in tight electoral and chamber margins between the parties — has combined with other key factors to cause the return of an old phenomenon in American politics that can best be described as *American style party government.*

Tight electoral and chamber margins between the parties and partisan polarization are not the only characteristics of contemporary American-style party government. Among other key features: (1) the respective congressional parties present meaningful and commonly agreed legislative agendas; (2) they are ideologically homogeneous and act cohesively under strong centralized and co-ordinated leadership, especially when in the majority; and 3) notwithstanding the constitutional constraints placed on party cohesion and leadership strength by the non-majoritarian Senate, majority leaders of the respective chambers and the same party co-ordinate their actions with the president, and typically accept his leadership, to link the constitutionally separated institutions together effectively in order to

Table 7.1: Tight Inter-Party Competition and Control of the Congress and the Presidency, 1990–2006

	House		Senate	Presidency		Pattern of Partisan Control
	Majority Party/seat plurality	Majority Party-Minority Party popular vote at previous elections	Majority Party/seat plurality	Party	Majority Party-Minority Party popular vote at previous elections	
102nd (1991–92)	Democrats–100	53–45	Democrats–12	Republican		Split
103rd (1993–94)	Democrats–82	51–46	Democrats–14	Democratic	43–37	Unified Democratic
104th (1995–96)	Republicans–26	52–45	Republicans–6	Democratic		Split
105th (1997–98)	Republicans–19	49–49	Republicans–10	Democratic	49–41	Split
106th (1999–2000)	Republicans–21	49–48	Republican–10	Democratic		Split
107th (2001–2002)	Republicans–9	48–48	Reps–0/Dems–2	Republican	48–48	Unified / Republican/Split
108th (2003–2004)	Republicans–24	51–49	Republicans–2	Republican		Unified Republican
109th (2005–2006)	Republicans–30	50–47	Republicans–10	Republican	51–48	Unified Republican

Sources: Richard M. Scammon, Alice V. McGillivray and Rhodes Cook (eds.), *America at the Polls* (Washington, DC: CQ Press, 2005); http://www.rhodescook.com/analysis.html

implement the most important priorities on their party agenda.[1] We could add other features relating to the party leaders' roles in candidate recruitment and election campaigning for federal office but these are not necessary for the purposes of this essay.[2] I also leave open the question whether contemporary American-style party government is a specifically Republican phenomenon tied to the GOP's more homogeneous political constituencies (Reichley, 2000) and a party culture that is more accepting of hierarchy and leadership (Peters, 1999) and more disciplined than Democrats who prefer more pluralistic organizations (Loomis, 1988).

Some of the features of party government were in place in the 1980s and 1990s under Democratic congressional majorities, but its full development was vitiated by frequent Republican control of the White House (Rohde, 1991; Sinclair, 1995; Owens, 1997; Smith and Lawrence, 1997; Pomper, 1999; Aldrich and Rohde, 2000; Smith and Gamm, 2001). It is really since the mid-term elections of 2002 and the return of single party Republican rule for the first time since the early 1950s that we have seen American-style party government in operation — and fairly near to its constitutional limits.

The Electoral Roots of Contemporary Party Government

This chapter focuses on the governance aspects of American-style party government since 2001. At the outset, however, it is important to emphasize that like its previous manifestations (Brady, 1973; Aldrich, Berger and Rohde, 2002), the contemporary phenomenon is rooted firmly in important developments in the American electorate. Indeed, inherent in and essential to the concept is the notion that the strength of partisanship depends on external factors. In consequence, there are periods of strong parties and strong party government and periods of weak parties and non-party or committee government. As we will see later, the electoral foundations of contemporary party government have carried important implications for Bush's relations with the Congress.

Since the 1970s, the electoral bases of the two main political parties (as well as party activists) have become much more homogeneous and grown much more disparate. As a consequence, split ticket voting declined sharply as patterns of presidential and House voting patterns became increasingly aligned. The same party won a majority of the votes cast in the House and presidential elections in 56 per cent of House districts in 1984. A voting majority supported the same party for the House as for the presidency in 80 per cent of districts in 2000 and 86 per cent in 2004 (Figure 7.1). This is truly a remarkable development, one mirrored by the voting pattern in Senate and presidential elections (Figure 7.2). The consequences for congressional-presidential relations are obvious.

Figure 7.1: Growing Partisan Consistency in House-Presidential Election Results, 1952–2004

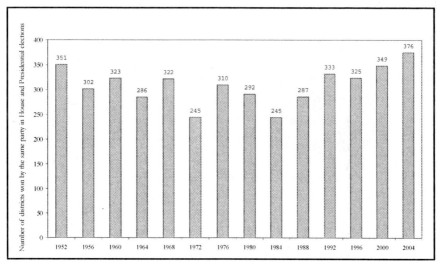

Source: *Congressional Quarterly Weekly*, various dates and http://www.polidata.org/prcd/default.htm

At the same time as partisan consistency in congressional and presidential elections has increased, voting support for the two main parties has increasingly diverged. The causes of electoral polarization are multiple but the southern realignment and redistricting are major factors. Whereas the percentage difference in votes for the president between House districts won by Republicans and Democrats was just 7.5 per cent in 1972, it had increased to 18 per cent in 2000, and to 21 per cent in 2004 (Jacobson, 2005). The popular vote in the 2004 presidential election was quite closely divided between Bush, who took 50.7 per cent, and Kerry, who took 48.3 per cent. In contrast, the results in almost half (215) of the House districts were decided by margins of at least 20 per cent (Polidata, 2005). A similar, increasingly polarized pattern of results obtains for the Senate, but the gap is smaller than for the House because statewide constituencies tend to be more heterogeneous (Jacobson, 2005).

Figure 7.2: Growing Partisan Consistency in Senate-Presidential Results, 1952–2004

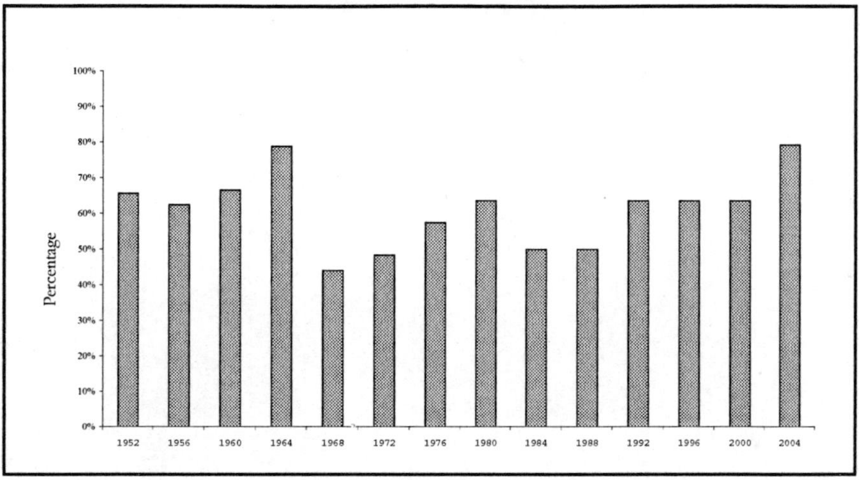

Sources: *Congressional Quartlerly's Guide to US Elections 1994; CQ Weekly*, various dates

Partisan Cohesion and Polarization in the Congress

More congruent congressional and presidential results and increasingly polarized electoral constituencies have produced stronger, more cohesive, and more polarized congressional parties. Whereas a majority of House Republicans opposed a majority of House Democrats on just two out every five votes as recently as the late 1970s, this was the case in two out of every three votes by the early 1990s. A similar development occurred in the Senate, where the percentage of party votes increased from just above 40 per cent to 60 per cent over the same period. As the number of party votes increased in each chamber, so did the frequency with which House members and senators voted with their co-partisans on party votes. For both the congressional parties, party unity rose from about 75 per cent between the 1960s and the early 1980s to above 85 per cent in the 1990s and sometimes above 90 per cent (Figure 7. 3 shows the House data). Inevitably, as the congressional parties became more homogeneous and polarized, the number of House and Senate centrists declined (Fleischer and Bond, 2003).

Figure 7.3: Strengthening Partisan Cohesion on Party Votes in the US House, 1945–2004

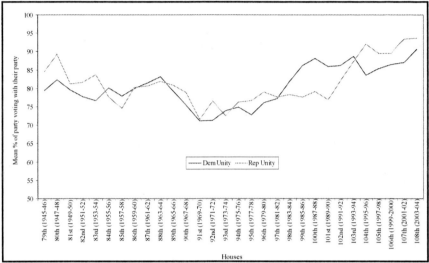

Source: *Congressional Quarterly Weekly*, various dates.

Figure 7.4: Increasing Partisan Polarization in the US House, 1945–2004

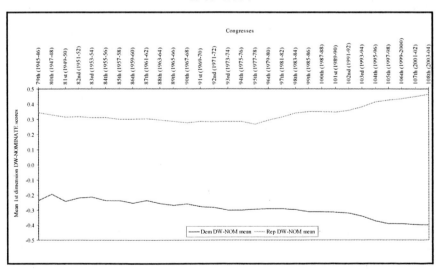

Source: http://voteview.com/dwnl.htm and updated data provided by Keith Poole.

As the Republican and Democratic parties grew more united and ideologically homogenized, they became more polarized. The mean scores of
House Republicans and Democrats' DW-NOMINATE scores — which
seek to locate party members' policy preferences along a single left-right
policy dimension — increasingly diverged after the mid-1970s (Poole and
Rosenthal, 1997; http://voteview.com/dwnl.htm, 2005). The same pattern prevailed in the Senate. Between the 90th and 107th Houses (1968
and 2002), the gap between the two parties' mean DW-NOMINATE
scores grew by a remarkable 71 per cent in the House and by 56 per cent
in the Senate.

American-Style Party Government, 2001–04

American-style party government implies that parties in control of the
government — and especially under conditions of single-party government — act cohesively within the Congress and in tandem with the White
House to promote commonly agreed agendas and policies, and to enact
those policies into law. The central thrust of the concept is that parties —
and particularly parties controlling the organs of government — are the
most significant organizations in Washington politics.

As a consequence of increased congressional partisanization and polarization since the late 1970s, congressional parties became the most significant organizational structures on Capitol Hill. They grew more cohesive
and more polarized, and as a consequence strengthened the hands of their
leaders, especially in the House. The power and prestige of Republican
House Speaker Dennis Hastert (Illinois), in particular, approaches — perhaps even surpasses — that of Thomas Brackett Reed and Joseph Cannon
in the late nineteenth and early twentieth era of Boss rule (Rohde, 1991;
Sinclair, 1995; Peters, 1997; Owens, 2002, 2004). When their party forms
the majority, rank and file members *require* and depend on their central
party leaders to: set and promote an agenda that reflects the party's priorities; to deliver legislative products that reflect the collective positions and
priorities of the majority party and diverge significantly from the chamber
median (Aldrich and Rohde, 1997, 2000); and to promote the party's collective reputation among voters (Aldrich and Rohde, 2001). Even in the
non-majoritarian Senate — and notwithstanding the pervasive obstruction-
ism that characterizes the contemporary chamber (Evans and Lipinski, 2005,
p. 228; Sinclair, 1989, 2000b) — similar developments have been afoot
(Sinclair, 2000b, pp. 64, 75; 2001, pp. 68–76; Owens, 2002, 2004). Majority
Leader Bill Frist's (Tennessee) establishment of greater control over

Republican committee assignments was one example of this. As the subsequent discussion will show, the styles, governing strategies and relations of congressional leaders with the Bush White House have been crucial agents in the development of American-style party government since 2001. In large part, this reflected the positive and negative agenda control that accrued to leaders (Rohde, 1991; Sinclair, 1995; Cox and McCubbins, 1993, 2005) and the pressures to toe the party line that they can bring to bear.

The GOP's stunning success in the 1994 mid-term elections gave it control of both chambers of Congress for the first time since 1953–54. Newt Gingrich (Georgia) and his House Republicans subsequently promoted their *Contract With America* manifesto in opposition to Bill Clinton's Democratic agenda as a means of projecting how contemporary Republican party government might work (Owens, 1997, 2000). This attempt ended in failure for the very good reason that Republicans did not win the White House in 1996. Modern American presidents are typically better placed to set the governmental agenda, as Gingrich discovered, not only because of their political and institutional powers, but also because of their considerable ability to set or influence the wider political agenda and 'go public'.

Interrupted Party Government: Bush and the 107th Congress

George W. Bush entered the White House in 2001 critical of Clinton's leadership and his administration's failure to stem the erosion of executive power (Simendinger, 2004). Disregarding the closeness of his own election as president, he was determined to exercise strong policy leadership *as head of his party in the Congress* in the way that Franklin Roosevelt had done in the 1930s. However, events in his first term — notably the defection from GOP ranks of Senator James Jeffords (Vermont) in May 2001 and then the 9/11 attacks — necessitated changes to this party governing strategy.

The results of the 2000 elections hardly warranted assertive party leadership. Bush encountered surprisingly effective resistance from Senator John McCain (Arizona) in the contest for the Republican nomination. He polled a minority of votes cast (and less than Democratic candidate Al Gore) in the presidential election. Before he could claim the White House, there was a prolonged legal wrangle over the disputed vote count in Florida, which ended with the Supreme Court rather than the people effectively deciding the election. He produced negative coattails in the congressional elections and the narrowest House majority for either party since 1953. Moreover, his party depended on Vice President Cheney's casting vote to control an evenly-divided Senate, whose ideological centre of gravity had shifted away from the right (Schwab 2003, pp. 243–5). Nevertheless, for the first time since the 1950s, Republicans now controlled the presidency and both chambers of Congress. For the Bush White House this was sufficient justification for the assertive party government strategy that it pursued until the Jeffords' defection precipitated an unprecedented shift in partisan control of the Senate.

As president, Bush took full advantage of his greatest institutional and political asset — to designate the agenda — and exerted forthright legislative leadership in pursuit of a hard-line, highly partisan, policy agenda. 'There's a new sheriff in town', the president's press spokesperson boasted. But, more significantly, Bush and his White House staff correctly anticipated that under conditions of unified party control House and Senate Republican leaders would expect the president to lead. In these circumstances, congressional leaders were willing to play accommodative roles in the shared belief that in making the president look good and in producing some kind of policy record the party would be well placed in the 2002 elections (Owens, 2004). 'We all have to remember that now Bush is the leader', Republican Congresswoman Jennifer Dunn (Washington) noted. 'We've got a president now. A lot of the work that we will be doing ... will be the interpretation of the Bush agenda' (Nitschke, 2000, p. 2845). 'In the past ... everybody was focused on their own agendas and there was no overriding agenda that anybody would say was Republican,' Senator Judd Gregg (New Hampshire) acknowledged. '*Now, we have the defining agenda. It's the president's agenda*' (My emphasis. Taylor, 2001).

The legislative agenda that Republican congressional leaders and the Bush White House agreed to pursue was actually quite small. The bulk of it had been incubating in the Congress for several years before being co-opted by Bush. The banner item was a ten-year US$1.7 trillion programme of tax cuts, which had been the centrepiece of Bush's 2000 election campaign and built on earlier GOP proposals thwarted by Clinton and the Democrats. Some education reform measures embodied new initiatives from Bush's campaign, including his reading and testing recommendations. Others, including the proposed merging of more than 50 programmes in the 1965 Elementary and Secondary Education Act into five block grants and a school voucher system, reflected traditional congressional Republican preferences. Bush's proposals to increase military expenditure, introduce a national missile defence system, overhaul Medicare and add a new prescription drug benefit, reform immigration legislation, strengthen patients' rights, reverse many of Clinton's executive orders and rules strengthening environmental protection also traced their pedigree to the unfinished business of the GOP congressional agenda of the 1990s. The same was largely true of his proposals for bankruptcy reform, banning e-mail spam, fast-track trade authority, restructuring the electricity industry and opening up the Alaskan wilderness to oil drilling. Other initiatives, notably the president's commitment to 'faith-based' policies, were new. So, here was a common party agenda that included Republican congressional and presidential priorities.

Here too was the first clear evidence of Republican party government in operation. The GOP had a well-defined governing strategy. It aimed to pursue the president's policy priorities on issues central to his campaign and highly salient to voters — especially, tax cuts and education reform. It simultaneously pushed legislation (such as foetal protection, 'faith'-based initiatives, human cloning prohibition) that appealed to the party's base. It also adopted hard-line conservative positions from the outset. GOP leaders anticipated that their agenda would be subject to centrist influences in the non-majoritarian Senate. Accordingly, House leaders determined to take full advantage of their chamber's majoritarian rules and legislative organization to win approval for the most conservative proposals possible. They would also eschew premature or unnecessary legislative compromises in conference unless absolutely necessary to gain an acceptable result. Finally, the party would declare victory once it had achieved a successful legislative outcome.[3]

One interpretation of party government might also imply close co-ordination between the White House and the Congress, with each branch carefully nurturing close relations with the other throughout the legislative process. Certainly, it is an essential condition of American party government that the president and congressional leaders of the same party must effectively bridge the separated system to enact a shared programme. To this end, there was an open phone line to the Speaker from the White House, and congressional leaders made desks available for White House staff in the their offices in the Capitol when crucial floor votes were held (Martinez, 2001). Nevertheless, the typical White House strategy was to announce very broad policy principles on major legislation — for example, on Medicare reform/prescription drugs and intelligence reform legislation — but leave congressional leaders to carry the issue to the floor vote, typically with little help from the White House's legislative liaison team. As was the case over intelligence reform, congressional leaders frequently expressed irritation that they received precious little help barring last-minute presidential calls to shift a few votes.[4] Even so — and this point is very important — congressional Republican leaders were compliant and extremely loyal to the Bush White House. They ultimately shared a common interest in the party and the president being successful. As Hastert's press secretary observed, 'The Speaker is not going to schedule bills that the president can't sign.'

This partisan governing strategy was clearly apparent during the enactment of Republican tax cuts in 2001. Bush followed Hastert's tactical advice. Instead of a single tax-cutting package, the president agreed to send Congress individual bills that included elimination of the so-called 'marriage penalty', abolition of estates taxes and new tax incentives for retirement savings, all of which had been approved by the Republican-controlled House with significant Democratic support in previous congresses.

Bush announced his tax plan in early February 2001. Three weeks later the House Ways and Means Committee approved income tax cuts without any Democratic support. Shortly afterwards, in a move closely co-ordinated with the Bush White House, House leaders sanctioned a special rule that tilted the legislative odds in their favour. This waived all points of order, including congressional budget legislation requirements that the House approve its annual budget resolution before passing tax or spending legislation. Additionally, it allowed the Democrats to make only one substitute amendment and one motion to recommit. Every single House Republican voted for the unamended bill with support from only ten Democrats. In the Senate, Majority Leader Trent Lott (Mississippi) attempted a similarly partisan strategy but was undercut by bipartisan opposition that reduced the tax cuts to US$1.35 trillion. His partisan strategy helped precipitate Jeffords' defection, which gave the Democrats control of the Senate. Nevertheless, Bush and congressional Republican leaders declared victory on the grounds that they had achieved some 85 per cent of the president's proposals. As in the House, every single Republican senator voted for the final compromise at the urging of the White House (Nitschke, 2001, p. 1251).

During this first phase of Republican party government, the House considered eight bills identified as 'major bills' by *CQ Weekly*.[5] These were: bankruptcy overhaul, overturn of Clinton administration's regulations on workplace ergonomics; income tax cuts; foetal protection; the FY 2002 budget resolution; reauthorization of the State Department's FY 2002 budget (which included eliminating US support for international family planning programmes); reauthorization of educational programme budgets; and tax cut reconciliation. All except the education reform legislation was approved along strict partisan lines with a mean 96 per cent of Republicans supporting passage of the remaining seven measures. On the education bill, Bush and Republican congressional leaders pursued a variation of their partisan strategy. They agreed to drop conservative

Republicans' proposals for school vouchers and other provisions and worked with George Miller (California) — the liberal ranking Democrat on the House Education and Workforce Committee to secure a major victory with bipartisan support (Nather, 2001).

After Jeffords' defection handed control of the Senate to the Democrats, party government was necessarily suspended. Republicans now had to compete with Democrats to set the public and legislative agendas. In these circumstances, Bush led congressional Republican chiefs in adjusting the GOP's governing strategy — just as Bill Clinton did with Democrats after the 1994 elections. They looked to respond pragmatically to the new strategic context by promoting Republican prescriptions on traditionally Democratic agenda items. Accordingly, new or revamped proposals were advanced for prescription drugs benefits for Medicare recipients, for medical malpractice, and for patients' rights. The GOP agenda stood little chance of enactment by the Democratic-controlled Senate. However, its very existence affirmed the party's capacity to address salient public issues in the new context of competitive agenda setting. It also demonstrated the GOP's continued political relevance and ability to compete effectively in the forthcoming mid-term elections. Most significantly, the revised agenda represented a pragmatic ploy to pre-empt the Democrats' appeal by co-opting some of their issues as Republican ones. Thus, on what was potentially one of Republicans' most vulnerable issues, the White House cleverly forged a deal with Congressman Charles Norwood (Georgia), the leading Republican sponsor of patients' rights legislation in the House. This manoeuvre shifted the agenda off an essentially Democratic proposal that Bush had threatened to veto to one that most Republicans could support and which gave the GOP an important political victory at a crucial moment.

If we examine the pattern of House and Senate decision-making between the Jeffords defection and September 11, we see the beginning of what would become a familiar pattern in the remainder of the 107th Congress and, to some extent, in the 108th Congress. Major issues were voted through the Republican-controlled House along partisan lines, albeit — as in the case of Bush's 'faith' initiative and patients' rights — in heavily amended form. Meanwhile, Senate decision-making was just as likely to be bipartisan (as on education reform and the overhaul of bankruptcy laws) as partisan. Even so, the percentage of Senate party unity votes in the period before 9/11 was one of the highest since the early 1970s (Benenson, 2001).

The change in the strategic context precipitated by the 9/11 attacks provided an enormous political boost to Republican political fortunes. The

congressional agenda was substantially reformed. Bipartisan homeland and
national security issues took precedence at a time of great national crisis
over the shrinking budget surplus, social security reform, and other domestic issues. This catapulted the Republican president into the role of preponderant agenda setter and impressive national leader.

All the major bills presented to the House as a consequence of 9/11
were approved on bipartisan votes, even though partisanship remained as
strong as before in committee and at the pre-floor stage (Foerstel and
Nather, 2001, pp. 2188–9). These included authorization for presidential
use of force against the Taliban, emergency supplemental spending for the
military and New York City, the airline industry bail-out, the PATRIOT
Act, aviation security and terrorism insurance. The White House continued
to rely on the House to enact more acceptable final measures. In the
Senate, however, bipartisanship grew stronger. Nowhere was this more the
case than in the 100–0 vote to place 30,000 airport security staff on federal payrolls, ultimately forcing an unwanted compromise on the House and
the White House. Other significant compromises were needed to enact
anti-terrorism legislation and establish a new Homeland Security
Department. Even so, the administration obtained most of what it wanted,
including a very broad authorization (dubbed a 'blank cheque' by some) for
use of force against the Taliban and the wide-ranging PATRIOT Act. Once
again, the Speaker provided loyal service to the president. In order to align
the House's position better with the president's on the PATRIOT Act,
Hastert effectively overruled the Judiciary Committee and other House
Republican leaders, wrote his own bill and then with presidential support
ushered it through the chamber under suspension of the rules (Palmer,
2001; Berke, 2001).

By late 2001, the political effects of September 11 were wearing thin and
the return to normal partisan politics ushered in a fourth phase of party government. The key legislative issues were the US$100billion economic stimu-
lus, the largest increase in military spending in 20 years, and budgetary matters. Led by the White House, Republicans reinstated their party government
strategy. Of the 18 House votes on major bills, 12 were approved along party
lines. Mean Republican unity on the latter reached an astonishing 96 per cent,
which underlined the weak position of the declining number of Republican
centrists in the lower chamber. House Republicans, whose unity averaged 91
per cent throughout the entire 107th Congress, were Bush's staunchest allies
under Hastert's loyal leadership — reinforced by Majority Whip Tom DeLay
(Texas), who ran the most effective whipping operation of modern times. In
July 2002, for example, the House Appropriations Committee cut its supple-

mental appropriations legislation by US$1.5 billion in response to what was effectively an instruction from the president (Martinez, 2001, p. 1923). Similarly, House Republicans were obliged by the White House to swallow a farm bill that most of their leaders opposed.

Republican priorities had less chance of enactment in the Senate, where decision-making patterns on major legislation that came to a vote remained predominantly bipartisan. Nevertheless, the GOP's partisan strategy remained in place. Senate Republican leaders rarely afforded opportunities for bipartisan centrists to exercise pivotal influence. In the 2001 session of the Senate, moderates certainly helped to trim the tax cuts of 2001, but the majority party only needed support from opposition party centrists to win in ten percent of total votes (Schwab, 2003, p. 248). In 2002, moreover, just 28 party unity votes were decided by five votes or less and eight of these were cloture votes that all failed.

Republicans' mean party unity score was an impressive 86 per cent in the 107th Senate. Party centrists rarely deserted their party on these votes. Moreover, their efforts to negotiate compromises were usually ignored or circumvented by skilful party leaders determined to work with the Bush White House. At one juncture a bipartisan initiative to create a new homeland security department seemed about to win Senate approval and go to conference with the House version, which more closely followed White House preferences. Bush quickly shifted his party's position and insisted on new legislation giving give him exceptionally broad authority to recruit, dismiss and promote the 170,000 federal employees transferred to the new department. Urged on by the White House, Senate Republicans staged a filibuster against the bipartisan measure. This served the dual purpose of preventing enactment and keeping homeland security a live and effective issue for Republicans in the 2002 elections (Bettelheim, 2002). House and Senate Republicans also worked effectively in tandem with the Bush White House to exploit Democratic divisions on proposed pre-emptive military action against Iraq. As a result, homeland security and Iraq — the kind of issues on which Republicans traditionally do well — were much more prominent in the 2002 elections than the weakening economy and rising fiscal deficit, issues that usually helped Democrats (Abramson, Aldrich and Rohde, 2003, pp. 258–60).

Finally, there was a notable shift in Republicans' governing strategy during this fourth phase — one that was less important for allowing the party to maintain its political momentum into the 2002 elections, but politically significant in the next congress and subsequently. As fierce partisan battles ensued over the budget and national security issues during the 2002 election campaign, Bush and his congressional Republican allies shifted the party's agenda towards a subtler, less harsh, brand of conservatism, which often allowed bipartisan outcomes. Much of this repositioning was signalled in Bush's 2002 State of the Union message and his FY 2003 budget. Most of the press attention focused on the foreign and national security policy aspects of this address, especially its denunciation of an 'axis of evil'. More interesting from the party government perspective, however, was Bush's enunciation of a Republican domestic agenda that was almost Clintonesque in its commitment to a more 'positive government'.

This new agenda laid greater emphasis on using federal outlays to ease the economic recession, produce jobs and provide some protection for those workers without health insurance, even to the extent of endorsing deficit spending. In a similar vein, the White House and congressional Republicans published and promoted proposals for a new prescription drug entitlement for the elderly (albeit linked to reform of Medicare), unemployment benefits, minimum wage levels for welfare jobs, post-Enron corporate reform and patients' rights in managed care plans. Many of these initiatives were approved by the Republican House, notwithstanding some conservative Republican opposition, but were blocked in the Democratic Senate. GOP leaders forbore from wasting political capital on trying to win enactment of these proposals or accepting unpalatable compromises. Nevertheless their support for such measures revived party momentum after the Jeffords setback. The Republicans had shown a willingness to address issues of concern to many voters, which would benefit them in the forthcoming elections.

Fully-Fledged Party Government: Bush and the 108th Congress

In the 2002 mid-term elections, Bush emulated Franklin Roosevelt in 1934 in audaciously assuming leadership of his party's campaign. By linking his presidency with congressional Republicans, he could call on voters to elect a Republican Congress that would loyally support his policy agenda.[6] Republicans picked up eight seats in the House and increased their representation in the Senate by two seats to regain partisan control. Bush thereby became the first president since Roosevelt to assist his party in gaining seats in both houses. In the last five days of the campaign, he visited 15 states in support of Republican congressional candidates. While most were in Republican-leaning states, the president's appearances and support probably made the difference in very tight races.[7] Bush's reward was the restoration of the unified party control of government that the

Republicans had fleetingly enjoyed in 2001, albeit with very narrow majorities in both chambers of the legislature.

Notwithstanding the return of single party Republican government, the 2002 elections intensified partisan polarization, because more conservative partisans replaced a number of centrist Republicans and Democrats who had either retired or lost (Jacobson, 2003, p. 17). Changes in House and Senate leadership and organization further consolidated party government. In the House, while Hastert remained Speaker, the acerbic Tom DeLay moved up to majority leader and Roy Blunt (Missouri) replaced him as whip. Blunt had been chief liaison person between Bush's 2000 campaign and House Republicans and, like Hastert, had a reputation for being very close to the White House. Republican leaders also strengthened party control over committees and Appropriations subcommittees: all chairs in the new Congress were to be selected on demonstrated loyalty to the party through a competitive interview process. As a result, several Republicans who might otherwise have become chairs through seniority were not selected.

Significant changes also occurred in the Senate following Trent Lott's downfall over his egregious comments in support of racial segregation. The inexperienced but politically ambitious Bill Frist became leader. Bush demonstrably refused to support Lott and then strongly encouraged the 'emergence' of Frist, who assumed the leadership without election. Despite his inexperience with Senate procedures and floor manoeuvring, Frist's elevation promised even closer Senate Republican co-operation and loyalty to Bush. Like Blunt, Frist had worked closely with the Bush White House. As National Republican Senatorial Committee chair, he had been joint architect of the party's 2002 campaign. Frist fitted better the public persona and 'compassionate' conservative moniker that the Bush White House sought for the party. It was thought that he could relate better to Senate centrists (Perrine, 2003, p. 20).

With conservative Republicans dominating the Congress to a greater extent than at any time since 1930, Bush and his congressional allies were determined to push the separated system to the limits. Bush's successful participation in the 2002 campaign and the surge in his approval ratings following the Iraq invasion made congressional Republicans all the more willing to follow his lead. With his confidence riding high, the president moved to implement his party's conservative agenda through resurrection of the party government strategy that had worked so well during his first months in office.

For the lame duck session immediately following the elections, Bush and congressional Republicans manufactured a policy mandate for enacting the delayed homeland security legislation and other measures. A raft of domestic agenda items was then placed before the new Congress. Few, if any, had featured prominently in the GOP election campaign. Among the new initiatives were: Medicare/prescription drugs benefits for the elderly, including private competition with the government programme; reauthorization of the 1996 welfare reform legislation; tort reform to limit class action damages for medical negligence; the overhaul of energy policy and opening up of environmentally sensitive public lands to mineral exploration and other commercial activities; 'faith'-based initiatives; pensions overhaul; Senate consent for Bush's conservative judicial nominations (all previously stymied in the 107th Senate); and new restrictions on abortion rights. Given the lacklustre state of the economy (which had not been a major issue in the campaign) and the increased costs of the 'war' on terrorism and the prospective war in Iraq, the Republican programme also gave prominence to economic stimulus. The top priority would be more tax cuts. In 2001 the president had bowed to the Speaker's tactical advice in this policy area, but in a clear indication of Bush's enhanced political reputation, the White House simply announced the party's tax programme without consulting congressional Republican leaders (Barshay and Ota, 2003, pp. 68–9).

Again, Bush kept his legislative agenda small with clear priorities; and, again, the party's broader domestic agenda co-opted congressional Republican proposals. In total, one or both chambers considered 64 major pieces of legislation in the 108th Congress. Just over half were initiated by the Republican Congress, 21 jointly by both branches and only ten by Bush. Irrespective of the institutional origin of these proposals, however, Bush provided strong leadership of his congressional party on almost two-thirds of these issues.[8] With few exceptions — the most notable being the tax cut bill, Bush's strategy was to establish the broad principles rather the specifics of GOP legislative goals. As exemplified by the new prescription drug entitlements for Medicare recipients, he allowed House and Senate Republicans to produce legislation that in most cases he would accept. In this way, and notwithstanding complaints from congressional Republicans that the White House was not sufficiently engaged in the legislative process, Bush exercised deft leadership of his party and allowed the Republican Congress to share in the party's legislative successes. Partly as a result of this strategy, Bush became the first president since John Quincy Adams to serve a full first term without employing his veto, although he threatened its use on several occasions (notably, over media ownership rules and military base closures).

By the end of the 108th Congress, Republicans in the White House and on the Hill could claim political credit for the enactment of significant parts of their party programme. Although hard-line Republican conservatives might demur, top of their list of achievements — and against the background of a burgeoning fiscal deficit — was the monumental prescription drug entitlement programme costing at least US$400 billion. Democrats had promised and fought for such a programme for decades without delivering. The Republicans had also enacted the third largest tax cut in US history (at US$350 billion, admittedly less than half the amount originally proposed but still sufficient, they claimed, to stimulate the economy). In addition they had: provided US$87.5 billion in supplemental appropriations requested by the administration for the war efforts in Afghanistan and Iraq; enacted Bush's global HIV/AIDS programme; abolished tobacco subsidies; enacted corporate tax reform and re-authorized programmes for educating disabled students. At the same time, the GOP had delivered to its core supporters a long awaited prohibition on late-term abortions, stronger guarantees of crime victims' rights and protection of foetuses, and DNA testing. Notwithstanding several false starts and sharp differences between congressional Republicans and the Bush White House, the party had also finally approved a major overhaul of US intelligence agencies. By the end of 2004, therefore, Republicans could claim with some justification that they were 'getting the job done'.

During the 108th Congress, moreover, Republicans had enacted much of their programme as a strongly cohesive party. At different times, party centrists and hard-line conservatives had swallowed their lumps in the interests of the party. Fully-fledged American-style party government was clearly in place as House (and Senate) voting patterns on party unity votes matched levels commonly found in the British House of Commons. Such was the strength of Republican party government that *CQ Weekly* identified 2003 as the most partisan year in the Congress since it began publication in 1945 (Poole, 2004). House and Senate Republicans' combined mean party unity score reached 92.5 per cent in 2003 and only dipped slightly to 89 per cent in 2004. Republican party discipline was so strong on party unity votes that no House or Senate Republican voted with his/her party less than 65 per cent of the time, and only seven House and six Senate Republicans voted with their party on fewer than 80 per cent of party votes.

As in the previous congress, partisanship on major legislation was stronger in the House than in the Senate: 63 per cent of House floor votes were partisan, while partisan and bipartisan votes were even in the Senate, producing a slight overall shift towards greater partisanship from the previous congress. Thus, partisan votes on such issues as tax cuts, foetal protection, energy policy and class action suits were largely balanced by bipartisan votes on Medicare/prescription drugs, healthy forests and Iraq reconstruction. Even so, House voting was five times more likely to be partisan and the Senate bipartisan than *vice versa*. This confirmed once again the persistence — even under single party Republican government — of significant inter-cameral policy differences, based on familiar institutional and constituency differences (Binder, 2002).

As in the previous congress, the White House was more closely aligned with the Republican House than the Republican Senate. Nevertheless, both House and Senate Republican leaders were highly sensitive to White House requests and often used the threat of potential damage to the president's political reputation as a reason to prevent unwanted legislation from reaching a floor vote or as a persuasive tool to keep co-partisans on board. Thus, when Bush identified a piece of major legislation as a priority or took a public position on it, 60 per cent of the time he was in agreement with the House outcome; and in only 20 per cent of cases did he disagree.[9] As centrist Republican Michael Castle (Delaware) observed in late 2004, 'I don't think a lot passes here that the White House has not at least given its tacit consent to' (Schatz, 2004, p. 2904).

To be sure, Hastert and other House leaders were in a better position to deliver for the president than their Senate counterparts. Their partisan strategy made full use of significant procedural advantages and institutional assets to maximize majority party control. 'You see', one of Hastert's most senior staffers explained, 'the leadership made an early decision to run the place only with Republicans' (Interview with author, 31 October 2003). Though the Republican majority was a slim one, the Speaker and his allies effectively excluded the Democrats from any real role in setting the agenda and formulating legislation. Rather than seek compromise, they aimed to push through — by however narrow a margin — the most conservative measures that had broadest support among House Republicans. Their intent was to shift the legislative debate and the ultimate legislative outcome to the right in order to strengthen the House's case in any negotiations with the Senate, where centrists exerted greater influence. 'That's why it's a one-vote victory rather than an overwhelming victory,' explained Majority Whip Blunt (Allen, 2003, p. 746). 'That's one of our guiding tenets,' House Republican Conference chair, Congresswoman Deborah Pryce (Ohio) argued. 'Let's do it our way, if we possibly can' (Eilperin, 2003, A1).

Hastert also reinforced majority party rule through extensive use of omnibus legislative packaging and special rules, devices previously used by majority Democrats.[10] These limited the opportunities for deliberation and prevented the minority from offering alternatives for floor vote that might expose majority party divisions. House leaders successfully pursued this strategy on several occasions in the 108th Congress: on the Medicare–Prescription Drugs Bill; on the FY 2004 Congressional Budget Resolution in March 2003; and on Head Start funding and DC school vouchers. In late 2004, Hastert was constrained by party opposition to pull the intelligence overhaul bill from the floor because *a majority of Republicans* did not support it, although a bipartisan House majority did (Babington, 2004).

At times Republican use of procedural tactics was nothing short of ruthless. During consideration of the party's totemic Medicare reform/prescription drugs bill in 2003, the Speaker held open the floor vote for almost three hours until enough supporters of the bill could be found. When the measure went to conference, Ways and Means chair Bill Thomas (California) and Republican leaders took advantage of rules that do not require minority representation on conference committees to lock out Democratic conferees. Republican leaders also played hardball when a widely supported Democratic floor amendment preventing the Justice Department from reviewing library and book store records was offered to the FY 2005 Commerce-Justice-State Appropriations Bill. Hastert and DeLay pointedly rejected the softer option, which would have been to allow it to pass and then ensure that it was dropped in conference. Instead, they launched a formidable whipping effort to rally Republican opposition and then held open the vote until they had rounded up enough votes to defeat the amendment on a 210-210 tie (Morgan and Babington, 2004).

Even so, just as party government in the British House of Commons is not perfect,[11] neither was it in the 108th House. House leaders had to contend with a number of revolts on unwanted floor amendments on issues such as base closings in the FY 2005 defence authorization bill, on Cuban travel in the FY 2004 Transportation-Treasury Appropriations bill, on Mexican ID cards in the same bill for the following fiscal year, and on the Justice Department's anti-terrorism powers in the FY 2004 Commerce, Justice and State Department Appropriations bill.

While the House and the White House typically agreed on major legislative outcomes, Bush disagreed with Senate outcomes on major legislation 41 per cent of the time, and agreed in only 34 per cent of cases. In the 108th Senate, the votes of six or seven centrist Republicans were crucial on several issues of importance to the GOP. In 2003 the House approved Bush's ambitious tax-cut proposal, following impressive whipping by DeLay and Blunt and appeals by Hastert and other leaders not to hand the president an embarrassing defeat at the outbreak of the war with Iraq (Rosenbaum, 2003). In the Senate, by contrast, three Republicans deserted their party on a crucial Democratic amendment to the budget resolution, and cut US$100 billion from the White House's proposals. Five days later, Republicans again joined with Democrats to reduce the president's tax cuts by half, a defeat that Majority Leader Frist failed to reverse on a second vote. This outcome resulted in major conflict with Republican House leaders (Dewar, 2003). GOP Senate unity also broke down over other party measures, such as avoiding budget enforcement rules, overturning the assault weapon ban and privatizing citizenship and immigration services.

In 22 per cent of cases, Senate Republican leaders could not even bring the party's priority legislation to a final vote. With the Congressional Budget Office projecting a new deficit of US$480 billion, House and Senate Republicans left Washington at the end of 2003 without completing action on all 13 FY 2004 appropriations bills. The following year, the White House and Senate leaders were unable to win passage of the FY 2005 budget resolution because of a major dispute over budget enforcement provisions and failed to complete any of the nine domestic appropriations bills before the new fiscal year began. Majority Leader Frist was obliged to pull other top Republican priorities that were controversial. These included: energy overhaul legislation mandating oil drilling in the Alaska Wilderness National Reserve (because six Republicans joined Democrats in opposing cloture); reauthorization of the 1996 welfare legislation (after Democrats successfully added amendments); rewriting of bankruptcy law (over a Democratic amendment affecting anti-abortion activists); tort reform/class actions (to avoid Democratic amendments); capping medical malpractice damages (Republican leaders failed three times to invoke cloture); protection of the gun industry from gun violence liability suits (defeated after gun control amendments were added); reauthorization of surface transportation programmes (because of House-Senate disagreements in conference and the threat of a possible White House veto); a constitutional ban on same-sex marriages (failure to invoke cloture); and confirmation of eleven of Bush's appeal court nominees to the federal bench.

Bush's Second Term and the 109th Congress

GOP success at presidential and congressional levels in the 2004 elections appeared to augur well for Republican party government in Bush's second term. The Republicans had won their largest majority in the House since the 80th Congress of 1947–49 and in the Senate since the 70th Congress of 1929–31. All six of the new Republican senators who replaced Democrats were more conservative than the mean Democratic senator, and four of them had more conservative DW NOMINATE scores than Republican senators' mean score. Their election therefore pushed the upper chamber's ideological mean to the right. Moreover, six of the seven newly elected Republican senators (including four of the five who replaced southern Democrats) had recently experienced party government in the House. The ideological composition of the already solidly conservative House Republican conference was unchanged. All five of the Texas Democrats who were casualties of DeLay's redistricting strategy were replaced by Republicans who were more conservative than their party's House mean, but partisan turnover elsewhere counterbalanced the effect of this.

Underpinning the 2004 membership changes was a further strengthening of the consistency in partisan support for Republican candidates in their constituencies across the different branches of government. As Figure 7.2 showed, 27 of the 34 Senate elections in 2004 were won by the same party whose presidential candidate won the state's electoral votes. As a consequence, three quarters of the 2005 Senate represented states where their party's candidate won the most recent presidential election. This represents the most consistent pattern in president-Senate election results over the last 50 years (Jacobson, 2005). The same pattern was also evident for the 109th House. As Figure 7.1 showed, 86 per cent of members represented districts that their party's presidential candidate won. There were only 59 split-ticket districts, of which 41 were held by Democrats but won by Bush and 18 were held by Republicans but won by John Kerry.

Threats to Strong Party Government

Nevertheless, the success of Republican party government in the 109th Congress could not be taken for granted. There was the danger that their very success in the 2004 elections would cause Bush and the Republicans to overreach in the manner of Clinton and the Democrats in 1993-94. In the wider strategic context, it was also significant that Bush, in contrast to his three Republican predecessors who had gained re-election since 1945 (Eisenhower, Nixon and Reagan), had not won by a landslide in 2004. His Electoral College majority was the smallest for any re-elected president since Woodrow Wilson in 1916. His 50.7 per cent share of the popular vote was higher than any Democrat had won since 1964 but still testified to the broadly even division of the electorate once the unifying effects of September 11 had worn off. Nor did re-election provide him with the normal popularity boost. Even at the time of his second inauguration, a *Washington Post/ABC News* poll showed that his approval/disapproval ratings were only plus six per cent. Moreover, there were growing signs of dissatisfaction with his leadership among conservative Republicans in Congress, who had been asked to swallow some very large lumps on Medicare reform/prescription drugs, education reform, patients' rights, the burgeoning fiscal deficit and most recently on intelligence reform. If Bush pushed his congressional party hard on another bold legislative agenda, the risk of further alienation and overreach would increase considerably.

Beyond these immediate dangers, historical experience further suggested that Republican party government might be less effective after 2004. Second-term presidents and entrenched congressional majorities bring greater experience to the task of governing and deftness of political touch, but they have to address problems that they have either created or postponed dealing with. For Bush and congressional Republicans, these problems included most significantly the state of America's economy, the burgeoning fiscal and trade deficits, and Iraq. Moreover, second-term presidents tend not to enjoy the benefits of a political honeymoon that they are given — in Bush's case, a very generous one — at the beginning of their first term. Worse still, two years into his second term, the president's party typically faces the prospect of an electoral setback in the mid-term elections. Since the beginning of the twentieth century, only once — Bill Clinton's Democratic Party in 1998 — has a president's party gained seats in these elections. In the five mid-term elections that fell in a president's second term since 1945, the party not controlling the White House picked up a mean of 29 House seats and six Senate seats. Finally, of course, legislative leadership is inevitably constrained by the president's 'lame duck' status. In the second term, power flows from the White House, the ties that bind congressional partisans to their president weaken, and — most importantly — the willingness of congressional allies to take political risks for the president diminish, especially if they perceive that the party's brand and reputation might be damaged. In addition, several Republican senators, including most importantly Bill Frist, have their own presidential ambitions to consider.

The New 'Bolder Is Better' Strategy

Immediately after the 2004 elections, Bush boasted: 'I earned capital in the campaign — political capital — and now I intend to spend it.' Either overlooking or dismissing historical experience and some of the apparent realities of his strategic context, he continued, 'I really didn't come here to hold the office just to say, "Gosh, it was fun to serve". I came here to get some things done, and we are doing it.' The party's governing strategy would be unmistakably partisan: 'I welcome the participation of Democrats,' the president declared, but then added '*in support of my agenda*' (My emphasis). As an anonymous Bush advisor later commented, 'This [president] isn't a guy who pivots. There's no point in a lot of outreach in the next 90 days that would be rendered moot by the first retirement from the court, and he's not going to do it' (Allen, 2004).

As in his first term, Bush set his sights on a 'bolder-is-better' Republican legislative strategy in the expectation that this would produce greater and more lasting political impact. The party's top domestic legislative priority would be nothing less than the wholesale reform of America's 70-year old social security system, with the aim of introducing private pension accounts for younger workers and cutting long-term federal obligations. Estimates by the Washington-based Center on Budget and Policy Priorities showed that Bush's audacious proposal would add as much as US$4.5 trillion to the federal government's budget over its first 20 years of operation. Meanwhile, the president also proposed to halve the fiscal deficit by the end of his second term by cutting or consolidating 150 federal programmes while also extending the first-term temporary tax cuts. In addition, the White House wanted to privatize parts of some federal programmes, change civil service employment rules and limit issues that could be negotiated with federal unions. Bush was determined, furthermore, to finish the unfinished business left over from the previous Senate. Top of his list was the appointment of conservative nominees to the federal bench, but he also sought enactment of bills pertaining to overhaul of energy legislation, restrictive class action suits, enhanced participation by religious charities in federal programmes, education reform, tax reform, bankruptcy reform and immigration reform. As if all this was not enough, congressional Republican leaders had their own wish list that included legislation to protect the US from bio-terrorism and new initiatives to restrict abortion. They also had a raft of items that had been objects of conflict with the White House in previous congresses, including reauthorization of surface transportation (which Bush had threatened to veto), Head Start, training programmes and reauthorization of the 1996 welfare legislation.

As in the previous congresses, congressional Republican leaders largely accepted Bush's legislative leadership — helped by the close relationships they had developed with him in the first term (Kaplan, 2004). Following the conflicts over the 2003 and 2004 tax cuts, the Bush White House made renewed efforts to keep the congressional party on board (VandeHei and Babington, 2004, A1). Also, Republican leaders of the House and Senate agreed to attend each other's strategy meetings and confer regularly to try to ensure close co-ordination (Kane and Pershing, 2005).

The Policy Limits of Republican Party Government?

For a second-term president to enunciate such a bold agenda for his party on social security and the deficit, especially when the US was heavily committed to equally bold foreign and military policies, was unusual, to say the least. Indeed, there were hints in public and private White House statements that Bush wanted his party to match the magnitude of the New Deal domestic policy agenda. Certainly, the Bush White House intended a qualitative shift from previous Republican proposals.

Following their 1994 take-over of the Congress, Republicans had emphasised the need to *reduce* the size and scope of the federal government. After 2001, this party thinking led to the enactment of tax cuts and increased military spending for the 'war' on terrorism, and resources were found by 'starving the beast' in domestic programmes (Rudder, 2005), as well as through partial privatizing of some government services. However, much to the chagrin of Republican conservatives, this post-2001 reordering of federal government priorities represented only part of the party's agenda and only part of the one outlined by the Bush White House in late 2004 and early 2005. The other part of the post-2001 Republican agenda entertained a larger, more activist, albeit more conservative-oriented federal government in education (e.g. testing), new entitlements (e.g. Medicare/prescription drugs costing an estimated US$720 billion over the next ten years), and federal funding of faith-based and other community initiatives. These significant expansions of federal responsibilities occurred, moreover, in addition to the creation of a large Homeland Security Department, a substantially larger military budget and significantly enhanced government surveillance powers enacted in the USA PATRIOT Act. In the space of just four years, federal spending increased by 28 per cent, and an US$86 billion budget surplus in the last full year of the Clinton administration was transformed into a deficit of US$412 billion in FY2004. Despite the gripes of some Republican conservatives, the party's post-2004 agenda anticipated more of the same: more tax cuts, more cuts in domestic programmes but also shifting rather than reducing federal government priorities in education, law suits, marriage and other areas of social policy. Even Republicans' proposals to introduce private social security accounts would necessitate a larger federal bureaucracy.

By June 2005, the effects of the strengthening Republican party government were evident. House and Senate Republicans approved budget resolution that kept to the Bush administrations spending limits and, after eight years of frustration, the party finally passed their bankruptcy and class action legislation over Democratic opposition. Indeed, indicative of the new conditions was the 53–46 vote to defeat a proposed amendment to the bankruptcy bill that would have made unlawful protesters liable for their debts, which Democrats had previously used to stymie the legislation.

In the first five months of the 109th Congress, decision-making patterns generally followed those of Republican party government in the previous Congress. While the House approved two-thirds of Republican party priorities on partisan votes, just over half the Senate's votes were along party lines. Interchamber differences were especially evident on the budget resolution. The House approved a budget similar to Bush's FY 2006 plan and cut back domestic programmes to a greater extent than requested, but the Senate resisted the requested Medicaid cuts and added US$5.4 billion in education spending. Sometimes, Republicans' highly reflexive reaction to situations produced ultra-partisan responses that showed alarming disdain for the Madisonian system, as in the Schiavo euthanasia case[12] and Frist's 'nuclear option' filibuster proposal.

In spite of their continued cohesion on many issues, however, the Republicans encountered some significant problems. Most importantly, Bush's social security proposals (especially the introduction of private accounts loved by conservatives) brewed up a political storm. Aware that Republican legislation tended to become even more conservative after it had left the upper house, Senate Democrats absolutely refused to negotiate with Republicans leaders on social security until the president agreed to withdraw his private accounts proposal. With the American Association of Retired Persons and other major interest groups campaigning against the proposals, GOP congressional leaders showed mark reluctance to move the legislation forward out of concern for the damage it might do the party in the 2006 and 2008 elections. Early on, House leaders indicated their preference that the Senate should act first on the issue, but Frist voiced a preference to delay the legislation until 2006 before having to recant as a result of White House and other party criticism (Allen and Babington, 2005). In early June 2005, however, social security reform was notably absent from the list of policy priorities that House Majority Whip Blunt e-mailed to Republicans staffers and lobbyists (O'Connor, 2005). Even if the legislation were voted out of committee or otherwise brought to the Senate floor, it appeared highly likely that the Democrats would employ their filibuster power to prevent the bill coming to a vote in the 109th Congress.

Other issues also cast something of a cloud over GOP unity. There was evidence of growing Republican concern over the fiscal effects of Bush's intention to make permanent his first-term tax cuts. The White House plan to cut the deficit through an unprecedented five-year freeze

on discretionary domestic outlays was another bone of intra-party contention. It appeared questionable that Bush had sufficient political capital
to achieve this scale of retrenchment (Weissman, 2005, p. A6). Indicative
of the difficulties that Republicans faced on this issue, in March 2005 both
houses approved surface transportation bills on lopsided bipartisan votes,
daring a veto as spending exceeded the president's recommendation by
US$11 billion. A week later centrist Republicans and Democrats com-
bined to reject proposed cuts in Medicaid and actually increased education
spending in the Senate budget resolution. A similar Senate coalition also
delayed the confirmation of the White House's ultra-conservative nominee, John Bolton, to the United Nations. In a sharp rebuke to Majority
Leader Frist, it then reached a bipartisan compromise on Bush's court
nominations so as to avoid revising the Senate's filibuster rule. Even in the
House, leaders lost key votes easing the Bush restrictions on stem cell
research and rejecting parts of the administration's second PATRIOT Act.
The threat of White House vetoes failed to persuade 50 Republicans to
stick with their leaders on the former and 38 to do so on the latter.

Opinion polls ratings also showed high public disapproval of
Republicans' performance. In April 2005, a CNN/USA Today/Gallup poll
showed that Bush's approval/disapproval ratings were minus four per cent
(45 per cent approval/49 per cent disapproval), the lowest for any president
at that early point in his second term since polls began. Only 31 per cent
of respondents supported his proposals on social security, while 56 per
cent disapproved of his performance on the economy. Bush's handling of
the Schiavo case and the Iraq war also drew negative ratings. Congress's
approval rating was even lower: minus 27 per cent, according to a Gallup
poll taken in the same month. In June 2005 a *Washington Post/ABC News*
poll found that six out of ten respondents thought that Bush and congressional Republicans were 'not making good progress on the nation's problems', and of those two-thirds blamed the president and Republicans for
this. Echoing Clinton's appeal that he was 'still relevant' in the face of the
Republican legislative juggernaut in 1995, Bush too was obliged to dismiss
publicly claims that his influence was waning (VandeHei, 2005b).

Conclusion

Midway through the first year of Bush's second term, there were signs that
the Republicans' scope for further major legislative achievements was
diminishing, but this did not negate the significance of what they had
already achieved. Ever since Bush took office — but particularly after the

2002 mid-term elections, the co-ordination of Republican agenda and policy formulation across the different branches of government has been so
extensive, the extent of majority party cohesion so strong and the enactment of partisan priorities so impressive, that it is valid to speak of the
return of American-style party government, especially since the mid-2002
elections. It is all the more remarkable that such strong party government
has been implemented at a time when American voters and political parties
are so polarized and electoral participation is barely above 50 percent. No
less impressive is the firm rightward shift that Republicans have wrought in
the centre of gravity of American government in these unpromising circumstances. Charles O. Jones (2003, p. 196) recently observed of the contemporary political context that 'achievement is less having won in the classic sense than having designated the agenda, determined the sequence of
agenda items, prepared credible proposals that serve as the basis for legislative action and inoculated yourself on issues of vulnerability'. Measured on
this basis, the early twenty-first century Republicans have been truly successful in restoring the American style of party government that until
recently looked to have become extinct.

Notes

*   I am grateful to Joe Cooper and Garry Young for providing me with
    up to date data on congressional party unity and to Keith Poole for up
    to date data on DW-NOMINATE scores. I would also like to thank
    Jim Thurber of the Center for Congressional and Presidential Studies
    at the American University for providing me with office accommoda-
    tion and a congenial base for my fieldwork in Washington DC.
    The data on contemporary developments in the Congress and the
    White House was taken from *The New York Times*, *The Washington Post*,
    The National Journal, *CQ Weekly* and *CQ Today* and were supplemented
    with unattributed interviews conducted by the author between 2000
    and 2005. The usual disclaimers apply.

1   Butler (2003, p. 256) suggests that responsible party government
    requires that the opposition party be made 'irrelevant'. This seems to
    me an unrealistically high standard that does not account for size of
    majority, as recent British experience between 1992 and 1997 illus-
    trates, and begs important measurement questions.

2   My concept of American-style party government shares common fea-
    tures with Pomper's concept of parliamentary government in the US

(2000). For reasons of space and focus, I will not discuss the parties' efforts to co-ordinate and centralize candidate recruitment and election campaigning for federal office.

3 This schema is compatible with the Bush White House's operating rules, as interpreted by Jones (2003, pp. 193–4).

4 One journalist interviewed for this article spoke of a blazing row between DeLay and Bush's chief legislative liaison assistance, David Hobbs, during the vote on the intelligence reform legislation in 2004.

5 Here and throughout the analysis, the list of 'major bills' for each Congress was compiled from *CQ*'s regular 'Bills To Watch' list together with 'Key Votes' on measures not included therein: 49 such measures were identified for the 10th Congress (2001–02) and 64 for the 108th Congress.

6 Parenthetically, we can note that the party government strategy pursued by the Bush White House and congressional leaders did not apply an ideological litmus test to determine which Republican candidates were worthy of support. Thus, they campaigned for centrists like Senator Susan Collins (Maine) or Congressman Chris Shays (Connecticut), both of whom had frequently opposed party leader's policy positions.

7 Overall, 43 per cent of those who voted said that their vote was a vote for Bush; only 17 per cent said they were voting against him (New York Times/CBS News Poll, 2002).

8 That is, either by the White House identifying measures as a presidential priority or by taking public positions on measures voted by the Congress.

9 In a further 20 per cent of cases, Bush did not declare a position or the House did not take action.

10 A report published in 2005 by House Rules Committee Democrats showed that the number of closed rules doubled between the 103rd House, the last congress controlled by Democrats, and the 108th House. See US Congress House, *Broken Promises* (2005, p. 13).

11 Although the first two Blair governments — with unprecedented Commons majorities of more than 165 — were not defeated in seven years, the previous Major government — with a small and dwindling majority — lost nine votes between 1992 and 1997.

12 As Terri Schiavo lay dying and her family squabbled over her future, Republican leaders pressured the House and Senate into substituting their opinion on a highly complex conscience issue for the considered judgements of five courts in Florida (Murray and Allen, 2005, p. A1).

8

Constitutional Issues, Rights and Supreme Court Appointments

Robert McKeever

George W. Bush consciously set out to defy political gravity in his second term as president. In order to achieve his major foreign and domestic policy goals, he faced the challenge of overcoming some of the most important constraints placed upon second-term presidential power by political dynamics, tradition and culture. Most obviously, it is axiomatic that second-term presidents have less sway over the political system than first-term presidents and that their power in this regard is also of a shorter duration. For this reason alone, second-term presidents are expected to be even more selective and focused in choosing their vanguard policies than in their first term. In other words, because resources, including time, are short, agendas have to be pared down.

The Bush administration and its congressional allies established an ambitious agenda for the second term. Its main elements included: the pursuit of the war on terror towards victory, possibly including further pre-emptive military action; winning the struggle for Iraqi democracy; reduction of the dangerously high budget and trade deficits; the radical reform of social security; ensuring that the economy produced more jobs; and transforming the taxation system. Bush also placed issues concerning the federal judiciary and constitutional rights at the core of his agenda, but some observers of American politics questioned whether he would have either the will or the political resources to advance along these fronts as well.

While political convention counselled caution and moderation on Bush's part, other factors suggested that he would be aggressive in judicial and constitutional policy. Firstly, the agenda was not entirely his to control. He was already engaged in a 'constitutional dialogue' with the Supreme Court on the rights of enemy combatants which would not disappear without a presidential volte-face. Moreover, his political allies expected — and his opponents were equally determined to resist — major advances on

issues such as abortion, same-sex marriage and the appointment of conservative judges who could realize the Christian Right's agenda through the
federal judiciary. Bush's ideology and character also shaped his stand on
judicial issues. Not only was he the most conservative president since the
New Deal, but he also had the strongest support in Congress enjoyed by
any conservative president since Herbert Hoover in 1929–30.
Furthermore, he appeared to share with neo-conservatives in his administration the belief that if reality counselled caution, then that reality could
be changed through an act of will.

Accordingly, Bush's second term promised to be a fascinating clash of
the tensions between, on the one hand, powerful forces of immobility and
continuity in the American political system and, on the other, a president
determined to advance the cause of conservative change on a wide front.
Taking this dichotomy as its analytic framework, this chapter focuses on
judicial appointments; abortion; gay rights; and the rights of enemy combatants. The analysis will explore whether the judicial goals of the second
Bush administration were visionary or hubris.

Conceptualizing the Bush Presidency

Before examining the prospects for the second term, it is valuable to consider the kind of presidency George W. Bush established in his first. For while
the political dynamics of first and second terms are different, there is no reason to suppose that a re-elected president will be inclined to alter a fundamentally successful *modus operandi*.

In comparative terms, many have observed that if George W. Bush has
a role model, it is Ronald Reagan. This is true both in terms of the forty-
third president's ideology and his presidential strategy (Graubard, 2004, p.
665; Aberbach, 2004, p. 59). Indeed there is considerable merit in the argument that President Bush should be viewed as a kind of 'Reagan-plus'. In
comparison with his conservative precursor, he has taken ideological entrepreneurship further (Campbell, 2004, p. 8), incorporated right-wing interest groups into his 'governing party' strategy more effectively (Peterson,
2004, p. 244), and made more extensive use of his powers of appointment
to ensure that his social and judicial values were embedded in presidential
decision-making (O'Brien, 2004).

Borrowing from Stephen Skowronek (1997), Stephen Schier's concep-
tualization of George Bush as an 'orthodox innovator' offers an insightful
means of analyzing his presidency. Such presidents take the values, goals and
policies of an earlier regime and articulate them in ways that will prove per-

suasive in a new and changed political environment. According to Schier, Bush has both resurrected failed policies of the Reagan administration and taken some of the successful ones beyond their original parameters (2004, pp. 4–5) Historically, however, orthodox innovators have operated high risk presidencies and most have come to grief, often because '... their innovations spawned dissension within the established political regimes with which they were affiliated' (Schier, 2004, p. 5) Indeed, the only successful president of this type was William McKinley, whose innovations in foreign and domestic policy assured a partisan realignment and 30 years of Republican ascendancy. The potential rewards are thus high for orthodox innovation in the presidency, but then so are the risks.[1]

For this reason, most presidents who come to the White House with a weak mandate eschew this approach, opting instead for a conciliatory approach to the opposition in the quest for legitimation and re-election. Not so George W. Bush. Despite having the weakest mandate of any president since at least 1876, he conducted himself in his first term as if he had been empowered by the electorate to implement a right-wing agenda, with tax cuts that disproportionately favoured the rich as its centrepiece. He also followed the high-risk strategy of campaigning hard for Republican Senate candidates in the mid-term elections of 2002. This strategy has often backfired on presidents, leaving them weakened by their high-profile failure to influence the electorate. Benefiting from the patriotic upsurge that followed the terrorist attacks of 11 September 2001, however, Bush gambled and won. The prize was the restoration of Republican control of the Senate.

One need not belabour the point. In his first term in office, George W. Bush proved to be an aggressive and confident president, with a clear preference for high risk strategies that advanced his strongly ideological agenda over low risk alternatives that held little promise of promoting substantive change. He was rewarded with some striking policy successes and electoral victories in 2002 and, above all, 2004.

The Second-Term Approach

Conventional wisdom and historical experience nevertheless offered some reasons to anticipate that Bush might temper his approach in his second term. The fact, for example, that he cannot seek another term in office could have inclined him to consolidate what he had already achieved rather than to seek further significant change. His lame-duck status might have instilled doubt that the congressional Republicans would follow him as readily as in his first term. Some GOP legislative leaders, notably Senate Majority Leader

Bill Frist (Tennessee), were known to be contemplating running for president in 2008, which would likely make them cautious of putting their ambitions at risk by supporting unpopular elements of the current incumbent's agenda. Moreover, rank-and-file members of Congress might gravitate towards a potential new leader since a lame-duck president could offer little assistance to their re-election. Well aware that previous presidents had more or less accepted as a fact of life that second terms were more difficult and less productive than first terms, President Bush might have bowed to the 'inevitable' and moderated his ambitions.

Turning now to the substantive policy area with which this chapter is directly concerned, we will encounter powerful evidence to suggest that rather than rest on his laurels, George W. Bush has signalled his clear intent to extend, if not complete, the triumphs of his orthodox innovation in judicial and constitutional issues.

Judicial Appointments

It was widely anticipated from the outset that the second Bush term would see a battle royal over judicial appointments, notably in the event of any seat falling vacant on the US Supreme Court. It appeared equally probable that Bush's approach to these appointments would confirm him to be an orthodox innovator.

A review of Ronald Reagan's record shows that he set out in systematic fashion to reverse the liberal-activist direction of the Court that had been prevalent since the 1960s.[2] This was to be achieved by rigorous scrutiny and selection of federal court nominees in order to ensure that only those who shared the president's judicial philosophy would be appointed to the bench. The strategy came unstuck, however, when Reagan put forward Robert Bork for a seat on the Court. Although eminently qualified for the position in most respects, the nominee's radically conservative writings on sensitive issues such as the race equality decisions of the Warren Court prompted an all-out 'stop Bork' drive. He eventually went down to a crushing defeat and after a second failed nomination for the seat, Reagan was obliged to compromise and nominate the moderate conservative, Anthony Kennedy (Bronner, 1989; Schwarz, 1988).

Reagan's successor, George Bush Sr., learned the lessons of that episode and his first nominee to the Court was another moderate, David Souter. In order to placate his right-wing constituency, the first President Bush did subsequently nominate a radical conservative to the Court, Clarence Thomas, but it took a major battle to secure his narrow confirmation (Mayer and

Abramson, 1994). Two moderately liberal appointments by President Clinton, Ruth Bader Ginsburg and Stephen Breyer, left the Court precariously balanced, with either Justice Sandra Day O'Connor or Justice Kennedy, or both, sometimes joining their more liberal colleagues on key issues such as abortion, gay rights, Church-State separation and the death penalty. The Reagan revolution had certainly put an end to virtually all liberal activism, but it did not secure the reversal of past decisions thought abominable by the Christian Right. Nevertheless, the decisions of the Rehnquist Court re-balanced the constitutional settlement on issues like abortion and gay rights in ways that were broadly acceptable to the majority of Americans.

President George W. Bush was not content to leave it there, however. He wanted to complete the Reagan revolution by nominating more radical conservatives to the Court. Although frustrated in his first term by the lack of vacancies on the Supreme Court, he repeatedly made it clear that he would nominate conservative judges in the mould of Justices Antonin Scalia and Clarence Thomas when the opportunity arose. This intent was signalled in his combative stand on nominations to the federal district and appeals courts.

By the time Bush entered the White House in 2001, the judicial confirmation process had already become bitterly adversarial. By the time he completed his first term, it had virtually broken down altogether. The contemporary presidential-Senate disharmony over lower federal court nominations dated back at least to the Carter administration. The data show that it is taking ever longer to get judgeships filled and that the more important the position, the longer it takes to fill it. As one analyst noted, 'it took almost three times longer for Circuit Court judges to be confirmed under George W. Bush than under his father' (Lott, 2005, p. 22).

Despite being fully aware of the difficult and acrimonious state of the judicial confirmation process and despite entering office with a weak mandate and a precarious hold on the Senate, Bush nominated many controversial judges whom he knew would meet furious resistance from Senate Democrats and perhaps arouse disquiet among moderate Senate Republicans. Why adopt such a combative strategy? The key is the president's connection to the Christian Right. Not only is George W. Bush an evangelical Christian himself, but the Christian Right is one of the core elements of contemporary Republicanism and the president's successful electoral coalition. In George W. Bush, personal conviction is intertwined with governing and electoral strategy in a way that was never true of either his father or Ronald Reagan. In his first term, therefore, he went beyond symbolic appeals to evangelical Christian values and '...sought to make public policy align with his own values and those of his religious coalition' (Guth, 2004, p. 131). Because so many of the issues that matter most to evangelicals are determined in whole or in part by the federal judiciary, the only means of achieving their agenda is through the appointment of judges whose constitutional views coincide with the policy goals of that agenda. More than any other reason, this was why Bush fought so doggedly for his judicial nominees in his first term and why he was likely to do so again in his second.

What illustrated Bush's judicial strategy above all else was the filibuster battle in the Senate. Senate Democrats were just as determined to delay and prevent the confirmation of President Bush's judicial nominees as Senate Republicans had been to deny President Clinton his choice of federal judge. However, they introduced a new weapon into their armoury in the form of the filibuster.[3] Whereas confirmation votes require a simple majority for or against, a cloture vote to end a filibuster in the Senate requires 60 votes, making it an ideal weapon for use by an obstructive minority. The Democrats employed the filibuster to prevent a confirmation vote on ten of President Bush's judicial nominees in his first term.

Armed with an indisputable personal victory in the presidential election of 2004 and an increased Republican majority in the Senate, Bush saw no reason to succumb to or compromise with the Democrats in his second term. While the Democrats held 45 seats in the upper chamber — more than enough to sustain a filibuster — the president acted as if the opposition to his nominees could be bulldozed and, indeed, humiliated. In February 2005, he re-nominated seven of the previously filibustered nominees.[4] Most emblematic amongst them was Justice Priscilla Owen of the Texas Supreme Court, an extreme conservative-activist in the eyes of her critics and the subject of four failed cloture votes in 2003. Most damaging to her in the confirmation battle was the comment of a fellow Justice in a Texas Supreme Court case involving the abortion rights of minors. He accused Owen of 'an unconscionable act of judicial activism' for her argument that sought to evade the clear letter of the statute at issue in requiring that a minor should be made aware of religious arguments against abortion.[5] This fellow Justice was Alberto Gonzales, whom President Bush appointed as Attorney-General in his second term

Like the other re-nominees, Owen was virtually guaranteed to provoke the Democrats into a second series of filibusters. As Senator Edward Kennedy (Massachusetts) commented, 'The president looks like he is still more interested in picking fights than picking judges' (Newsday.com, 2005). The ranking Democrat on the Senate Judiciary Committee, Patrick Leahy (Vermont), similarly charged, 'In re-nominating some of their most controversial nominees, the Bush administration has again chosen confrontation over co-operation and ideology over moderation' (Civil Rights Coalition for the 21st Century, 2005).

Although undoubtedly motivated by partisanship, the comments by Senators Kennedy and Leahy were accurate in that the president chose a fight where he could have chosen compromise. After all, the Senate had confirmed over 200 of his judicial nominees in his first term, many of them clear conservatives. Facing tough battles ahead on other issues such as social security reform, he could easily have chosen to bargain over judicial nominations. Instead, he chose escalation. With the president's explicit backing, Majority Leader Bill Frist threatened a change in Senate rules to end the right to filibuster on judicial nominations by requiring a simple majority of those present to bring a nomination to a confirmation vote. This so-called 'nuclear option' reinforced the perception that Bush was not interested in compromise. Neither did the president seem moved when the Democrats threatened to retaliate by effectively bringing Senate business grinding to a halt, thus jeopardizing the rest of his agenda.

Bush's high-risk strategy on judicial nominations bordered on the irrational. To adopt a 'governing party' strategy was one thing: to expect party unanimity in the face of controversial nominations was another. Even more unreasonable, however, was the apparent belief that all Republican Senators would go along with a sweeping change of the filibuster, a Senate privilege that has been used by both parties in the past on issues of deep concern to them. Indeed, even as the president pressed ahead, there was no guarantee that he had the votes to secure confirmation of his nominees, never mind to change the filibuster rule. By the end of April 2005, the administration believed it had 'lost' three Republican Senators and that several others were wavering (*Washington Post*, 2005a). Even the Republican chair of the Senate Judiciary Committee, Arlen Specter (Pennsylvania), was known to be uncomfortable with both the re-nominations and the filibuster threat (*New York Times*, 2005a).

In the end, the White House was forced to accept a compromise when seven Republican Senators joined seven Democrats (who were quickly dubbed 'the gang of 14') to negotiate an agreement that preserved the filibuster right in return for the confirmation of certain nominees. Initially, the Democrats believed that they had come out on top, especially as the filibuster remained available to them in the event of an objectionable nomination to the Supreme Court. However, their outlook changed when highly conservative judges such as Priscilla Owen were confirmed to the Courts of Appeal shortly after the deal was struck. For all the administration's genuine disappointment with the filibuster compromise, it had for the most part won the battle of the lower court judges. In that sense, the president's confrontational strategy had paid off.

The victory was not cost-free, however. Not only did the strategy push Republican loyalty to the limits and harden Democrat unity, it also damaged the president's standing with the public.[6] It remained to be seen whether the administration still had the resources and the political will to pursue another confrontational strategy when the much bigger prize of a Supreme Court vacancy became available to fill.

The Terri Schiavo Case

The demands of the president's evangelical allies, which had driven his confrontational strategy over judicial nominations, also shaped his response to the Terri Schiavo case in early 2005. Having been in a persistent vegetative state for fifteen years, Schiavo was kept alive by artificial life support. While her husband and her doctors wished to disconnect the life support, others in her family did not and the case ended up being heard several times in the Florida state courts and the federal courts. When a Florida judge insisted that a deadline for switching off the life support be met, Bush and congressional Republican leaders called for action to support a 'culture of life'. They took the extraordinary step of passing in a matter of days a private bill pertaining only to the Schiavo case. This permitted a federal court to review the last Florida court decision.

When that manoeuvre failed and Terri Schiavo eventually died, House Majority Leader Tom DeLay (Texas) launched a bitter attack on the judiciary. Vowing that state and federal judges involved in the case would one day have to pay for what they had done, he called for an investigation that would 'look at an arrogant, out-of-control, unaccountable judiciary that thumbed their nose at Congress and the president' (*Washington Post*, 2005b). Perhaps the clearest expression of the political and moral nexus that linked the Christian Right and the Republican national leadership came, however, with Justice Sunday. On 24 April 2005, a televised rally was organized by evangelical groups such as the Family Research Council to attack the Democrats for the use of the filibuster. Senate Leader Frist, the most prominent speaker to address the rally, was more temperate in his remarks than DeLay had been in his comments on the Schiavo case, but his very presence at the event underlined the Republicans' intention to use every resource at their disposal to win the struggle for control of the judiciary.

Through their words and actions, Bush, Frist and DeLay clearly signalled their intent to mobilize the Christian Right on behalf of the administration's federal and district court nominees. In part, this was because all had political ambitions that made the support of the evangelical movement highly desirable. It also reflected the genuine religious and moral values that the three Republican leaders shared with the Christian Right. However, neither of these factors would have been sufficient to have summoned forth such a mighty effort over lower court appointments if it were not for one other calculation. The appeals and district court nominations were merely the prelude to the far greater prize of completing the Reaganite campaign for control of the Supreme Court.

The Supreme Court

The lower court nominations seemed destined to be as nothing compared to the conflicts that were widely anticipated over the Supreme Court vacancies created by the resignation of Justice O'Connor in July 2005 and the death of Chief Justice Rehnquist shortly afterwards. The modern history of Supreme Court nominations showed that presidents who avoided unnecessary provocation in their choice of nominee got an easy and largely cost-free confirmation process: O'Connor, Anthony Kennedy, David Souter and Stephen Breyer all illustrate the point. In contrast, the nomination of someone perceived as 'extreme' tended to provoke a no holds-barred confirmation battle that drained the considerable resources of both sides, left the political atmosphere poisoned and was of uncertain outcome (McKeever, 2004). The nominations of Robert Bork and Clarence Thomas exemplified this. William H. Rehnquist was also given a mauling when President Reagan elevated him to Chief Justice in 1986.

It is evident that modern presidents are well-advised to undertake a careful cost-benefit analysis before settling on a nomination to the Court. A controversial nominee requires a huge effort in terms of public relations, advertizing, mobilizing and co-ordinating interest groups, keeping one's supporters united and keeping one's opponents on the defensive. A non-controversial nominee usually benefits from a bi-partisan confirmation process in the Senate, leaving hard-line opponents marginalized and the president free to pursue other goals with his unspent political capital.

If the costs are clearly very different in these two scenarios, the benefits are not so easy to distinguish. O'Connor and Kennedy may not have delivered all that Reagan hoped of them but they did enough to be considered successful choices. Scalia and Thomas were more committed to the full conservative agenda, but they had limited success in advancing its more controversial elements.

Take, for example, the situation pertaining on the Court at the start of Bush's second term. In order to be sure of overturning *Roe v. Wade*, the president needed two of the following justices to retire before he left office: Justices Stevens, O'Connor, Kennedy, Souter, Ginsburg and Breyer. This was possible, but not probable. Justices of the Supreme Court appear to think strategically about their retirements, if their health allows, and Justice Stevens, the oldest member of the Court and a staunch liberal, would not wish to place his seat in the hands of President Bush and Bill Frist. Even if Stevens did follow O'Connor into retirement, Bush would have to find two nominees whom he could be certain would overturn *Roe*. Inevitably, however, such nominees would require him to fight two costly confirmation battles in perhaps as many years — a tall order for a second-term president who could not even be sure of holding all his Republican Senators in line.

In short, for President Bush to seek to fill any vacancy with someone akin to Scalia or Thomas would be a high-risk strategy, offering significant but by no means certain rewards. If on the other hand, he settled for a moderate conservative to replace O'Connor in like-for-like fashion, he could conserve his political resources and consolidate the conservative hold on the Court, but would be unlikely to score a slam-dunk on abortion, homosexual equality or Church–State relations.

Unless he could find a way to finesse the situation, all the evidence indicated that Bush would go for broke. Apart from the tendency revealed by his approach to lower court nominations, the president had staked a great deal of his reputation on winning the war for control of the federal judiciary. Having risked so much in the skirmishes and battles to date, it would do untold damage to his presidency, his 'governing party' strategy and his electoral coalition to step back in his second term. A Supreme Court nominee perceived as having been chosen to give the White House an easy ride in the Senate at the expense of its declared socio-moral policies would severely damage presidential credibility and, perhaps, the electoral ambitions of Senate Republicans.

It has to be understood, too, that one of the core concerns of the Bush presidency is to strengthen presidential power within the American political system. This has shaped his approach towards federal court appointments. Bush subscribes particularly strongly to a familiar White House view that presidential prerogative in judicial appointments has been undermined since the 1960s by a re-assertive Congress. From this perspective, the increasing delays in confirming nominees under a series of presidents indicated more than just the partisan problem highlighted by the Bork and Thomas confirmation battles. Rather, they were seen as resulting from an exaggerated and unwarranted view of Senatorial power. According to the Bush administration's credo, the Constitution assigns initiative and therefore preponderant power in the selection of federal judges to the president and the Senate role in the process is confined to ascertaining that nominees are fit for office in terms of judicial character.

This outlook explained Bush's enthusiasm for the 'nuclear option' of changing Senate rules to circumvent the use of the filibuster in the case of judicial nominations. The removal of this weapon would mean that any president would no longer be so constrained ideologically in his choice of nominee, simply because only 50 votes, rather than 60, would be sufficient for confirmation. Moreover, the successful removal of the filibuster on judicial appointments might well spill over into other areas, again aiding the cause of presidential government. It may well be the case that Bush and his allies will resurrect the 'nuclear option' threat if faced with Democratic opposition to the nominee he puts forward to replace O'Connor. This would be certain to cause concern among the ranks of Republican senators, especially moderates. However the temptation to kill two birds with one stone — that is to secure a conservative justice and enhance presidential power at the same time — may prove too strong for Bush.

Supreme Court Strategy

Abiding by his conservative beliefs with regard to Supreme Court nominations did not mean that Bush's appointment strategy could be free from subtlety. To nominate someone akin to Robert Bork would invite disaster. Bork was an extremely intelligent and able judge, but his controversial opinions were not offset by any other political assets. Chief among these assets in recent decades has been the race-ethnicity-gender issue. Simply put, if the nominee comes from a sub-community whose voters, activists and politicians usually adhere to the president's opposition party in the Senate, enough of those Senators will vote for confirmation despite their ideological misgivings. Both Sandra Day O'Connor, as the first female nominee, and Antonin Scalia, as the first Italian-American nominee, benefited from this. The greatest beneficiary, however, was Clarence Thomas. As an African-American, Thomas posed a particularly difficult problem for white Southern Democrats in the Senate. A vote against confirmation would not only raise the ghost of segregation and discrimination, but alienate some of the black voters on whom such Democrats were dependent for re-election. Thus, despite the ferocious anti-Thomas movement that almost destroyed his nomination, Southern Democrats provided the crucial votes in his confirmation.[7]

However, the most recent evidence suggests that this factor is of dwindling significance. Priscilla Owen and Janice Rogers Brown were among the most controversial of the stalled nominees to the appeals courts. The latter, as an African-American, was often compared to Justice Thomas, particularly as some of her off-court pronouncements indicated radical views. Yet gender and race seemed not to help either candidate, as Democrats and liberal interest groups focused more intently on the ideology of nominees. Indeed, when Democrat Senator Joseph Biden (Delaware) floated a compromise on the filibuster whereby all but the two most extreme of the stalled judges would be given a straight confirmation vote, Owen and Rogers appear to be the two 'extremists' he had in mind (*Washington Post*, 2005c; *New York Times*, 2005b). Ironically both these 'extremists' were eventually confirmed as a result of the compromise struck between the Democratic and Republican moderates to break the deadlock caused by the hard-line positions of their respective party leaders

The most striking evidence of the dwindling salience of race, ethnicity and gender in judicial nominations, however, was the failed nomination of conservative jurist Miguel Estrada in Bush's first term. When nominated to the District of Columbia Court of Appeals in May 2001, Estrada appeared to have everything going for him. He embodied the American Dream: born in Honduras, he emigrated to the United States at age 15 barely able to speak English and went on to obtain his J.D. from Harvard Law School. He clerked for Supreme Court Justice Anthony Kennedy and served as assistant to the Solicitor General of the United States in the Clinton administration. He was ranked by the American Bar Association as 'well-qualified' to serve on the Court of Appeals. He had the backing of moderate Republican Senators such as Lincoln Chafee (Rhode Island), Susan Collins (Maine) and Olympia Snowe (Maine). He would also have been the first Hispanic to sit on the DC Circuit Court. The conservative Estrada therefore appeared to have all the off-setting characteristics required to ensure his confirmation.

Instead, this Hispanic nominee became the first victim of the Democrats' new use of the filibuster. Estrada's major weakness was not that he had a record as an arch-conservative, but that he obfuscated when asked questions about abortion and other key issues (Alliance for Justice, 2003). Second, although he had the support of some Hispanic organizations, he was opposed by others, including the Hispanic Congressional

Caucus (Slate, 2003). Underlying the filibuster, however, was an apparent determination by Democrats to show the Bush administration that the Senate was not to be taken for granted. On no less than seven occasions between March and July 2003, they sustained the filibuster in cloture votes. As Senator Edward Kennedy commented after the withdrawal of Estrada's nomination in April 2003: 'It reflects a clear recognition by Miguel Estrada and, hopefully, this White House that under the Constitution the Senate has shared power over judicial appointments'(CNN, 2003)

By the time he had two nominations to make, Bush's options had evidently narrowed over the course of his first term. In order to please his Christian conservative base and fulfil his own policy agenda, he needed to nominate justices who would swing the court to the right. If he did so, however, he might provoke either resistance from the Gang of 14 or a Democratic filibuster and risk losing his nominees in the Senate. Nominating moderate conservatives, however, would cause disarray and disaffection in many conservative circles and put at serious risk the electoral fortunes of the Republican Party. One familiar ruse for evading this dilemma — playing the race-gender-ethnicity card — no longer seemed to work.

Predictably, Bush responded unpredictably. Relying heavily on his governing party strategy, he nominated Judge John G. Roberts as Chief Justice (but initially as O'Connor's replacement) and White House counsel Harriet Miers to take O'Connor's seat. Both could best be described as 'insider-stealth' candidates. Neither was a classic stealth candidate, in that both were well known in Washington political circles. However, unlike most of the names usually cited as potential Supreme Court nominees, neither had made any public pronouncements on the controversial issues of the Court's agenda. Moreover, both were Republican insiders, which suited Bush's governing party strategy. Thus, although Judge Roberts gave little away during his confirmation hearings regarding how he might vote on particular issues, the administration was able to assure its constituency that he was 'one of us'. With Roberts' impressive judicial credentials providing him with further protection, the Democrats had little of substance to aim at. As a result the minority party split almost down the middle with 19 of its ranks voting to confirm Roberts, whose appointment was approved by 78 votes to 22. All 55 Republicans supported the confirmation of the new Chief Justice and no right-wing interest group opposed him.

However, Bush ran into immediate trouble when he tried to repeat the strategy with the Miers nomination. Despite the fact that Miers was a born-again Christian who was known to believe that life begins at conception, the evangelical wing of the Republican movement was very reluctant to take her on trust. It wanted certainty that the O'Connor seat would be filled by a nominee who would move the Court to the right on key issues. Within days of her nomination, the press reported scepticism, and in some cases outright hostility, among conservatives. William Kristol described his own reaction as 'disappointed, depressed and demoralized' (Babington and Edsall, 2005, p. A11). Some conservative Senators, such as Sam Brownback (Kansas), pronounced themselves unconvinced even after meeting with the nominee (Stollberg, 2005c).

The revolt on the Right against Miers overpowered the White House. While some, like Kristol, objected to her lack of judicial experience and gravitas, the Christian wing of the Republican Party wanted a nominee already established as being in the Scalia mould. Using the leverage afforded to them by the president's governing party strategy, the social conservatives forced Miers to withdraw. A chastened George W. Bush then gave them exactly what they had wanted all along in the form of Judge Samuel A. Alito, sometimes referred to as 'Scalito' because of the similarity of his judicial views to those of Justice Scalia. Thus, albeit with the diversion of the Miers debacle, the Bush administration eventually followed the political logic outlined earlier in this chapter. The nomination of Judge Alito was immediately greeted as a *causus belli* among liberal groups and a fierce Senate battle loomed. For George W. Bush, however, a major fight with the Democrats was less risky than a fight with his Republican base.

Abortion

The ultimate aim of the pro-life movement is the reversal of *Roe v. Wade*, the 1973 Supreme Court decision that decriminalized abortion, but this victory was unlikely to be achieved during Bush's term in office. The fact that attainment of this goal proved more difficult than campaigners ever imagined did much to engender a second level of abortion politics. This consisted of guerrilla warfare in which the anti-abortion insurgents struck at the most vulnerable secondary targets available. At this lower level of abortion politics, the president was expected not to lead, so much as to encourage the troops and set the seal on their victories through signing bills and administrative orders.

The classic illustration of secondary abortion politics in Bush's first administration was the enactment of legislation outlawing partial-birth abortion. This rarely-used procedure was undeniably gruesome when described, which helped make it easy to attack and difficult to defend.[8] Nevertheless, the pro-life drive to ban it, which began in the 1990s, encountered firm opposition from pro-choice groups, who feared that the real motive of the campaign was to undermine the legitimacy of all abortion rights. Although Congress approved a prohibition in 1995 and again in 1997, President Clinton used his veto to thwart it from becoming law on both occasions.

Bush's election ended presidential resistance to the ban. Once again both chambers in Congress passed by large majorities the Partial Birth Abortion Ban Act of 2003, which the president signed into law. At the signing ceremony, President Bush once again referred to the need to build 'a culture of life' in America. In discussing 'the rights of the unborn', he also referred to them as 'children' and 'persons'. In short, his rhetoric was designed to signal his opposition to abortion and the Supreme Court's decision in *Roe v. Wade*. Unsurprisingly, he vowed that '... the executive branch will vigorously defend this law against any who would try to overturn it in the courts' (White House, 2003).

The guerrilla warfare continued when the pro-life coalition secured passage of the Unborn Victims of Violence Act of 2004. This legislation gave legal recognition to a foetus by making the murder of an unborn child a separate crime from the murder of the pregnant mother. In *Roe v. Wade*, the Supreme Court ruled that a foetus had no legal status, since it was not a person within the meaning of the law. Hence, like the Partial Birth Abortion Act, the constitutionality of the Unborn Victims Act faced challenge in the federal courts, and possibly the Supreme Court, during the second George W. Bush administration.

The administration could easily lose both cases. For example, in *Stenberg v. Carhart* (2000), a five–four majority of the US Supreme Court struck down a Nebraska statute very similar to that enacted by Congress in 2003. The Court held that the state statute was unconstitutional because the ban allowed no exception where the mother's health would otherwise be threatened. The 2003 Act, however, directly challenged the medical evidence on which the Supreme Court relied in allowing no exception to the ban. In effect, this legislation posed a challenge to the Court to reverse *Sternberg v. Carhart* on the basis of Congress' own evaluation of the medical factors. If the Court were to uphold the 2003 statute, it would undermine key elements of the *Roe* decision and some of its progeny. A decision upholding the Unborn Victims Act of 2004 would have similar implications. If, however, both measures were declared unconstitutional, this would simply emphasize once more that the key to the triumph of the pro-life movement lay in Bush's ability to appoint the judges he wanted. Again, then, we see the fundamental reason why he was willing to court confrontation on the filibuster issue and on the ideology of any Supreme Court nominee.

Political development early in Bush's second term indicated that the president, the pro-life movement and its congressional allies would take every opportunity to restrict abortion rights. Early in 2005, the House passed the Child Interstate Abortion Notification Act, which received the president's public endorsement. This measure imposed criminal sanctions on adults who accompany pregnant girls aged 17 or under across state lines for the purpose of circumventing strict abortion laws in the home state (*New York Times*, 2005c). The abortion conflict also bedevilled consideration of a bankruptcy bill, which was held up because pro-choice members of Congress sought to close a loophole allowing anti-abortion clinic protestors to avoid paying fines by declaring themselves bankrupt (*New York Times*, 2005d). For its part, the administration continued its efforts to prevent abortions being performed throughout the world. Early in 2005 it unsuccessfully attempted to insert an anti-abortion clause into a one-page declaration by the United Nations Commission on the Status of Women that actually made no mention of abortion rights (*New York Times*, 2005e).

It was clear that the pro-life campaign would be more relentless than ever in Bush's second term. The pro-life element in Congress had been strengthened by the election in 2004 of new members staunchly opposed to abortion rights, notably Senators Jim DeMint (South Carolina), John Thune (South Dakota) and Tom Coburn (Oklahoma). The congressional leadership, particularly Bill Frist and Tom DeLay, was passionately pro-life. And anti-abortion groups, the Republican Party and the White House liaised more closely on the issue than ever before. This political and religious alliance was evidently intent on total victory through confrontation, rather than incremental change through bargaining and compromise.

Homosexual Equality

If abortion rights constituted the oldest policy preoccupation of the Christian Right and its Republican supporters, same-sex marriage was the newest of its targets. While there was nothing new in traditionalist disapproval of homosexuality, the issue became explosive following the Supreme Court's 2003 decision in *Lawrence v. Texas*. Reversing its decision in *Bowers v. Hardwick* (1986), a six–three majority of the Court ruled that states could not criminalize private, consensual homosexual acts simply because a majority of its residents disapproved of such acts on moral grounds.

That decision in itself was not particularly controversial: very few states had retained such legislation, public opinion was clearly tolerant on the issue, and such laws were highly impractical to enforce. What triggered the explosion was Justice Scalia's dissenting opinion that if majoritarian morality did not legitimize a ban on homosexual sodomy, neither could it justify a ban on other morality-based laws, such as homosexual marriage. Although the Court's opinion, and Justice O'Connor's concurring opinion, explicitly stated that the case had no bearing on same-sex marriage, Scalia wrote: 'Do not believe it ... Today's opinion dismantles the structure of constitutional law that has permitted a distinction to be made between heterosexual and homosexual unions, insofar as formal recognition in marriage is concerned' (Scalia, 2003).

That there was a powerful logic to Justice Scalia's argument was borne out by the fact that it energized *both* sides of the gay rights battle. Local officials in various parts of the country announced that they were ready to perform gay marriages, an offer that thousands of gay couples took up. Those opposed to same-sex marriage worked to pass state constitutional amendments outlawing it. Despite enormous success in these efforts,[9] it soon became clear that only an amendment to the United States Constitution would eliminate the possibility of gay marriage throughout the country. The problem from the traditionalist point of view was that some states might permit the practice and other states would have to recognize the legitimacy of those marriages through the Full Faith and Credit clause of the Constitution. Such fears appeared to be confirmed when the Massachusetts Supreme Judicial Court declared in November 2003 that disallowing same-sex marriage amounted to violation of the state constitution's due process and equal protection clauses.[10] This aroused conservative concern that the 1996 Defence of Marriage Act, which declares that the federal government only recognizes heterosexual marriage, was itself vulnerable to constitutional challenge and might be struck down by the courts.

In these circumstances enactment of the Marriage Protection Amendment to the federal constitution became one of the top priorities of the Christian Right.[11] At first glance, the amendment appeared to have good prospects of success. The Defence of Marriage Act of 1996 had passed with congressional majorities well over the two-thirds needed to approve a constitutional amendment: 342–67 in the House and 85–14 in the Senate. Polls at the outset of Bush's second term showed that public opinion was opposed to gay marriage in a ratio of about 3:1.[12] Moreover, with some 43 states having either statutory or constitutional prohibitions on same-sex marriage, a federal constitutional amendment to this end would seem well-placed to gain the approval of the required three-quarters majority of states.

However, the Marriage Protection Amendment had limited prospects of enactment because of the enormous effort and resources required to change the Constitution over the resistance of a determined minority. Liberal and left groups learned this lesson from the failed attempt to secure adoption of the Equal Rights Amendment in the 1970s and early 1980s. Conservative opponents of same-sex marriage experienced the unique difficulties of the amendment process in Bush's first term. While few legislators hesitated to support the Defense of Marriage Act in 1996, far more opposed a federal constitutional amendment to the same end. In July 2004, the Senate failed by a cloture vote of 48 for and 50 against to bring the proposed amendment to a vote. In September the House of Representatives cast 227 votes for the amendment and 186 against, but this fell far short of the two-thirds majority required.

Even the election in 2004 of new members of Congress devoted to the Christian Right agenda did not provide the additional votes to achieve the supermajorities necessary for the passage of the amendment. It appeared certain that the Marriage Protection Amendment would remain a bone of contention for some time and be used in future Republican electoral campaigns to embarrass Democrats. However, even so ardent an administration as that of George W. Bush appeared unlikely to devote substantial resources to a campaign for the enactment of a measure that had such little chance of bearing fruit.

Liberty and Security: The Rights of 'Unlawful Combatants'

Another major issue that pitted the White House against the courts was the impact of the 'war on terror' on civil liberties. George W. Bush — and presidential power in general — suffered a significant blow from the Supreme Court's decisions in 2004 on the due process rights of those detained as 'unlawful combatants' in Guantanamo Bay and other prisons in the United States.[13] These judgements adversely affected both the administration's policy on dealing with enemy combatants and its attempt to re-assert presidential power in the federal system.

One of the striking features of the decisions was that eight of the nine Justices rejected the administration's claim to plenary power when it came to fighting the war on terror. Only Justice Thomas accepted the solicitor-general's argument that the only requirement needed to justify the indefinite detention of enemy combatants and the refusal to grant them basic due process rights was a good-faith assertion by the executive branch that the policy was necessary to the conduct of the war. The Court majority in all three cases, however, insisted that the federal judiciary had jurisdiction over such issues and that the detainees were entitled to due process.

The scale of this defeat meant that the president could do little to change the Supreme Court's position on the issue through new judicial appointments. However, this did not mean that he intended to comply with the adverse rulings. Instead, the Bush administration showed every intention to evade the Court's ruling where it could and minimize its impact where this was not possible. Its stance offered the prospect of an interesting 'constitutional dialogue' between the executive and judicial branches of government on this relatively new subject.

One of the justifications that the administration advanced for the indefinite detention of enemy combatants was the need for their ongoing interrogation in order to gather maximum intelligence on the terrorist forces. On the other hand it was deeply reluctant to produce in court evidence of sufficient strength to persuade a judge of the necessity of continued detention. Whether the evidence was too sensitive or whether convincing evidence was actually absent remained unclear. Instead of bowing to the Court's ruling, however, in some cases the administration chose to circumvent it by sending detainees abroad into the custody of other jurisdictions.

This practice, sometimes referred to as 'extraordinary rendition' was defended by the administration, even though detainees were sent to countries such as Saudi Arabia, Afghanistan, Yemen and Egypt, which the State Department itself condemned for their brutal treatment of prisoners. Nevertheless, Attorney-General Alberto Gonzales publicly stated that the administration did not send prisoners to countries which it believes would mistreat them (*Washington Post*, 2005d). Moral and legal doubts about extraordinary rendition were heightened by evidence suggesting that the practice had been stepped up in order to circumvent the Supreme Court's 2004 rulings. An anonymous senior Defense Department spokesman was reported as saying in March 2005, 'It's fair to say that the calculus now is different than it was before, because the legal landscape has changed …' (*New York Times*, 2005f). The same report suggested that 65 Guantanamo prisoners had been dealt with in this way, though a Human Rights Watch dossier claimed that the number of Guantanamo and other post-9/11 detainees sent to Egypt alone could have been as high as 200 (*Human Rights Watch*, 2005).

However, 'extraordinary rendition' was uncharted legal territory, so it remained to be seen how the administration's actions could effectively be challenged.[14] For even if the executive is vulnerable to the charge that it knowingly sent prisoners to countries where they were likely to suffer abuse, there are obvious practical difficulties to mounting a legal challenge.

Accordingly, the administration looked set to continue this practice, with the prospect that most prisoners will have been removed from Guantanamo before any suit reaches the Supreme Court.

The administration also offered only the most grudging compliance with the Supreme Court's 2004 decisions. In asserting that enemy combatants were entitled to a measure of due process, the Court left it vague as to exactly what this might consist of. The plurality opinion of Justice O'Connor in *Hamdi v. Rumsfeld* concluded: 'We therefore hold that a citizen-detainee seeking to challenge his classification as an enemy combatant must receive notice of the factual basis for his classification and a fair opportunity to rebut the Government's factual assertions before a neutral decision-maker.' She added, however: 'At the same time, the exigencies of the circumstances may demand that, aside from these core elements, enemy combatant proceedings may be tailored to alleviate their uncommon potential to burden the Executive at a time of ongoing military conflict.'

The administration's response was to establish Combatant Status Review Tribunals. The 'neutral decison-maker' called for in the Supreme Court's opinion would be three commissioned officers of the US armed forces who had had nothing to do with the detainee's case. Legal counsel provided to each detainee would also be a military officer, who would have 30 days to prepare the case. Detainees would have access to evidence that was 'reasonably available' and likewise could confront witnesses who were 'reasonably available'. However, tribunals were not bound by the rules of evidence that would apply in a court of law and could, for example, consider hearsay. Decisions would be made on the preponderance of evidence and there would be a rebuttable presumption in favour of the Government's evidence.[15]

Many analysts thought that the tribunals were loaded against the detainees, so it was unsurprising that the district court for the District of Columbia ruled in January 2005 that the tribunals violated the detainees' due process rights.[16] By that time, however, these bodies had completed their work and the Department of Defence had taken final action in 330 cases. In all but three of these cases, the determination supported the government's position that the prisoners were rightfully detained (*Washington Post*, 2005e).

The administration was expected to vigorously defend the tribunals when its appeal against the district court ruling was heard. Should it succeed in convincing the Supreme Court that it had complied with its 2004 rulings, it will have successfully retained its hard-line policy on enemy combatants. Should it fail to do so, the record suggests it will once again comply with any new instructions in the most unco-operative manner and yield as little as possible to the judicial branch of government.

Conclusion

George W. Bush's second administration promised to be uncompromising on issues relating to the judiciary and constitutional rights. Much of its governing party strategy, electoral coalition and prospects and ideological predilections were based on achieving significant success in these policy areas. Indeed, so much of the president's credibility was staked on achieving this success that many believed he considered 'noble defeat' preferable to 'cowardly compromise'. Bush intended to rule rather reign in his second term, but the odds were stacked against him. On constitutional issues and judicial appointments, his attempt to beat the odds by selecting 'insider-stealth' nominees was both ingenious and risky. While this tactic worked well with Judge Roberts, it could not be sustained with Miers. As a result, the President was forced back to his destiny as an orthodox innovator. The nomination of Samuel Alito was a means to make good the divisions he caused in his own ranks with the Miers nomination. Accordingly George W. Bush may escape the fate of other orthodox innovators whose presidencies provoked dissent and division within the regime to which they were affiliated.

Notes

1   Perhaps the most interesting comparison with a negative outcome is the presidency of Lyndon B. Johnson. Like Bush, Johnson came to the presidency in a fortuitous (if tragic) manner and set out to complete the New Deal regime of his hero, Franklin D. Roosevelt. While his domestic agenda caused dissension both in the country at large and within the Democratic alliance, it was his determination to pursue a complicated foreign war in Vietnam that did most to shatter a regime that had held sway for some 30 years.

2   President Richard Nixon had earlier attempted to bring a halt to judicial activism through the appointment of such judges as William H. Rehnquist to the Supreme Court, but he was neither as systematic nor as determined as the Reagan administration.

3   This was not the first time that filibuster tactics had been used to thwart a judicial nomination. Much the same happened in 1968, for example, when the Senate delayed a vote on President Lyndon Johnson's nomination of Justice Abe Fortas to be Chief Justice of the

United States Supreme Court. The Fortas nomination was withdrawn as a result.

4   The re-nominees whom Senate Democrats had successfully blocked in cloture votes were: Priscilla Owen (Fifth Circuit); Richard Griffin, David McKeague and Henry Saad (all Sixth Circuit); William G. Myers III (Ninth Circuit); William H. Pryor (Eleventh Circuit); Janice Rogers Brown (DC Circuit).

5   *In re Jane Doe 1 (II)*, 19 S.W.3d 346 (Tex. 2000).

6   A *Washington Post*–ABC News poll in April 2005 suggested that the public was opposed to a change in the filibuster rules by a margin of 2–1. *Washington Post*, 26 April 2005.

7   Justice Thomas was confirmed by a vote of 52–48. Eleven Democrats voted for his confirmation. They were mostly from the South and had strong electoral reasons for supporting the nominee: Boren (Oklahoma), Breaux (Louisiana), DeConcini (Arizona), Dixon (Illinois), Exon (Nebraska), Fowler (Georgia), Hollings (South Carolina), Johnston (Louisiana), Nunn (Georgia), Robb (Virginia), Shelby (Alabama).

8   'Partial birth abortion is a common term for the Intact Dilation and Extraction (D&X) abortion procedure. In the partial birth abortion (D&X) procedure, a physician delivers a baby to the point where only the head remains inside the womb but then punctures the back of the skull and removes the brain before completing delivery. Partial birth abortion (D&X) makes up only one per cent of all abortions performed', http://womensissues.about.com.

9   For example, on 2 November 2004, eleven states voted on and passed state constitutional amendments banning same-sex marriage: Arkansas, Georgia, Kentucky, Michigan, Mississippi, Montana, North Dakota, Ohio, Oklahoma, Oregon and Utah. Earlier in 2004, similar proposals were passed by referenda in Louisiana and Missouri, CNN.Com, 3/11/04.

10 *Goodridge v. Department of Public Health*, 440 Mass. 309 (2003).

11 The pertinent part of the measure introduced into the Senate in January 2005 reads: 'Marriage in the United States shall consist only of the union of a man and a woman. Neither this Constitution, not the constitution of any State, shall be construed to require that marriage or the legal incidents thereof be conferred upon any union other than the union of a man and a woman'. 109th Congress, S.J.RES. 1, 24 January 2005.

12 One poll showed 27 per cent supporting gay marriage, a further 29 per cent supporting civil unions and 40 per cent opposing any legal recognition of same-sex relationships, *Washington Post–ABC News Poll*, April 2005. Another showed figures of 23 per cent, 34 per cent and 41 per cent respectively, *New York Times/CBS News Poll*, March, 2005.

13 *Hamdi v. Rumsfeld*; *Rasul et al. v. Bush*; *Rumsfeld v. Padilla*.

14 For a discussion of possible legal constraints on extraordinary rendition, see Garcia (2005).

15 'Order Establishing Combatant Status Review Tribunal', Office of the Deputy Secretary of Defence, 7 July 2004.

16 *In re* Guantanamo Detainees Cases, United States District Court for the District of Columbia, 31 January 2005.

9

A New Republican Majority?

Philip Davies

Election Results at the Turn of the Century

'The Thief of Bagdad' was a hit film in 1924. In this silent movie Douglas Fairbanks' character used all his magic skills to outwit the evil Caliph on his native soil. Halliwell applauds this classic action adventure, especially 'its leading performance and driving narrative energy', even if the tricks intended to shock and awe the Caliph and the audience were 'a little timeworn' (Halliwell, 1998, p. 800).

In the same year Ramsay MacDonald formed the first Labour government in the United Kingdom, only to be thrashed at the subsequent election. J. Edgar Hoover became director of the Bureau of Investigation. The First Winter Olympics took place. Knute Rockne coached the Green Tide of Notre Dame to nine wins out of nine games and just 2.5 million of America's households owned radios.

And it was the last time before 2004 that an incumbent Republican president was returned to the White House with a majority of his party in the US House of Representatives and in the US Senate.

It is not at all clear that George W. Bush would appreciate the comparison with President Calvin Coolidge. Like Bush, Coolidge could have trouble with words. With his northern New England twang he was reputed to be able to say cow in four syllables. But unlike Bush he is remembered more for the times when he said nothing at all. During the 1924 campaign Coolidge is reported to have been asked by a newsman for his thoughts about Prohibition, and to have replied 'No comment'. 'Will you say something about unemployment?' 'No', said the president. '... your views about the world situation?' 'No'. 'About your message to Congress?' 'No'. Then, 'Wait', the newsman perked up, 'remember — don't quote me' (Boller, 1981, p. 234).

But there are parallels. Coolidge took over a presidency that had been stained by corruption and personal hypocrisy in the White House, and took seriously the job of re-establishing the reputation of the presidency and protecting the party. He was committed to limited central government, lower taxes and, even in a post-war atmosphere heavily influenced by isolationism, he recognized the necessity and inevitability of America's involvement in international affairs. His was a campaign that stressed the virtue of sticking with the known quantity, suggesting that the electorate should 'Keep cool with Coolidge'. After his victory *The Boston Transcript* argued effectively that the new president had a personal mandate: 'Calvin Coolidge was the issue, and to the president belongs the victory' (Boller, 1984, p. 220).

Unlike Bush, Coolidge was not elected president twice. He was incumbent by virtue of promotion, having inherited his presidency on the death of Warren Gamaliel Harding. In fact in order to find an elected Republican president re-elected with simultaneous majorities for his party in both chambers we have to go back to the second victory of William McKinley, in 1900, after the apparently realigning election of 1896.

If the election result of 1924 looks something like that of 2004, it was nonetheless achieved at a time when Republican political dominance was about to founder on the rocks of the Great Depression. It may well be that the Bush-era GOP would therefore prefer to look beyond the time when Mickey Mouse made his first appearance and Amelia Earhart was impressing the world to the *fin de siècle* era that saw the McKinley elections lay firm foundations for a generation of predominantly Republican electoral success.

Election Results in the Twenty-first Century

Bush also had to wait until his second term to be able to make a strong claim that his elections could have a long-term institutional impact. His 2000 victory in the Electoral College was undermined by the plurality for Al Gore in the popular vote and the need for judicial intervention to create a winner in Florida. A week after the 2002 US mid-term elections Karl Rove, Special Assistant to the President, gave a speech at the University of Utah that praised George Bush for leading the Republican Party to an unusual victory. Against the tide of history the presidential party had gained congressional seats at the first mid-term in both the House of Representatives and the Senate. Even though more Republican-held than Democratic-held constituencies were up for election both in Congress and at gubernatorial level, the party's candidates had beaten the statistical odds on defeat in holding on to a majority of governorships as well as making legislative gains.

Some of the individual victories were close, but the fact that the balance of power had tilted towards the Republicans at every level, and in every branch, was clear by the morning after election day. There was no 36-day wait for a result in 2002, and Rove was quick to claim a mandate for George Bush. Having become president in an election where he did not gain a plurality of the popular votes that were cast, George W. Bush picked up the mantle of a mandate from an election in which he was not on the ballot at all.

While he was pleased with the short term impact of the November 2002 results, Rove saw much more potential in this victory. 'Nothing stays in gridlock in American politics ... things are beginning to move in one direction ... Something else more fundamental is happening there', claimed Rove, 'but we will only know it retrospectively, in two years or four years or six years [when] we look back and say the dam began to break in 2002.' In particular he claimed there was a 'pretty dramatic' growth in Republican identification among young voters, a shift in the gender gap and indications of Republican attraction to Hispanic voters, each of which 'could be a significant trend' for the building of a generation-long Republican majority (Rove, 2002).

Overdue Realignment

This is a scenario that some Republicans feel is long overdue. Through all of US political history until the last third of the twentieth century the electorate tended to vote for a government united by political party, and when electoral opinion shifted, even for short periods, the effect was generally felt on all parts of federal government simultaneously. The pattern after 1968 was quite different.

Previous eras in the balance of party political power have been typified by unified control by the dominant party across the branches of federal government, albeit broken by occasional temporary electoral swings, but this pattern was not replicated in the late twentieth century. In an attempt to encompass this, different authors have identified the contemporary party political system as realigned, but 'hollow', 'weak', 'casual', 'soft', 'rolling' or 'by default', bringing to mind a kind of era of weak feelings. Others have argued that the realignment concept has outlived its usefulness, basing their case on the prolonged era of almost continuous divided party control of government in the late twentieth century (Shafer, 1991).

The reasons posited were varied. It may be that the electorate wishes for different attributes to be represented in the different branches and chambers of government, and recognizes these attributes as best represented by different political parties. It may be that voters have a sense of 'cognitive Madisonianism' — a belief in the value of maximizing the oppositions that are already institutionalized within the checks and balances system. An electorate that was increasingly suspicious of all institutions of authority over the last part of the twentieth century appeared generally comfortable with divided government. This knowledge underpinned campaigns by both parties that have leaped to defend their candidates for one branch by arguing the dangers of handing 'unlimited' power to a single party. In particular, the National Republican Congressional Committee, apparently giving up on Bob Dole's chances of being elected president as the 1996 campaign entered its final week, sought to tap into the perceived public valuation of the checks provided by divided government. On 26 October, it began running a television spot advertisement asking 'What would happen if the Democrats controlled Congress and the White House? ... The liberal special interests aligned with Clinton desperately want to buy back control of Congress. If we give the special interests a blank cheque in Congress, who's going to represent us?' Republican party leaders rather disingenuously denied that this was anything less than supportive of the Dole re-election effort (Davies, 1999, p. 215). It is not an approach that one would expect to see in the campaigns of the early twenty-first century, which in itself suggests that, whether driven by ideology or pragmatism, the context of campaigning has shifted.

By 1985 Everett Carll Ladd was one of those leading the argument that 'The New Deal type of realignment is not likely to occur again'. He posited five components of a new type of realignment: voting changes by a variety of groups; the emergence of Republican dominance in presidential elections; a changed mix of national issues; a weakening of voters' ties to parties; and split ticket voting for races at different levels of government (Ladd, 1985, p. 19). In his analysis of the following presidential election, Ladd was inclined to say that these changes constituted a realignment, but also moved to reject the debate as unproductive. Rather, he saw the 'post-New Deal system' as 'A transformed parties and elections system ... firmly in place in the United States. It has no historic counterpart ...' (Ladd, 1989, p. 18).

Walter Dean Burnham maintains the value of realignment as a conceptual tool, but in 1985 he too felt that a sixth party system, dating from the late 1960s, was without historic counterpart. He claimed that the emerging weakness of political parties was perhaps an immutable part of this new system. In his view, the historic structure of party coalitions had given way to a state of 'permanent campaign' in which new features of the political environment — professionalized, personalized campaigns, the demands of the electronic media and the increased financial obligations of running for office — had become paramount.

There appears to have emerged a shared belief that something had happened in party politics, even though the name and shape of what had happened was in dispute. Ladd's argument that too much time had been spent waiting for realignment — the Godot of American political science — has some force. But it was not just political scientists who were waiting for it. Candidates, office-holders and political parties were increasingly using consultants both internal and external to their normal operations staff. Consultants and other political actors were increasingly aware of political science research. The language of political science crossed over into the political parties. One could be excused for thinking that the orchestration of realignment had become a target of the major parties as their relationship with the electorate weakened and they looked to experts to advise them.

Perhaps something had happened in the late 1960s, but if it was to mirror earlier equivalent happenings it should have resulted in a new pattern of party domination, to last for a generation. A pattern of that kind reduces the unpredictability of election results and increases the efficiency with which a party can expend its campaigning resources. It is especially welcome if yours is the dominant party. But whatever had happened had not followed the usual pattern. Those in the Republican Party who believed that realignment in their favour was clearly signalled in the late 1960s found their expectations rudely interrupted when the Nixon administration ended in ignominious resignation. They were really quite disturbed that this cycle of history had not taken its hoped for turn, and they especially were eager to give realignment a helping hand.

The winning of elections is essentially a short-term task. A date is fixed. A plurality of the vote in the constituency is required for victory. But US political party leaders were faced with a system that was no longer working predictably and according to received wisdom. Simultaneously there was a suspicion that the opportunity might exist to create a new voting pattern that could last for a generation, rather than an election. It is not clear that the party leaders were trying to 'win realignment', but the need to respond to changes both in electoral behaviour and in the legislated structure of the elections process meant that they certainly had to think of doing more than the short term aim of winning the next election. For example, while he was Republican Party chairman in the 1980s Frank Fahrenkopf's '1991 Plan' injected resources into local party organizations around the country in an attempt to stimulate party growth from the grass roots. This effort was prompted by his belief that realignment 'is already underway ... and is in the process [of] making Republicans the majority party, the party of the future' (Fahrenkopf, 1986b, p. 28). At the national level the Republican Party began generic television advertizing in 1980. Both the significance accorded to realignment and the extent to which it had impinged on the consciousness of political leaders was signally indicated in 1984, when, upon winning re-election, President Ronald Reagan himself declared that 'realignment is real' (White, 1985, p. 18).

But Reagan's perception was faulty. The political landscape remained very competitive. The Republicans failed to unify their party control of government during the last years of the twentieth century by losing the executive precisely as they gained the legislature. For many Republicans, the abiding feeling of the last generation has been that this unique pattern of party competitiveness was a startling aberration. In their opinion it was not so much a new kind of realignment, as it was a Republican realignment irritatingly stalled, or rudely interrupted. However Republican leaders saw the election results of 2000 as their opportunity to bring to an end the post-New Deal era of party competition and institute an era of GOP control more akin to earlier party alignments.

On 7 November 2000 National Republican Congressional Committee Chairman Thomas M. Davis III (Virginia) claimed that the Democrats 'have lost their once-in-a-generation chance to win back control of the House'. This boast certainly gave expression to party efforts to 'win realignment' and offered insight into the emerging structural context of national elections in the USA (Eilperin and Vita, 2000, p. A1). Rove's 2002 speech further highlighted an electoral battle that has increasingly been fought between a Republican Party machine determined to achieve its destined realignment and a Democratic Party determined to resist.

After 2002, Republicans hoped that this was not another false dawn, but many Democrats felt that the newly built temple of long-term Republican domination was founded on shifting sands. After all, they could argue, the 2000 victory was based on an historical technicality, a toss up that went the wrong way. In 2002, gains in the House of Representatives could be explained almost entirely by post-census redistricting, and the national aggregate vote was a dead heat. Even in 2004 House losses may be substantially explained by the re-redistricting of Texas, losses in the Senate passed off as the culmination of a southern shift that has been underway for decades and the gubernatorial elections appear to have left the party distribution unchanged. According to this interpretation local conditions and small temporary shifts in national mood can account for everything that we have seen, and the Democrats are poised to take advantage of a swing back to conditions more similar to those of the last generation.

Republicans Raise High the Red Map

In the wake of the 2004 election the traditional presidential electoral map showed an apparently strong dominance of Republican states. The thirty-one Bush states, stretching across the centre of the USA, made an impressive visual statement of the GOP's election success. The South and Border states, the Mountain states and most of the agricultural Midwest had voted for Bush, providing a contiguous mass of the red with which the electoral cartographers in the USA denote Republican victories. At the county level Bush's victory put even more red on the map, with 2,575 of the nation's 3,155 counties going for him over Kerry, while the Democrat's victories concentrated in the most populous localities (Cook, 2005c).

It might have been close, but the map indicated that Bush had clearly won. According to Rhodes Cook's figures, Bush took 50.7 per cent of the presidential vote, a 2.4 per cent lead over Kerry.[1] In addition Republicans took 50.1 per cent of the aggregate House vote, a 2.7 per cent lead in the popular vote that resulted in a Republican margin over the Democrats of 232 to 202 seats, with one Independent, Bernie Sanders of Vermont. A net gain of four Senate seats gave the Republicans 55 seats to the Democrats' 44, again with an Independent from Vermont, Jim Jeffords. The Republicans retained their pre-election 28 to 22 advantage among state governorships, failing to take Washington by only a few dozen votes out of the two and three-quarter million cast in the state. GOP leaders claimed that the red map was an accurate representation of a personal victory for George W. Bush and a party victory for the Republicans that was evidence of the fundamental shift whose existence Karl Rove had asserted two years earlier.

Exit polls showed the GOP vote up among suburbanites, women, Jews, Roman Catholics and Hispanics. This rise in Hispanic support attracted particular note in the immediate aftermath of the 2004 election because Rove had identified this group as a critical element in his target audience. Almost immediately, however, Ruy Teixeira indicated his misgivings about this poll result (2004). Leal, Barreto, Lee and de la Garza (2005) took this further, claiming that other indicators challenged the accuracy of the exit polls. In contrast, Warren Mitofsky (2005) entered the debate to defend the exit polls as most likely to give a fair picture of the vote. While the appeal of the Democrats to the non-Cuban Latino populations may have slipped, the jury still seems to be out on the extent of their shift towards Republicanism.

The voting divide at a family income of US$50,000 was evident in 2004, as it had been four years earlier, with 55 per cent of voters in the below US$50,000 category voting for Kerry, and 56 per cent of those above this line voting for Bush. But the proportions of the whole population divided by this line had been shifted, by inflation if nothing else, from 47:53 in 2000, to 45:55 in 2004, proportionately reducing the size of the Democrats' target audience. Also in 2004, for the first time in decades, the Democrats lost their party identification advantage. After this election party political identification split the country's voters evenly, with 37 per cent for each major party and the rest self-assigning as independents.

In 2004 George W. Bush received more votes than any presidential candidate in US history. Compared to 2000, his vote increased by almost 23 per cent at the same time as turnout increased by 16 per cent. Republican vote gains were higher than those for the Democratic presidential candidate in 38 states, and were at least double those of the Democrat opposition in 16 states. In a year when the Democrats had committed to mobilizing and getting out their vote, and when they did add over eight million voters to their 2000 presidential candidate's tally, President Bush's election team added almost three extra Republican voters for every two additional Democrats.

The re-elected President Bush opined that 'there is a feeling that the people have spoken and embraced your point of view, and that's what I intend to tell the Congress, that I made it clear what I intended to do as president ... and the people made it clear what they wanted, now let's work together'. House Majority Leader Tom DeLay (Texas) felt that the message of the election had potentially a much larger footprint. 'The Republican Party is a permanent majority for the future of this country ...' he avowed, 'We are going to be able to lead this country in the direction we've been dreaming of for years' (Harris and VandeHei, 2005, p. A1).

Democrats See a Purple Haze

Democrats generally make up the voting majority in densely populated states. Republican strength often lies in states with large areas and relatively small populations. On the traditional map the swatches of colour represent the area taken up by the states. As a result, while over 48 per cent of the population voted Democratic, substantially less than one-quarter of the map of the United States shows the blue that indicates a Democratic state. Alarmed that the visual concreteness of the electoral map may be misleading, cartographers have developed alternative ways of illustrating the vote. These cartograms can manipulate state borders to represent the size of electorate, rather than its acreage, can adopt shades and mixings of red and blue to represent the mix of voters and can drill the data to local precinct level (Gastner, Shalizi and Newman, 2004). The resulting diagrammatic representations of the election show a picture in which the red is much less striking. Democrats have seized on this as showing the two-party vote distribution in a more visually accurate fashion, in shades ranging from red to blue through myriad intervening shades of purple.

Conceding that 2004 was a George W. Bush victory does not mean that the Democrats see its significance as anything more than providing the president with a reasonably good bargaining position in the separated, checked and balanced political structure inside the Beltway. They could draw comfort from more than cartographic re-design. The two-thirds of states with US Senate elections inevitably do not form an accurate sample of all states, but the 34 Senate elections in 2004 achieved 70 per cent as many voters as the presidential election. Democrat candidates for the US Senate ended up with 51 per cent of the vote in these races, 4.7 per cent ahead of the Republicans. The Democrats won six of the 11 gubernatorial contests held in 2004 and took 49.5 per cent of the aggregate vote, compared with the Republican share of 48.9 per cent.

A Democratic analysis of the election results can also draw on historical evidence to question whether it represented a significant endorsement of Bush. Since the beginning of the twentieth century incumbent presidents have run for re-election on 19 occasions. Of the 14 incumbents who won a second term, Bush occupied only eleventh place in terms of the size of his popular vote, which was below the median achieved by re-election victors. His 35 Electoral College majority was the second lowest re-election margin ever achieved in the Electoral College, after his first election margin was the third lowest in US history.

Some Democrats also drew comfort from the narrowness of the results in key states that gave Bush his overall victory. A swing of only 59,500 popular votes would have put Ohio in John Kerry's column to give him an overall majority of 273 to 266 votes in the Electoral College. A switch of fewer than 58,000 votes, appropriately distributed, would have enabled Kerry to win Iowa, New Mexico and Colorado, whose combined total of 21 Electoral College votes would have been enough to put him in the White House. The popular majority would have remained with Bush in both these hypothetical cases, but the Electoral College win would have been validated by the experience of 2000.

For an even more intriguing result, fewer than 19,000 votes switching from Bush to Kerry in Iowa, Nevada and New Mexico would have provided a 269 to 269 vote dead heat in the Electoral College, throwing the choice of president into the House of Representatives and of vice president into the US Senate. At the very least, such a result would have challenged the confident claim of the administration and the Republican Party that their mandate was strong and clear.[2] The past may not be changed, but these tantalizing hints of what might have been help maintain a Democratic vision of George W. Bush as an accidental president and the Executive as an achievable Democratic target in the near future.

Re-mapping the Terrain: Campaign Finance, Technology and Electoral Speech

The 2004 election itself was taking place on a political landscape already terraformed by new campaign finance legislation. The Bipartisan Campaign Reform Act (BCRA) went into operation on the day following the 2002 mid-term elections, making the 2004 election the first to take place under its auspices. The authors of the BCRA wanted to divorce candidate and party campaigns for federal office from the use of soft money, and simultaneously to discourage the use of attack advertizing in political campaigns (Davies, 2006; Kaid and Jones, 2004). Soft money receipts by the national committees of the two major parties increased almost six-fold over the decade to 2002, while hard-money donations rose only by a factor of about 1.5 times. By 2002 soft money receipts accounted for about 44 per cent of the money that the political parties had to spend, a situation that was seen as creating an unregulated context and an atmosphere of irresponsibility in which campaigning was taking place.

Eliminating party and candidate access to soft money was intended to encourage responsible campaign spending. The legislation complements this by insisting in addition that campaign advertisements include an explicit statement authorizing the campaign message, including a full screen picture of the authorizing candidate in the case of television advertizing.

Regulation has unanticipated consequences, however, and the BCRA was being launched into a political world that was familiar since the 1970s both with campaign finance regulation and with political and legal searches for ways of working efficiently within those regulatory regimes. Inevitably the law was challenged in the courts. Eleven different lawsuits, involving more than 80 plaintiffs, were consolidated into one case (*McConnell v. FEC*, 2003).

The Supreme Court, by the slimmest 5–4 majority, upheld virtually the whole of the new legislation. Its ruling declared that 'the statute's two principal, complementary features — Congress's effort to plug the soft money loophole and its regulation of electioneering communications — must be upheld in the main'. In particular the Supreme Court upheld the ban that the law contained on national parties raising and spending soft money. With limited exceptions federal candidates and office-holders are also required by the new law to avoid raising and spending soft money, and these limits too were upheld in the Court's decision. Requirements limiting soft money spending by state parties on most federal election activities were upheld. The Court agreed that corporations and labour organizations may not use soft money to broadcast electioneering advertisements within 30 days of a primary election or 60 days of a general election, and that the sponsors of any significant electioneering communications cannot remain anonymous, but must be disclosed. Special interest groups, which had become particularly adept at using soft money to interject their own narrow agendas into election campaigns, were required to use only hard money to pay for electioneering communications.

The Court's decision was nevertheless concerned about the future of regulation under the BCRA. The main opinion, authored by Justices Stevens and O'Connor, expressed apparently deeply held suspicion of the role that campaign money had attained in US politics. 'Just as troubling ... as classic quid pro quo corruption', their opinion said, 'is the danger that officeholders will decide issues not on the merits or the desires of their constituencies but according to the wishes of those who have made large financial contributions valued by the officeholder.' While this feeling undoubtedly contributed to their decision, they went on to comment that 'We are under no illusion that BCRA will be the last congressional statement on the matter. Money, like water, will always find an outlet.'

Seasoned campaign staff may have preferred the status quo ante, but they did not so much examine the new laws in terms of their restrictions as use them as blueprints that showed exactly how money could be spent, especially soft money. The matters that now preoccupied them were finding the vehicle for the displaced soft money and creating the machinery to fill with hard money any gaps left by the soft money diversion (Mason, 2005). The campaign spending system achieved both of these objectives with commendable skill in the two years available between the implementation of the legislation and the first presidential campaign that it covered.

There are few signs that the rhetorical tenor of campaigning was very much modified by this legislation. Campaigns remained direct in their attacks and candidates seemed unembarrassed to have their names and images attached to firm attacks on their opponents. President Bush was in a position to indicate this through his own campaign. His refusal of the federal matching funds available to primary election candidates left his campaign free to raise and spend primary election funds unlimited by the matching funds regulations. When the Democratic national convention nominated John Kerry, the Bush campaign still had money in the bank, and, with the Republican convention a month away, was able to count its spending as primary electioneering, rather than setting it against the general election limits. The Bush campaign shifted smoothly and rapidly into attack mode, free to run against Kerry for almost a month in the summer of 2004 while the Democrat's campaign held back, marshalling its general election fund.

The official Republican campaign and its allies worked well to define John Kerry, especially in critical marginal states like Ohio, and destabilized the Kerry campaign in a crucial period of the summer. These allies operated through the main soft money development consequent on the BCRA, the emergence of 'Section 527' political organizations, sometimes called 'stealth PACs'. These groups, named for the relevant section of the Internal Revenue Service (IRS) Code, are acknowledged as having the purpose of influencing elections. They neither donate funds to candidate and party campaigns nor make explicit recommendations to the public to 'vote for' or to 'vote against' an office-seeker. They do, however, engage in public education around issues that may well promote or oppose some part of the agenda being debated between candidates, and thereby retain the ability to raise and spend soft money on their efforts.

By summer 2004 the routing of soft money through 527s was emerging as a serious issue. Supporters of the Democrats were quickest to use 527s, through groups such as the America Coming Together, New Democrat Network and The Media Fund. Republican supporters struck back through groups such as Swift Boat Veterans for Truth (SBVT) and People of Color United. The former bankrolled advertisements in key election states that attacked Kerry's record as a veteran of the Vietnam War and the latter did likewise to challenge the commitment of Kerry and his wife Teresa Heinz Kerry to the black American community. The Kerry campaign slipped up in its response to the attack in allowing its opponents the space to encourage the growth of any doubts that existed about their candidate.

The Democrats should have been well aware that Bush campaigners take no prisoners, if for no other reason than through reference to the attacks made against Democrat Michael Dukakis by George Bush Sr.'s team in the 1988 presidential election. Also, Kerry was accustomed to hard-nosed partisan give and take. A *Boston Globe* article on his 1996 US Senate re-election race against popular Republican Governor of Massachusetts, William H. Weld, gave this word picture of the two campaigns' messages: 'You can vote for the heartless liar who wants to destroy the environment, shred Medicare, attack innocent children and throw Grandma on the street. Or you can vote for the tax-happy freeloader who supports cop-killers, terrorists, drug addicts, welfare cheats, gang members, unemployment and gridlock' (Grunwald, 1996, p. 1). Kerry won that race, which was a fairly good-natured affair on the whole, but his team seemed unprepared for the attacks that came in 2004.

The top fifty 527 committees spent a total of over US$500 million in the run up to the 2004 campaign, but this appeared in no way to reduce the energy with which campaign related fund-raising and spending was pursued elsewhere.[3] The various party political national committees out-raised in total hard money their previous best hard and soft money total receipts, with the Democrats amassing over US$800 million, and the Republicans approaching US$900 million. Spending on the presidential race reached around US$1 billion, an increase of 56 per cent over 2000 levels, with House and Senate campaigns spending between them close to another billion dollars. Senate spending was 32 per cent higher than in 2002, with House spending up by ten per cent. 'Stealth PACs' notwithstanding, the traditional PACs were as busy as ever, raising over US$900 million, 34 per cent more than in 2002, increasing their contributions to federal candidates by ten per cent, with these funds accounting for 45 per cent of House campaign spending. PAC contributions were concentrated heavily on incumbents, with only 20 per cent of these funds going to challengers or candidates in open seats. In 2004 Republicans received 56 per cent of PAC contributions, and in the two years since the previous election cycle these contributions to Republicans had increased by 21 per cent, while there was only an increase of one per cent in giving to the Democrats.

US election campaigns have never hesitated to react with entrepreneurial enthusiasm to newly emerging technologies in the pursuit of their aims and objectives (Davies, 2002). In 2004 the Howard Dean campaign showed the growing power of Internet fund-raising and campaign communications. Larry Biddle and Stephanie Schriock (2005), two key members of Dean's team, pointed out that the number of on-line contributors doubled to four million between 2000 and 2004. They also emphasized the importance of this medium for political communication in 2004. Up to 34 million used the Internet to gain information on the candidate positions and 18 per cent of respondents to a Pew Research Centre poll claimed that the internet was one of their two major news sources. The Dean campaign took donations from almost 190,000 on-line donors and by February 2004 was communicating on-line with 630,000 supporters. It may have foundered early in the primary season but the skills it pioneered transferred rapidly to other campaigns, to be elaborated further — for example with weblogs and John Edwards's commencement of podcasting in 2005 to position himself for another presidential bid (Anderson, 2005). These developments may create new communities of activists connected to candidates, parties and issues. They also raise a difficulty for campaign regulators, since this growing advertising and communications market is not subject to those rules just recently imposed in an attempt to moderate traditional television and radio campaign rhetoric.

Re-mapping the Terrain: Declining Competition and Growing Polarization

Both campaigns in 2004 marshalled their resources carefully. Many states were effectively conceded as firmly in one or other camp at an early stage. Regardless of the success of both parties in raising more funds than in any previous presidential election year, and in spite of the anticipated closeness of the presidential race, there were swathes of the nation where voters were barely troubled by campaigners from the presidential election machines.

For the most part the Republicans remained strong in most states of the South, the Mountain West and the Great Plains, while the Democrats were pretty firmly planted in the Northeast and on the West Coast. The battleground was identified early as being about 17 or 18 states. The story that one campaign executive, when asked in early 2004 where he might be reached at a later date, was reported as muttering 'Ohio, Florida ... Florida, Ohio ... Ohio, Florida', may be apocryphal. Nevertheless it expresses accurately the central place that the political geography of the Electoral College has in presidential elections, especially when the evenly balanced nature of their popular support compels the major parties to develop new strategies to maximize their chance of victory. While voters in many states found 2004 a quiet year, the electorate in those states identified as critical may sometimes have felt transported to a virtual reality where they heard of little else but the presidential election. In some Ohio television markets two-thirds of all commercials shown in October 2004 were related to elections (Hadfield, 2005). When the presidential competition is localized in this way, large portions of the population can be artificially disengaged from the race.

Similarly in the House of Representatives close competition is not typical of most election races. Incumbent advantages in name recognition, fundraising, campaign resources and the delivery of constituency-favouring pork barrel have been evident for many years. In addition the partisan control of redistricting in most states makes gerrymandering part of the spoils of political success. Opposition party populations are corralled as much as possible into a small number of constituencies. Controlling party populations are used as efficiently as possible to maximize the number of safe seats. In such unpromising circumstances the recruitment of strong candidates becomes difficult. Making a hopeless bid for a US House of Representatives seat is a fairly desolate way of spending a year of one's life. It also entails considerable loss of money and requires an unreasonable amount of indulgence from family and friends. In 2004 only 32 of the 435 House races were so marginal that the victor took 55 per cent or less of the vote, and in 62 constituencies there was no major party opposition to the eventual winner (Cook, 2005d). In huge areas of the USA the voting population is barely being exposed to contemporary political debates through the electoral process.

It is clear, though, that in voting terms the 2004 election was the most partisan of recent times. In 2004, 93 per cent of self-described Republicans voted for Bush, compared to 91 per cent in 2000, 80 per cent in 1996 for Dole and 73 per cent in 1992 for Bush Sr. Meanwhile, 89 per cent of self-described Democrats voted for Kerry, compared to 86 per cent for Gore in 2000, and 84 per cent and 77 per cent for Clinton in 1996 and 1992 respectively. The 2004 loyalty rates were the highest in the eight elections since 1976 (Connelly, 2004). Moreover, having been tempted by third party candidates in recent elections, independents divided their votes in 2004 between the two major party candidates to give Kerry a one per cent edge.

Some analysts see a link between enhanced partisanship and the decline in publicly engaged competition. They point, in particular, to the decision by the Republican majority in the Texas legislature to redistrict that state in mid-decade solely in order to create an electoral map favouring the GOP. This form of 'rolling gerrymander', critics charged, was one of the factors driving centrists out of elective office and creating a more partisan, less co-operative legislature (Nivola, 2005). Recent House elections have seen Republican gains, but they have seen few incumbent losses. Incumbency re-election rates are at their highest ever, around 99 per cent in the most recent elections. In such a tightly managed duopoly, partisan change is slow in coming and likely to be slow to dislodge.

Twenty-first Century Opportunities

Recent Republican victories suggest that some climate change may be taking place in American electoral politics. The long forecast emergence of a new Republican majority may be at hand. Nevertheless, predictions of its arrival have to be hedged with qualification because the opposition is by no means down and out.

The Democrats have won 250 Electoral College votes and more in the last four presidential elections. They have also rolled up aggregate leads of over two million votes in the Nixon and Reagan megastates of California, New York and Illinois. There are other positive signs for the Democrats. Bush couched his campaign in the rhetoric of a war president and used symbolic events such as his landing on the USS Abraham Lincoln to reinforce his image as wartime commander-in-chief. He also had all the campaigning advantages that come with incumbency. He was leading a country that many believed was at least under threat of attack. He could appeal to Americans to remain with the president who had led the nation through its response to the attacks of September 2001 and did gain support from many who did not want to risk leadership change in the face of potential threat. He faced no nomination challenge from within his own political party. He refused federal support in the primaries, when his campaign raised more money than any presidential primary campaign in history, so he had open season to train the full force of his financial resources on John Kerry. With all these advantages, however, he barely shifted the political geography, with only three states changing hands, one of which was a Bush loss to Kerry.

In spite of this, the Republicans appear to possess some structural advantages in the post-2004 electoral environment. Their strength lies in many of the smaller states, giving them an immediate advantage in return on US Senators that they can get for their campaign resources. In tight races this also gives them a modest statistical advantage in the Electoral College. The GOP also has the lead in the fastest growing counties of the nation. They took all 25 of the nation's fastest growing counties in 2004, racking up 600,000 more votes than the Democrats in those counties alone — which might indicate a healthy future for the Republican party vote (Cook, 2005c). At presidential level the South shows every signs of being solidly Republican. If this remains so, then the GOP starts the presidential race with 168 Electoral College votes and needs just 102 from the other 370 to claim the White House. Most of the fastest-growing counties are in the Sunbelt. Accordingly, Republicans can look forward to the 2010 census bringing more Electoral College votes and more US House seats, into a South where they show every signs of remaining politically dominant.

The first decade of the new century gives Republicans a number of chances to achieve the 60 seats that would give them much stronger control of legislative decisions in Senate, and any such battles are likely to be well-resourced. The 2006 Senate races put more Democrat than Republican Senate seats on the line. Three of those Democrats won previously with only 49 per cent of the vote and three with 50 per cent or 51 per cent. Additionally, at least two other Democrats — Jeff Bingaman of New Mexico and Kent Conrad of North Dakota — have liberal Senate voting records far enough out of line with their state's political perspectives to make them tempting targets. The Republicans also will strive to punish Vermont's Jim Jeffords for his 2001 defection to Independent status. The Democrats have fewer obvious targets until later in the decade and even then will simultaneously have vulnerable seats of their own exposed.

In the House of Representatives the Republicans came out of the 2004 election with 232 of the 435 seats, but President Bush led his Democratic opponent in 255 House constituencies (Giroux, 2005). While there were 18 Republican members of Congress whose constituents gave a majority of their votes to Senator Kerry, the Democrats appear more vulnerable because Bush won a majority in 41 districts that they held. More of these Democratic seats have marginal majorities, and those in increasingly Republican regions, notably the South, appear especially vulnerable, particularly if they are affected by incumbent retirement. With Republican voters distributed relatively efficiently in contrast to the heavy Democratic concentration in urban areas, it will be a challenge for the Democrats to move seats back into their column.

A Responsible Republican Future?

The second George W. Bush victory was also accompanied by an apparent fall in split ticket voting. In total the voters in 59 House seats voted for the presidential candidate of one party, while choosing a Member of Congress from the other. At 14 per cent, this is the lowest proportion of split ticket seats at least since 1952. Only four years previously there had been 86 'split ticket' seats (20 per cent) (Giroux, 2005). In 1972, a generation earlier, the Democrats retained strong control of House and Senate seats in the Southern states and of Congress as a whole, at the same time that President Nixon gained a sweeping re-election victory. The Republicans may have had a 'southern strategy' to address this disparity, but they were starting from a position in which 192 House seats (44 per cent) were 'split ticket', mainly the result of Democratic strength at the local level even while the Republicans were developing the expertise of winning national elections.

The reduction in the proportion of 'split ticket' districts to its lowest point in modern times has come at the same time that the political parties on Capitol Hill are reported to be acting in a more organized partisan fashion. Voters in the 2004 election stayed more closely with their party identification than is commonly the case in US elections, and various voting groups were vocal in their claims that they would be holding the new administration to account on its policy agenda. And the Bush White House has certainly pressed an agenda of change. Over 50 years ago the

Committee on Political Parties of the American Political Science
Association expressed the opinion that the USA might benefit from a more
responsible party system. It could be that increased parallelism of party,
policy and ideological position suggests the potential for a period of
Republican dominance in an increasingly responsible party context.

Whether it was originally intended or prompted by circumstance,
President Bush's foreign policy has brought remarkable changes to
America's world position, but his administration has also had significant
impact on the domestic scene. First-term initiatives, notably regarding
homeland security, tax reduction and education reform, showed an unusual willingness on the part of Republicans to move strongly into domestic
policy guidance. Bush posed sweeping and potentially controversial initial
targets for a second administration, particularly the reform of social security. Simultaneously the Republican White House and Congress have
adopted more centralized policy-making and implementation processes
(VandeHei, 2005a). There are risks to such an approach, but in progressing
as though driven by a strong mandate, some Republicans perceived the
Bush administration's policy agenda as supplying the policy building blocks
of realigned support, using programmes to create an electoral coalition
invested into a Republican political future.

While its social security policies point America towards a debate about a
future where individuals need to be more careful with their money in order to
protect their long-term, pension-supported future, the Bush administration
was part of a new, spending Republicanism. As a share of GDP the federal
budget increased from 18.5 per cent to 20.3 per cent in the Bush first term
(Slivinski, 2005; Nather, 2005). The perceived terrorist threat and associated
expenditure accounted for much increased spending, but domestic outlays
also grew strongly. All cabinet-agency budgets increased in Bush budget
requests, and the Republican Congress was not shy in adding further spending on top of White House requests.

The 2004 Republican campaign worked hard to get out its vote, allocat-
ing three times its 2000 campaign spending to GOTV efforts (Abramson,
Aldrich and Rohde, 2005). The tradition is that increased turnout benefits
the Democratic Party, and certainly Kerry gained eight million more votes
than Gore in 2000, but this was more than offset by the growth of 11.5 million in the Republican vote. There could be reasons beyond party activity for
this increase, including the improvements in tabulating the vote that have
been implemented since the 2000 election (Wattenberg, 2005). Nevertheless
the difference in party political turnout improvement cannot be ignored. As
Democratic political consultant Dan Payne said after the election. 'We no

longer have the edge "on the ground".' There was a late rally of Bush support from independent groups, who spent US$30 million on TV and radio
ads in the final three weeks of the campaign, three times the Democratic
expenditure (Birnbaum and Edsall, 2004).

To be sure, independent groups promoting their agenda concerns can
be the core of a firm and long-lasting electoral coalition, but their expectations once victory is gained can be problematic. Different groups were
not hesitant in claiming credit for Bush's re-election. Richard Viguerie, a
conservative activist with a record of campaign innovation, attributed
Republican success in the presidential and congressional elections to
'conservative Christians and values voters'. He went on the pose a rhetorical question: 'If you don't implement a conservative agenda now, when
do you?' (Kirkpatrick, 2004, p. 1). In similar vein, James C. Dobson, of
the group Focus on the Family, pressed the point that 'the involvement
of millions of evangelicals, and mainline Protestants and Catholics' had
helped re-elect President Bush, obligating him to address their concerns
in his second term. Some of these groups have shown that they can be
hard taskmasters at least in the rhetoric of holding their elected officials
responsible. Without a majority of 60 the Republicans were still unable
to confirm all the judicial appointments that they wished to put through
the Senate. Republican threats to change the rules of procedure were followed by a compromise that had critics on both sides of the floor, but it
was James Dobson who went so far as decrying this as a 'complete
bailout and betrayal' (Balz, 2005, A11).

In a paper delivered in 1996 I said, 'The Democrats seem to have revert-
ed to Scammon and Wattenberg's Quadcali vision of victory — the
Northeast quadrant plus California. But it is even more clear now, as those
authors pointed out ... thirty years ago, that demographic shifts mean that
this coalition alone cannot win presidential elections ... broader national
coalitions are needed for consistent chance of victory.' With the South in
the Republican camp, I went on, 'It would be very exciting for observers, if
this culminates in a potential era of party competition. Certainly both sides
have plenty to fight for' (Davies, 1996). My opinion has not changed. The
GOP would appear to have an advantage in the House of Representatives
and the Senate, but in 2008 the 33 Senate seats up for election will include
21 held by Republicans. The party will not have an incumbent president
running. The Democrats may also face a hard primary season.

The Republicans have an opportunity to consolidate their position.
Walter Dean Burnham is sympathetic to the idea that the Republican
strength in all three branches could last a long time, 'if the Republicans

keep playing the religious card with the terrorism card' (Harris, 2004, p. 10). This resonates with John Kenneth White's assertion that the Democrats have to understand that issues and values are not the same thing, and therefore have either to adapt to the current value position or find ways of getting the voters to accept their issues within a values system (White, 2006). In similar vein, Ed Kilgore of the Democratic Leadership Council commented that his party needed 'to find a way ... to expand into hostile territory and that sure as hell is a challenge we face right now. We've got to become credible on issues where the people don't trust us' (Bresnahan, 2005).

Bush has the chance to end his administration with reviews like those for the 1924 *Thief of Bagdad*, 'compelling, deliberate', 'a work of rare genius'. But the Republican Party will be hoping that at the beginning of twenty-first century they can take the opportunity to consolidate their recent success and model the foreseeable political future on the earlier turn of the twentieth-century realignment that heralded decades of GOP dominance.

Notes

1. Much of the statistical data in this paper draws on information from issues of the *Rhodes Cook Letter*.
2. In Minnesota one of the ten Democrat electors cast a presidential vote for John Edwards in preference to John Kerry. I am assuming that if there was a real chance of a Democratic victory the 'faithless voter' would stick with the party choice, rather than clouding the waters in this way.
3. The statistics on campaign fundraising and spending are taken from various reports and press releases on the websites of the US Federal Election Commission (http://www.fec.gov), and the Centre for Responsive Politics (http://www.opensecrets.org).

10

Evangelicals and the Politics of Red America

Martin Durham

In the 2004 presidential election George W. Bush took 50.7 per cent of the popular vote for a lead of 2.4 per cent over his Democratic rival, John Kerry. On this occasion, he had avoided the embarrassment of winning an election without a popular vote majority, but his margin of victory was the smallest achieved by any incumbent president. Of the groups who made up the electorate, one was particularly significant in helping to put Bush back in the White House. Nearly one in four (23 per cent) of those who voted were white evangelicals, Christians who saw themselves as saved by their personal relationship to Christ. More than three out of every four (78 per cent) participating voters who shared this faith-based identity cast their ballots for George W. Bush.

For many years, the involvement of evangelicals in American politics has been the subject of considerable discussion, and much of the journalistic commentary that appeared in the aftermath of the president's re-election drew attention to the role of moral values and religious faith in the construction of a winning voting bloc. This was not the first time evangelicals had given a majority of their votes to Bush. An evangelical himself, he had gained 68 per cent of the votes cast in the 2000 presidential election by his fellow devotees. As commentators noted, however, the Bush organization had been disappointed by the failure of evangelicals to turn out in sufficient numbers to give the GOP standard-bearer a clear victory. In a speech in 2001 to the conservative American Enterprise Institute, the president's chief political adviser, Karl Rove, suggested that this was a crucial weakness in the Republicans' 2000 campaign (mindswell.org, 2001; Pew Research Center, 2004a). Much effort went into correcting this shortfall in the 2004 election, in which evangelical voter participation was higher.

In analyzing this development, discussion must focus not only the increased mobilization of evangelical voters but also the increased share of the evangelical vote won by Bush. How had this success been achieved? What role had evangelical groups themselves played in bringing evangelicals to the polls, and what role the Republican party? This in turn takes us to other questions. What do evangelicals expect from the political system? How had they seen the first term of the Bush presidency, and how were they likely to see the second? The 2004 election sheds a stark light on the role of evangelicals in American politics. Through examination of how the Republican White House (and the GOP party machinery) and the evangelicals responded to each other, we can better understand how and why the Bush administration was sustained in power.

It is important, however, to be cautious in linking the evangelical vote with the results in the so-called red states that went for Bush in 2004. Some 22 per cent of those evangelicals who voted did not cast their ballots for Bush. Nor did the size of his majority in the states which supported him correspond perfectly with the percentage of evangelicals in their populations. Alabama, for example, had 47 per cent of evangelicals in its electorate and gave a Bush majority of 62 per cent; Ohio had 27 per cent of evangelicals and a Bush majority of 51 per cent (Annenberg Public Policy Center, 2004; CQ Voting and Elections Collection, 2004). Furthermore, evangelicals were not the only religious group to cast a majority of votes for Bush. Though Kerry was a fellow-believer, 52 per cent of Catholics who voted backed Bush. So did 55 per cent of so-called mainline Protestant voters (those who did not claim a direct relationship with Christ). For all three of these religious groups, the key factor in support for Bush was the frequency of church attendance. A pre-election survey found that 52 per cent of intending voters in states that had gone for Bush in 2000 attended a religious service weekly compared with 34 per cent in states carried by Gore. A post-election survey similarly reported that 65 per cent of voters who attended church more than once a week supported Bush while only 45 per cent of those who attended only occasionally did so. In other words, Bush drew support from a range of faith-based groups, not just from evangelicals. Nor did religion represent the sole difference between blue states and red states — the latter, for example, had more gun owners than the former (Pew Research Center, 2004a; Newhouse News, 2004). Nevertheless evangelicals were a crucial element in Republican success, and to understand this better we need to turn to the role they played before the 2004 election.

Evangelicals first became a significant force in modern American politics in the 1970s. The increase in the legal abortion rate following the Supreme Court's 1973 *Roe v. Wade* decision to strike down restrictive laws on abortion, the rise of the gay movement and moves by the federal government to regulate Christian schools were all instrumental in the creation of a number of evangelical conservative organizations in the late 1970s.

This new movement, often described as the Christian Right, played a prominent role in Ronald Reagan's election victories of 1980 and 1984. In spite of this, failure to advance their substantive policy agenda resulted in the decline of Christian Right organizations by the late 1980s. Within a short time, however, a second wave of Christian Right mobilization had arisen, particularly helped by the election of Bill Clinton and resulting controversies over his support for both abortion and the right of gays to join the military. The most important of the new organizations, the Christian Coalition, was created by TV evangelist Pat Robertson following his unsuccessful bid for the Republican presidential nomination in 1988. Other key groups, such as Concerned Women for America and the Traditional Values Coalition, were survivors of the first wave. One of the most important organizations, Focus on the Family, represented a further permutation. Originating in the late 1970s, it had gradually become aligned with the Christian Right through itself taking up political issues and through forging an alliance with an explicitly political group, the Family Research Council. Its establishment of family policy councils in a large number of states provided an important boost for the second wave of mobilization of the Christian Right (Moen, 1992, pp. 52, 108–10; Boston, 2000, pp. 170, 200, 239; Diamond, 1996, pp. 68, 72).

Replicating the experience of the movement in the previous decade, the Christian Right of the 1990s found it extremely difficult to achieve goals such as banning abortion or restricting gay rights. Even the impeachment of President Clinton ended in disappointment. As a result Christian Right organizations again went into decline. But although organizational failings had weakened the movement, as they had in the 1980s, the second mobilization of the Christian Right had succeeded in penetrating the Republican Party. According to one estimate, in the early 1990s the Christian Right had strong influence (measured as 50 per cent or more of the seats on GOP central committees) in 18 states and moderate influence (measured as 25 to 49 per cent of seats) in 13 states. While the number of state committees with strong Christian Right presence remained the same in 2000, those with a moderate presence had doubled to 26 (Conger and Green, 2002, pp. 58–60, 64). As a complex of organizations, the Christian Right was weaker. Those who espoused its ideas within the Republican Party, however, had grown significantly stronger.

It is important to recognize, too, that the mobilization of evangelicals and the Christian Right is not always one and the same. Not all evangelicals supported the Republicans, as indicated by the sizeable minority who voted for Gore in 2000 and Kerry in 2004. Even those evangelicals who supported Bush should not be equated with the Christian Right, which is just one part of a broad evangelical milieu. The most important element in this wider sub-culture is the immense number of evangelical churches. Another sector is made up of parachurch ministries which cater to the different needs of evangelicals. (Focus on the Family, for instance, is best known for the advice it gives on child-rearing in a society seen as hostile to Christian values.) There are also national bodies set up to co-ordinate evangelical activity and to represent evangelical interests, of which three are particularly important. The National Association of Evangelicals has 30 million members from 45,000 churches. The National Religious Broadcasters bring together some 1,700 evangelical television and radio ministries. And while not solely composed of evangelicals, the 16 million strong conservative-led Southern Baptist Convention is the largest Protestant denomination in the United States (Kaplan, 2004, p. 40; Tumulty and Cooper, 2005, p. 43). It was through these and other channels, not just through the Christian Right, that evangelical views were brought to the GOP, and Republican views were conversely brought to evangelicals.

This had already become evident during Bush's first term. Evangelicals were crucial in securing the post of Attorney General for one of their own, John Ashcroft. Their importance was evident too in some of the venues at which the president spoke. In 2003, for instance, he addressed the National Religious Broadcasters conference, which subsequently went on to pass a resolution acknowledging the president's 'godly' leadership. The following year, he spoke at the National Association of Evangelicals convention, emphasizing his opposition to both abortion and gay marriage. Many Bush speeches were written by an evangelical, Michael Gerson, who drew on religious language for much of their power. This was particularly evident when he declared after 9/11 that good would prevail over evil because 'history has an author who fills time and eternity with his purpose'. Evangelicals' fellow-feeling with the president was particularly evident in the wake of the terrorist attacks. Ralph Reed, the former executive director of the Christian Coalition, declared that God had known that Bush could lead in such a moment. But still more was needed. Thus one of Rove's earliest actions after the 2000 victory was to recruit Tim Goeglein as deputy director of the White House Office of Public Liaison, a post whose responsibilities included forging a close relationship with evangelicals. As Richard Land, a leading figure in the Southern Baptist Convention, subsequently declared, 'In the Reagan administration, they would usually return our phone calls. In the Bush 41 administration, they often would return our phone calls, but not as quickly … In this administration, they call us' (Kaplan, 2004, pp. 34,

40–41, 84; Micklethwait and Wooldridge, 2004, p. 145; LifeSiteNews.com 2004; *New York Times*, 2004a; Campbell, 2004a, p. 79; Pastor Paul T. McCain Cyberbrethren, 2005; Frontline, 2004).

Most importantly, the forging of Bush administration policy was closely linked with the concerns of evangelicals, some of which pertained not to domestic issues but to foreign policy. The Christian Right, an enthusiastic supporter of Israel, believed that God had given the Holy Land to the Jews. An alliance between evangelical conservatives and human rights campaigners in the late 1990s had promoted enactment of legislation requiring the president to take action against countries violating religious rights. In Bush's first term this alliance successfully lobbied the administration to take up the Sudanese regime's persecution of Christians. As one campaigner explained, 'There are these issues below the radar screen that are of deep concern to the evangelical community, and while they are sincerely held by the administration, they also have the benefit of allowing the president to say, "I have responded to what you wanted me to do"' (Durham, 2004, pp. 150–1; Green, 2001, pp. 26–30; Bumiller, 2003, p.5).

Evangelicals saw much to admire in the Bush administration's foreign policy, but were far from uncritical. In the aftermath of 9/11, one of their leading figures, Franklin Graham, described Islam as an evil religion, only to have the White House distance itself from his view. Conversely, when Bush declared in 2003 that Muslims and Christians worshipped the same God, Richard Land replied that he was 'simply mistaken'. But if evangelicals disagreed with Bush's view of Islam, they were more disturbed by his policy towards Israel. Ralph Reed, who in 2002 had co-founded a pro-Israel group, declared that he was certain that Bush would never attack Israel's interests. Richard Land shared this belief. But in 2003 he and Moral Majority founder Jerry Falwell were among the signatories of a letter to the president expressing concern over his support for negotiations between Israel and the Palestinians. Pat Robertson, meanwhile, warned that Bush would be exposed to 'the wrath of the Lord' if he supported the division of Israel (Durham, 2004, pp. 148–52).

Bush's first term foreign policy, in other words, drew both support and criticism from conservative evangelicals. This was also the case with regard to the domestic issues most prominently associated with their campaigns. A number of Bush initiatives found particular favour with conservative evangelicals. One of his first acts as president was the reversal of Bill Clinton's decision to allocate government funds to organizations providing abortions overseas. In 2003, he signed into law the Partial-Birth Abortion

Ban Act, banning a particular operation which abortion opponents charac-terized as killing a child in the process of being born. The administration also allocated federal funds for sexual abstinence to be taught in schools. Finally, Bush supported the allocation of federal funds to religious chari-ties providing social services (Durham, 2005, pp. 91–2; Kaplan, 2004, pp. 40–53, 129–30, 209–15).

Other issues, however, were more problematic. Christian conservatives opposed federal funding of research on embryonic stem cells out of belief that it destroyed human life. Fearing that Bush would permit such funding, the Family Research Council warned in 2001 that he was in danger of frac-turing 'his pro-life base, which was essential to his election' and would be crucial for his re-election. The president's decision shortly afterwards to deny funds to such research except for those stem cells already gathered met with both praise and criticism from a divided Christian Right, with Dobson, for instance, taking the former position and the Family Research Council the latter. Commenting on this divide, one veteran conservative, Paul Weyrich, suggested that perhaps a quarter of social conservatives had become estranged from the president (Human Events, 2001; American Life League, 2002; lifeissues.net, 2001).

Most significantly, early attempts to build Republican support in the gay community were anathema to Christian conservatives. Eventually, the effort to secure both evangelical and gay support became impossible to continue because of the burgeoning controversy over gay marriage. In 1996, Congress had passed the Defense of Marriage Act declaring that for federal purposes marriage would be defined as between a man and a woman and allowing states to withhold recognition of a same-sex marriage conducted in another state. In 2003, however, the Massachusetts Supreme Judicial Court pronounced in favour of gay marriage and in the following year the Mayor of San Francisco issued marriage licences to same-sex cou-ples. Christian conservatives, who had long argued that the Defense of Marriage Act could fall prey to hostile judges, now urged that the only way to protect marriage was through a constitutional amendment. Bush's initial reluctance to promote such a measure exposed him to evangelical criticism (Durham, 2005, pp. 93–6).

In these circumstances, one conservative website reported in early 2003 that leading Christian conservatives were considering abandoning the Republican Party. The president of the Family Research Council, it noted, had declared that if Republican leaders would not vigorously defend mar-riage, then pro-family voters might reconsider their loyalty to the party. Michael Farris, a leading figure among those evangelicals who chose to teach their children at home, observed that discontented supporters of the family would not defect to the Democrats but might lose their enthusiasm for the Republicans (Newsmax. com, 2003).

As 2004 dawned, Christian Rightists remained unconvinced that the president was committed to the introduction of the Federal Marriage Amendment. A leading figure in Concerned Women for America warned of 'social conservatives who are not motivated to work for the ticket and to ensure their fellow Christians get to the polling booth'. The president of the Family Research Council also noted that 'our folks' might go 'AWOL when it comes time for the election' (*Washington Times*, 2004). Faced with this danger, the attempts to legalize gay marriage in Massachusetts and San Francisco finally gave Bush the opportunity to take a position that could shore up his evangelical support. In late February 2004, he declared himself in support of a constitutional amendment banning same-sex marriage.

To be sure, not all within the Christian Right, let alone all evangelicals, became estranged from the president during his first term. This was evident when Dobson, Falwell and the leader of the Traditional Values Coalition, Lou Sheldon, were among the evangelicals who attended the signing of the Partial-Birth Abortion Bill in 2002. Bush's signature, the Family Research Council declared, was 'a turning point in the debate over abortion' (Esther Kaplan, 2004, p. 129). In a subsequent meeting with the president, the participants joined hands in prayer. Shortly after, Falwell told the president that the people in the room represented around 200,000 pastors and 80 million believers who saw him as a man of God (Alternet, 2004).

The White House's outreach activities had helped to achieve this increasing closeness between the administration and conservative evangelicals. Land, Dobson and Ted Haggard, the president of the National Association of Evangelicals, were among the evangelical leaders who took part in a regular conference call with Tim Goeglein at 3.00 pm every Monday (Mobilization, 2004). The White House also deliberately targeted the most critical sections of the Christian Right. Thus in 2002, Rove was one of several administration officials who attended a meeting of the Family Research Council. Citing White House intent to fund state programmes encouraging marriage, Republican success in getting pro-life legislation through the House and Bush's nominations of conservatives to the federal courts, he called for closer co-operation. 'There will be some times you in this room and we over in the White House will find ourselves in agreement', Rove avowed, 'and there will be occasions when we don't. But we share a heck of a lot more in common than we don't' (Americans United, 2002).

To win re-election, the president needed not just to retain his 2000 level of support among evangelicals but to extend it. However, the Bush-Cheney campaign was not the only force seeking to win over evangelicals. Instead, three types of mobilization took place.

The first was what we can properly call the Christian Right, which intervened strongly in the election. The Christian Coalition claimed to have distributed 30 million of its voter guides which contrasted the policy stances of Bush and Kerry on issues ranging from gay marriage and abortion to child tax credits and the placing of American troops under UN control (Cochran, 2004, p. 2685; Christian Coalition, 2004). Both Pat Robertson and Ralph Reed had ceased to play central roles in the Coalition, and the most visible Christian Right figure was Focus on the Family's chairman, James Dobson. In the run-up to the 2004 election, leading figures in Focus on the Family were amongst those who signed an open letter which argued that the Bible gave guidance on such issues as the appointment of Supreme Court Justices, the fight against terrorism and gay marriage. The organization launched a website, iVotevalues.org, and created an offshoot, Focus on the Family Action, which organized rallies to get Christians to the polls. It was also was very active in many of the so-called battleground states. In Florida, for instance, the State Family Policy Council held around 25 gatherings of sympathetic pastors and worked with some 500 churches to mobilize voters (Church and State, 2002; CitizenLink, 2004; BP News, 2004b; Cochran, 2004, p. 2685). Among other Christian Right initiatives, Ohio pastor Rod Parsley, who had attended Bush's signing of the Partial-Birth Abortion Ban, launched a new organization, the Center for Moral Clarity, in 2004. He criss-crossed the country urging fellow-believers that they should vote and cast their ballots for a candidate who would protect the family. Meanwhile he gathered a list of 100,000 Ohio evangelicals to be telephoned by his church just before the election and reminded to vote (freerepublic.com, 2004; Parsley, 2005, p. 51; TheocracyWatch, 2004b).

A second mobilization centred on the Southern Baptist Convention, which set up an iVote Values website (the Focus on the Family site was based on it) and sent an 18-wheel tractor-trailer on the road as a mobile voter registration centre. Southern Baptist political education activities also focused on ensuring that registered voters knew where politicians stood on issues of concern to believers. 'Many Christians', Land declared, 'fail to consider biblical values when voting, often choosing candidates whose positions are at odds with their own beliefs.' Although officially non-partisan, such a stance clearly favoured conservative Republicans. At the Southern Baptists' 2003 annual convention, Tim Goeglein introduced a videotaped address from Bush, in which the president noted how he and Southern Baptists shared concern for marriage and pro-life values. The next day Ralph Reed, who had been made the Bush-Cheney campaign's Southeast regional co-ordinator, addressed a pastors' reception at the Convention, where names were taken of those willing to organize a voter registration Sunday, endorse Bush and organize a pastors' 'party for the president' (Cooperman, 2004; Cooperman and Edsall, 2004; BP News, 2004b; Florida Baptist Witness, 2003; TheocracyWatch, 2004a).

Reed's appearance at the Southern Baptist Convention was only one component of the GOP's own mobilization of evangelicals. At the 2004 Republican convention, he addressed a Faith, Family and Freedom Rally, which also heard a Bush video address setting out his opposition to abortion and gay marriage. A film, 'George W. Bush: Faith in the White House', was shown five times during the convention. For its own part, the Republican National Committee [RNC] appointed an evangelical outreach co-ordinator, Drew Ryun, the son of a Kansas Congressman. His role was to maximize evangelical turnout for the GOP through pastors' briefing meetings and providing churches with voter registration packets (Atlanta Journal-Constitution, 2004; Nieves, 2004; Post-Gazette, 2004; MASMinistries, 2004). The RNC also employed as a consultant David Barton, a vice-chairman of the Texas Republican Party. Barton was well known to evangelicals through his books and speeches which proclaimed that the separation of Church and State was a myth and that America had been born a Christian nation. In a report published shortly before the election Barton was described as having addressed pastors in some 300 RNC-sponsored lunches. He had told them, he explained to an interviewer, of 'the Biblical basis' of their involvement in civil government and the issues that were at stake. These meetings had been kept 'below the radar ... We work our tails off to stay out of the news'. But now, with voter registration largely ended and early voting already started, he declared that keeping quiet no longer mattered (Beliefnet, n.d.a).

At times Republican efforts to win over evangelicals caused offence to their target group. In July, Southern Baptists published an attack on a Bush-Cheney instruction sheet calling for church directories to be sent to state headquarters. To use such lists to contact possible Republican voters, Richard Land complained, was an unacceptable intrusion into the life of a congregation (BP News, 2004a). At other times, Republican efforts only offended opponents. Thus in two red states, Arkansas and West Virginia, the party sent out mailings warning voters that if 'Liberals' won, gay marriage would be allowed and the Bible would be banned (Kirkpatrick, 2004a).

Three forms of mobilization had taken place, by the Christian Right, the Southern Baptist Convention and the Bush-Cheney campaign itself. During the election, Reed had declared that the 2004 election was distinctive because 'for the first time, the effort to get out the socially conservative faith community has been fully integrated into the presidential campaign'. While recognizing that the GOP had not co-ordinated the whole gamut of activities to this end, he contended that it no longer expected someone else to mobilize 'the conservative faith vote' (Cooperman, 2004). Conversely, a post-election report in the *Washington Post* suggested that 'the untold story of the 2004 election' was not the mobilization of the evangelical vote by the Bush campaign but the independent campaigning of evangelicals themselves. Often, it suggested, these were better organized than the Republicans' efforts (Cooperman and Edsall, 2004). Reed may well have overstated the significance of the Republicans' mobilization. However, the *Washington Post* analysis conflated Republican electoral efforts to mobilize voters in the battle for the presidency with evangelical attempts to defeat gay marriage. It is important to distinguish between these different efforts, even at the same time as we try to inter-relate them.

In the aftermath of the presidential election, evangelical conservatives claimed that the approval of simultaneous referenda to prohibit gay marriage in 11 states (Arkansas, Georgia, Kentucky, Michigan, Mississippi, Montana, North Dakota, Ohio, Oklahoma, Oregon and Utah) had contributed to his re-election victory. In Ohio, the leader of a state Christian Right group commented that 'the president rode our coattails' (Hess and Dial, 2005, pp. 18–21; Americans United, 2004; *New York Times*, 2004b). As Bush's second term progressed, the prominence of the gay marriage issue and the unstable mixture of co-operation and conflict between the Republican Party and evangelicals continued to shape the unfolding of events.

The degree to which evangelicals and the GOP remained close was evident in the weeks following election victory. Whoever won, Richard Land declared, it would have been God's will, but Bush's victory had been a sign of His blessing. If Kerry had won, he went on, it would have shown God was cursing America (Beliefnet, n.d.b). Some evangelicals even credited the party for the mobilization of their followers. In his first post-election visit to the White House, Ted Haggard called in to congratulate Goeglein for his role in Bush's victory. 'He is the key person that actually produced the evangelical vote in America,' he subsequently commented. 'It was Karl Rove's initiative, but it was Tim that actually did it' (MediaTransparency, 2005).

Yet there were also tensions between the two camps. Responding to a White House telephone call thanking him for his efforts in the election,

James Dobson warned that the president needed to be 'more aggressive' about the issues evangelicals cared about. He subsequently made his views public: 'If the Republicans do what they've done in the past, which is to say, "Thanks so much for putting us in power, now we don't want to talk to you anymore," they will pay a severe price in four years and maybe two.' Tim Wildmon, the American Family Association's president, similarly declared that, 'We'll have to see what he does … I feel this time, with the strength of our groups, hopefully President Bush will do the right thing. If he wavers, we're here to let people know' (Slate, 2004; Hess and Dial, 2005, p. 21; *Western Recorder*, 2005).

In late January, Rove, Goeglein and others were among the attendees at a Christian Inaugural Eve Gala, where Rove thanked those attending for 'getting out the vote in a big way.' However, the gathering was not the love-in that had been anticipated because of recent remarks by Bush. Asked how strongly he would push for the Federal Marriage Amendment, the president declared that senators had made it clear to him that it would not pass so long as the Defense of Marriage Act was not ruled unconstitutional. Not all Christian Right leaders reacted negatively. Lou Sheldon, the leader of the Traditional Values Coalition, the Christian Gala's main sponsoring organization, expressed continued optimism about Bush's determination to secure passage of the amendment. In contrast, leading figures in Focus on the Family and the Family Research Council called the White House to protest. Many of the leading Christian conservatives also sent Rove a letter expressing their disappointment that the president was willing to spend a substantial amount of political capital on social security privatization when he was defeatist on the issue that was on the top of their agenda. Scott McClellan, the White House press secretary, issued immediate reassurances that the Federal Marriage Amendment remained a priority, and the text of his comments were e-mailed to the signatories of the letter (Slater, 2005; *Washington Times*, 2005a; TheocracyWatch, 2005; Tumulty and Cooper, 2005, pp. 30–1).

Other issues also came into play. A long-running controversy over a comatose Florida woman, Terri Schiavo, and moves to end her life finally came to a head. While primarily concerned with abortion and homosexuality, conservative evangelicals were also disturbed by euthanasia, whether voluntary or decided on by others. In the clash between Schiavo's husband, who sought the end of her life, and her parents, who opposed such a decision, evangelicals identified with the latter. A court decision to remove her feeding-tube led to frantic efforts to reverse or over-rule the decision, which resulted in Bush signing a hastily enacted congressional bill to take her case back to court.

'He's a man of faith and he acted as he did because it was the right thing to do,' Land commented. 'But the political reality is that if the president and pro-life leaders had not taken extraordinary action to address this extraordinary case, it would have had serious repercussions in our constituency on a whole range of issues.' In spite of this, Judge George Greer ordered the removal of the tube, and on 31 March Schiavo's life came to an end (Anon, 2005c; Campo-Flores, 2005, pp. 38–40; Dial, 2005, pp. 28–31).

As a result of the Schiavo case, evangelicals intensified action on a front that had already attracted their attention in Bush's first term. It was judges, Dobson declared in 2003, who were threatening to 'destroy the family and bring down this nation'. The Christian Coalition likewise argued that the judiciary had 'been overriding the will of the American people and legislating from the bench' (Esther Kaplan, 2004, pp. 260–61, 311, 313). This was not an attack on the judiciary as a whole. Instead, it was an argument about what view of judicial decision-making should prevail. For Christian conservatives, the choice was between judges who saw the Constitution as a living document and those who sought to return to the Founders' original intent. The former, they argued, were judicial activists, using their position to effect social change in a way that violated the Constitution; the judges that 'pro-family, pro-life folks' supported would defend it. Bush's first-term efforts to appoint conservative federal judges had been constrained by the Democrats' threat to filibuster Senate approval proceedings, a tactic that Land described as 'odious' (Cushman, 2005, pp. 22–6; Esther Kaplan, 2004, p. 261). The stand-off looked set to extend to Supreme Court nominations that were likely to come up in the second term, when a number of sitting justices of advanced years were expected to retire. Fear that Bush would be denied the opportunity to reshape the Supreme Court in support of their agenda mobilized conservative evangelicals into battle. In a fund-raising letter for the Family Research Council, James Dobson avowed: 'We didn't win the struggles and the battles that were before us on November 2. All we did was win the right to fight the battles … The judges have not changed. The Supreme Court is still the way it was' (Family Research Council, 2005).

As the conflict sharpened, Senate Majority Leader Bill Frist (Tennessee) participated in April 2005 in a Family Research Council-sponsored telecast, *Justice Sunday — Stopping the Filibuster against People of Faith*. He issued a stark warning that the right to filibuster should be removed if the Democrats continued to obstruct the president's judicial nominations. According to Paul Weyrich, Frist's appearance in the forum reflected his recognition that evangelical support was essential to his presidential ambitions in 2008. Meanwhile House Majority Leader Tom DeLay (Texas) sent a video message of support to a two-day conference on 'The Judicial War on Faith', in which the record of Supreme Court Justice Anthony Kennedy came under vigorous attack. One speaker charged that his opinion in *Lawrence v. Texas* (2003), which struck down the Lone Star state's anti-sodomy law, had drawn upon 'Satanic' principles derived from foreign law (*Washington Times*, 2005b; truthout.org, 2005).

As argued above, a range of issues will likely affect how evangelicals see the administration in Bush's second term. The president's policy towards Israel will continue to be important, and other aspects of foreign policy, for instance in Sudan, will still exercise evangelicals (Page, 2005; Nordlinger, 2005). But the core issues continue to centre on the family, the rights of evangelicals in the USA itself and, in both cases, the powers of the judiciary. Evangelicals have come into conflict with judges over such matters as the display of religious symbols or the Ten Commandments on public property (Anon, 2005b, p. 8; Anon, 2005d, p. 7). They have also returned to the offensive over abortion. The reversal of *Roe v. Wade* remains their goal and a central motive in their focus on how the administration might reshape the Supreme Court. But less dramatic measures continue to be pursued. In January 2005 Bush declared his support for two bills, one to require those carrying out late-term abortions to tell the woman that the unborn could feel pain, the other making it an offence for any adult other than a parent to take a girl across state lines to have an abortion (Anon, 2005a, p. 5). Even if enacted, such legislation could come under challenge in the courts, and it is around how judges are selected and how they reach their decisions that evangelicals will fight particularly hard. Across the range of the issues that have mobilized them, evangelicals will judge the Republican Party and the Bush administration. What conclusion might they reach?

As Karl Rove suggested in his 2002 speech to the Family Research Council, evangelical conservatives and the Bush White House had much in common. At the outset of Bush's second term, they shared a common concern for the federal encouragement of pre-marital abstinence, for denying government funding to agencies carrying out abortions abroad and for restrictions on abortion at home. They also faced a big battle, or more exactly a series of battles, to secure Senate approval of the conservative nominees they want to see placed on both the federal bench and the Supreme Court. As noted by *Christianity Today*, the leading evangelical magazine, Christian conservatives have raised millions of dollars ready to fight for the future composition of the Supreme Court (Carnes, 2005, pp. 66–7). Against that background, disappointment over the president's commitment to a Federal Marriage Amendment appeared likely to take second place. On the other hand, if Bush's judicial nominees fell short of their expectations, or if he did not show sufficient zeal in fighting for the approval of nominees acceptable to them, evangelical conservative support for the GOP could recede from its high level in 2004.

This is not to argue that evangelical support will be the deciding factor in 2008. When we consider Bush's two victories, we are inevitably drawn to the considerable support he received from evangelicals. But in addition to gaining 78 per cent of their votes in 2004, Bush gained a majority of Catholics. A report in 2001 had already noted that the White House was holding weekly conference calls with conservative Catholics, and that the administration had compiled a list of almost three million active Catholics in 14 states, each of whom had received at least two phone calls and two items of mail focusing on such issues as abortion and gay marriage. A report after the 2004 election suggested that the Catholic vote might have been at least as important as the evangelical vote in the president's victory. The Bush campaign, it noted, had appointed 50,000 Catholic team leaders at local level (Lizza, 2001; beliefnet, n.d.c). If the Catholic vote was crucial, Bush also achieved majority support among mainline Protestants, and voters defined in other ways, by income or gun-ownership, were part of a diverse coalition that brought the Republicans victory.

Yet, as we have seen, within that coalition, the support of conservative evangelicals has been crucial. Since they began to be mobilized in the late 1970s, they have prioritized such issues as opposition to abortion and homosexuality. This has not meant that they have failed to pursue a broader agenda that has included defence of institutions at home and advocacy of a Christian foreign policy abroad. Indeed, as a cursory glance at the Christian Coalition's 2004 voters' guide should remind us, it has even involved taking up economic issues, particularly if they were concerned with the family. But moral issues are at the core of a mobilization that has brought evangelicals close to the Republican Party and taken the Republican Party close to evangelicals. Each has adjusted how it pursues its objectives. Evangelicals have entered enthusiastically into both interest group politics and the internal life of the Republican Party itself. Conversely, the GOP has taken up evangelical concerns, partly in pursuit of evangelical votes but also because evangelicals who have become active within the party demanded that it take up their concerns.

This has not meant that Republicans and evangelicals have become indistinguishable. The GOP responds to a variety of pressures and pursues a variety of objectives, and the concerns of conservative evangelicals are but one factor in its calculations. To secure and maintain evangelical support has been crucial for Republican success, but it has also proved prob-

lematic. Conservative evangelicals fervently hope that a conservative
Republican president will adopt their priorities, but at the same time they
fear that just as Reagan proved a disappointment, so too will George W.
Bush. Yet if there are significant elements of continuity between evangelical politics in the 1980s and evangelical politics 20 years later, there are
also important elements of discontinuity. Opposition to stem cell research
is now a key issue. Concerns that had arisen in the earlier period, notably
evangelical support for Israel or opposition to euthanasia, have risen in
importance. Opposition to homosexuality was already important for evangelical mobilization in the Reagan years, but it has sharpened dramatically,
and campaigning against gay marriage has become central to conservative
evangelicals. The importance of the judiciary has escalated dramatically.
Seen as the reason why evangelical demands have often been unsuccessful, liberal judges are held to be the enemy, conservative judges as the solution. Against the background of these elements of continuity and discontinuity from the late 1970s to the early twenty-first century, evangelicals
have forged a relationship with the GOP which brings their demands to
the fore of American politics. It is a position which the second term of
the Bush administration could sorely test.

11

Whither Blue America?

Alex Waddan

The soul-searching that followed the election defeat of November 2004 was hardly a new experience for the Democratic Party. There have been important additional twists to the narrative in recent years, but what has been apparent to all observers of American politics over the last generation is that the Democrats have been mired in a prolonged identity crisis as the different factions that call the party 'home' have engaged in a drawn out blame game following the latest electoral setback. Much of this infighting is a product of the nature of American political parties which are broad tent coalitions made up of quite diverse elements. When things go wrong it is not surprising that there is a tendency for the different elements of the coalition to point the finger at each other; and in this context there has been good reason for the Democratic coalition to engage in angst as the long-term decline in the party's electoral fortunes has been stark. A generation ago the Democrats were still the majority party in American politics but that political order, driven by the New Deal, has manifestly ended. The votes cast in 2004, in producing unified Republican government in Washington DC, merely confirmed this once again. Moreover, opinion polls asking about party identification demonstrated that even on this measure, where the Democrats held sway even throughout the Reagan era, the party's advantage has evaporated (Dunn and Slann, 1994, p. 262: Exit Poll, 2004). Indeed, the most optimistic Democrat spin could only depict George Bush's America as an evenly divided political nation.

Not surprisingly, there was a further bout of Democratic introspection following the defeats in November 2004. In fact the recriminations were perhaps less acrimonious than usual since the party did largely ally itself with Senator Kerry's candidacy for the presidency. Historian Alan Brinkley noted that while Kerry was 'never anyone's idea of a perfect candidate ... he helped unite Democrats in a way they have not been united in a generation' (Brinkley, 2004, p. 18). The congressional results were disappointing but hopes had not been high for success in this arena (Cohen, 2004). Thus, while there were criticisms of Kerry's performance as a candidate and his some-times uncertain message (Kuttner, 2004), there was less ideological blood spilt on the carpet than following the defeats for Walter Mondale in 1984, Michael Dukakis in 1988 and Al Gore in 2000. In the aftermath of those reversals, and particularly the heavy beatings handed out to Mondale and Dukakis, the Democrats verged on ideological civil war as the party's liberals and centrists offered their quite different diagnoses of what had gone wrong and hence put forward quite distinct prescriptions for how to recuperate.

While the party's post-2004 self-analysis did not match the ferocity of the inquisitions that took place 20 years earlier, it did engage in important debates about how to move on. It was manifest that the Democrats need-ed to be more competitive across the US if more of the political map was to turn blue, but it was not so obvious how this is to be achieved. Some liber-als insisted that the party could win in red states by sending out a more pop-ulist economic message that is, 'us-versus-them red meat, straight talk about how the system is working against ordinary Americans' (Sirota, 2005, p. 28). Centrists cautioned against such an approach, warning that increased politi-cal polarization would only further alienate those voters who had turned their back on the Democrats. Instead, they wanted Democrats to woo Republican voters by emphasizing that they 'have much in common on many issues, like family values, not just economic concerns' (Range, 2004).

Nevertheless, there were some rays of hope for the Democrats. Political commentators John Judis and Ruy Teixeira caused a stir, at least within the party's elite circles, with their book *The Emerging Democratic Majority*, pub-lished in 2002. The title was a direct echo of Kevin Phillips' *The Emerging Republican Majority*, published in 1969 (Phillips, 1969). Judis and Teixeira based their prediction on two broadly defined trends (Judis and Teixeira, 2004, pp. 165–77). First, they regarded America's post-industrial economy as an uncertain one where many workers felt insecure about their jobs and associated fringe benefits, such as healthcare. In such circumstances, they anticipated that voters would turn to the Democrats who, through policies such as the Earned Income Tax Credit and investment in worker training, had demonstrated that they understood the fickle nature of the post-indus-trial economy and knew how to use government as a tool to regulate the inequities and excesses produced by modern capitalism. In contrast, the Republicans were deemed to be too committed to an unfettered free mar-ket to offer the protections that many people needed. Secondly, Judis and Teixeira argued that the GOP had become so far in hock to the religious right that they were now the extremists on issues such as gay rights and stem cell research. In their view more voters would be put off by this insistent cultural conservatism than would be attracted by it.

The broad sweep of Judis and Teixeira's argument is that the conservative political hegemony of the 1980s was a reaction to the social and economic tumult of the 1960s and 1970s. In the late 1960s the conservative movement gained political momentum as many Americans were turned off by the noisy demands made by the 'civil rights protesters, feminists, environmentalists, welfare rights organizers and community activists'. Then in the 1970s, as the economy stagnated, people questioned the value of 'government programmes that cost too much and accomplished too little'. The subsequent conservative policy backlash, however, in turn proved to be too extreme; and just as the Republicans were overplaying their hand, the Democrats recovered their equilibrium through the 1990s. Hence, the 'emerging Democratic majority is a corrective to this Republican counterrevolution' (Judis and Teixeira, 2004, p. 164). Clearly, if measured by electoral results from 2000 through 2004, these predictions have not materialized. Although the two analysts maintain that the fundamentals of their argument still stand, they acknowledge that the anticipated transformation of American politics was delayed by 9/11. In their opinion the events of that day disrupted the evolving political map by putting security back on the agenda to the advantage of the Republicans. This particularly helped George W. Bush to reinforce support among the white working class who had voted for Reagan but had been persuaded of the virtues of Clintonism (Judis and Teixeira, 2004; 2005).

The Two Majorities Thesis

One aspect of the Judis and Teixeira thesis that jars with the current conventional wisdom is its assertion that the Democrats will be the net beneficiaries of the so-called culture wars. Indeed the immediate aftermath of the 2004 defeats saw many Democrats ponder aloud about how to re-connect the party with those voters in red America who appear to have turned to the GOP not as a consequence of rational pocketbook calculations but because of a sense that the Republicans better represent traditional American values than the Democratic Party does. As it is, the debates about how exactly to interpret the data from the 2004 opinion polls continue but the suggestion that the Democrats are out of touch with many Americans on cultural questions is *not* new. Indeed, the question of how to balance and express the party's commitments on socio-economic matters and on cultural ones has been at the heart of much of the party's in-fighting since the 1960s.

In hindsight it is evident that Phillips' prediction in 1969 was a prescient one. The New Deal liberal consensus unravelled at the end of the 1960s and into the 1970s. Indeed, in retrospect, it is possible to trace the fault lines of the New Deal coalition back to its foundations as President Roosevelt built a winning majority that included northern liberals and African-Americans together with the white voters of the segregated southern states. The inherently unstable nature of this union was dramatically exposed in 1948 when Strom Thurmond, the Democratic Governor of South Carolina, stormed out of the party's national convention in protest against the commitment to undo racial discrimination. Thurmond then stood in the 1948 presidential election as the States' Rights Democratic candidate. This did not prevent Harry Truman's re-election but Thurmond did win his home state plus Louisiana, Mississippi and Alabama. According to Thomas and Mary Edsall, Thurmond's 1948 campaign was 'of profound importance', as it illustrated how the issue of race could, and would further, disrupt the Democratic Party (Edsall with Edsall, 1991, p. 34).

On the surface the party appeared to survive the dislocation of 1948 as Kennedy narrowly won the White House in 1960 and Johnson did so emphatically in 1964. Yet, even the 1964 triumph was clouded by evidence of the ongoing political transformation of the South where Republican candidate Barry Goldwater carried five states. And, by the end of the 1960s, race issues had combined with foreign policy and social issues — where compromise was difficult to come by — to wrench the Democratic Party apart (Lengle, 1981; Matusow, 1984; Morgan, 1994; Mayer, 1996). The war in Vietnam undermined the Cold War certainties of Kennedy's inaugural address; the Civil Rights Acts exposed the incompatible attitudes towards race within the party; and ghetto riots and in general the rise in violent crime pushed 'law and order' to the top of the political agenda to the benefit of Nixon and the Republicans.

What these new issues had in common was that they were not perceived primarily as economic problems.[1] Not being an obvious part of the New Deal package that had established the Democrats as the majority party, they generated a series of internal rifts. These divisions were highlighted in 1972 when, with new rules governing the primary election process, the Democrats gave a public display of all their agonies (Polsby, 1983; Shafer, 1983). The ultra-liberal George McGovern finally emerged as the party's candidate but he was crushed in the general election as at least one-third of Democratic party identifiers voted for Nixon (Mayer, 1996, p. 6). Nixon's misdemeanours gave the Democrats a chance to regroup but the concerns raised in the late 1960s and early 1970s about the nature of American life persisted after the end of the Vietnam war and after the white South had reconciled itself to the end of Jim Crow. Critically for the Democrats, this made it difficult to refocus political debate on economic progress for working Americans which had been the bedrock of the New Deal's electoral success.

What emerged in the late 1960s, and has become increasingly evident since then, is that American politics has divergent, if not quite distinct, dimensions that divide the American public in cross-cutting ways. This concept was comprehensively articulated in the mid-1990s by Byron Shafer and William Claggett. In *The Two Majorities* (1995), they argued that the American public had something of a split personality when popular attitudes across a range of issues were studied in terms of a standard liberal–conservative model. While partisan activists on both sides of the ideological divide were consistently liberal or conservative across issues, many of the public were not so logical in their preferences. Hence, Shafer and Claggett found that on economic and social welfare issues, such as Medicare and social security, the majority public preference was for liberal policy options, giving political advantage to the Democrats. On the other hand, they also found a presiding majority conservative sentiment on cultural and foreign policy issues which favoured the Republicans. Thus, if it was possible to identify a hypothetical single median voter, he or she would be moderately liberal on the economic and social welfare dimension of American politics, yet conservative on the cultural and foreign policy dimension. According to Shafer and Claggett, all things being equal, the former factor would be more likely to affect voting behaviour than the latter. This finding appeared to be good news for the Democrats and to give them a natural electoral advantage over their opponents. However, the proviso 'all things being equal' entailed an important qualification. While the issue contexts and the underlying preferences outlined by the 'two majorities' thesis have operated at a fundamental level, they could, and increasingly have been, disrupted by the fluctuations of political events, with a consequent dislocation of expected voting patterns. A sustained period of emphasis on cultural and foreign policy issues consequently handed the electoral edge to the GOP.

For Democrats the immediate question is why cultural issues have trumped socio-economic ones so regularly in recent elections. In reviewing the Clinton presidency Shafer reflected that the 'two majorities' thesis still held true inasmuch as Democrats remained better trusted 'to handle economic and welfare issues' and the Republicans were favoured on cultural matters. The problem for the Democrats was that the latter type of issue had come to have 'a substantially greater priority' (Shafer, 2000, p. 29). Indeed, a reprise of Clinton era policy and politics provides a revealing insight into opportunities and threats that the Democratic party faced as it came to terms with the redrawing of the political map in 2004.

Democratic Strengths: It's the Economy Stupid.

Clinton's 1992 campaign stands as a testimony to a political strategy which emphasized economic concerns and took a moderate tone on cultural ones. Primarily, his election and re-election demonstrated the value of being a challenger when the economy is in a downturn and an incumbent when the economy is healthy. In mid-1991 the Republican incumbent, President George Bush Sr., was assumed by many to be a shoo-in for re-election because of his foreign policy triumphs. By 1992, however, the electoral battleground was the state of the American economy and the Democrats were at last on comfortable terrain. The famous campaign mantra, 'It's the economy, stupid', made it clear that the Clinton team was focused on exploiting the perceived weakness of the US economy in 1992. In turn, the economic downturn and the prospect of rising unemployment exacerbated fears about access to healthcare for those Americans whose health insurance was related to their job (Shafer, 2003, p. 40). Clinton's effort to legislate health care reform turned sour through 1994 but in 1992 it appeared to be a winning issue for the Democrats (Skocpol, 1997). Furthermore, Clinton's political rehabilitation after the 1994 mid-terms came about when he vetoed Republican budget cuts to Medicare and Medicaid, as he symbolically used the same pen to veto the cuts as President Johnson had used when signing these programmes into law 30 years earlier. Towards the end of his presidency Clinton flirted with idea of social security reform but eventually settled for scoring political points by presenting himself as the protector of the traditional social security programme (Beland and Waddan, forthcoming).

On the other hand, there were signs through the 1990s that the complexities of the global economy could produce serious disruption within Democratic ranks. Most publicly, the White House battled with congressional Democrats over a series of trade issues. The disputes over NAFTA in 1993 (Livingston and Wink, 1997), reauthorization of so-called 'fast-track' authority in 1997 (Harris, 1997) and trade with China in 2000 (Nitschke with Tully, 2000) exposed a fundamental difference in ideas about how best to respond to the global economy and the uncertainties this brings with it (Destler, 1999). In 2004 Democrats papered over these disagreements, but John Edwards's espousal of the protectionist cause suggested that this may be an enduring fault line within the party.

Democratic Weaknesses: Security and Cultural Politics

In terms of dealing with cultural issues Clinton's time in office illustrated contrasting dynamics. Clinton's political identity in 1992 was very much tied to the Democratic Leadership Council (DLC). At the time of its formation in 1985 its centrist inclinations were apparent but it did attract people from across the party who agreed on the need for a rethink (Hale, 1995). After 1988, however, it became a more divisive grouping as it aggressively promoted itself and its message denouncing 'liberal fundamentalism'. A particularly significant expression of the DLC's perspective, published in 1989, was entitled *The Politics of Evasion* (Galston and Kamarck, 1989). In this William Galston and Elaine Kamarck, who both went on to work in the Clinton-Gore administration, attacked the liberal activists in the Democratic Party for alienating many voters by emphasizing their liberal credentials on issues such as crime and defence, while downplaying the party's more appealing message on 'social and economic progress' (Galston and Kamarck, 1989, p. 27). For the DLC, Dukakis's candidacy was an unmitigated disaster because it allowed the Bush team to portray him as soft on crime and reluctant to stand up for America's best interests.[2] As Wilson Carey McWilliams reflected, 'Where Democrats once ran against Hoover, Republicans ran against McGovern in 1988 and George Bush argued repeatedly that "neighbourhood Democrats" should prefer him to a leadership dominated by "the remnant of the '60s"' (2000, p. 58).

As a candidate, Clinton was aware of the need to not to leave himself vulnerable to accusations that he was a limousine liberal. One obvious manifestation of this was his support for the death penalty. Crime played a lesser role in the 2004 elections, but in the late 1980s and early 1990s it was a key issue. Opposition to the death penalty hurt Dukakis, as it did Mario Cuomo when he lost his re-election bid for governor of New York in 1994.

Once in office, however, Clinton was soon to realize that cultural issues can develop a life of their own and overshadow efforts to concentrate attention on the social welfare agenda. The early days of his presidency were blighted by the argument over whether or not to end the ban on gays in the military. Then in April and May 1993 the Lani Guinier affair took the headlines (Drew, 1994, pp. 204–10). The problem for the Clinton administration was that popular concern over these perceived displays of cultural liberalism spilled over to distort understanding of the administration's efforts elsewhere. As Baer reflects in his study of the New Democrat movement, these early episodes combined 'to send an Old Democratic, culturally liberal message to the public' and made it 'easier for Republicans to portray any of Clinton's initiatives as traditional Democratic policies' (2000, p. 213).

The issue of gays in the military in particular was seen as responsible for the early drop in Clinton's approval ratings (Drew, 1994, p. 48; Baer, 200, p. 212). Indeed, according to Sidney Blumenthal, 'Clinton's poll numbers fell twenty points in his first two weeks almost entirely on the basis of this one issue' (Blumenthal, 2003, p. 53). Clinton himself later reflected on polling done at the time which illustrated why the issue was such a bad one for the administration: 'Only 16 per cent of the electorate strongly approved of lifting the ban [on gays serving in the military], while 33 per cent strongly disapproved' (Clinton, 2004, p. 485). Hence, John White's conclusion that by 1994 the combination of the gays-in-the-military, the Brady Bill and the healthcare plan 'reminded voters why they disliked Democrats in the first place. Many began to suspect they had elected George McGovern rather than Bill Clinton' (2003, p. 127).

In the end Clinton did reassert some control over the cultural agenda by downsizing the debate and concentrating on a series of micro-issues to get on the right side of the family values debate. He thus championed school uniforms and the V-chip as a means of giving parents control over what their children watched on television. He also signed into the law the Defense of Marriage Act of 1996 (DOMA), which stated that the federal government would only recognize heterosexual marriages. The gay community disapproved, but preferred Clinton to Dole, who was the original sponsor of DOMA (Carney, 1996). Apart from continuing questions about his character Clinton 'had otherwise succeeded in putting the cultural-values cluster to sleep, neutralizing Democratic disadvantages within it' (Shafer and Claggett, 2003, p. 45). Thus in 1996 values issues did not play loud enough to drown out the harmonious mood music made by the purring economy. Of course, in the end Clinton's own behaviour undermined his effort to be a champion of family values. The Lewinsky affair also made it difficult for Al Gore to exploit fully the positive aspects of Clinton's legacy in 2000. Indeed it was widely speculated that Gore chose Jo Lieberman as his vice presidential candidate because the Connecticut senator was the first prominent Democrat to make a public attack on Clinton for his behaviour (Sapiro, 2002, p. 16).

In 2000 Gore and Lieberman aggressively protested their own personal morality and their faith (Hansen, 2002, p. 274). In doing so, they succeeded in countering the Lewinsky legacy as polls showed Gore tied with Bush when respondents were asked who would provide the strongest moral leadership for the country (White, 2003, p. 162). On the downside, however, the Democratic *Party* fared poorly when contrasted with the Republicans. Polling showed the Democrats trailing the GOP significantly when voters were asked which party best knew right from wrong, which party they trusted most to uphold traditional family values and which would best protect religious values (White, 2003, p. 162). A Pew Research Center poll in the aftermath of the 2000 elections 'found that 49 per cent of Americans trusted the Republicans to improve moral values, while only 26 per cent trusted the Democrats to do so' (Greenberg, 2001).

When examining the political dynamics of the 1990s, and explaining Clinton's success in keeping the focus on socio-economic affairs, it is important to reflect on the dog that lost its political bark throughout the decade. Foreign policy had minimal impact on domestic electoral politics during the Clinton era. It was particularly beneficial to Clinton that the end of the Cold War diminished the scrutiny of his credibility as a potential commander-in-chief. Even in the 2000 campaign George W. Bush preferred to keep foreign policy, traditionally a Republican strength, off the agenda. In hindsight, however, it seems likely that the 1990s was an anomalous era. The 9/11 attacks, the ensuing war on terror and the Iraq war restored national security issues to the forefront of American politics (Yglesias, 2004).

The Two Majorities in 2004

In many ways the 2004 election conformed to the two majorities thesis. The exit polls showed that Kerry, like Gore, did best amongst those voters who prioritized issues along the socio-economic dimension. For example, of the 52 per cent of respondents who thought that the economy was 'not good' or 'poor', 79 per cent voted for Kerry. Furthermore, of those voters who prioritized health care as a key issue, 77 per cent voted for Kerry (Exit Poll, 2004). Most efforts to explain the result, however, have focused on Bush and his majorities amongst those who felt cultural and/or security issues to be the most important.

In the immediate aftermath of the 2004 elections two pieces of evidence emerged that were quickly interpreted to support the assertion that the Democrats were out of touch on culture issues. First, the exit poll result which showed 22 per cent of voters citing 'moral values' as the most important issue in the presidential election, with 80 per cent of their number voting for Bush (Exit Poll, 2004). Second, was the fact that all 11 states conducting ballots on gay marriage voted to bar the practice, with the corresponding assumption that the issue had been important in mobilizing social conservatives. The presence of Ohio, which had lost over 230,000 jobs during the Bush years, among those 11 states certainly gave added piquancy to the perception that culture and values were critical factors in determining the election outcome. Indiana GOP representative Mark Souder explained:

'Those issues were clearly overpowering economic issues in the Midwest' (Nather, 2004, p. 2588). Certainly some liberals were angry about the manner in which the Massachusetts Supreme Court and San Francisco officials put the gay marriage issue on the political agenda. The day after the election California Senator Dianne Feinstein lamented that the topic had arisen 'too fast, too soon, too much' (Wildman, 2004, p. 39). According to the liberal commentator Paul Starr, 'the reaction against gay marriage ... triggered a huge evangelical turnout, probably tipping Ohio and thus the electoral college' (Starr, 2004, p. 4). Bill Clinton also concluded that 'the gay-marriage issue ... was an overwhelming factor in the defeat of John Kerry' (Schneider, 2004).

However, there have been more sceptical reflections on the significance of the moral values and gay marriage issues. First, the methodology of the National Election Pool exit poll has been queried. Voters identifying 'moral values' as their key concern were responding to a multiple-choice question. In more open-ended polls conducted prior to the election, respondents did not specify 'moral values' as a prominent concern. Furthermore, the actual term 'moral values' was hardly a precise one with an unequivocal meaning. There was room for dispute over the significance of the various gay marriage initiatives. For example, in 2004 Bush gained one point in Ohio against his performance in 2000, but this was below his average national improvement of 3.1 per cent (Giroux, 2004).[3] Moreover, while the number of evangelical voters increased in 2004, the same was true for most categories of voter.

Nevertheless, it would be wrong for Democrats to use such methodological niceties to deny the force of these issues. The phrase 'moral values' may be vague, but it surely conveyed a message. In any case, there were a series of other voting gaps that reinforced the impression that the electorate was divided along cultural or value lines. There was clearly a 'God gap', with more regular church attendance correlated to likelihood of being a Bush voter. The 'marriage gap' was also significant, with 57 per cent of married voters (63 per cent of the electorate) supporting Bush. The 'gun gap' saw 63 per cent of households with a gun owner vote for Bush, whereas only 43 per cent of those without a gun owner did so (Exit Poll, 2004). Moreover, these gaps cannot be dismissed as one-off blips as many of the same trends were apparent in 2000 (Greenberg, 2001; Wolfe, 2001).

This data has led to much Democratic soul-searching. In 2004 gay rights was a core party commitment, but it was clear that gay marriage was not acceptable to the majority of Americans. Kerry did come out publicly against gay marriage, but if it is true that Clinton suggested to him that he should support the state initiatives to ban it, then he did not follow this advice

(Wildman, 2004). In this regard it is worth noting that Kerry was one of only 14 senators to vote against the 1996 DOMA (Schneider, 2004). Abortion, too, surfaced in the post-defeat debate as pro-life Democrats claimed that they had been effectively silenced by the strident pro-choice wing of the party. Tim Roemer, a former Democratic congressman from Indiana and a pro-life advocate, complained that the image of the party was not so much 'pro-choice' as 'pro-abortion' which hurt it among 'churchgoing African-American, Latino, Catholic, rural and suburban voters' (Roemer, 2005).

The challenge facing Democrats with regard to these contentious cultural and moral issues is to craft compromise positions that defuse the passion of the opposition yet satisfy the party's own base and which are robust enough to stand up in the heat of partisan competition. On gay rights, the data suggested that it might be possible to develop a conciliatory message. The exit polls found that the 37 per cent of respondents who opposed any legal recognition for gay couples voted overwhelmingly (70 per cent) for Bush. Against this, however, a majority favoured some legal recognition, with 25 per cent supporting gay marriage (77 per cent voted for Kerry) and 35 per cent supporting civil unions. Interestingly of the latter group, 52 per cent voted for Bush (Exit Poll, 2004). It can be deduced from this that the culture debate is more nuanced than is sometimes assumed.

On the other hand, the difficulty in finding the route to compromise is well illustrated by the post-election debate about abortion. Shortly after the election Senator Hillary Clinton of New York suggested that the Democrats emphasize that abortion should be 'safe, legal and rare' rather than just championing the legal part of this equation. Her point was that Democrats should not give up a principle, but should express their regret over the number of abortions taking place. At the same time, however, pro-choice groups made it clear that they would oppose anti-abortion candidates running in Democratic primaries (Babington, 2005; Kirkpatrick, 2005). Furthermore, the politics of abortion is not a one-way street running in the GOP's direction. In 2000 Gore's pollster, Stanley Greenberg, found that Bush's opposition to abortion was the single biggest reason that women opposed him (Judis and Teixeira, 2004, p. 55).

Hence, the 2004 elections and their aftermath revealed that the overall picture on the culture question was a complex one. Democrats needed to avoid alienating culturally conservative Americans, but without simply abandoning their own base. Nevertheless it was evident that, while the politics of cultural issues could be cross-cutting, the prediction that cultural issues would backfire on the Republicans had not yet transpired. Judis and Teixeira contended that the GOP, 'goaded by the religious right, have become the defenders of the mores of Middletown against those of the post-industrial metropolis' (2004, p. 174). The evidence from 2004 showed that Middletown's values still carry plenty of punch.

On the question of security, Judis and Teixeira echoed the two majorities thesis. Indeed, of the 19 per cent of voters who named terrorism as their prime concern, 86 per cent voted for Bush. In the opinion of former presidential candidate, Michael Dukakis, Bush 'won it ... on the national security issue' not on gay marriage or the appeal to the religious right (Schneider, 2004). Regardless of whether cultural or security issues were more decisive with voters, the problem from the Democrats' perspective was that the combination of these topics, at the centre of the campaign, exposed the party's weakest flank. Of course, part of Kerry's appeal in the primaries was his military record and the Democratic convention was dominated by messages about Kerry's military service. Amongst the 15 per cent of voters who prioritized the Iraq war as an election issue, he won 73 per cent support. Fundamentally, however, Kerry failed to convince the electorate of his credentials as a leader in the war on terror. The Republican convention was devoted to promoting Bush's qualities as just such a leader. The president emerged from the New York gathering with a lead in the polls that he maintained through the remainder of the election campaign (Judis and Teixeira, 2005, p. 24).

The Democratic Coalition

Of course, the bottom line from an electoral perspective is that the Democratic Party must put together a winning coalition for the 2008 presidential election. In comparison with the winning Republican coalition, this will inevitably have to be a more heterogeneous coalition, which carries attendant problems. The GOP has its ideological dilemmas but these have tended to be overshadowed by the Democrats' internal conflicts. In addition any Democrat coalition for 2008 and beyond is bound to be ethnically and racially diverse. In this sense it might help that the country is becoming more diverse, but the Democrats cannot take for granted that minority groups will automatically ally with them and, critically, they must still do better with the majority white population.

Judis and Teixeira (2004) argued that the winning Democratic coalition would consist of significant majorities among the following groups of voters: 'post-industrial professionals' who include teachers, nurses, engineers and computer analysts; women; minorities; and an equal share of the white working class. They labelled the first three groups as the McGovern constituencies, all of whom are growing as a proportion of the electorate. The post-industrial professionals, historically a Republican clan, were attracted to the Democrats because of their sympathy for the civil rights, feminist and environmental causes. Their political transition was then accelerated in the 1990s as they saw the Democrats forcibly emerge as the party of fiscal responsibility.

Historically women, too, have been more likely to vote Republican, but as more and more women entered the workforce, they looked to government to protect them against discrimination and the vagaries of the marketplace. Hence, a feature of recent elections has been the so-called 'gender gap' that saw women disproportionately aligned with Democratic candidates and men more supportive of the Republicans. This peaked in 1996, when there was an 11-point gap in the voting behaviour of women and men, with 54 per cent of the former voting for Clinton and Dole just winning a plurality of the latter (Pomper, 1997).[4] Women's support for the Democrats has not been uniform, but was especially strong among 'the working, single and highly educated' (Judis and Teixeira, 2004, p. 66). If, however, women are a critical part of any future Democratic majority, the evidence from 2004 should concern party strategists. Kerry gained only 51 per cent of the overall women's vote.[5] This loss of the Democratic advantage amongst women voters is best explained by the prominence of terrorism and security concerns and the feeling that President Bush was better able to deal with these issues. One post-election poll found that 35 per cent of 'white working-class women voters ... chose terrorism and security ... as their most important voting issue' (Judis and Teixeira, 2005, p. 24).

If Democratic presidential candidates have recently come to rely on winning a majority of women voters they are equally dependent on winning big majorities of the minority vote. No Democrat since Lyndon Johnson in 1964 has won a majority of the overall white vote. Even in 1992 and 1996 Clinton trailed Bush Sr. and Dole amongst white voters (Pomper, 1997, p. 180). Hence, the absolute requirement for Democrats to maintain high levels of support from African-Americans, with an increasing emphasis also on the Latino vote.

African-Americans

The African-American population has been loyal to the Democratic Party. Indeed the data would be startling were it not so familiar. The Democrats have been able to count on 90 per cent support in presidential elections from black America since the 1970s. No other identifiable group of the electorate has such a level of fidelity to either party. In some ways, of course, this makes African-American voters appealing to Republican strategists. Even if only a relatively small proportion of blacks could be persuaded to the GOP cause, this would do real damage to the Democrats.

There was little evidence from the 2004 election to suggest that the Republicans have engineered any real change in the voting patterns of black Americans as Bush gained only 11 per cent of black votes, up just two points on 2000 (Exit Poll, 2004). Nevertheless, it is worth noting one area of administration activity that has, relatively speaking, slipped under the political radar. The much maligned faith-based initiative has been used as a means of channelling federal money through black churches. As leading Republican strategist Matthew Dowd reflected: 'The minister is the No. 1 influencer in the African American community' (Wallsten et al, 2005). Although the lines of causality are unclear, there is some indication that the administration's efforts promoting faith-based programmes to black churches had a degree of pay off in battleground states. In 2004 Bush took 13 per cent of the African-American vote in Florida, up six per cent on 2000, 14 per cent in Wisconsin, and perhaps most interestingly 16 per cent in Ohio. According to one analysis by the Joint Center for Political and Economic Studies, a think tank on black issues, Bush's victory margin in Ohio could have been as low as 25,000 if African-American voters had cast their votes in the same ratios as in 2000 (Wallsten et al, 2005). Nevertheless, the prospect of black voters transferring their party loyalties in any great numbers seems remote. The Democrats, however, do need to be much concerned about the behaviour of another block of voters that they had perhaps too comfortably assumed would rally to their cause.

Latino America

According to Judis and Teixeira, 'Hispanic support is a crucial part of the new Democratic majority. Hispanics are the minority group that is growing the most in terms of both absolute numbers and percentage of the population' (2004, p. 59). Indeed, the 2000 census revealed that Latinos are already the biggest minority group in the US (Pachon, 2001). While it is important to distinguish between the Latino population and the eligible electorate, Latinos constituted nearly 30 per cent of eligible voters in Texas and California in 2004. As yet, they are underrepresented in terms of turnout, constituting eight per cent of voters in 2004 as against the 11 per cent of voters who were African-Americans, but as the political engagement of the community increases so their political allegiances will become more crucial. It was therefore particularly frustrating that the exit polls did such a bad job in measuring the behaviour of Latinos in 2004. The initial release of figures suggested that Bush had captured 44 per cent of the Latino vote (Exit Poll, 2004). This would have represented a nine-point gain since 2000, when Bush captured 35 per cent of the Latino vote and would have been a real blow to any notion of Latinos being a building block for future Democrat success. Subsequently, however, there have been revisions of this estimate as state-by-state exit polls did not aggregate up to this figure (Meyerson, 2004). Furthermore, the various pre-election surveys never hinted at such a strong performance by the president amongst Latinos (Leal et al., 2005, p. 43). Hence, it is not entirely clear to what extent Bush advanced on his performance in 2000. According to Judis and Teixeira, 'Bush probably increased his support among Hispanics by no more than four or five per cent' (2005, p. 25). Even this figure, however, would mean that the increase in Bush's support from Latinos tipped the balance in New Mexico.

More generally, two patterns seemed to be emerging in Latino voting trends. First, that the Latino population is split along religious lines. Catholics, who comprise about 70 per cent of Latinos, were strongly pro-Kerry, while non-Catholics favoured Bush (Leal et al, 2005, p. 44). Second, the evidence from the 1980s and 1990s suggested that the Latino vote is relatively fickle, especially when compared to the partisan constancy of the African-American vote (Gersh, 2004). About 37 per cent of the Latino vote went to Reagan in 1984, but support for Republicans subsequently diminished toward a low of 21 per cent in 1996, when Bob Dole made little play for it and the GOP was strongly associated with anti-immigrant sentiment, exemplified by Governor Pete Wilson in California (Leal et al., 2005). The former Governor of Texas, however, has been a strong messenger in terms of GOP efforts to win over Latinos. From the moment he started running for president, Bush explicitly targeted Latino voters. He ran Spanish language radio advertisements when campaigning for the Iowa caucus in 2000 (Pachon, 2001). His first foray abroad as president was to Mexico City and Latinos, like African Americans, have high profile jobs in the current administration.

Overall, especially given their volatility, Latinos represent a test case for the Democrats' ability to win voters on economic issues while not losing them on cultural ones. National studies show that most Latinos identify themselves as 'working families' with concerns about wages, worker training and access to healthcare. On the other hand, they manifest conservative views on issues such as abortion and gay rights (Pachon, 2001).

White Americans

In 1970 Richard Scammon and Ben Wattenberg famously noted that America was '*un*young, *un*poor and *un*black' (1970).[6] Thirty years on, as John White points out, this assertion has less validity if taken as a statement that most Americans are middle-aged, middle-class whites living in the suburbs (White, 2003, p. 2). On the other hand, white voters remain in the majority and ultimately Bush's victory in 2004 came down to the fact that whites, who comprised 77 per cent of the electorate, voted for him by a 58 to 41 per cent margin. White men, at 36 per cent of the electorate, went for Bush by 62 to 37 per cent and white women gave him 55 per cent of their votes. One factor that must disturb Democrats is that both Gore in 2000 and Kerry in 2004 failed to better Clinton's performance amongst white men, even though independent candidate Ross Perot picked up 22 per cent of the white male vote in 1992 and 11 per cent in 1996. These Perot voters, in effect, moved en masse to the Bush camp (Galston, 2001).

Furthermore, Bush won working class whites by 23 points in 2004. Most alarmingly for Democrats, this group thought Bush would better manage the economy by a margin of 55 to 39 per cent (Meyerson, 2005). These numbers would almost suggest that lower income whites with less than college education are a lost cause for the Democrats, but the party simply cannot afford to surrender such a significant group, whose socio-economic status should make them one of its core constituencies. One problem that the Democrats must resolve is how to communicate better with working class voters. The de-unionization of America and the decline in the number of Democratic identifiers from union families has undermined a key element of New Deal politics (Roy and Denzau, 2004, p. 74). According to Meyerson, 'Today's working class isn't found largely in factories; it's in nursing homes, on construction sites, in Wal-Marts. Republicans talk to its members about guns, gays and God. Democrats often just stammer' (Meyerson, 2005, p. A19).

Prospects

To get a sense of where the Democrats stood at the outset of Bush's second term, it is instructive to look back to the 1980s when the party lost three successive presidential elections. At that point some commentators began to talk of a Republican lock on the electoral college. In comparison to the conclusive defeats of 1980, 1984 and 1988, the losses in 2000 and 2004 appeared less overwhelming and the road back to the White House looked less intimidating. Whereas in the 1980s Reagan turned California, Illinois and New Jersey into Republican states, these have since become relative Democrat strongholds. On the other hand, only Lyndon Johnson and Jimmy Carter have won over 50 per cent of the popular vote in presidential elections for the Democrats since FDR in 1944. This record suggests that the heyday of the New Deal coalition had a short shelf life at presidential level and that while Clinton proved that Democrats can still win the White House, this is unlikely to be done decisively in a two-horse race.

Furthermore, the Congressional picture is bleak. The lack of competitive House seats renders a partisan turnaround to the Democrats on the scale of 1994 to the Republicans most unlikely. The cycle of Senate elections also suggests that the Democrats will be once again be the hunted rather than the hunter in 2006. If post 1994 trends continue, the danger is that defeat at congressional level becomes a self-fulfilling prophecy. As the party becomes less competitive, particularly across the South, its infrastructure will deteriorate. Consequently even if there is a change in the political climate, the Democrats may have neither the political apparatus nor the quality of candidate to hand to exploit this. Early in 2005 there was a fair amount of chatter about the ideological implications of Howard Dean's ascent to the chair of the Democratic National Committee, but his job is less to act as a leader of the opposition than to make sure that the party machinery functions effectively (Dionne, 2004; Nagourney and Kornblut, 2005).

On the other hand, the ideological battle lines remain crucial. In 2004 Kerry won a majority of self-described moderates and a plurality of self-described independents, while self-identified Democrats and liberals overwhelmingly backed their candidate. At a glance this would seem to constitute a decisive winning coalition. The piece that is missing from this jigsaw is the disparity in those calling themselves liberals against those calling themselves conservatives. That is, while 21 per cent of voters were happy with the liberal tag, 34 per cent proclaimed themselves conservatives. In the long term this is ominous for the Democrats and suggests that they must reinterpret the values debate in ways more compatible with liberal positions — even if the 'L-word' itself remains unspoken. In other words, regardless of the party's stand on gay rights, Democrats need to shift the debate away from one about gay families and onto terrain that emphasizes help to working families through policies on family leave, healthcare and childcare.

Notes

1   Liberals might insist that crime is a product of economic circumstance but that is a two-step argument that many Americans had little patience with.

2   The Bush camp found plenty of ammunition to attack their opponent
     when they put Dukakis's record as Governor of Massachusetts under
     the microscope. For example, Bush championed the American flag
     and his own patriotism in contrast to Dukakis's decision, as Governor,
     to veto a law passed by the state legislature that would have mandated
     the recital of the Pledge of Allegiance in the state's schools. Most
     notoriously, the Bush campaign highlighted the case of Willie Horton,
     a convicted first degree murderer, who attacked a man and viciously
     raped his fiancee after disappearing while on a weekend furlough from
     a Massachusetts prison. Dukakis had previously vetoed a bill that
     would have ended the furlough programme. When he learned of the
     Horton case, Lee Atwater, Bush's chief campaign strategist, was bare-
     ly able to contain his joy (Edsall and Edsall, 1991, pp. 222–4).
3   Of course Starr still might be correct that the gay marriage issue
     tipped it for Bush in Ohio by providing a counterweight to the decline
     of the state's economy.
4   As Pomper explains, at least in 1996, the gender gap was truly about
     gender: 'Gender differences in the vote are real, not the result of other
     social influences. The gender gap remained stable among both blacks
     and whites, among all age groups and in suburbs, and across levels of
     education and income' (Pomper, 1997, p. 183).
5   There did remain a notable gender gap in the 2004 presidential elec-
     tion with a seven-point difference in the voting behaviour of women
     and men, but this was because men voted strongly for Bush.
6   In many ways Scammon and Wattenberg's book, entitled *The Real
     Majority*, was a precursor to Galston and Kamarck's *The Politics of
     Evasion* (1989).

BIBLIOGRAPHY

Presidential Debate, Winston-Salem, North Carolina, 11 October 2000, www.washingtonpost.com/politics/elections/debattext101100.htm.

Aberbach, J.D. (2004) 'The State of the Contemporary American Presidency: Or, is Bush II Actually Ronald Reagan's Heir?' in Colin Campbell and Bert Rockman (eds.), *The George W. Bush Presidency: Appraisals and Prospects* (Washington, DC: CQ Press), pp. 46–72.

Abrams, E. (1995) *Security and Sacrifice: Isolation, Intervention and American Foreign Policy* (Indianapolis: Hudson Institute).

Abramson, Paul R., Aldrich, John H. and Rohde, David W. (2003) *Change and Continuity in the 2000 and 2002 Elections* (Washington, DC: CQ Press).

Abramson, P., Aldrich, J.H. and Rohde, D.W. (2005) 'The 2004 Presidential Election: The Emergence of a Permanent Majority?' *Political Science Quarterly*, vol. 120, no. 1, pp. 33–57.

Ajami, Fouad (2005) 'The Autumn of the Autocrats,' *Foreign Affairs*, vol. 84 (May/June), pp. 20–35.

Aldrich, John H (1995) *Why Parties? The Origin and Transformation of Party Politics in America* (Chicago and London: The University of Chicago Press).

Aldrich, John H., and Rohde, David W. (2000), 'The Consequences of Party Organization in the House: The Role of the Majority and Minority Parties in Conditional Party Government,' in Jon R. Bond and Richard Fleisher (eds.), *Polarized Politics: Congress and the President in a Partisan Era* (Washington, DC: CQ Press).

Aldrich, John H., Berger, Mark W. and Rohde, David W. (2002) 'The Historical Variability of Conditional Party Government, 1887–1994,' in David W. Brady and Mathew McCubbins (eds.), *Party, Process, and Political Change in Congress. New Perspectives on the History of Congress* (Stanford, CA: Stanford University Press), pp. 17–35.

5

AlJazeera.com (2005), 'Blair Wins Election, Admits Iraq Divided Britons' (6 May), http://www.aljazeera.com/me.asp?service_ID=8432

Allen, Jonathan (2003). 'Effective House Leadership Makes the Most of Majority,' *CQ Weekly* (29 March), p. 746.

Allen, Mike (2004) 'Confident Bush Vows to Move Aggressively. Second-Term Agenda Includes Social Security, Tax Code,' *The Washington Post* (5 November), p. A1.

Allen, Mike and Babington, Charles (2005) 'Social Security Vote May be Delayed Critics Could Force Proposal to Change,' *The Washington Post* (2 March), p. A1

Allen, Mike and Baker, Peter (2005) '$2.5 Trillion Budget Plan Cuts Many Programs,' *The Washington Post* (7 February), p. A1.

Alliance for Justice (2003) 'Statement on Miguel Estrada,' www.independentjudiciary.com (30 January).

Alternet (2004), 'The Christian Right's Humble Servant,' http://www.alternet.org/election04/20499.

Altman, Daniel (2004) *Neoconomy: George Bush's Revolutionary Gamble with America's Future* (New York: Public Affairs Books).

American Life League (2002), 'Assisted Suicide,' http://www.all.org/issues/broken.htm.

Americans United (2002), 'All in the Family', http://www.au.org/site/News2?page=NewsArticle&id=5580&abbr+cs_.

Americans United (2004) 'The Religious Right and Election 2004,' http://www.au.org/site/News2?page=NewsArticle&id=7078&abbr=cs_.

Anderson, K. (2005) 'US Politicians Embrace Podcasts,' *BBC News*, http://newsvote.bbc.co.uk/mpapps/pagetools/print/news.bbc.co.uk/2/hi/americas/444, 13 April 2005

Anderson, Martin (1988) *Revolution* (New York: Harcourt Brace Jovanovich).

Andrews, Edmund L. (2005) 'In Plan to Reduce the Deficit, White House Turns to Old Projections,' *New York Times* (2 January).

Annenberg Public Policy Center (2004) 'White Evangelical or Born-Again Protestants by State,' http://www.annenbergpublicpolicycenter. org/naes/2004_03_evangelical-table_09_27_pr.pdf.

Anon (2005a) 'Bush Supports Senate's Pro-life Bills,' *Focus on the Family Citizen* (April), p. 5.

Anon (2005b) 'Fate of San Diego's Cross Still Being Worked Out,' *Focus on the Family Citizen* (April), p. 8.

Anon (2005c) 'Following Their Own Path,' *Economist* (2 April), pp. 43–4.

Anon (2005d) 'San Diegans Want Cross to Stay Put,' *Focus on the Family Citizen* (June), p. 7.

APS Diplomat Recorder (2001) 'Bush Gives Opposition the Go Ahead,' *APS Diplomat Recorder*, vol. 54, no. 5.

Arnold, Peri (2004) 'One President, Two Presidencies: George W. Bush in Peace and War,' in Stephen E. Schier (ed.), *High Risk and Big Ambition: The Presidency of George W. Bush* (Pittsburgh: University of Pittsburgh Press), pp. 145–66.

Asmus, Ronald (2002) *Opening NATO's Door: How the Alliance Remade itself for a New Era* (New York: Columbia UP).

Atlanta Journal-Constitution (2004) 'Evangelicals Satisfied with GOP Convention,' http://www.ajc.com/search/contents/shared/news/ politics/stories/GOP_EVANGELICALS_0904_COX.html.

Babington, Charles (2004) 'Hastert Launches a Partisan Policy,' *Washington Post* (27 November), p. A1.

Babington, Charles (2005) 'Democrats Wrestle with Choice and Choices,' *The Washington Post* (13 February).

Babington, Charles and Edsall, Thomas (2005) 'Conservative Republicans Divided over Nominees,' *Washington Post* (4 October), p. A11.

Baer, K.S. (2000) *Reinventing Democrats: the Politics of Liberalism from Reagan to Clinton* (Lawrence: University of Kansas Press).

Baker, Peter (2005) 'President Sends '06 Budget to Congress,' *Washington Post* (8 February), p. A1.

Balz, Dan (1999) 'Bush Favours Internationalism,' *Washington Post* (20 November), p. A1.

Balz, Dan (2001) 'Next on Bush Agenda: Bigger Policy Changes,' *Washington Post* (6 May), p. A1.

Balz, Dan (2005) 'For GOP, Deeper Fissures and a Looming Power Struggle,' *Washington Post* (25 May), p. A11.

Balz, Dan (2005a) 'Issue Expected to be Toughest Domestic Battle,' *Washington Post* (3 February).

Barone, M. (2004) 'The Stakes in 2004,' *The Atlantic Monthly* (September), pp. 27–8.

Barshay, Jill and Ota, Alan K. (2003) 'White House Tax Cut Package Gets a Wary Hill Reception,' *CQ Weekly* (11 January), pp. 2515–16.

Bauer, G L. (1997) 'A Reaganaut's View,'*The Weekly Standard* (24 February), pp. 14–15.

Beachler, Donald (2004) 'Ordinary Events and Extraordinary Times: The 2002 Congressional Elections,' in Jon Kraus, Kevin J. McMahon and David M. Rankin (eds.), *Transformed by Crisis: The Presidency of George Bush and American Politics* (New York: Palgrave Macmillan), pp. 29–50.

Becker, Elizabeth (2005) ''04 Trade Deficit Sets Record, $617 billion,' *New York Times* (11 February).

Beland, D and Waddan, A. (forthcoming) 'The Social Policies Presidents Make: Pre-emptive Leadership Under Nixon and Clinton,' in *Political Studies*.

Belasco, Amy (2005) 'The Costs of Operations in Iraq, Afghanistan and Enhanced Security,' *Congressional Research Service* (9 February).

Beliefnet (n.d.a), 'David Barton and the "Myth" of Church–State Separation,' http://www.beliefnet.com/story/154/story_15469.html.

Beliefnet (n.d.b), 'Did God Intervene?' http://www.beliefnet.com/story/156/story_15602.html.

Beliefnet (n.d.c) 'It Wasn't Just (Or Even Mostly) the "Religious Right",' http://www.beliefnet.com/story/155/story_15598.html.

Benenson, Bob (ed.) (2001) 'Between the Lines,' *CQ Weekly* (20 October), p. 2446.

Berger, S.R. (2004) 'Foreign Policy for a Democratic President,' *Foreign Affairs*, vol. 83, no. 1, pp. 47–63.

Berke, Richard L. (2001) 'A Flurry of Hugs for "Gang of Five" in Capital,' *The New York Times* (23 October).

Bettelheim, Adriel (2001) 'Personnel Issues Have Senate Stumbling on Homeland Security,' *CQ Weekly* (28 September), pp. 2515–16.

Biddle, L. and Schriock, S. (2005) 'Politics in the Real World: How Campaign Fund-raising Gets Done in the Internet Age,' panel presentation, 'Money and Politics: Are Elections for Sale,' symposium sponsored by the Lou Frey Institute of Politics and Government at the University of Central Florida

Binder, Sarah A. (1997) *Minority Rights, Majority Rule* (New York: Cambridge University Press).

Birnbaum, J.H. and Edsall, T. B. (2004) 'Bush Backers Had Edge in Stretch,' *The Boston Globe* (7 November), p. A11

Birnbaum, Jeffrey H. (2005) 'Bracing for Battle, Bush to Move Slowly on Social Security,' *Washington Post* (5 January).

Blumenthal, S. (1982) *The Permanent Campaign* (New York: Simon and Schuster).

Blumenthal, S. (2003) *The Clinton Wars* (London: Penguin Books).

Blumenthal, Sidney (2005) 'Nixon's Empire Strikes Back,' *The Guardian* (9 June), p. 26.

Blustain, S. (2004) 'Choice Language,' in *The American Prospect*, vol.15, no.12, pp. 36–7

Boller, P.F. Jr. (1981) *Presidential Anecdotes* (Harmondsworth, Middlesex: Penguin).

Boller, P.F., Jr. (1984), *Presidential Campaigns* (New York and Oxford: Oxford University Press).

Boston, Robert (2000) *Close Encounters with the Religious Right* (Amherst: Prometheus Books).

BP News (2004a) 'Land "Appalled" by Bush Campaign Strategy for Churches,' http://www.sbcbaptistpress.org/bpnews.asp?ID=18624.

BP News (2004b) 'Focus on the Family Signs on to ERLC's iVote Values Initiative,' http://www.baptistpress.com/bpnews.asp?ID=18853.

Brady, David W. (1973) *Congressional Voting in a Partisan Era* (Lawrence: University Press of Kansas).

Brenner, Robert (2002) *The Boom and the Bubble: The US in the World Economy* (London: Verso).

Bresnahan, J. (2005) 'Centrist Democrats Search for Direction,' *Roll Call* (14 February).

Brinkley, A. (2004) 'What's Next?' in *The American Prospect*, vol. 15, no. 12, pp. 18–23.

Brinkley, Douglas (2004) *Tour of Duty: John F. Kerry and the Vietnam War* (New York: Morrow).

Broder, David (2005) 'The Heat Is On the GOP,' *Washington Post* (3 April), p. B7.

Bronner, E. (1989) *Battle for Justice: How the Bork Nomination Shook America* (New York: Norton).

Brownlee, W. Elliott and Graham, Hugh Davis (eds.) (2003) *The Reagan Presidency: Pragmatic Conservatism and its Legacies* (Lawrence, KS: University Press of Kansas).

Brownlee, W. Elliott and Steuerle, C. Eugene (2003) 'Taxation,' in W. Elliott Brownlee and Hugh Davis Graham (eds.), *The Reagan Presidency: Pragmatic Conservatism and Its Legacies* (Lawrence, KS: University Press of Kansas), pp. 155–81.

Brownstein, Ronald (2002) 'Loyal to the Core, Bush Knows How to Play to the Crucial Outsiders,' *Los Angeles Times* (27 May), p. A1.

Brzezinski, Zbigniew (1983) *Power and Principle: Memoirs of the National Security Adviser, 1977–1981* (New York: Farrar, Straus, Giroux).

Buckley Jr., W.F. (1997) 'Conservatives Split on China,' *National Review* (19 May), pp. 62–3.

Buckley, Mary and Singh, Robert (eds.) (2005) *The Bush Doctrine and the War on Terrorism* (London: Routledge).

Bumiller, Elisabeth (2003), 'Religious Lobby Finds a Good Friend in Bush,' *International Herald Tribune* (27 October), p. 5.

Buni, F. (1999) 'Bush Has Tough Words and Rough Enunciation for Iraqi Chief,' *New York Times* (4 December), p. A12.

Burnham, J. (1947) *The Struggle for the World* (London: Jonathan Cape).

Burnham, J. (1953) *Containment or Liberation? An Inquiry into the Aims of United States Foreign Policy* (New York: The John Day Company).

Burnham, J. (1965) *The War We Are In: The Last Decade and the Next* (New Rochelle: Arlington House).

Burnham, W.D. (1985) 'The 1984 Election and the Future of American Politics,' in E. Sandoz and C.V. Crabbe Jr. (eds.), *Election 84: Landslide Without a Mandate?* (New York: New American Library), pp. 204–60.

Burns, Nicholas (2005) 'A Transatlantic Agenda for the Year Ahead,' speech transcript (available on the Chatham House website), delivered at Chatham House (Royal Institute for International Affairs), 6 April 2005.

Bush, George W. (1999) 'A Period of Consequences,' *The Citadel* (23 September), www.fas.org/spp/starwars/program/news99/92399_defense.htm.

Bush, George W. (2002) 'Remarks by the President at a Reception for Senator Susan Collins,' 3 August. http://www.whitehouse.gov/

Bush, George W. (2002a) 'The President's State of the Union Address,' Washington DC (29 January), www.whitehouse.gov/news/releases/2002/01/20020129–11.html.

Bush, George W. (2002b) 'Remarks by the President at 2002 Graduation Exercise of the United States Military Academy,' West Point, New York (1 June), www.whitehouse.gov/news/releases/2002/06/20020601-3.html.

Bush, George W. (2002c) 'President's Remarks at the United Nations General Assembly,' New York, New York (12 September), www.whitehouse.gov/news/releases/2002/09/20020912-1.html.

Bush, George W. (2003) 'President Delivers State of the Union,' Washington, DC (28 January), www.whitehouse.gov/news/releases/2003/0l/20030128-19.html.

Bush, George W. (2005) 'Brussels Speech: Bush Calls For New Era Of Transatlantic Unity To Advance Peace' (21 February), http://usinfo.state.gov/eur/Archive/2005/Feb/21-770552.html

Bush, George W. (2005a) 'State of the Union Address' (2 February), www.whitehouse.gov/news/releases/2005/02/20050202-11.html.

Bush, George W.   (2005b) 'The President Discusses War on Terror,' National Defense University, Fort Lesley J. McNair (8 March), www.whitehouse.gov/news/releases/2005/03/20050308-3.html.

Bush, George W. (2005c) 'United States Wants Diplomacy to Work with Iran, Bush says' (18 February), http://www.parstimes.com/news/archive/2005/washfile/diplomacy_iran.html

Bush, George H.W. and Scowcroft, Brent (1998) *A World Transformed* (New York: Knopf).

Bush, George W. and Schröder, Gerhard (2001), 'Joint Statement by President George W. Bush and Chancellor Gerhard Schröder on a Transatlantic Vision for the 21st Century' (29 March), http://usa.usembassy.de/etexts/docs/ga1-032901e.htm

Bush, George W. and Schröder, Gerhard (2004) 'The German-American Alliance for the 21st Century. Joint Statement by President George W. Bush and Chancellor Gerhard Schroeder' (27 February), http://www.whitehouse.gov/news/releases/2004/02/print/20040 227-10.html

Butler, R. Lawrence (2003) 'Taking Responsible Party Government Seriously: Assessing Party Strength in the House of Representatives,' in John C. Green and Daniel M. Shea (eds.), *The State of the Parties*, 4th edition (Lanham, MD: Rowman and Littlefield), pp. 254–63.

Calleo, David P.   (1992) *The Bankrupting of America: How the Federal Budget is Impoverishing the Nation* (New York: William Morrow).

Campbell, C. (2004) 'Managing the Presidency or the President?' in Colin Campbell and Bert Rockman (eds.), *The George W. Bush Presidency: Appraisals and Prospects* (Washington, DC: CQ Press), pp. 1–15.

Campbell, Colin (2004a) 'Unrestrained Ideological Entrepreneurship in the Bush II Advisory System' in Colin Campbell and Bert A. Rockman (eds.), *The George W. Bush Presidency. Appraisals and Prospects* (Washington DC: CQ Press), pp. 73–104.

Campo-Flores, Arian (2005) 'The Legacy of Terri Schiavo,' *Newsweek* (4 April), pp. 38–40.

Cannon, Lou (2000) *President Reagan: The Role of a Lifetime* (New York: Public Affairs).

Caridi, R.J.   (1968) *The Korean War and American Politics: The Republican Party as a Case Study* (Philadelphia: University of Pennsylvania Press).

Carnes, Tony (2005) 'Opportunity of a Generation,' *Christianity Today*, February, pp. 66–8.

Carney, D. (1996) 'GOP Bill Restricting Gay Unions Clears — But Does Not Yield Political Dividends,' *Congressional Quarterly Weekly Report* (14 September), pp. 2598–9

Cassidy, John (2004) 'Tax Code,' *New Yorker* (9 June), p. 9.

CBS News (2004) 'France, US, Buddies vs Syria' (7 September), http://www.cbsnews.com/stories/2004/09/07/world/main641781.shtml.

Chamberlain, Lawrence H. (1946) *The President, Congress and Legislation* (New York: Columbia University Press).

Cheney, R. (2002) 'Vice-President speaks at VFW 103rd National Convention,' (26 August), www.whitehouse.gov/news/releases/2002/o8/20020826.html.

Chicago Council on Foreign Relations (2004) 'Global Views 2004' (available on the CCFR website, accessed 1 December 2004).

Christian Coalition (2004) '2004 Voter Guide Presidential Election,' http://www.cc.org/voterguides2004/national.pdf.

Church and State (2002) 'The Christian Coalition: Born Again?' http://www.au.org/churchstate/cs11021.htm.

CitizenLink (2004) 'A Must-Read Election Message,' http://www.family.org/cforum/extras/a0034053.cfm.

Civil Rights Coalition for the 21st Century (2005) 'President Sends Previously-Rejected Judicial Nominees to Senate,' www.civilrights.org (15 February).

Clarke, Richard A. (2004) *Against all Enemies: Inside America's War on Terror* (New York: Free Press).

Clarke, Richard A., et al. (2004) *Defeating the Jihadists: A Blueprint for Action* (New York: The Century Foundation Press).

Clinton, J.D., Jackman, S. and Rivers, D. (2004) '"The Most Liberal Senator"? Analyzing and Interpreting Congressional Roll Calls,' *PSOnline* (www.apsanet.org) (October), pp. 815–11.

Clinton, W.J. (2004) *My Life*, (London: Hutchinson).

CNN (2003) 'Estrada Withdraws as Judicial Nominee,' Cnn.com (4 September).

Cochran, John (2004) 'Religious Right Lays Claim to Big Role in GOP Agenda,' *CQ Weekly* (13 November),, pp. 2684–9.

Cohen, R.E. (2004) 'To Soul Search, Or Not to Soul Search,' in *National Journal* (20 November), p. 3566.

Committee on Political Parties of the American Political Science Association (1950) *Toward a More Responsible Two-Party System* (New York, Rinehart).

Concord Coalition (2005a) 'A Real Fix for Social Security Requires an Increase in National Saving,' *Concord Coalition Social Security Briefing*, no. 5 (13 April).

Concord Coalition (2005b) 'Concord Coalition Warns against Fiscal Euphoria,' concordcoalition.org (13 July).

Concord Coalition (2005c) 'Concord Coalition Calls for "Pork" Rescission and Tax Cut Freeze in Response to Katrina,' concordcoalition.org (16 September).

Conger, Kimberley H. and Green, John H. (2002) 'Spreading and Digging in,' *Campaigns and Elections* (February), pp. 58–60, 64.

Congressional Budget Office (2005) *The Budget and Economic Outlook: Fiscal Years 2005–2014*.

Connelly, M. (2004) 'How Americans Voted: A Political Portrait,' *The New York Times*, 7 November 2004, p. 4.

Cook, R. (2005a) *The Rhodes Cook Letter January 2005*.

Cook, R. (2005b) *The Rhodes Cook Letter March 2005*.

Cook, R. (2005c) *The Rhodes Cook Letter May 2005*.

Cook, R. (2005d) 'Campaign Finance: The Good, Bad and the Ugly,' panel presentation, 'Money and Politics: Are Elections for Sale,' symposium sponsored by the Lou Frey Institute of Politics and Government at the University of Central Florida.

Cooper, Joseph and Young, Garry (2005) *Congressional Voting Data*, http://jhunix.hcf.jhu.edu/%7Ejcooper/papers.html

Cooper, Joseph (2005) 'From Congressional to Presidential Preeminence. Power and Politics in Late Nineteenth Century America and Today,' in Lawrence C. Dodd and Bruce I. Oppenheimer (eds.), *Congress Reconsidered*, 7th edition (Washington, DC: CQ Press), pp. 363–93.

Cooperman, Alan (2004) 'Evangelical Leaders Appeal to Followers To Go to Polls,' *Washington Post* (15 October), p. A6.

Cooperman, Alan and Edsall, Thomas B. (2004) 'Evangelicals Say They Led Charge for the GOP,' *Washington Post* (8 November), p. A1.

Council on Foreign Relations (2003), 'Address by John Kerry' (3 December) (available on John Kerry official website, accessed 18 June 2004).

Cox, Gary W. and McCubbins, Matthew D. (1993) *Legislative Leviathan* (Berkeley, CA: University of California Press).

Cox, Gary W. and McCubbins, Matthew D. (2005) *Setting the Agenda: Responsible Party Government in the US House of Representatives* (New York: Cambridge University Press).

Cox, Michael (2002) 'American Power before and after 11 September: Dizzy with Success?' *International Affairs*, vol. 78 (April), pp. 261–76.

Cox, Michael (2004) 'The Empire Votes Back,' *The World Today*, August/September, pp. 13–15.

Coy, Peter (2005) 'That Trade Deficit is no Debacle,' *Business Week* (31 January).

CQ Voting and Elections Collection (2004) '2004 Presidential Elections: National Results,' http://www.cqpress.com/docs/2004Elections/2004Pres.htm.

Cushman, Candi (2005) 'Bad Behavior,' *Focus on the Family Citizen* (June), pp. 22–6.

Daalder, Ivo H. and Lindsay, James M. (2003) *America Unbound: The Bush Revolution in Foreign Policy* (Washington, DC: The Brookings Institution).

Danforth, John C. (2005) 'In the Name of Politics,' *New York Times* (17 April).

Danner, Mark (2005) 'The Secret Way to War,' *New York Review of Books*, vol. LII/10 (9 June), pp. 70–4.

Dao, James (2005) 'Mayors Urge Bush Not to Cut Aid Program,' *New York Times* (19 January), p. A5.

Davies, P.J. (1996) 'Electoral Causes and Electoral Consequences,' paper presented to 'Towards the Millennium: Elections 1996,' the annual colloquium of the American Politics Group of the Political Studies Association and the British Association for American Studies, at the United States Embassy, London (22 November).

Davies, P.J. (1999) *US Elections Today* (Manchester and New York: Manchester University Press).

Davies, P.J. (2002) 'The Material Culture of US Elections: Artisanship, Entrepreneurship, Ephemera and Two Centuries of Trans-Atlantic Exchange,' in B.I. Newman and D. Vervic (eds.), *Communication of Politics: Cross-Cultural Theory Building in the Practice of Public Relations and Political Marketing* (New York: Haworth Political Press), pp. 9–24.

Davies, Philip J. (2003) 'A New Republican Generation?' *Contemporary Review* (March), pp. 139–46.

Davies, P. J. (2006, forthcoming) 'Reforming Campaign Finance in the 21st Century,' in J. West (ed.), *The USA and Canada 2006* (London: Europa Publications).

Destler, I.M. (1999) 'Trade Policy at a Crossroads,' in H.J. Aaron and R. Reischauer (eds.), *Setting National Priorities: the 2000 Election and Beyond* (Washington DC: Brookings Institution Press), pp. 73–96.

Deutsche Welle (2003) 'Rumsfeld Repeats "Old Europe" Comments,' 11 June, *Deutsche Welle:* http://www.dw-world.de/dw/article/0,,890806,00.html

Deutsche Welle (2004) 'Germany Signals Shift on Iraq Policy' (13 October), http://www.dw-world.de/dw/article/0,1564,1359991,00.html.

Dewar, Helen (2003) 'Senate GOP Slashes Tax Cut House Leaders Upset at Lid Put on Bush Proposal,' *The Washington Post* (12 April), p. A1.

Dewar, Helen and Allen, Mike (2004) 'GOP May Target Use of Filibuster,' *Washington Post* (13 December).

Dial, Karla (2005) 'Vital Signs,' *Focus on the Family Citizen* (June), pp. 28–31.

Diamond, Sara (1996) *Facing the Wrath* (Monroe: Common Courage Press).

Dion, Douglas (1997) *Turning the Legislative Thumbscrew: Minority Rights and Procedural Change in Legislative Politics* (Ann Arbor: University of Michigan Press).

Dionne, E.J. (2004) 'The Democrats' Rove Envy,' *The Washington Post* (14 December).

Dircksen, Jeff (2004) 'A Reality TV Show Out of Touch with Fiscal Realities,' *National Taxpayers Union Foundation*, Policy Paper no. 151, Vote Tally Report 108–1 (17 June).

Doyle, M. (1986) 'Liberalism and World Politics,' *American Political Science Review*, vol. 80 (December), pp. 1151–69.

Drew, E. (1994) *On the Edge: The Clinton Presidency* (New York: Simon and Schuster).

Duffy, M. and Shannon, E. (2005) 'Condi on the Rise,' *Time* (28 March), pp. 23–5.

Dumbrell, John (2002) 'Was There a Clinton Doctrine? President Clinton's Foreign Policy Reconsidered,' *Diplomacy and Statecraft*, vol. 13, no. 2, pp. 43–56.

Dunn, C. and Slann, M. (1994) *American Government: A Comparative Approach* (New York: Harper Collins).

Dunn, D.H. (2003) 'Myths, Motivations and Misunderestimations: The Bush Administration and Iraq,' *International Affairs*, vol. 79 (April), pp. 279–97.

Durham, Martin (2004) 'Evangelical Protestantism and Foreign Policy in the United States after September 11,' *Patterns of Prejudice*, vol. 38, no. 2, pp. 145–58.

Durham, Martin (2005) 'Abortion, Gay Rights and Politics in Britain and America,' *Parliamentary Affairs*, vol. 58, no. 1, pp. 89–103.

Economic Report of the President (2004) (Washington, DC: Government Printing Office).

Edsall, Thomas B. and Edsall, Mary D. (1991), *Chain Reaction: the Impact of Race, Rights and Taxes on American Politics* (New York: W.W. Norton and Company).

Edwards, Chris (2005) 'Social Policy, Supply-Side, and Fundamental Reform: Republican Tax Policy, 1994–2004,' in Chris Edwards and

John Samples (eds.), *The Republican Revolution 10 Years Later: Smaller Government or Business as Usual* (Washington DC: Cato Institute), pp. 37–58.

Edwards, Chris (2005a) 'Options for Tax Reform,' *Cato Institute Policy Analysis*, no. 536 (24 February).

Eilperin, J. and Vita, M. (2000) 'Elections Narrow GOP Advantage in House,' *Washington Post* (8 November).

Eilperin, Juliet (2003) 'House GOP Practices Art of One-Vote Victories,' *Washington Post* (14 October), p. A1.

Epstein, J. (2003) 'Leviathan,' *The New York Review of Books* (1 May), pp. 13–14.

Evans, C. Lawrence and Lipinski, Daniel (2003) 'Obstruction and Leadership in the US Senate,' in Lawrence C. Dodd and Bruce I. Oppenheimer (eds.), *Congress Reconsidered*, 6th edition (Washington, DC: CQ Press), pp. 227–48.

Exit Poll (2004) National Election Pool exit poll.

Fahrenkopf, F. J. (1986a) 'Address at Harvard University, 31/1/86'.

Fahrenkopf, F.J. (1986b) 'Address at Yale University, 10/9/86'.

Family Research Council (2005) 'Dear Friend of FRC,' direct mail letter (April).

Fineman, Howard and Rosenberg, Debra (2005) 'The Holy War Begins,' *Newsweek* (11 July), pp. 29–30.

Fischer, Joschka (1999) 'Serbien gehört zu Europa,' *Die Zeit*, 1999, http://www.zeit.de/archiv/1999/16/199916.fischer_.xml

Fleisher, Richard and Bond, Jon R. (2003) 'The Shrinking Middle in Congress,' *British Journal of Political Science*, vol. 34, no. 3 (July), pp. 429–51.

Fletcher, Michael and Weisman, Jonathan (2005) 'Bush Says Spending Cuts Will be Needed,' *Washington Post* (17 September), p. A1.

Florida Baptist Witness (2003) 'Pres. Bush Thanks Southern Baptists for Prayers,' http://www.floridabaptistwitness.com/1149.article.

Foerstel, Karen and Nather, David (2001) 'Beneath Capitol's Harmony, Debate Simmers Patiently,' *CQ Weekly* (22 September), pp. 2186–9.

Fox News (2005) 'Frist: Social Security Votes This Year' (3 March).

freerepublic.com (2004) 'Battle Cry of Faithful Pits Believers Against the Rest,' *New York Times*, http://www.freerepublic.com/focus/f-news/1263316/posts.

Friedman, Benjamin (1988) *Day of Reckoning: The Consequences of American Economic Policy under Reagan and After* (New York: Random House).

Friedman, Joel (2005) *Dividend and Capital Gains Tax Cuts Unlikely to Yield Touted Economic Gains*, Centre on Budget and Policy Priorities (10 March).

Friedman, Thomas (2001) 'Reforming Success,' *New York Times* (7 September).

Frontline (2004) 'The Jesus Factor: Interview Richard Land,' http://www.pbs.org/wgbh/pages/frontline/shows/jesus/interviews/land.html.

Frum, David (2003) *The Right Man: The Surprise Presidency of George W. Bush* (New York: Random House).

Fukuyama, Francis (2004) 'The Neoconservative Moment,' *The National Interest*, vol. 76, no. 2, pp. 57–68.

Gaddis, John L. (1982) *Strategies of Containment: A Critical Appraisal of Post-war American Security Policy* (Oxford: Oxford University Press).

Gaddis, John L. (2002) 'Grand Strategy,' *Foreign Policy* (November–December), pp. 50–7.

Gaddis, John L. (2004) *Surprise, Security, and the American Experience* (Cambridge, MA: Harvard University Press).

Gaddis, John L. (2005) 'Grand Strategy in the Second Term,' *Foreign Affairs*, 84 (January/February), pp. 2–16.

Gale, William and Orszag, Peter (2004a) 'An Economic Assessment of Tax Policy in the Bush Administration, 2000–2004,' *Boston College Law Review*, vol. 45, no. 5, pp. 1157–1232.

Gale, William and Orszag, Peter (2004b) 'The US Budget Deficit: On An Unsustainable Path,' *New Economy*, vol. 11 (December), pp. 236–42.

Galston, W. (2001) 'The White Male Problem,' in *Blueprint Magazine* (12 July), http://www.ndol.org.

Galston, W. and Kamarck, E. (1989) *The Politics of Evasion: Democrats and the Presidency* (Washington, DC: Progressive Policy Institute).

Gannon, K. (2003) 'Afghanistan Unbound,' *Foreign Affairs*, vol. 83 (May–June), pp. 35–47.

Garcia, M.J. (2005) *Renditions: Constraints Imposed by Laws on Torture* (Washington, DC: Congressional Research Service).

Garfinkle, A. (2001) 'Strategy and Preventive Diplomacy,' *Orbis*, vol. 45, no. 3, pp. 503–18.

Garrett, Major (2004) *The Enduring Revolution: How the Contract with America Continues to Shape the Nation* (New York: Crown Forum).

Garton Ash, Timothy (2005) 'The Sobering of America,' *The Guardian* (30 June).

Gastner, M., Shalizi, C. and Newman, M. (2004) 'Maps and Cartograms of the 2004 US Presidential Election Results,' http://www-personal.umich.edu/~mejn/election/

Gersh, M. (2004) 'Swing Voters,' in *Blueprint Magazine*, 25 July, http://www.ndol.org.

Gingrich, Newt (2005) 'The GOP Revolution Holds Powerful Lessons for Changing Washington,' in Chris Edwards and John Samples (eds.), *The Republican Revolution 10 Years Later: Smaller Government or Business as Usual?* (Washington, DC: Cato Institute), p. 1–4.

Giroux, G.L. (2004) 'Effect of "Moral Values" Exaggerated, Say Analysts,' *Congressional Quarterly Weekly* (13 November), p.2688

Giroux, G.L. (2005), 'Odds Still Heavily Against Midterm House Takeover,' *CQ Weekly* (11 April), pp. 878–9.

Goodnough, Abby and Yardley, William (2005) 'Federal Judge Condemns Intervention in Schiavo Case,' *New York Times* (31 March).

Gordon, Philip H. and Shapiro, Jeremy (2004), Allies at War: America, Europe and the Crisis over Iraq (Washington, DC: Brookings Institution Press).

Gourevitch, P. (2004) 'Damage Control,' *The New Yorker* (26 July), pp. 50–63.

Grant, Charles (2004) 'Manifesto for Optimists,' *Prospect* (December), pp. 15–17.

Graubard, S. (2004) *The Presidents: The Transformation of the American Presidency from Theodore Roosevelt to George W. Bush* (London: Allen Lane).

Gravelle, Jane (2005) *Dividend Tax Relief: Effects on Economic Recovery, Long-Term Growth and the Stock Market,*' Congressional Research Service RL31824 (14 February).

Green, Joshua (2001) 'God's Foreign Policy,' *Washington Monthly* (November), pp. 58–60, 64.

Greenberg, A. (2001) 'The Marriage Gap,' *Blueprint Magazine* (12 July), http:www.ndol.org.

Grunwald, M. (1996) 'It's Clear: Ad Spots Tarnish Reputations,' *Boston Globe* (3 November), p. 1

Guth, J.L. (2004) 'George W. Bush and Religious Politics,' in Stephen Schier (ed.), *High Risk and Big Ambition: The Presidency of George W. Bush* (Pittsburgh: University of Pittsburgh Press), pp. 117–41

Hadfield, J. (2005), 'More Than Survive, Parties Thrive Under New Campaign Finance Rules,' *Campaigns & Elections*, April 2005, pp. 22–4.

Hale, J. (1995) 'The Making of the New Democrats,' *Political Science Quarterly*, vol. 110, no. 2, pp 207–32.

Halliwell, L. (1998) *Halliwell's Film and Video Guide 1999* (edited by John Walker) (London: Harper Collins Publishers).

Halper, Stefan and Clarke, Jonathan (2004) *America Alone: The Neo-Conservatives and the Global Order* (Cambridge: Cambridge University Press).

Hansen, S.B. (2002) 'Religion and Morality' in G. Peele, C. Bailey, B. Cain and B.G. Peters (eds.), *Developments in American Politics 4* (Basingstoke: Palgrave Macmillan), pp. 264–77.

Harding, James (2005) 'A Polarizing President Gets his Chance to Become a Republican Roosevelt,' *Financial Times* (19 January), p. 17.

Harnisch, Sebastian and Maull, Hanns W. (eds.) (2001), *Gemany as a Civilian Power: the Foreign Power of the Berlin Republic* (Manchester: Manchester UP).

Harris, J.F. (1997) 'President Takes Blame for Fast Track Delay,' *The Washington Post* (11 November), p. A1

Harris, J.F. (2004) 'Blame – or Praise – the Swing Voters,' *The Washington Post National Weekly Edition* (6–12 December), p. 10

Harris, John (2005) 'Deficit Worries Threaten Bush Agenda,' *Washington Post* (7 February), p. A5.

Harris, J.F. and VandeHei, J. (2005) 'Doubts about Mandate for Bush, GOP,' *Washington Post* (2 May), p. A1.

Heclo, Hugh (2003) 'Ronald Reagan and the American Public Philosophy,' in W. Elliott Brownlee and Hugh Davis Graham (eds.), *The Reagan Presidency: Pragmatic Conservatism and its Legacies* (Lawrence, KS: University Press of Kansas).

Heilbrunn, Jacob (2000) 'President Gore's Foreign Policy,' *World Policy Journal,* vol. 27, no. 2, pp. 48–55.

Heins, Volker (2002) 'Germany's New War: 11 September and its Aftermath in German Quality Newspapers,' *German Politics*, vol.11, no. 2 (August), pp. 128–45.

Hersh, Seymour M. (2005) 'The Coming Wars,' *The New Yorker* (24 and 31 January), pp. 40–47.

Hess, Tom and Dial, Karla (2005) 'Year of the Values Voter,' *Focus on the Family Citizen* (January), pp. 18–21.

Hill, Dilys, Moore, Raymond and Williams, Phil (eds.) (1990) *The Reagan Presidency: An Incomplete Revolution* (Basingstoke: Macmillan).

Hodgson, Godfrey (1996) *The World Turned Right Side Up: A History of the Conservative Ascendancy in America* (New York: Houghton Mifflin).

Hoffman, S. (2003) 'The High and the Mighty: Bush's National Security Strategy and the New American Hubris,' *The American Prospect*, vol. 13, no. 24, pp. 28–31.

Hook, Janet (2005) 'President Putting "Big" Back in Government,' *Los Angeles Times* (8 February), p. A1.

Hooper, John (2002) 'German Leader Says No to Iraq War,' *The Guardian* (6 August).

Horney, James and Kogan, Richard (2005) 'OMB's Mid-Session Review: Does an Increase in Revenues This Year Really Mean Future Deficits are Under Control?' *Center on Budget and Policy Priorities* (13 July).

Human Events (2001) 'Pro-Lifers to Bush: Don't Flip on Embryo Research,' http://www.humanevents.org/articles/08-06-01/gizzi.htm.

Hurst, Steven (1999) *The Foreign Policy of the Bush Administration. In Search of a New World Order* (London: Cassell).

Ignatieff, Michael (2005) 'Dreams of Liberty,' *The Observer* (3 July), p. 25.

Ignatius, David (2005) 'Beirut's Berlin Wall,' *The Washington Post* (23 February), p. A19.

Ikenberry, G. John (2002) 'America's Imperial Ambition,' *Foreign Affairs*, vol. 81 (Sept/Oct), pp. 44–60.

Ikenberry, G. John (2004) 'A Liberal Leviathan,' *Prospect*, October, pp. 46–51.

Ikenberry, G. John and Kupchen, Charles (2004) 'Liberal Realism,' *The National Interest*, vol. 77, no. 3, pp. 38–49.

Ippolito, Dennis S. (2003) *Why Budgets Matter: Budget Policy and American Politics* (University Park PA: University of Pennsylvania Press).

Jacobson, Gary C. (2003) 'Terror, Terrain, and Turnout: Explaining the 2002 Midterm Elections,' *Political Science Quarterly*, vol. 118, no. 1 (April), pp. 1–22.

Jacobson, Gary C. (2005) 'The Congress: The Structural Basis of Republican Success,' in Michael Nelson (ed.), *The Elections of 2004* (Washington, DC: Congressional Quarterly Press).

Jauvert, Vincent (2005) 'Chirac-Bush. The Cordial Mistrust,' *Le Nouvel Observateuer* (17 February), p. 2.

Joint Economic Committee (2004) *What Happened to the Surplus?* (20 September), www.jec.senate.gov.

Jones, Charles O. (1994) *The Presidency in a Separated System* (Washington, DC: The Brookings Institution Press).

Jones, Charles O. (1999a) *Clinton and Congress 1993–1996* (Norman, OK: University of Oklahoma Press).

Jones, Charles O. (1999b) *Separate But Equal Branches. Congress and the Presidency*, 2nd edition (New York and London: Chatham House Publishers).

Jones, Charles O. (2003) 'Capitalizing on Position in a Perfect Tie,' in Fred I. Greenstein (ed.), *The George W. Bush Presidency. An Early Assessment* (Baltimore, MD and London: The Johns Hopkins University Press), pp. 173–96.

Judis, J. and Teixeira, R. (2004) *The Emerging Democratic Majority* (New York: Lisa Drew/Scribner), revised edition.

Judis, J. and Teixeira, R. (2005) 'Movement Interruptus,' *The American Prospect*, vol. 16, no. 1, pp. 23–7

Junker, Detlef (ed.) (2004) *The United States and Germany in the Era of Cold War, 1945–1990* (Cambridge: Cambridge UP).

Kady, David (2004) 'Defense: A Deficit Driver,' *CQ Weekly*, vol. 62 (17 January), pp. 154–6.

Kagan, R. and Kristol, W. (2000) 'Introduction: National Interest And Global Responsibility,' in R. Kagan and W. Kristol (eds.), *Present Dangers: Crisis and Opportunity in American Foreign and Defense Policy* (San Francisco: Encounter Books), pp. 3–24.

Kagan, R. and Schmitt, G. (1998) 'Now May We Please Defend Ourselves?' *Commentary*, vol. 106, no. 1, pp. 21–5.

Kaid, L.L. and Jones, C.A. (2004) 'The New US Campaign Regulations and Political Advertising,' *Journal of Political Marketing*, vol. 3, no. 4, pp. 1105–10

Kane, Paul and Pershing, Ben. (2005) 'GOP Leaders Reaching Out,' *Roll Call* (2 March).

Kaplan, Esther (2004) *With God on their Side* (New York: New Press).

Kaplan, Jonathan (2004) 'House GOP Says the Way is Paved for Bush Agenda. Pence: 'Dems Lost their Leader. That Speaks Spades,' *The Hill* (4 November).

Kaplan, Lawrence F. and Kristol, William (2003) *The War over Iraq: Saddam's Tyranny and America's Mission* (San Francisco: Encounter Books).

Keegan, John (2004) *The Iraq War* (New York: Knopf).

Keller, Bill (2003) 'Reagan's Son,' *New York Times* (26 January), p. A7.

Kerry, Richard J. (1990) *The Star-Spangled Mirror* (New York: Rowman and Littlefield).

Kessler, Glenn and Eilperin, Juliet (2001) 'Congress Passes $1.35 Billion Tax Cut,' *Washington Post* (7 April), p. A9.

Kirkpatrick, D.D. (2004) 'Some Backers Say They Anticipate a "Revolution",' *The New York Times* (4 November), p. A1

Kirkpatrick, David D. (2004a) 'Republicans Admit Mailing Campaign Literature saying Liberals Will Ban the Bible,' *New York Times* (24 September), p. A20.

Kirkpatrick, D. (2005) 'For Democrats, Rethinking Abortion Runs Risks,' *The New York Times*, 16th February.

Klein, Joe (2005) 'The End of Rose-Petal Fantasies,' *Time* (7 February), p. 25.

Kogan, Richard and Greenstein, Robert (2005) 'President Portrays Social Security Shortfall as Enormous, but His Tax Cuts and Drug Benefit Will Cost at Least Five Times as Much,' *Centre on Budget and Policy Priorities* (11 February).

Kohl, Helmut (2004) *Erinnerungen 1930–1982* (Munich: Droemer).

Kranish, M., Mooney, B. and Easton, N. (2004) *John F. Kerry: The Complete Biography* (Boston: Public Affairs).

Kraus, Jon, McMahon, Kevin J. and Rankin, David M. (2004) *Transformed by Crisis: The Presidency of George Bush and American Politics* (New York: Palgrave Macmillan).

Krauthammer, C. (1991) 'The Unipolar Moment,' *Foreign Affairs*, vol. 70 (January–February), pp. 23–33.

Kristol, W. and Kagan, R. (1999) 'The Senate Republicans' Finest Hour,' *The Weekly Standard* (25 October), pp. 11–12.

Krugman, Paul (2005) 'Privatizers Can't Explain Away Their Catch-22,' *New York Times* (26 January).

Kupchan, Charles (2003) *The End of the American Era: US Foreign Policy and the Geopolitics of the 21st Century* (New York: Vintage Books).

Kuttner, R. (2004) 'An Uncertain Trumpet,' *The American Prospect*, vol. 15, no. 12, p. 5.

Ladd, E.C. (1985) *The Ladd Report: The Election of 1984* (New York: W.W. Norton).

Ladd, E.C. (1989) 'The 1988 Elections: Continuation of the Post-New Deal System,' *Political Science Quarterly*, vol. 104, no. 1, pp. 1–18.

Larres, Klaus (2003) 'Mutual Incomprehension: US-German Value Gaps beyond Iraq,' *Washington Quarterly*, vol. 26, no. 2 (Spring), pp. 23–42.

Larres, Klaus (2004a) 'Bloody as Hell'. Bush, Clinton and the Abdication of American Leadership in the Former Yugoslavia,' *Journal of European Integration History*, vol. 10, no. 1, pp. 179–202.

Larres, Klaus (2004b) 'Time for a Threesome: European Leadership and America. Europe's New Ménage à Trois,' *The World Today* (April), pp. 7–9.

Larres, Klaus and Torsten Oppelland (eds.) (1997) *Deutschland und die USA im 20. Jahrhundert. Geschichte der politischen Beziehungen* (Darmstadt: WBG).

Leal, D.L., Barreto, M. A., Lee, J. and de la Garza, R.O. (2005) 'The Latino Vote in the 2004 Election,' *PS: Political Science & Politics*, vol. 38, no. 1, pp. 41–9.

Leffler, Melvyn P. (2004) 'Bush's Foreign Policy,' *Foreign Policy* (September–October, 2004), pp. 22–8.

Lengle, J. (1981) *Representation and Presidential Primaries: the Democratic Party in the Post-Reform Era* (Westport, CT: Greenwood Press).

Lewis, Bernard (2005) 'Freedom and Justice in the Modern Middle East,' *Foreign Affairs*, vol. 84 (May/June), pp. 36–51.

lifeissues.net (2001) 'Breaking Abortion News for September 10–16, 2001,' http://www.lifeissues.net/abortion/news/010910-16.html.

LifeSiteNews.com (2004) 'President Bush Speaks out for Life and Family in Remarks to Evangelicals,' http://www.lifesite.net/ldn/2004/mar/04031104.html.

Lind, Michael (2003) 'The Weird Men behind George Bush's War,' *The New Statesman* (7 April), pp. 10–13.

Lind, Michael *Made in Texas: George W. Bush and the Southern Takeover of American Politics* (New York: New America Books).

Livingston, C.D. and Wink, K.A. (1997) 'The Passage of the North American Free Trade Agreement in the U.S. House of Representatives: Presidential Leadership or Presidential Luck?,' *Presidential Studies Quarterly*, vol. 27, no.1, pp. 52–70.

Lizza, Ryan (2001) 'Salvation,' *New Republic* (23 April), pp. 12–14.

Loomis, Burdett A. (ed.) (2000) *Esteemed Colleagues. Civility and Deliberation in the US Senate* (Washington, DC: The Brookings Institution Press).

Lott, J. (2005) *The Judicial Confirmation Process: The Difficulty in Being Smart* (Washington, D.C: American Enterprise Institute).

Lowell, A Lawrence (1902) 'The Influence of Party upon Legislation,' *Annual Report of the American Historical Association for 1901*, vol. 1, pp. 321–545.

Madsen, Wayne (2005), 'Bush Administration's 'Ministry Of Truth' Attacks American Journalists who Fail to Adhere to the Official Line', Onlinejournal.com, 18 April, http://www.onlinejournal.com/Special_Reports/041805Madsen/041805madsen.html

Maltese, John Anthony (2004) 'Confirmation Gridlock: The Federal Judicial Appointment Process under Bill Clinton and George W. Bush,' *Journal of Appellate Practice and Process*, www.ualr.edu/~japp/maltese.html.

Martinez, Gebe. (2001) 'House GOP Keeps the Faith, *CQ Weekly* (20 July), pp. 1923–25.

Martinez, G. (2005) 'GOP Pans for Political Gold in Kerry's Voting Record,' *Congressional Quarterly Weekly Report* (21 February), pp. 458–64.

MasMinistries (2004), 'IMPORTANT: Voter Registration,' http://www.injesus.com/Groups/ViewMessage.cfm?MessageId=0 A008FLU&GroupID=MB005YP1&UCD=j4c.

Mason, D. (2005) 'Campaign Finance: The Good, Bad and the Ugly,' panel presentation, 'Money and Politics: Are Elections for Sale,' symposium sponsored by the Lou Frey Institute of Politics and Government at the University of Central Florida.

Matusow, A.J. (1984) *The Unravelling of America: A History of Liberalism in the 1960s* (New York: Harper and Row)

Maull, Hanns W., Harnisch, Sebastian and Grund, Constantin (eds.) (2003) *Deutschland im Abseits? Rot-grüne Außenpolitik 1998–2003* (Baden-Baden: Nomos).

Mayer, J. and Abramson, J. (1994) *Strange Justice: The Selling of Clarence Thomas* (New York: Houghton Mifflin).

Mayer, W.G. (1996) *The Divided Democrats: Ideological Unity, Party Reform, and Presidential Elections* (Boulder, CO: Westview Press).

Maynes, C.W. (2001) 'Contending Schools,' *The National Interest*, vol. 69 (Spring), pp. 49–58

McConnell v FEC (2003) (124 S.Ct. 619).

McGrory, Mary (2002) 'Winning on the War,' *Washington Post*, 7 November, p. A25.

McKeever, R. (2004) 'Presidential Strategies in the New Politics of Supreme Court Appointments,' in George C. Edwards III and Philip John Davies (eds.), *New Challenges for the American Presidency* (New York: Pearson), pp. 144–60.

McPherson, Harry (1972) *A Political Education* (Boston: Little Brown).

McWilliams, W.C. (2000), *Beyond the Politics of Disappointment: American Elections 1980–1998* (New York: Seven Bridges Press).

MediaTransparency (2005) 'Tim Goeglein: Selling Brand Bush to the Christian Right,' http://www.mediatransparency.com/stories/goeglein.html.

Meyerson, H. (2004) 'Uno, Dos, Tres …' *The American Prospect*, vol. 15, no. 12, p. 10

Meyerson, H. (2005) 'ISO: Working-Class Democrats,' *The Washington Post* (23 February).

Micklethwait, John and Wooldridge, Adrian (2004) *The Right Nation* (London: Allen Lane).

Milbank, Dana (2005) 'GOP, Democrats Look for Symbolism in Schiavo Case,' *Washington Post* (1 April).

Milbank, Dana (2005a) 'From Some Bush Supporters, Anger Over Budget,' *Washington* Post (14 February), p. A15.

Milbank, Dana (2005b) 'Almost Unnoticed, Bipartisan Budget Anxiety,' *Washington Post* (18 May), p. A4.

mindswell.org (2001) 'A Discussion with Karl Rove,' http://www.mindswell.org/news/A%20Discussion%20with%20Karl%20Rove.htm.

Mitofsky, W.J. (2005) 'Comment on "The Latino Vote in 2004",' *PS: Political Science & Politics*, vol. 38, no. 2, pp. 187–8.

Mobilization 2004 (2004) 'All the Candidates' Clergy,' *Wall Street Journal*, http://www.mobilization2004.org/site/pp.asp?c=cfINIUMDG&b +139793.

Moe, Ronald C. and Teel, Steven C. (1970) 'Congress as Policymaker: A Necessary Reappraisal,' *Political Science Quarterly*, vol. 85, pp. 443–70.

Moen, Matthew C. (1992) *The Transformation of the Christian Right* (Tuscaloosa: University of Alabama Press).

Morgan, Dan (2005) 'An End to the Days of High Cotton?' *Washington Post* (8 March), p. A1.

Morgan, Dan and Babington, Charles (2004) 'House GOP Defends Patriot Act Powers. Partisan Rancor High as Plan to Soften Anti-Terror Law Is Defeated,' *The Washington Post* (9 July), p. A1.

Morgan, I.W. (1994) *Beyond the Liberal Consensus: A Political History of the United States Since 1965* (London: Hurst and Company).

Mucciaroni, Gary and Quirk, Paul J. (2004) 'Deliberations of a "Compassionate Conservative": George W. Bush's Domestic Presidency,' in Colin Campell and Bert A. Rockman (eds.), *The George W. Bush Presidency: Appraisals and Prospects* (Washington, DC: CQ Press), pp. 158–90.

Mufson, S. (2001) 'A Worldview of His Own,' *Washington Post*, (11 August), p. A1.

Muntaglio, Bill (1999) *First Son: George W. Bush and the Bush Family Dynasty* (New York: Times Books).

Muravchik, J. (1996) *The Imperative of American Leadership: A Challenge to Neo-Isolationism* (Washington, DC: AEI Press).

Murray, Shailaigth and Allen, Mike (2005) 'Schiavo Case Tests Priorities of GOP,' *The Washington Post* (26 March), p. A1.

Naeck, L. (2004) 'Peacekeeping, Bloody Peacekeeping,' *Bulletin of the Atomic Scientists*, vol. 60, no. 4, pp. 40–7.

Nagourney, A. and Kornblut, A.E. (2005) 'Dean Emerging as Likely Chief for Democrats,' *The New York Times* (2 February).

Nash, G.H. (1996) *The Conservative Intellectual Movement in America Since 1945* (Wilmington: Intercollegiate Studies Institute).

Nather, David (2001) 'Boehner and Miller: Bipartisan Allies Determined to Pass ESEA Overhaul,' *CQ Weekly* (2 June), pp. 1314–15.

Nather, David (2004) 'Social Conservatives Propel Bush, Republicans to Victory,' *CQ Weekly* (6 November), pp. 2586–91

Nather, David (2005) 'Reinventing Bush Country,' *CQ Weekly*, vol. 63, 24 January, pp. 174–77.

National Election Pool (ABC News, Fox News, CBS News, CNN, Associated Press and NBC News), *US General Election. 2004 National Exit Poll.* Data collected by Edison Media Research and Mitofsky International http://www.exit-poll.net/faq.html

National Review (1995) 'Keep America First' (31 July), pp. 12–13.

National Review (2003) 'Left Turn: Is the GOP Conservative?' (23 July), p. 7.

Nelson, Michael (2004) 'George W. Bush and Congress: The Electoral Connection,' in Gary L. Gregg and Mark J. Rozell (eds.), *Considering the Bush Presidency* (Oxford and New York: Oxford University Press), pp. 141–59.

New York Times (2004a), 'Aide is Bush's Eyes and Ears on the Right,' http://www.nytimes.com/2004/06/28/politics/28ROVE.ready.html.

New York Times (2004b), 'Some Bush Supporters Say They Anticipate a "Revolution",' http://www.nytimes.com/2004/11/04/politics/campaign/04conserve.html.

New York Times (2005a) 'Senator Critical of Proposal on Filibusters' (28 April).

New York Times (2005b) 'In Telecast, Frist Defends his Efforts to Stop Filibusters' (25 April).

New York Times (2005c) 'House Passes Bill Tightening Parental Rule for Abortions' (28 April).

New York Times (2005d) 'Bankruptcy Bill is Arena for Abortion Fight' (8 March).

New York Times (2005e) 'US Drops Effort on Abortion Proviso at UN Meeting of Women' (4 March).

New York Times (2005f) 'Pentagon Seeks to Transfer More Detainees from Base in Cuba' (11 May).

New York Times/CBS News (2002) *Poll. Perception of Parties*, taken 27–31 October, http://www.nytimes.com/pages/politics/index.html.

Newhouse News (2004) 'Presidential Politics Confronts a Values Divide in Red and Blue America,' http://www.newhousenews.com/archive/okeefe012104.html.

Newsday (2005) 'Senate Democrats Criticize President on Judges,' *Newsday*.com (3 March).

Newsmax.com (2003) 'Christian Right Talks of Bolting GOP in 2004,' http://www.newsmax.com/archives/articles/2003/5/6/110046.shtml.

Nieves, Evelyn (2004) 'The Religious Right, Out of the Spotlight,' *Washington Post* (3 September), p. A23.

Niskanen, William A. (1988) *Reaganomics: An Insider's Account of the Policies and the People* (New York: Oxford University Press).

Niskanen, William A. (2003) 'A Case for Divided Government,' *Cato Institute Policy Report*, vol. 25, no. 2 (March–April).

Nitschke, Lori (2000) 'Bush's Capitol Course Relies on Cheney's Steadying Hand,' *CQ Weekly* (16 December), pp. 2842–46.

Nitschke, Lori (2001) 'Tax Cut Deal Reached Quickly As Appetite for Battle Fades,' *CQ Weekly* (26 May), pp. 1251–55.

Nitschke, L. with Tully, M. (2000) 'Big Victory For China Trade Needs Senate Blessing' (27 May), *Congressional Quarterly Weekly Report*, pp. 1244–52.

Nivola, P.S. (2005) 'Thinking about Political Polarization,' *The Brookings Institution Policy Brief*, no. 139.

Noonan, M.P. (1999) 'Conservative Opinions on US Foreign Policy,' *Orbis*, vol. 43, no. 3, pp. 621–32.

Nordlinger, Jay (2005) 'About Sudan,' *National Review* (23 May), pp. 39–42.

O'Brien, D.M. (2004) 'Ironies and Disappointments: Bush and Federal Judgeships,' in Colin Campbell and Bert Rockman (eds.), *The George W. Bush Presidency: Appraisals and Prospects* (Washington, DC: CQ Press), pp. 133–57.

O'Connor, Brendon and Griffiths, Martin (eds.) (2005) *The Rise of Anti-Americanism* (London: Routledge).

O'Connor, Patrick (2005) 'Social Security in Limbo,' *The Hill* (3 June).

Office of Management and Budget (2005a) *Budget of the United States Government: Fiscal Year 2006: Historical Tables* (Washington, DC: Government Printing Office).

Office of Management and Budget (2005b) 'Major Savings in the President's 2006 Budget' (11 February), pp. 7–151.

Ota, Alan K. (2004) 'Business Newly Tolerant of "Manageable" Deficit,' *CQ Weekly*, vol. 62 (17 January), pp. 162–4.

Owens, John E. (1997) 'The Return of Party Government in the US House of Representatives: Central Leadership Committee Relations in the 104th Congress,' *British Journal of Political Science*, vol. 27 (April), pp. 249–53.

Owens, John E. (2000) 'Congress after the "Revolution": The Continuing Problems of Governance in a Partisan Era,' in Alan Grant (ed.), *American Politics: 2000 and Beyond* (Aldershot and Burlington, VT: Ashgate Publishing).

Owen, John E. (2002) 'Late Twentieth Century Congressional Leaders as Shapers of and Hostages to Political Context: Gingrich, Hastert and Lott,' *Politics and Policy*, vol. 30 (June), pp. 236–81.

Owens, John E (2004) 'Challenging (and Acting For) the President: Congressional Leadership in an Era of Partisan Polarization,' in George C. Edwards and Philip John Davies (eds.), *New Challenges for the American Presidency* (New York and London: Longman).

Pachon, H.P. (2001) 'Seizing the Latino Moment,' in *Blueprint Magazine*, July, http:www.ndol.org

Page, Susan (2005), 'Christian Right's Alliances Bend Political Spectrum,' *USA Today* (15 June), pp. 1A–2A.

Palmer, Elizabeth A. (2001) 'House Passes Anti-Terrorism Bill that Tracks White House Wishes,' *CQ Weekly* (13 October), pp. 2399–400.

Palmer, Elizabeth A. (2001a) 'Terrorism Bill's Sparse Paper Trail May Cause Legal Vulnerabilities,' *CQ Weekly* (27 October), pp. 2533–5.

Parmar, Inderjeet (2005) 'Catalysing Events, Think Tanks and American Foreign Policy Shifts: A Comparative Analysis of the Impacts of Pearl Harbor 1941 and 11 September 2001,' *Government and Opposition*, vol. 40, no. 1, pp. 1–25.

Parrott, Sharon et al. (2005) 'Where Would the Cuts Be Made under the President's Budget,' *Center on Budget and Policy* Priorities (28 February).

Parsley, Rod (2005), 'I'm Drawing the Line,' *Charisma* (April), pp. 48–51, 96.

Pastor Paul T. McCain Cyberbrethren (2005) 'Liaison for the President of the USA,' http://paulmccain.worldmagblog.com/paulmccain/archives/011721.html.

Paterson, T.G. Clifford, J.G. and Hagan, K.J. (1995) *American Foreign Relations: A History since 1895,* vol. 2, 4th edition (Lexington, MA: D.C. Heath).

Payne, D. (2004), 'Whaddaya gonna do?,' *The Boston Globe* (6 November) , p. A15.

Perle, R. (2000) 'Iraq: Saddam Unbound,' in R. Kagan and W. Kristol (eds.), *Present Dangers: Crisis and Opportunity in American Foreign and Defense Policy* (San Francisco: Encounter Books), pp. 99–110.

Perrine, Keith (2003) 'Frist's Senate Voting Record Shows Blend of Partisanship and Pragmatism,' *CQ Weekly* (4 January).

Peters, Ronald M. (1997) *The American Speakership. The Office in Historical Perspective*, 2nd edition (Baltimore and London: The Johns Hopkins University Press).

Peters, Ronald M. (1999) 'Institutional Context and Leadership Style: The Case of Newt Gingrich,' in Nicol Rae and Colton Campbell. (eds.), *New Majority or Old Minority: The Impact of Republicans on Congress* (Lanham, MD: Rowman and Littlefield).

Peterson, Mark A. (1990) *Legislating Together: The White House and Capitol Hill from Eisenhower to Reagan* (Cambridge, MA and London: Harvard University Press).

Peterson, Peter G. (2004) *Running on Empty: How the Democratic and Republican Parties are Bankrupting Our Future and What Americans Can Do About It* (New York: Farrar, Strauss and Giroux).

Pew Research Center (2004), 'Foreign Policy Attitudes Now Driven by 9/11 *and* Iraq' (available on Pew Research Center website, accessed 1 December 2004).

Pew Research Center (2004a) 'Religion and the Presidential Vote', http://people-press.org/commentary/display.php3? AnalysisID=103.

Phillips, K. (1969) *The Emerging Republican Majority* (New York: Doubleday).

Pilger, John (2004) 'The Warlords of America,' *The New Statesman*, 23 August, pp. 14–15.

PNAC (Project for a New American Century) (1998) 'Letter to President Clinton on Iraq' (26 January), www.newamericancentury.org/ iraq-clintonletter.htm.

PNAC (Project for a New American Century) (2000) 'Rebuilding America's Defenses,' September 2000 www.newamericancentury.org/ RebuildingAmericasDefenses.pdf.

Podhoretz, N. (1999) 'Strange Bedfellows: A Guide to the New Foreign Policy Debates,' *Commentary*, vol. 108, no. 5, pp. 19–31.

Polsby, Nelson W. (1983) 'Some Landmarks in Modern Presidential-Congressional Relations', in Anthony King (ed.), *Both Ends of the Avenue. The Presidency, the Executive Branch, and the Congress in the 1980s.*(Washington, DC and London: American Enterprise Institute for Public Policy Research), pp. 1–25.

Polsby, N. (1983a) *Consequences of Party Reform* (New York: Oxford University Press).

Pomper, G.M. (1997) 'The Presidential Election,' in G.M. Pomper (ed.), *The Election of 1996* (New Jersey: Chatham House), pp. 173–204.

Pomper, Gerald M. (2003) 'Parliamentary Government in the United States?' in John C. Green and Daniel M. Shea (eds.), *The State of the Parties,* 4th edition (Lanham, MD: Rowman and Littlefield), pp. 267–86.

Poole, Isaiah J. (2004) 'Votes Echo Electoral Themes,' *CQ Weekly* (11 December), pp. 2906–08.

Poole, Keith T. (2005) http://voteview.com/dwnl.htm.

Poole, Keith T. and Rosenthal, Howard (1997) *Congress: A Political-Economic History of Roll Call Voting.* (New York: Oxford University Press).

Post-Gazette (2004), 'Churches a Good Place to Round up Votes,' http://www.post-gazette.com/pg/04277/388984.stm.

Price, Kevin S. and Coleman, John J. (2004) 'The Party Base of Presidential Leadership and Legitimacy,' in Stephen E. Schier (ed.), *High Risk and Big Ambition: The Presidency of George W. Bush* (Pittsburgh: University of Pittsburgh Press), pp. 55–76.

Quandt, William (1986) 'The Electoral Cycle and the Conduct of Foreign Policy,' *Political Science Quarterly*, vol. 101, no. 3, pp. 825–37.

Rae, Nicol (2004) 'The George W. Bush Presidency in Historical Context,' in Stephen E. Schier (ed.), *High Risk and Big Ambition: The Presidency of George W. Bush* (Pittsburgh: University of Pittsburgh Press), pp. 17–36.

Range, P.R. (2004) 'Lessons for Liberals,' in *Blueprint Magazine* (13 December), http:www.ndol.org.

Rauch, Jonathan (2004) 'Epochal Election?' *Prospect* (November), pp. 12–14 (originally published in *National Journal*).

Reid, T.R. (2004) *The United States of Europe: The New Superpower and the End of American Supremacy* (New York: Penguin, 2004).

Renshon, Stanley (2004) *In his Father's Shadow: The Transformations of George W. Bush* (New York: Palgrave Macmillan).

Rice, Condoleezza (2000) 'Promoting the National Interest,' *Foreign Affairs*, vol. 79 (January–February), pp. 45–62.

Rice, Condoleezza (2005), interview of Condoleezza Rice with *Washington Post* journalists, http://www.WashingtonPost.com/wp–dyn/articles/A2015–2005Mar25:html (25 March).

Richey, Warren (2005) 'Judicial Aftershocks from the Schiavo Case,' *Christian Science Monitor* (4 April).

Riechmann, Deb (2005), 'Bush trying to win over Americans on Iraq' Associated Press report on Bush's weekly radio address and the Democratic response by Zbigniew Brzezinski, Saturday, 25 June 2005, http://news.yahoo.com/news?tmpl=story&u=/ap/20050625/ap_on_go_pr_wh/bush.

Roberts, Paul Craig (1984) *The Supply-Side Revolution: An Insider's Account of Policymaking in Washington* (Cambridge MS: Harvard University Press).

Roemer, T. (2005) 'Repairing the Democratic Tent,' *Washington Post* (10 February).

Rohde, David W. (1991) *Parties and Leaders in the Post Reform House* (Chicago and London: The University of Chicago Press).

Rosenbaum, David (2001) 'Doing the Math on Bush's Tax Cut,' *New York Times* (15 February), p. A12.

Rosenbaum, David (2003) 'White House Sees a $455 Billion Gap in '03 Budget,' *New York Times* (16 July), p. A1.

Rosenbaum, David E. (2003a) 'Both Chambers Back Tax Cuts,' *The New York Times* (22 March), p. A1.

Roubini, Noriel and Setser, Brad (2004) *The US as a Net Debtor: The Sustainability of External Imbalances*, http://www.stern.nyu.edu/global-macro/Roubini-Setser-US-External-Imbalances.pdf

Rove, K. (2002), 'What Makes a Great President?' lecture at the University of Utah's Rocco C. Siciliano Forum.

Roy, R.K. and Denzau, A. (2004) *Fiscal Policy Convergence from Reagan to Blair: The Left Veers Right* (London: Routledge).

Rubin, Barry (2002) 'The Real Roots of Arab Anti-Americanism,' *Foreign Affairs*, vol. 81 (November/December), pp. 73–85.

Rubin, Barry and Rubin, Judith Colp (2004) *Hating America: A History* (Oxford: Oxford University Press).

Rubin, Robert E. (2005) 'Attention: Deficit Disorder,' www.nytimes.com/2005/5/13/opinion/12rubin.html

Rubin, Robert, Gale, William and Orszag, Peter (2004) 'Sustained Budget Deficits: Longer-Run U.S. Economic Performance and the Risk of Financial and Fiscal disarray,' Allied Social Science Annual Meetings, The Andrew Brimmer Policy Forum, 'National Economic and Financial Policies for Growth and Stability' (4 January).

Rudder, Catherine E. (2005) 'The Politics of Taxing and Spending in Congress: Ideas, Strategy and Policy,' in Lawrence C. Dodd and Bruce I. Oppenheimer (eds.), *Congress Reconsidered*, 7th edition. (Washington, DC: CQ Press), pp. 319–42.

Rumsfeld, D.H. (2001a) 'Prepared Testimony to the Senate Armed Services Committee by Secretary of Defense Donald H. Rumsfeld' (21 June), www.defenselink.mil/speeches/2001/s20010621-secdef.html.

Rumsfeld, D.H. (2001b), 'Press Briefing on Afghanistan,' Secretary of Defense Donald H. Rumsfeld, The Pentagon (9 October), www.defenselink.mil/news/oct2001/tl10092001-tl1009sd.html.

Rumsfeld, D.H. (2002), 'Prepared Testimony of US Secretary of Defense Donald H. Rumsfeld before the House and Senate Armed Service

Committees regarding Iraq' (18 and 19 September), www.defenselink.mil/speeches/2002/s20020918-secdef.html.

Russett, B. (1993), *Grasping the Democratic Peace: Principles for a Post-Cold War World* (Princeton: Princeton University Press).

Sapiro, V. (2002) 'The 2000 Elections and Beyond,' in G. Peele, C. Bailey, B. Cain and B.G. Peters (eds.), *Developments in American Politics 4* (Basingstoke: Palgrave Macmillan), pp. 15–34.

Scammon, R. and Wattenberg, B. (1970) *The Real Majority* (New York: Coward McCann).

Scammon, Richard M., McGillivray, Alice V. and Cook, Rhodes (eds.) (2005) *America At The Polls* (Washington, DC: CQ Press).

Schatz, Joseph J. (2004) 'With a Deft and Light Touch, Bush Finds Ways to Win,' *CQ Weekly* (11 December), pp. 2900–04.

Schier, Steven E. (2004) 'Introduction: George W. Bush's Project,' in Stephen E. Schier (ed.), *High Risk and Big Ambition: The Presidency of George W. Bush* (Pittsburgh: University of Pittsburgh Press), pp. 1–14.

Schneider, W. (2004) 'On This, Clinton and Rove Agree,' in *National Journal* (20 November), p. 3568.

Schöllgen, Gregor (2003) *Der Auftritt. Deutschlands Rückkehr auf die Weltbühne* (Berlin: Propyläen).

Schwab, Larry. (2003) 'The Unprecedented Senate: Political Parties in the Senate after the 2001 Election,' in John C. Green and Daniel M. Shea (eds.), *The State of the Parties*, 4th edition (Lanham, MD: Rowman and Littlefield), pp. 241–53.

Schwarz, H.(1988) *Packing the Courts: The Conservative Campaign to Rewrite the Constitution* (New York: Charles Scribner's Sons).

Segal, A. (2004) 'Is America Losing its Edge?' *Foreign Affairs*, vol. 83, no. 4, pp. 2–8.

Sestanovich, Stephen (2005) 'Not Much Kinder and Gentler,' *New York Times* (3 February).

Shafer, B. (1983) *The Quiet Revolution: The Struggle for the Democratic Party and the Shaping of Post-Reform Politics* (New York: Russell Sage Foundation).

Shafer, B.E. (1991) *The End of Realignment? Interpreting American Electoral Eras* (Madison, Wisconsin: University of Wisconsin Press).

Shafer, B. (2000) 'The Partisan Legacy: Are there any New Democrats? (And by the way, was there a Republican Revolution?),' in C. Campbell and B. Rockman (eds.), *The Clinton Legacy* (New York: Chatham House), pp. 1–32.

Shafer, B. and Claggett, W. (1995) *The Two Majorities: The Issue Context of Modern American Politics* (Baltimore: the John Hopkins University Press).

Shapiro, Isaac and Greenstein, Robert (2005) 'Cuts to Low-Income Programs May Far Exceed the Contribution of These Programs to Deficit's Return,' *Centre on Budget and Policy Priorities* (9 February).

Sharansky, Natan (2004) *The Case for Democracy: The Power of Freedom to Overcome Tyranny and Terror* (New York: Public Affairs).

Shawcross, William (2003) *Allies: The United States, Britain, Europe and the War in Iraq* (London: Atlantic Books).

Simendinger, Alexis (2002) 'Power of One,' *National Journal* (26 January), p. 230.

Simendinger, Alexis (2004) 'Andy Card on Power and Privilege,' *National Journal* (17 April), p. 1173.

Sinclair, Barbara (1983) *Majority Leadership in the House* (Baltimore, MD: The John Hopkins University Press).

Sinclair, Barbara (1989) *The Transformation of the US Senate* (Baltimore, MD and London: The John Hopkins University Press).

Sinclair, Barbara (1995) *Legislators, Leaders, and Lawmaking. The US House of Representatives in the Post-reform Era* (Baltimore and London: The Johns Hopkins University Press).

Sinclair, Barbara (2000a) 'The President as Legislative Leader,' in Colin Campbell and Bert A. Rockman (eds.), *The Clinton Legacy* (New York and London: Chatham House Publishers), pp. 70–95.

Sinclair, Barbara.(2000b) 'Individualism, Partisanship, and Cooperation in the Senate,' in Burdett A. Loomis (ed.), *Esteemed Colleagues. Civility and Deliberation in the US Senate* (Washington, DC: The Brookings Institution Press), pp. 59–77.

Sinclair, Barbara (2000c) *Unorthodox Lawmaking: New Legislative Processes in the US Congress* (Washington, DC: CQ Press).

Sirota, D. (2005) 'The Democrats' Da Vinci Code,' in *The American Prospect*, vol. 16, no. 1, pp. 28–32.

Skocpol, T. (1997) *Boomerang: Health Care Reform and the Turn Against Government* (New York: W.W. Norton and Company).

Skowronek, Stephen (1997) *The Politics Presidents Make: Presidential Leadership from John Adams to Bill Clinton* (Cambridge, MS: Harvard University Press).

Slate (2003) 'Miguel, Ma Belle: The Racial Ugliness under the Miguel Estrada Nomination,' slate.msn.com (27 February).

Slate (2004) 'James Dobson. The Religious Right's New Kingmaker,' http://slate.msn.com/id/2109621/.

Slater, Wayne (2005) 'Religious Conservatives Expect Bush to Deliver,' *Dallas Morning News* (29 January), p. 1A.

Slevin, Peter (2005) 'In North Dakota, Farmers Wary of Cuts to Subsidies,' *Washington Post*, p. A3.

Slivinski, Stephen (2005) 'The Grand Old Spending Party: How Republicans Became Big Spenders,' *Cato Institute Policy Analysis*, no. 543 (3 May).

Sloan, John (1999) *The Reagan Effect: Economics and Presidential Leadership* (Lawrence: University Press of Kansas).

Small, Melvyn (2004) 'The Election of 1968,' *Diplomatic History*, vol. 28, no. 4, pp. 513–28.

Smith, Steven S. and Gamm, Gerald (2005) 'The Dynamics of Party Government in Congress,' in Lawrence C. Dodd and Bruce I. Oppenheimer (eds.), *Congress Reconsidered*, 7th edition. (Washington, DC: CQ Press), pp. 181–206.

Smith, Steven S. and Lawrence, Eric D. (1997) 'Party Control of Committees,' in Lawrence C. Dodd and Bruce I. Oppenheimer (eds.), *Congress Reconsidered*, 6th edition. (Washington, DC: CQ Press), pp. 163–92.

Starobin, P. (2004) 'John Kerry: Leader of the Free World,' *National Journal* (18 September), pp. 1280–85.

Starr, P. (2004) 'Morals of the Election,' in *The American Prospect*, vol. 15, no. 12, p. 4.

Stein, Herbert (1994) *Presidential Economics: The Making of Economic Policy from Roosevelt to Clinton*, 3rd revised edition (Washington DC: AEI Press).

Stevenson, Jonathan (2004) *Counter-Terrorism: Containment and Beyond*, International Institute (Oxford: Oxford University Press).

Stevenson, Richard W. (2005) 'Bush Finds a Backer in Moynihan, Who's Not Talking,' *New York Times* (26 January).

Stockman, David (1986) *The Triumph of Politics: The Crisis in American Government and How it Affects the World* (London: Bodley Head).

Stolberg, Sheryl Gay (2005a) 'Oregon Republican in Revolt Over Budget,' *New York Times* (28 April), p. A3.

Stolberg, Sheryl Gay (2005b) 'Congress Passes Budget With Cuts in Medicaid and Taxes,' *New York Times* (29 April), p. A1.

Stolberg, Sheryl Gay (2005c) 'Foe of Abortion, Senator is Cool to Court Choice' (7 October).

Strahan, Randall and Palazzolo, Daniel J. (2004) 'The Gingrich Effect,' *Political Science Quarterly*, vol. 119 (Spring), pp. 89–114.

Styan, David (2004) 'Jacques Chirac's "Non": France, Iraq and the United Nations, 1991–2003,' *Modern and Contemporary France*, vol.12, no. 3 (August), pp. 371–85.

Sullivan, Steven (2002) 'Wag the Dove: German Chancellor Gerhard Schröder Wins on Peace — and Little Else,' *The National Interest*, vol.1, no. 3.

Suskind, Ron (2004) *The Price of Loyalty: George W. Bush, the White House, and the Education of Paul O'Neill* (New York: Simon & Schuster).

Swink, Margaret (2005) 'French Ambassador Speaks at Yale Center for International and Area Studies' (22 March), http: www.yale.edu/ycias/publications/articles/frenchamb.htm

Szabo, Steven F. (2004), *Parting Ways: The Crisis in German-American Relations* (Washington, DC: Brookings Institution Press).

Tatalovich, Raymond and Frendreis, John (2004) 'The Persistent Mandate: George W. Bush and Economic Leadership,' in Stephen E. Schier (ed.), *High Risk and Big Ambition: The Presidency of George W. Bush* (Pittsburgh: University of Pittsburgh Press), pp. 224–45.

Taxpayers for Common Sense (2004) 'Statement by Jill Lancelot on the Omnibus Spending Bill' (22 January), www.taxpayer.net.

Taylor, Andrew (2001) 'GOP Team Players Grapple With Roles As Bush Team Players' *CQ Weekly* (3 February), p. 269.

Teather, David and Elliott, Larry (2005) 'Poor to Pay the Price of US Deficit,' *The Guardian* (8 February), p. 16.

Teixeira, R. (2004) '44 Percent of Hispanics Voted for Bush?' http://www.alternet.org/election04/20606/

The Economist (2004) 'The Passing of the Buck?' (4 December), pp. 77–80.

The National Security Strategy of the United States of America, September 2002, www.whitehouse.gov/nsc/nss.pdf.

TheocracyWatch (2004a) 'Bush Allies Till Fertile Soil, Among Baptists, for Votes,' *New York Times*, http://www.theocracywatch.org/ bush_reed_times_june18_04.htm.

TheocracyWatch (2004b) 'Ohio's Anti-gay Marriage Amendment,' http://www.theocracywatch.org/homo_ohio_salon_oct16.htm.

TheocracyWatch (2005) 'Backers of Gay Marriage Ban Use Social Security as Cudgel,' *New York Times*, http://www.theocracywatch.org/ homo_ban_cudgel_times_jan25_05.htm.

Toner, Robin (2001) 'Conservatives Savor their Role as Insiders at the White House,' *New York Times* (March 19), p. A1.

Toner, Robin (2002) 'Social Security is Rattling Races for Congress,' *New York Times* (4 June), p. A1.

Toner, Robin (2004) 'Changing Senate Looks Better to Abortion Foes,' *New York Times* (2 December).

truthout.org, 'In Theocracy They Trust,' http://www.truthout.org/ docs_2005/printer_041105F.shtml.

Tucker, Robert and Hendrickson, David (2004) 'The Sources of American Legitimacy,' *Foreign Affairs*, vol. 83, no. 4, pp. 18–32.

Tulis, Jeffrey J. (2003) 'The Two Constitutional Presidencies,' in Michael Nelson (ed.), *The Presidency and the Political System*, 7th edition (Washington, DC: *CQ* Press), pp. 79–110.

Tumulty, Karen and Cooper, Matthew (2005) 'What Does Bush Owe the Religious Right?' *Time* (7 February), pp. 29–32.

United Nations (2003) http://www.undp.org/rbas/ahdr/english2003.html.

US Congress House (2005) *Broken Promises: The Death of Deliberative Democracy. A Congressional Report on the Unprecedented Erosion of the Democratic Process in the 108th Congress*, Compiled by the House Rules Committee Minority Office. The Honorable Louise M. Slaughter, Ranking Member.

van Biema, David et al. (2005) 'The 25 Most Influential Evangelicals in America,' *Time* (7 February), pp. 34–45.

Van Oudenaren, John (2005), 'The German Seat on the UN Security Council. A Tough Call,' *AICGS Advisor* (7 April) http://www.aicgs.org/c/vanoudenaren040705.shtml.

VandeHei, Jim (2005) 'Blueprint Calls for Bigger, More Powerful Government,' *Washington Post* (9 February), p. A1.

VandeHei, Jim (2005a) 'GOP Tilting Balance of Power to the Right,' *The Washington Post* (26 May), p. A1.

VandeHei, Jim. (2005b) 'Bush Rejects Talk of Waning Influence', *The Washington Post* (1 June), p. A1.

VandeHei, Jim and Babington, Charles (2004) 'More Aggressive Congress Could Hinder Bush's Plans,' *The Washington Post* (20 December), p. A1.

VandeHei, Jim and Weisman, Jonathan (2005) 'Partisan Social Security Claims Questioned,' *The Washington Post* (27 February), p. A5.

Volcker, Paul (2005) 'An Economy on Thin Ice,' *Washington Post* (31 January).

Wahl, Nicholas and Paxton, Robert O. (eds.) (1994) *De Gaulle and the United States, 1930–1970: A Centennial Reappraisal* (Oxford: Berg).

Walker, Martin (2000) 'What Europeans Think of America', *World Policy Journal*, vol. XVII, no. 2.

Wallsten, P., Hamburger, T. and Riccardi, N. (2005) 'Bush Rewarded by Black Pastors' Faith,' *Los Angeles Times* (18 January).

Waltz, Kenneth (1979) *Theory of International Politics* (New York: Addison-Wesley).

Warshaw, Shirley Anne (2004) 'Mastering Presidential Government: Executive Power and the Bush Administration,' in Jon Kraus, Kevin J. McMahon and David M. Rankin (eds.), *Transformed by Crisis: The Presidency of George Bush and American Politics* (New York: Palgrave Macmillan), pp. 101–18.

Washington Post (2005a) 'Filibuster Vote will be Hard to Predict: Undecided Republicans are Big Unknown' (28 April).

Washington Post (2005b) 'DeLay wants Panel to Review Role of Courts' (2 April).

Washington Post (2005c) 'Senate GOP Sets Up Filibuster Showdown' (22 April).

Washington Post (2005d) 'Gonzalez Defends Transfer of Detainees' (8 March).

Washington Post (2005e) 'Judge Rules Detainee Tribunals Illegal' (1 February).

Washington Times (2004) 'Evangelicals Frustrated by Bush,' http://www.washingtontimes.com/functions/print.php?StoryID=2 0040219–115609–3712r.

Washington Times (2005a) 'Second-term Values Agenda,' http://www.washingtontimes.com/functions/print.php?StoryID=200050126–09420 2–1140r.

Washington Times (2005b) 'Frist Takes Filibuster Fight to Christians,' http://www.washingtontimes.com/functions/print.php?StoryID=2 0050424-112051–12.

Wattenberg, Martin P. (2004) '*Elections*: Tax Cut Versus Lockbox: Did the Voters Grasp the Tradeoff in 2000?' *Presidential Studies Quarterly*, vol. 34 (December), pp. 838–48.

Wattenberg, M. (2005) 'Elections: Turnout in the 2004 Presidential Election,' *Presidential Studies Quarterly*, vol. 35, no. 1, pp. 138–46.

Wayne, Stephen J. (2004) 'Bush and Congress: Old Problems and New Challenges,' in George C. Edwards and Philip John Davies (eds.), *New Challenges for the American Presidency* (New York and London: Pearson Education Inc.), pp. 101–22.

Weinstein, Henry (1997) 'Drive to Block Clinton Judicial Nominees,' *Los Angeles Times* (26 October).

Weisman, Jonathan (2005) 'Skepticism of Bush's Social Security Plan as the Right One,' *Washington Post* (15 March).

Weisman, Jonathan (2005a) 'Senate Rejects GOP Budget Cuts,' *Washington Post* (18 March), p. A4.

Weisman, Jonathan (2005b) 'Budget Deal Sets Stage for Arctic Drilling and Tax Cuts,' *Washington Post* (29 April), p. A1.

Weisman, Jonathan (2005c) 'Congress Unlikely to Embrace Bush Wish List,' *The Washington Post* (8 February), p. A6.

Weisman, Jonathan and Baker, Peter (2005) 'After Bush Leaves Office, His Budget Costs Balloon,' *Washington Post* (14 February).

Weller, Christian (2004) 'The US Current Account Deficit: On an Unsustainable Path,' *New Economy*, vol. 11 (December), pp. 18–31.

Western Recorder (2005) 'Christian Conservatives Expecting More this Term,' http://www.westernrecorder.org/wr/WRSITE.nsf/stories/200504-Bush.

White House (2003) 'President Bush Signs Partial Birth Abortion Ban Act of 2003,' www.whitehouse.gov/news (5 November).

White House (2004), 'Bush to meet with NATO, EU Leaders in February' (9 December) http://www.usembassy.org.uk/nato188.html.

White, J.K. (1985), 'Partisanship in the 1984 Presidential Election: The Rolling Republican Realignment,' paper delivered at the 1985 Northwestern Political Science Association annual meeting.

White, J.K. (2003) *The Values Divide: American Culture and Politics in Transition* (New York: Chatham House).

White, J.K. (2004) 'Ronald Reagan, Bill Clinton, and the Democratic Party's Values Dilemma,' chapter in progress, Catholic University of America.

White, Joseph and Wildavsky, Aaron (1989) *The Deficit and the Public Interest: The Search for Responsible Budgeting in the 1980s* (Berkeley: University of California Press).

Wildman, S. (2004) 'Wedding-Bell Blues,' *The American Prospect*, vol. 15, no.12, pp. 39–40.

Will, George (2004) 'Foreign Policy Requires More Optimism than Force,' *Washington Post* (30 May), p. A7.

Wolfe, A. (2001) 'Faith Matters,' in *Blueprint Magazine* (12 July), http:www.ndol.org.

Wolfowitz, P. (2001) 'Remarks by Deputy Secretary of Defense Paul Wolfowitz to the American Jewish Committee,' Capitol Hilton, Washington, DC (4 May), www.defenselink.mil/speeches/2001/s20010504-dpsecdef.html.

Wolfowitz, P. (2003) 'Deputy Secretary of Defense Paul Wolfowitz Interview with Sam Tannenhaus, Vanity Fair,' www.defenselink.mil/transcripts/2003/tr20030509-depsecdef0223.html.

Woodward, Bob (1994) *The Agenda: Inside the Clinton White House* (New York: Simon & Schuster).

Woodward, B. (2003) *Bush at War* (London: Pocket Books).

Woodward, Bob (2004), *Plan of Attack: The Road to War* (New York: Simon and Schuster).

Yglesias, M. (2004) 'Insecurity Blanket,' *The American Prospect*, vol. 15, no. 12, pp. 37–9.

Printed in the United Kingdom
by Lightning Source UK Ltd.
109268UKS00001B/79-99